European Dictatorships, 1918–1945

European Dictatorships, 1918–1945

Second edition

Stephen J. Lee

London and New York

First published 1987 by Methuen & Co. Ltd

Reprinted 1988, 1989, 1990, 1991, 1992, 1994, 1995, 1996, 1998, 1999
by Routledge
11 New Fetter Lane, London EC4P 4EE
29 West 35th Street, New York, NY 10001

Routledge is an imprint of the Taylor & Francis Group

Second edition, 2000

© 1987, 2000 Stephen J. Lee

Typeset in Times by
Florence Production Ltd, Stoodleigh, Devon
Printed and bound in Great Britain by
TJ International Ltd, Padstow, Cornwall

British Library Cataloguing in Publication Data
A catalogue record for this book is available from the British
Library

Library of Congress Cataloging in Publication Data
Lee, Stephen J., 1945–
  European dictatorships, 1918–1945 / Stephen J. Lee.–2nd ed.
  p. cm.
  Includes bibliographical references and index.
  1. Europe–Politics and government–1918–1945. 2. Dictators–
  Europe. I. Title.
  D727 .L37 2000
  940.5—dc21
  99-059922

ISBN 0-415-23045-4 (hbk)
ISBN 0-415-23046-2 (pbk)

Again, for Margaret and Charlotte

Contents

Illustrations

Maps

Preface to the second edition

Extensive alterations have been made in the second edition of *European Dictatorships, 1918–1945*, which may surprise some readers familiar with the first. They are, however, broadly in line with recent historical research.

The first edition was published in 1987. Within four years of this there occurred one of the most sudden and dramatic events of the twentieth century: the collapse of the Soviet Union and, with it, the transformation of the map of Europe. This has had a major impact on the way in which the earlier history of the Soviet state is now being seen by historians. There are, therefore, some real reversals of interpretation in Chapter 2 of this edition by comparison with the original version.

Elsewhere, changes in interpretation have been more gradual – sometimes even predictable. Earlier work on Italy and Germany has been taken further in the same overall direction, although with some unexpected twists. Here revised views are due less to political upheaval than to the cumulative research of individual historians receptive to new insights. Chapters 3 and 4 will therefore be much more recognizable, although with some shifts in emphasis. This applies even more to Chapter 5 on the minor dictatorships.

Finally, this edition hints at a broader chronological perspective on the inter-war regimes. It places more emphasis on influences from before the First World War and looks again at the period after the Second. The result is another look at styles of dictatorship often described as 'authoritarian' and 'totalitarian'.

A comment on the term 'dictatorship'

Dictatorship is not a modern concept. Two thousand years ago, during the period of the Roman Republic, exceptional powers were sometimes given by the Senate to individual dictators such as Sulla and Julius Caesar. The intention was that the dictatorship would be temporary and that it would make it possible to take swift and effective action to deal with an emergency.

There appears to be some disagreement as to how the term should be applied today. Should it be used in its original form to describe the temporary exercise of emergency powers? Or can it now be used in a much broader sense?

Let us take two typical views. One is put forward by H. Buchheim in *Totalitarian Rule: Its Nature and Characteristics*.[1] Buchheim argues that dictatorship should be seen as a temporary device. It is equally present in contemporary democratic republics and involves the short-term suspension of the democratic process when quick and vigorous action is necessary. An alternative position is adopted by M.R. Curtis in an entry in *Encyclopedia Americana*.[2] He maintains that the meaning of the term has changed since Roman times. The essential ingredient of modern dictatorship is power; an emergency is not necessarily present.

In this book I have opted for the broader approach of Curtis. The reason is not that I consider it to be sounder or more accurate; while preparing my material I came across very different analyses of the term 'dictatorship', most of which were highly convincing and formidably supported. My aim is to reflect common usage and to conform to the approach of general books on the twentieth century and the inter-war period.

Introduction

The sixteen dictatorships, 1918–45

Europe between the two World Wars consisted of a total of twenty-eight states. In 1920 all but two of these could be described as democracies in that they possessed a parliamentary system with elected governments, a range of political parties and at least some guarantees of individual rights. By the end of 1938, no fewer than sixteen of these had become dictatorships. Their leaders now had absolute power which was beyond the constraints of any constitution and which no longer depended upon elections. The dictators sought to perpetuate their authority by removing effective opposition, by restricting personal liberties and by applying heavy persuasion and force. Of the remaining twelve democracies, seven were torn apart between 1939 and 1940. Thus, by late 1940, only five democracies remained intact: the United Kingdom, Ireland, Sweden, Finland and Switzerland (see Map 1).

The first dictatorships were those of the far left, and involved the use of the term 'dictatorship of the proletariat' to indicate a phase in the development of the principles of communism (see p. 16). Lenin established the Bolshevik regime in Russia in October 1917 after the overthrow by force of the semi-liberal Provisional Government which, in turn, had disposed of the Tsarist Empire in March. Lenin's dictatorship was subsequently enlarged by Stalin, who came to power in 1924. Meanwhile, Hungary experienced a communist revolution in 1919 as Béla Kun tried to repeat the Bolshevik achievement. His regime, however, lasted only 133 days and eventually fell to counter-revolutionary forces. Although there were to be further attempts at installing a dictatorship of the proletariat in several other European countries during the 1920s and 1930s, none succeeded.

In fact, all the other dictatorships came from the right of the political spectrum. Two of these, the most powerful, have been described as revolutionary. In 1922 Mussolini set the pattern for a number of other leaders by assuming control of Italy, and proceeded to impose the basic principles of Fascism. Eleven years later, in 1933, Hitler was appointed Chancellor in Germany and established a more ruthless regime – the Nazi Third Reich. Italy and Germany, initially rivals for control over central Europe, developed from the mid-1930s a working diplomatic partnership known as the Rome–Berlin Axis. With this they spread their influence widely in an effort to undermine the remaining democracies on the one hand and, on the other, to checkmate Soviet Russia.

The right also produced a series of more conservative dictatorships; these are often called authoritarian, in contrast to the totalitarian regimes of Italy and Germany and, indeed, of Stalin's Russia (see Chapter 6). Central and eastern Europe,

Dictatorships by 1938

Democracies dismantled by dictatorships 1938–40

Remaining democracies in 1940

Map 1 The European dictatorships 1918–38/40

completely reorganized after the First World War, succumbed to a series of strong men who promised an escape from the chaos of party conflict or the threat of communism. Hence, Horthy established control over Hungary in 1920 and Piłsudski over Poland in 1926. Austria moved to the right in 1932 under Dollfuss, whose regime was continued by Schuschnigg from 1934 until Austria's eventual absorption into Germany (1938). Even the tiny Baltic states adopted an authoritarian system: Lithuania fell to Smetona in 1926, Latvia to Ulmanis in 1934 and Estonia to Päts in the same year.

Dictatorships also emerged in all the states of south-eastern Europe, or the Balkans. Four of these were monarchies: Ahmet Zogu proclaimed himself King Zog of

Albania in 1928; King Alexander assumed personal control of Yugoslavia in 1929; King Boris followed suit in Bulgaria in 1934; and, finally, King Carol dispensed with parliamentary government in Romania in 1938. The fifth Balkan state, Greece, experienced under Metaxas (1936–40) a more systematically organized form of authoritarianism which was influenced to some extent by Nazi methods.

The Iberian peninsula, meanwhile, had produced three strong men. The first was General Miguel Primo de Rivera, Spanish dictator between 1923 and 1930. His regime, it is true, was succeeded by a democratic republic but this, in turn, was brought down by General Franco who led the Nationalists to victory over the Republicans in the Spanish Civil War. This conflict, which lasted from 1936 to 1939, also gave an opportunity to Hitler and Mussolini to pour military support into Franco's war effort and launch a combined offensive against the leftist supporters of the Republic; it did much, therefore, to increase the confidence and aggression of German and Italian diplomacy. Portugal's experience was less turbulent. From 1932 she was under the iron rule of Dr Antonio Salazar, who remained in power until 1968.

Between 1939 and 1941 no fewer than seven dictatorships (Poland, Lithuania, Albania, Yugoslavia, Greece, Latvia and Estonia) came under the direct rule of Germany or Italy. During the same period, seven democracies were dismantled – Czechoslovakia, Norway, Denmark, Holland, Belgium, Luxembourg and France – while, from 1941, the Third Reich made substantial inroads into Soviet Russia. Almost the entire continent, therefore, became part of the Nazi order, ruled either by governors appointed by Hitler or by puppet dictators. The latter were often leaders of fascist movements which had not succeeded in gaining power before 1939 but which now benefited from the military support of Germany. Examples included the Quisling regime in Norway, the Vichy administration in France, the Ustashi movement in Croatia, and Szálasi's Arrow Cross dictatorship in Hungary.

The fate of these regimes was tied to that of Nazi Germany; between 1944 and 1945 they all fell to the invading armies of the Soviet Union or Western Allies and to the internal resistance movements. After 1945, parliamentary democracy made a major comeback in western and central Europe, while Stalin's version of communism prevailed in eastern Europe. Right-wing dictatorship was therefore squeezed out of all but Spain and Portugal, and even here residual authoritarianism ended in 1975.

All the developments outlined in this Introduction will be given more detailed treatment throughout the rest of this book. Chapter 1 will look at the overall situation in Europe between the wars and focus on the general preconditions for dictatorship. Chapters 2, 3 and 4 will examine the main developments in Russia, Italy and Germany, while Chapter 5 will cover the different manifestations of dictatorship elsewhere in Europe. The purpose of Chapter 6 will be to draw together some of the main themes in a general survey.

The overall aim will be to examine ideas as well as details. Many of the issues dealt with are highly controversial, and will therefore be looked at from a variety of angles. During the past few decades there has been a vast outpouring of books on the inter-war period, initially on Nazi Germany and more recently on Soviet Russia. It is intended that the following chapters should reflect at least some of the more important theories: the current second edition has updated these in line with recent research and will therefore contain a number of arguments that differ substantially from those in the first edition. That is the way in which the study of history progresses.

This approach is based on the conviction, or hope, that most readers will find explanations as interesting and as important to them as factual detail. Where there are several explanations in direct conflict with each other there is plenty of scope for the reader to reflect and come to a personal decision.

Here are a few examples of the sorts of controversy addressed. Was the Bolshevik Revolution of 1917 followed by a counter-revolution between 1918 and 1921? Why was Lenin not succeeded by Trotsky? Was Stalin ever fully in control of the Soviet Union? Was Stalin intending to invade Nazi Germany? Why did Stalin purge his party even of his loyal supporters? Was Mussolini a statesman or a mere buffoon? Was Hitler's foreign policy improvised or based on a master-plan? Was Hitler a more or less effective dictator than Stalin? Was Hitler a strong or a weak leader? Can any of the other dictators legitimately be called fascist? Which dictatorships were totalitarian and which authoritarian? How much were all the dictators influenced by pressures from ordinary people?

Chapter 1

The setting for dictatorship

Europe experienced, between the wars, an unprecedented upheaval. Boundaries were altered in the most drastic way and numerous new states came into existence. Old-fashioned empires and the last remnants of autocracy had been swept away, to be replaced by constitutional democracies and the principle that each major ethnic group should be given the right to form its own nation. Naturally there was a heady optimism about the future and many shared the belief of H.G. Wells that the struggle between 1914 and 1918 had been the war to end wars. Yet the collapse of the old order was also a precondition for movements that were anti-democratic, and there was no guarantee that the new constitutions or boundaries would be indefinitely preserved.

The overall argument of this chapter is developed in six stages. First, Europe before the First World War was in a state of uncertainty, in many places in crisis. Trends were already in place that were released by the First World War and the peace settlement which followed it. The events of 1914–20 acted as a powerful catalyst, second, for internal change and, third, for the redrawing of boundaries. Fourth, these developments were in most cases associated with constitutional democracy and national self-determination. Such ideals were, however, soon threatened by serious underlying problems that, fifth, gave a boost to alternative systems in the form of left- or right-wing dictatorship. Finally, this process was accelerated by the worst economic crisis in recent history and by a complex international situation that saw the eventual association of dictatorship with militarism and war.

THE PERIOD BEFORE 1914

There has always been a tendency to see the period to 1914 as the climax of an order that was fundamentally stable when Europe had experienced the longest period of peace between major powers in its history. This was destroyed by the upheaval of the First World War, the radical effects of which created the environment for instability and dictatorship between 1918 and 1939. This picture is partly true, but it conceals major changes that were already taking place beneath the surface in pre-1914 Europe, and that were to provide at least some of the roots for inter-war developments. From this approach, the First World War cleared the way for changes that were already under way. These affected economies, societies and political trends.

The pre-war period saw rapid technological development which amounted to a second wave of industrialization, along with an acceleration of communications and transport and an enhancement of scientific and medical knowledge. At the same time, there was also a massive population growth within Europe which more than offset the emigration from it. In most countries the most obvious social change was the growth of the working class, the result of industrialization. This was becoming increasingly politically aware, as was the more traditional peasant class. Both exerted increasing influence, either through being enfranchised and participating in the early stages of mass politics or by the way in which the upper levels of society tried to shape policies to contain them. Either way, the politicization of the masses was proceeding before 1914.

So far, there has been little to dispel the positive image of the pre-war era. A great deal of attention, however, has been given by historians to a phenomenon associated with the so-called '*fin de siècle*'. According to Sternhell and others, there was a far-reaching 'intellectual crisis of the 1890s'.[1] This was beginning to shake the established thought of most of the nineteenth century which had been based on liberalism and materialism and which had pointed towards rational and progressive change. Examples of the new wave of anti-rationalism in philosophy and political thought are to be found in the works of Nietzsche in Germany, Bergson in France, Croce in Italy – all showing a reaction against positivism. The arts were also affected in a new wave of romanticism, epitomized by the operas of Wagner in Germany and by the departure from the accepted harmonic system in concertos and symphonies. There was a new interest in social psychology, especially in the emotional behaviour of the masses: the leading influence here was Le Bon in France. Throughout society, and especially in the universities, there was a growing emphasis placed on youth and renewal: this had enormous potential for the mass involvement of youth movements.

Politically, there were powerful critics of liberal parliamentarism, especially among Italian writers such as Mosca and Pareto. Even Marxism was affected by the transformation of ideas. Before the 1890s most Marxist organizations had aimed at a progressive change to a workers' state through the medium of social democratic parties. By the turn of the century, however, there was a growing force advocating violent revolution, which meant a pre-war split within many social democratic movements. The most obvious case was the crisis of the Russian Social Democrats in 1903 and the separation of the moderate Mensheviks from the more radical Bolsheviks under Lenin. Another major influence emerging on the far left was revolutionary syndicalism, developed by Sorel in France as an alternative to Marxism and using trade unionism as a revolutionary device to achieve political objectives. One of its early pre-war converts was Mussolini.

The far right also had its roots in this period. This adapted ideas relating to biology and evolution to generalized conceptions of humanity. The resultant Social Darwinism transformed the more traditional patterns of racism and anti-Semitism. Especially influential were writers like Haeckel in Germany, Soury in France, and H.S. Chamberlain in Britain. Many far-right movements were already developing before the outbreak of the First World War. Action Française, set up in 1899, appealed to the masses in the form of 'integral nationalism'. Social Darwinism was highly influential elsewhere: for instance, in the Portuguese Integralismo Lusitano, and also in Spain and Greece. Germany experienced a series of movements and leagues which grew up during the 1890s, especially the Pan-German League and the Society for Germandom Abroad. There were also strong pressure for expansionism into eastern Europe and for the achievement of a continental Lebensraum as well as an overseas empire. Almost all of the far-right influences were *völkisch* and anti-Semitic: pre-1914 examples included the anti-semitic People's Party. Similar parties developed in Austria-Hungary, a diverse empire which comprised a dozen different ethnic groups. Particularly active were pan-German groups which favoured union between German-speaking Austria and Germany itself; Hitler came under the influence of these when he scratched out a living in pre-war Vienna.

Another, and even more complex, pre-1914 development was the convergence of the far left and the far right. This occurred especially in France, where the revolutionary syndicalism of Sorel synthesized with the radical nationalism of Maurras. The result was a dynamic conception of the state which would combine a corporatist society with expansionist militarism. This synthesis was to prove important in the development of Fascism in Italy as the syndicalism of Mussolini came eventually to fuse with the activism of D'Annunzio (see pp. 104–6).

Traditional influences in Europe were also changing before the First World War. There was far more general instability than is often thought, especially in those regimes which were to become dictatorships during the 1920s and 1930s. As can be seen in Chapter 2, Tsarist Russia was in crisis in the sense that it was threatened by social and political upheaval. Austria-Hungary was also confronted by the possibility of internal collapse as the German and Magyar ruling groups were coming increasingly under pressure from the Slavs. Although more secure politically than Russia and more homogeneous than Austria-Hungary, Germany too had problems in the form of an increasingly assertive and numerous working class: this was considered intolerable by the ruling industrial and agricultural aristocracy. Italy's liberal regime had become increasingly unstable during the 1890s and attempted an unsuccessful experiment with a more authoritarian political structure. Even France and Britain were vulnerable – the former to pressures from the radical left and right, the latter to an unprecedented combination of constitutional and social crises between 1910 and 1914.

Since 1870 new states had come into existence in south-eastern Europe, while others struggled to be born. The whole process influenced the post-war settlement between 1919 and 1920. Already independent were Greece (1830) and, since 1878, Serbia, Romania and Bulgaria. Each of these considered itself incomplete and aimed for territorial fulfilment. There were also nationalist movements for independence among the Poles in Russia and among the the different Slav groups in Austria-Hungary. Whether or not these aspirations were achieved depended on which side they found themselves on during the First World War. The Balkan states had also alternated between constitutionalism and political upheaval which produced periods of autocracy, a pattern which was similar to developments in Spain and Portugal.

Europe was therefore seething with unresolved problems and tensions. These were subsumed in 1914 by the greater emergency of war, only to re-emerge, considerably strengthened, in the peace which followed.

THE IMPACT OF THE FIRST WORLD WAR

The First World War was fought between the Entente powers and the Central powers. The former comprised Britain, France, Russia, Belgium, Serbia, Portugal and Montenegro, joined by Italy (1915), Romania (1916) and Greece (1917). The Central powers were Germany, Austria-Hungary, the Ottoman Empire and Bulgaria. Both sides expected at the outset a swift victory after a limited, nineteenth-century-style war. What in fact occurred was a massive onslaught, with a mobile front in eastern Europe and stalemate in the trenches of the western front. The total losses amounted to 13 million dead, of whom 2 million were Germans, 1.75 million Russians, 1.5 million Frenchmen, 1 million British and half a million Italians. Economies were drained, resources depleted, armies exhausted. Europe proved incapable of ending the conflict and it took the eventual involvement of the United States to tip the balance in favour of the Entente powers.

The impact of the struggle was considerable. During the 1920s the Great War epitomized all the evils to be avoided in the future. Twenty years later, however, it seemed to be eclipsed by the Second World War, particularly since the latter involved considerably greater loss of life and destruction. Then, as J.S. Hughes has argued, the further passage of time restored the original perspective. The First World War now appears fully as important as the Second – indeed, in certain respects, still more decisive in its effects.[2] It was, for example, a catalyst for revolution. It has long been accepted that military failure destabilizes a political system, destroys economic viability, mobilizes the masses, and undermines the normal capacity of the regime to deal with disturbances. The European state system was profoundly altered by the collapse of three empires, induced by defeat and privation.

The first of these was Tsarist Russia. By 1916 the German armies had penetrated deep into Russian territory on the Baltic, in Poland and the Ukraine. The Russian military response proved inadequate, and the supply of foodstuffs and raw materials was severely disrupted by communications difficulties. The government proved unable to cope, badly affected as it was by the periodic absences of the Tsar at the front. In February 1917 food riots erupted spontaneously in Petrograd, to which the official response was entirely inadequate; the regime's stability was destroyed by desertions from a destabilized army. The result was the abdication of the Tsar and the emergence of a Provisional Government which aimed eventually to operate a Western-style constitutional democracy. But this also made the mistake of seeking to snatch victory from defeat; further military disasters severely reduced its credibility and assisted the Bolsheviks in their revolution of October 1917. Within eight months, Russia had moved from autocracy, via a limited constitutional democracy, to communism: a remarkable transformation for a state which had historically been renowned for its resistance to political changes. Lenin made peace with the victorious Germans at Brest-Litovsk. The price he had to pay was to abandon Russian control over Finland, Estonia, Latvia, Lithuania and Poland – a very considerable loss of territory.

Of similar magnitude was the collapse of the Austro-Hungarian Empire. This had been Europe's most heterogeneous state, comprising thirteen separate ethnic groups, all of whom pulled in different directions. Two of these, the Germans of Austria and the Magyars of Hungary, had benefited most from the Ausgleich of 1867 which had created a Dual Monarchy, effectively under their control. The majority of the population, however, had been excluded from this agreement; Austria-Hungary contained a large proportion of Slavs, who could be subdivided into Czechs, Slovaks, Poles, Ukrainians, Serbs, Croats and Slovenes. These were already pressing for full political recognition, even autonomy, by 1914. The First World War wrecked the Austro-Hungarian economy and tore apart the political fabric of the empire as the various Slav leaders decided in 1918 to set up independent states rather than persist with a multiracial federation. By the time that the emperor surrendered to the Allies on 3 November 1918, his empire had dissolved into three smaller states – Austria, Hungary and Czechoslovakia – while the remaining areas were given up to Italy, Romania, Poland and the newly formed Southern Slav nation, eventually to be known as Yugoslavia.

The third empire to be destroyed as a direct result of the First World War was the Kaiser's Germany, or the Second Reich. The German war offensive, so successful against Russia, had been contained on the western front. The Western Allies, greatly assisted by American intervention, came close to breaking through the German lines in September 1918. Meanwhile, the German economy was being strangled by a British naval blockade. Under the threat of military defeat, the Second Reich was transformed into a constitutional republic, the Kaiser having no option but to abdicate on 9 November, two days before the German surrender.

By the end of 1918, eleven states covered the area once occupied by the three great empires (see Map 2). All but Russia were trying to adapt to Western-style parliamentary systems and this seemed to justify the belief of many that the war had become a struggle for democracy. Victory carried with it an element of idealism. The different peoples of Europe would be guaranteed separate statehood and given democratic constitutions. These, in turn, would ensure lasting peace by removing the irritants which had caused so many of Europe's most recent conflicts: harsh autocracy and unfulfilled nationalism. There is, therefore, a strong case for arguing that the First World War had a liberating effect. Further evidence for this can be seen in the profound social changes that occurred in all the states which took part. Particularly important was the increased influence of the middle class at the expense of the traditional aristocracy, the possibility of agrarian reforms and improved conditions for the peasantry, allowance for a greater political role for the working class and trade unionism and, finally, the emancipation and enfranchisement of women.

There is, however, another side to the picture. The First World War may well have created the conditions for the establishment of democratic regimes. But, at the same time it produced a series of obstacles which these new democracies proved unable to surmount. One of these was an underlying resentment of the terms of the peace settlements, which particularly affected Germany, Austria, Hungary and Russia; there was, from the outset, a powerful drive to revise them. Another obstacle was the prolonged economic instability which was aggravated by war debts and reparations payments. Even the destruction of the three empires had unintended side-effects. Some of the new dictatorships which emerged between the wars were built upon the mobilized masses and upon the ideologies which these autocracies had helped restrain – especially communism and fascism. It is arguable, therefore, that the war cleared the way for twentieth-century dictatorships by smashing nineteenth-century autocracies without providing a viable alternative.

Former extent of Tsarist Russia

Former extent of Austria-Hungary

Former extent of the Second Reich
(Boundaries shown are those after the First World War)

Map 2 The collapse of three empires and the emergence of the successor states

Was the First World War more important for inter-war changes than the developments which were already under way before 1914? Bracher certainly thinks so, going so far as to say that 'In spite of their ideological prehistory, there can be no doubt that the new dictatorships of our century were principally a result of the 1914–18 war.'[3] On the other hand, recent research has pointed to the extreme vulnerability of Tsarist Russia even by 1914, to the pre-war ethnic crisis of Austria-Hungary, to the potential for social explosion in Germany, and to the emergence of the radical right and revolutionary left. Hence the war did not *cause* fascist or communist regimes. According to Payne, 'The War nonetheless introduced a new brutalization of public life, a routinization of violence and authoritarianism, and a heightening of nationalist conflict and ambition, without which fascism could not have triumphed in key countries during the generation that followed.'[4]

THE PEACE SETTLEMENT AND ITS SIGNIFICANCE

Ten months before the end of the First World War, President Wilson announced in his Fourteen Points the expectations which he had for any future settlement:

> What we demand in this war . . . is that the world be made fit and safe to live in; and particularly that it be made safe for every peace-loving nation which, like our own, wishes to live its own life, determine its own institutions, be assured of justice and fair dealing by the other peoples of the world as against force and selfish aggression.[5]

What was needed, he continued, was a ban on secret diplomacy, guarantees of freedom of navigation on the high seas, the removal of economic barriers, the lowering of armaments levels, the evacuation of all occupied territory, the granting of self-determination to Europe's different peoples and the formation of a 'general association of nations'. This programme provided the set of ideals upon which the peace settlement was to be based.

Idealism, however, mingled with other motives. One was the satisfaction of wartime expansionist ambitions; the Secret Treaty of London (1915) had, for example, promised Italy extensive territorial gains at the expense of the Ottoman Empire and Austria-Hungary – a reward for joining the Entente powers rather than fulfilling an earlier commitment to Germany. Could such promises be squared with the principle of national self-determination? Another factor was public opinion. All the representatives gathering in Paris were under constant pressure from the media at home and from exhortations from politicians like Geddes to 'squeeze the German lemon until the pips squeak'. Finally, some delegates were obsessed with the need for providing security in the future, and regarded their priority as a settlement which would destroy Germany's military strength.

The actual negotiations were carried out in Paris by the Council of Ten. This consisted of two representatives from each of five powers: Britain and the dominions, France, the United States, Italy and Japan. But most of the work was done by President Wilson of the United States, British Prime Minister Lloyd George and French Premier Clemenceau. The usual picture of this trio is that Wilson was the idealist, having the advantage of American detachment from European problems. Clemenceau was concerned primarily with French security and revenge against Germany, while Lloyd George adopted a pragmatic approach, endeavouring to steer between Wilson and Clemenceau and to achieve by compromise a moderate and lasting solution. The Paris Settlement, therefore, reflected these three broad strategies, which can be seen at work in the individual treaties, named after the ring of towns around the outskirts of Paris or parts of the complex of Versailles.

Germany was dealt with by the Treaty of Versailles, signed on 28 June 1919. It affirmed, by Article 231, the prime responsibility of Germany and her allies for the outbreak of the First World War and, accordingly, made provision for territorial adjustments, demilitarization and economic compensation to the victorious Allies for the losses they had incurred. Germany was deprived of Alsace-Lorraine, Eupen and Malamedy, Northern Schleswig, Posen, West Prussia, parts of Southern Silesia, and all her overseas colonies. Limits were placed on her naval capacity, her army was restricted to 100,000 volunteers, and the Rhineland was demilitarized. A considerable quantity of rolling-stock and merchant shipping was also removed, while France was given exclusive rights to the coal-mines of the Saar region. Finally, provision was made for the payment of reparations by the German government, the total amount eventually being fixed in 1921 at 136,000 million gold marks. Altogether, Germany lost 13 per cent of her area, 12 per cent of her population, 16 per cent of her coal, 48 per cent of her iron, 15 per cent of her agricultural land and 10 per cent of her manufactures.

Opinion is divided as to whether this was a fair settlement. Historians of the 1920s, like W.H. Dawson, emphasized the harshness of a treaty which cut into German territory in a way which discriminated blatantly in favour of non-German populations. The result was that Germany's frontiers 'are literally bleeding. From them oozes out the life-blood, physical, spiritual and material of large populations.' More recent historiography has tended to redress the balance. Writers like J. Néré, M. Trachtenberg and W.A. McDougall put the case that France suffered far more heavily than Germany from the impact of war and that she therefore had a powerful claim to compensation and security. Indeed, considering that a German victory would have meant German control over much of Europe, the settlement drawn up by the Allies was remarkably moderate.

Time has therefore enabled a perspective to emerge. But perhaps the most important point is that contemporary statesmen strongly attacked the treaty, thereby giving ammunition to the German case that the treaty should be revised, even evaded. J.M. Keynes, the economist, was particularly critical; he argued that the settlement lacked wisdom, that the coal and iron provisions were 'inexpedient and disastrous' and that the indemnity being considered was far beyond Germany's means to pay. He considered, indeed, that the treaty, 'by overstepping the limits of the possible, has in practice settled nothing'. This accorded very much with the German view that the treaty was a diktat, forced upon a defeated power, rather than a genuine negotiated settlement. By 1930 it was evident that a wide cross-section of the German political spectrum was extremely hostile to the Treaty of Versailles and that British politicians were increasingly aware of its shortcomings. The ultimate beneficiaries of both these trends were the parties of the right – the conservative National Party and the more radical Nazis. Hitler, especially, was to exploit the underlying resentment in Germany, while British politicians, affected by a belated attack of conscience, made excuses for his activities against the settlement. As will be shown in Chapter 4, the failure to uphold Versailles in the 1930s contributed greatly to the growing confidence and aggression of Nazi foreign policy.

The rest of the peace settlement concerned central and eastern Europe. Austria-Hungary was dealt with by the Treaties of St Germain (10 July 1919) and Trianon (4 June 1920), which were largely a recognition of a fait accompli, the collapse of the Habsburg monarchy. Czechoslovakia was formed out of the provinces of Bohemia, Moravia, Slovakia and Ruthenia; Transylvania and Bukovina were given to an enlarged Romania; Serbia received the Dalmatian coastline, Bosnia-Herzegovina, Croatia and Slovenia; while Trentino and South Tyrol were transferred to Italy. Bulgaria, meanwhile, was covered by the Treaty of Neuilly (27 November 1919) by which she lost the Aegean coastline, or Western Thrace, to Greece, parts of Macedonia to Yugoslavia, and Dobrudja to Romania. Elsewhere in eastern Europe, 1918 saw the emergence of Poland, Finland, Estonia, Latvia and Lithuania as independent states. Although the victorious Allies cancelled the Treaty of Brest-Litovsk between Germany and Russia, no attempt was made to return to Russia the territory which had been given up. Taken as a whole, all these settlements amounted to the greatest territorial transformation in European history.

The accompanying problems were also considerable. The new nations (or successor states) that replaced Austria-Hungary faced a series of crises, examined at length in Chapter 5. They all contained large disaffected ethnic minorities and struggled to achieve economic viability in cut-throat competition against each other. Austria and Hungary sought to revise the whole settlement, Austria by seeking union with Germany (prohibited by the Treaty of St Germain) and Hungary by trying to extend her frontiers at the expense of her neighbours. The overall result was that eastern Europe was fundamentally unstable and therefore vulnerable to political extremes. Italy, meanwhile, was thoroughly dissatisfied with her meagre gains at St Germain – certainly far fewer than had been guaranteed by the Secret Treaty of London (1915). Indeed, Mussolini found that resentment against the settlement had, by 1922, become a significant factor in boosting support for Fascism. Another resentful, and hence revisionist, power was Russia; Stalin had no intention of conceding permanently the territory lost at Brest-Litovsk or that lost to Poland by the Treaty of Riga (1920). He, too, had no underlying commitment to the post-war settlement and was not averse to helping upset it.

THE CRISIS OF DEMOCRACY

The nineteenth century had seen the growth of parliamentary institutions in almost every European state. In many cases, however, there had been severe constraints on democracy, such as a limited franchise, strong executives, weak legislatures and, in central and eastern Europe, the persistence of royal autocracy. As we have seen, the First World War swept away these constraints, while President Wilson based his views of future stability on entrusting the different peoples of Europe not only with new states but with the power to run them. Cobban argues that 'The key to the understanding of Wilson's conception of self-determination is the fact that for him it was entirely a corollary of democratic theory.'[6] The basic assumption of many was that democracy could work and that it was the best guarantee of lasting peace.

What was meant by the democratic state? H. Köhn has listed some of the main characteristics of the democratic way of life. These include 'open minded critical enquiry' and 'mutual regard and compromise'; an opposition which functions as 'a legitimate partner in the democratic process'; a 'pluralistic view of values and associations'; a refusal to identify totally with 'one party or with one dogma'; recognition of the fundamental values of 'individual liberty'; and 'freedom of the enquiring mind'.[7] These features are common to all open democracies, whether republics or monarchies, and several devices were introduced after the First World War to try to give them effect.

These included the extension of the suffrage and the strengthening of the powers of parliaments. In much of central and eastern Europe a deliberate decision was made to use proportional representation, in the belief that this was the best means of conveying the popular will. The most influential type was the Belgian system, as adapted in 1918 by the Dutch. This related the number of votes cast to the size of party representation in parliament while, at the same time, allowing a national pool in which smaller groups could be included alongside the main parties. The general principle here was that the harmony and stability of the new democracies would be best served by a complete range of parties and interests. This device was therefore used in Germany, Poland, Austria, Czechoslovakia, Finland, Lithuania, Latvia and Estonia. Italy, Spain, Portugal and the Balkan states tried other variations on the democratic theme.

Unfortunately, democracy everywhere soon came under serious strain. Economic crises included inflation in the early 1920s in Germany, and a universal depression from 1929 onwards, aggravated by the raising of tariff barriers and the disruption of trade. Some states suffered racial instability as a result of conflicting ethnic groups. Others experienced social disruption caused by the growing hostility towards the regime of the different social classes – the business groups and capitalists, the professional middle class and small traders, peasants, farmers and workers. Economic, racial and social crises had a serious effect on political parties. Liberal parties were drained of supporters, especially in Germany; populist and Catholic parties managed to keep theirs, but consciously moved their policies to the right; conservatives became increasingly anti-democratic and authoritarian; and the parties of the left were torn between socialism and communism. In this state of flux what was needed everywhere was a secure political framework to restore stability and stiffen the resolve to preserve democracy.

This is precisely what was missing. The creators of the constitutions had been unduly optimistic in assuming that the expression of different viewpoints through party politics would automatically guarantee harmony. The unhappy experience of proportional representation demonstrated quite the reverse. K.J. Newman considers that proportional representation led to the disintegration of Italian democracy and seriously destabilized Germany. In multi-ethnic states like Poland and Yugoslavia it ensured that 'national, religious, ideological and regional groups' were irreconcilable.[8] It could certainly be argued that the majority voting system (or winner takes all) was more likely than proportional representation to maintain harmony. The reason was that it tended to produce a two-party system, in which each party was an alliance of interest groups prepared to compromise in order to present an acceptable image to the electorate; failure to do this would mean severe defeat, as seats in parliament were not designated in proportion to votes received. Proportional representation, by contrast, removed the necessity for groups to compromise within parties; the emphasis, rather, was on parties presenting as specific an image as possible and making a bid for a place in a subsequent coalition government. In other words, the majority voting system forced co-operation within parties before elections, while proportional representation relied on co-operation between parties *after* elections.

It is, of course, possible to criticize the majority voting system for being inadequately representative and for distorting electorates' decisions. It is also significant that most European democracies have, since 1945, reintroduced proportional representation. The important point, however, remains that the type of proportional representation adopted between the wars had no means of preventing splinter parties (a shortcoming now largely corrected) and coincided with an unusual number of crises. As a result, democracy became less a matter of how to deal with problems than of how to put together a government. A considerable amount of time and effort was spent trying to find a majority, necessitating exhaustive negotiation and horse-trading. In the process, the role of the prime minister or chancellor changed significantly; instead of acting as the head of a government putting across a package of proposals, he became a mediator between conflicting groups, desperately trying to retain power. This situation would be difficult enough in normal circumstances. At a time of national crisis it proved intolerable. The result was that, in some cases, the head of the government had many of his powers taken out of his hands by the head of state – the king in a monarchy, the president in a republic.

The trend away from democracy towards authoritarian rule was assisted by another defect which existed in some of the new constitutions. The constitution of the Weimar Republic in Germany was typical in that it provided a safeguard if things went wrong; Article 48 gave the president exceptional emergency powers when he needed them. Thus Germany became authoritarian during the Great Depression from 1931, providing a more amenable political atmosphere for the rise of Hitler. Over most of Europe it proved possible to graft dictatorship on to earlier democratic foundations. Only one regime, Bolshevik Russia, made a clean sweep of previous institutions. Others, including even Nazi Germany, retained much of the original constitutional framework until the very end. They did, however, amend the constitutions so as to make a mockery of the original principles and intentions. The main amendments were a ban on party politics and the strengthening of the executive at the expense of the legislature.

Finally, democracy was severely weakened by the absence of any really popular statesmen during the inter-war years. The talent of men like Briand and Stresemann was unostentatious diplomacy which, although effective, rarely caught the public imagination. Churchill, who eventually did fill this gap, did not come into his own until 1940; indeed, R. Rhodes James has called his earlier career 'The Years of Failure'. Almost all the great personalities of the period were critics of democracy – Mussolini, Hitler, Piłsudski, Dollfuss, Primo de Rivera and many others. The masses were tempted by their charisma, sweeping promises and simple solutions. The nations' policies were increasingly taken out of the hands of larger political groups and the key decisions were personalized. This was to be one of the main characteristics of dictatorship and applies everywhere, including in Stalin's Russia.

DICTATORSHIP AS AN ALTERNATIVE

It is now time to turn to the main ideas and influences underlying these dictatorships, starting with the communist left and moving to the more varied radical right.

The communist movements were based on a carefully formulated set of principles. The original ideas derived from Marx and Engels, who argued that all societies comprised two main parts – the base and the superstructure. The former was the prevailing economic structure (for example capitalism), the latter the political and social institutions of the ruling class. In order to change the institutions, or superstructure, it was essential to transform the base. This, in turn, involved the notion of class conflict, as the exploited classes sought to bring down their oppressors. Indeed, according to the *Communist Manifesto* (1848), 'The history of all human society, past and present, has been the history of class struggles.' This struggle operated by a dialectical process, by which the capitalist system inevitably developed its own opposite which would eventually destroy it. Hence, 'the bourgeoisie produces its own gravediggers'. Revolution, Marx considered, was a necessary function of this change for, in his words, 'force is the midwife of every old society pregnant with a new one'. After the revolution had been accomplished, a period known as the 'dictatorship of the proletariat' would begin, during which the bourgeois superstructure would be dismantled, private property would be abolished, production would be socialized and the proletariat would proclaim its triumph by eliminating all other classes. Gradually the 'dictatorship of the proletariat' would be transformed into the 'classless society' which would see an end to all need for force and coercion. According to Engels, 'The interference of the state power in social relations becomes superfluous in one sphere after another, and then dies away of itself.' The result is that state powers would be confined to purely administrative functions. In every other respect the state 'withers away'.

These ideas needed substantial alteration before they could become the basis for revolutionary action. Lenin developed the practical means for the proletariat to overthrow the capitalist system. His main contribution was to develop a revolutionary party to act as 'the proletariat's advance guard'.[9] He regarded organization as essential, for 'Just as a blacksmith cannot seize the red hot iron, so the proletariat cannot directly seize power.' Marxism–Leninism, as the new synthesis came to be called, succeeded in overthrowing the western-style Provisional Government in Russia in October 1917. Between 1918 and 1919 it looked as though it might, in the wake of the First World War, make spectacular gains elsewhere. The British Prime Minister, Lloyd George, said in 1919: 'The whole of Europe is filled with the spirit of revolution.' Yet, by 1929, the failure of the non-Russian Communist Parties to seize control had become apparent. Revolutions of the far left had collapsed in Bavaria, Hungary, Austria and the Po Valley in Italy. After 1920, communism, while remaining a spectre and constant threat, never succeeded in gaining power. Among the reasons, examined in Chapter 2, were the inconsistencies and defects of Stalin's foreign policy, which eventually weakened communism everywhere.

The most extreme movement of the right is generally called fascism. This was more diffuse than Marxism–Leninism and certainly much more difficult to define. There were, however, several obvious characteristics. First, there was a deep hatred of the British and French traditions of democracy; Hitler claimed, in *Mein Kampf*, that 'There is no principle which . . . is as false as that of parliamentarianism.'[10] Second, fascism was antagonistic to Marxism, and E. Nolte has argued that 'The origin of the Right lies always in the challenge of the Left.'[11] Third, fascism was seen as an alternative economic strategy to socialism and trade union power on the one hand and capitalism and big business on the other. It therefore offered a 'third way' which would seek to eliminate class conflict. Fourth, fascists believed that traditional social values, based on Christian morality and ethics, were impediments to the achievement of domination and power. Instead, the emphasis should be placed on conflict. Fascism applied the theory of the survival of the fittest to the social and political spheres, justifying both the crushing of the weak and ruthless military expansion. The result was a glorification of war which led to 'hypernationalist' policies. In Germany, this Social Darwinism also underlay Hitler's racism and anti-Semitism. In terms of organization, fascist parties were presided over by an absolute leader who, in turn, was surrounded by all the trappings of a personality cult. At the lower levels were cadres and para-military outfits, intended to mobilize the masses and turn them against the establishment: in this sense, fascism was potentially revolutionary.

Fascist movements drew support from a wide cross-section of the population, although with varying degrees of success from area to area. One receptive social group was the 'lumpenproletariat', the unemployed and displaced, although it should be said that most workers tended to support socialist or communist parties. Another was the rural population – both the peasantry and the estate owners. A third was the large number of former army officers and demobilized soldiers, veterans who were disillusioned by their treatment immediately after the First World War and, in some instances, shocked by the terms of the peace settlement. In the more industrialized countries, fascism drew its main support from the middle classes, who were profoundly affected and destabilized by the economic crises of the early 1920s and 1930s. Finally, capital and big business joined the bandwagon to try to find security against the threat of communism. Overall, fascism benefited greatly from the instability of the inter-war period and made the most of the 'flabbiness and the failures of the existing regimes'.[12]

At this stage it is necessary to sort out the various regimes of the right and establish which were fascist. The most obvious instance was Mussolini's Italy, where the term Fascism originated, and which showed all the components already mentioned. Germany may also be included; although Nazism did not consciously imitate Italian Fascism, there was considerable common ground in both organization and ideas. The most important differences were Hitler's emphasis on the racial community and anti-Semitism – neither of which was an integral part of Italian Fascism until 1938.

The other dictatorships of the right can be divided, before the Second World War, into two types. The first did have significant fascist influences but these were mixed, in varying concentrations, with other factors. An example is Spain, where Franco balanced the fascist Falange with the more traditional interests of the army,

Church and monarchists; certainly the Falange never dominated the regime in the way that the Fascist Party prevailed in Italy. Another instance of a regime partially influenced by fascism can be seen in Austria, where Dollfuss introduced a conservative and clerical-inspired variant which has been dubbed both 'clerico-fascist' and 'Austrofascist'. A case has also been made for the existence of a quasi-fascist regime under Metaxas in Greece. The second type of dictatorship was fundamentally non-fascist, although not immune to occasional fascist influences. These were much more traditional regimes and lacked any mass or mobilized support. They included Poland under Piłsudski, Portugal under Salazar, the Baltic states of Estonia, Latvia and Lithuania, and the Balkan countries of Albania, Romania, Bulgaria and Yugoslavia.

Fascist movements and fascist states were not necessarily one and the same thing; before the Second World War the former, more often than not, failed to develop into the latter. In fact, the majority of dictatorships regarded fascist movements as disruptive and dangerous. Horthy had little sympathy with the Hungarian Arrow Cross, while King Carol of Romania tried to suppress the Iron Guard. There were also struggles between Päts and the Estonian Freedom Fighters, between Smetona and the Iron Wolf of Lithuania and between Latvia's Ulmanis and the Thunder Cross. Minority fascist movements also tried to cause upheaval in the democracies: for example, Action Française, the Dutch National Socialist Movement, the British Fascist Movement, Rex in Belgium and Lapua in Finland. There were also, in some countries, subnational or regionally based fascist parties; these included the Slovak People's Party and Ustashi in Croatia. Every one of these movements failed to gain power – until an opportunity was provided during the upheaval of the Second World War. From 1941 onwards a series of Fascist regimes came into existence as Nazi puppets – the Iron Guard, Szálasi's Arrow Cross, the Slovak People's Party and Ustashi. All proved far more oppressive and vicious than the more traditional dictatorships which they replaced, but none survived the collapse of Nazi Germany in 1945.

THE ECONOMIC CATALYST

J.M. Keynes observed in 1931: 'We are today in the middle of the greatest economic catastrophe – the greatest catastrophe due almost entirely to economic causes – of the modern world.'[13] He was referring to events generally known as the Great Depression. This was the nadir of the inter-war economy but, at the same time was part of a broader economic picture which needs to be examined. It is generally accepted that economic crises had profound political effects; although they were rarely the sole or specific cause of dictatorship, they certainly accelerated the process.

The first major crisis followed the First World War and the peace settlement. Before 1913, Europe had dominated world trade and industrial production. Concentration of four years of total war, however, meant the loss of ground to the United States. Some European countries also experienced major upheavals as a result of revolution or the peace settlement. Russia, for example, went through a period of War Communism, followed by the New Economic Policy. The Bolsheviks also decided to repudiate all of Russia's pre-war debts, which particularly affected France. The emergence of eleven new states in eastern and central Europe destroyed the previous customs union in the area, impeded industrial development and promoted intense rivalry. In western Europe there was a considerable variation in post-war economic conditions. Italy underwent economic collapse which contributed to the rapid decline of effective parliamentary democracy and the rise of Mussolini. Britain and France both experienced post-war booms, but these were followed, after 1922, by a temporary general recession. Germany, meanwhile, was saddled by the Treaty of Versailles with reparations payments. The German government resented these deeply, and defaulted in 1923, at the same time printing paper money and effectively bringing about the collapse of the mark. In fact, the situation in the Weimar Republic epitomized everything which seemed most dangerous to Europe's economies: hyperinflation with threats to jobs and savings and a potential social upheaval.

In many cases, however, this first phase of economic malaise was dealt with effectively. The slump and inflation were both reversed and western Europe experienced a rapid increase in prosperity between 1924 and 1929. Several factors contributed to this. One was a more stable international situation; another was the resolution of the German reparations crisis by the Dawes Plan of 1924. But the most important reason was the beneficent influence of the United States – which contributed between 1925 and 1929 approximately $2,900 million in the form of investment in Europe. This helped settle the complex problem of post-war debts. American loans enabled Germany to make reparations payments to her former enemies in Europe, which, in turn, could make repayments on war loans to the United States. The more stable and rational system meant that industrial and agricultural output increased, while shipping and transport expanded rapidly. This was also a period of industrial rationalization or scientific management, which included the use of assembly-line techniques and the more economic employment of labour. In the international sphere attempts were made to restore a fully functioning and stable exchange. Britain returned to the gold standard in 1925, followed by most other European countries by 1928. Meanwhile, in 1927, a conference met at Geneva to try to remove any remaining impediments to international trade. Overall, it seemed that Europe was experiencing unprecedented – and permanent – prosperity.

Our retrospective knowledge shows just how misplaced this confidence was. The recovery proved extremely fragile and a potential crisis lurked behind every apparent gain.

In the first place, much of eastern Europe was less affected by the upswing in prosperity. The Soviet Union was almost completely isolated, while the less industrialized economies of the successor states and the Balkans suffered severely from lower agricultural prices which benefited the consumer at the expense of the producer. Indeed, Poland, Albania and Lithuania were all lost to dictatorship during this period, the result of an interaction between economic stagnation and political crisis.

Second, western European industrial growth was not accompanied by a proportionate increase in the volume of trade. By 1925 Europe's industrial production was the same as that of 1913, but her share of world trade was down from 63 per cent to 52 per cent. It was clear, therefore, that Europe had not succeeded in fully replacing the markets lost during the First World War. The United States, in fact, hoped to prevent Europe from doing so. Experiencing itself a massive increase in industrial production and fearing competition from Europe, the USA imposed higher tariffs on imports. European countries, with the exception of Britain, followed suit. The result was a series of major obstacles to international trade which did much to reduce its overall volume.

A third problem was that the agricultural sector in western Europe and the United States went through a period of overproduction, largely because of more efficient farming methods. The result was a fall in agricultural prices of up to 30 per cent between the end of 1925 and autumn 1929. As in eastern Europe, the producer suffered and the erosion of his spending power eventually reduced the market for industrial goods. There were also political implications. In Germany, for example, small farmers had become destabilized and a prey to Nazism long before the onset of the Great Depression.

Fourth, industrial growth – the great economic achievement of the 1920s – was itself unsteady. It depended too heavily on American loans, mostly short term, and Germany borrowed at 2 per cent above normal interest rates. Any large-scale withdrawal of this investment would have devastating results. Even industrial rationalization or scientific management had its perils. By making it possible to reduce the size of the workforce, it added, even in prosperous times, to the unemployment figures. Before the onset of the depression, Britain already had 1 million out of work and Germany 2 million.

Finally, even the improvements made in international economic relations proved short-lived. The gold standard, for example, did not provide the anticipated stability, as its operation was distorted by the accumulation of most of the world's gold reserves in the United States. In general, Europe's recovery was so closely linked to the prosperity of the United States that the relationship could transmit disadvantages as well as benefits. To repeat the old metaphor, 'when America sneezes, the rest of the world catches cold'.

The more negative impact of the United States began to be felt from mid-1928. The quantity of American loans to Europe began to decrease, largely because of a boom in the domestic stock market. Investors were convinced that this would last indefinitely and that the prospects for returns on investment were far better at home than they were abroad. European economic growth was therefore already affected when, in October 1929, another savage blow was dealt by the Wall Street Crash. The sudden collapse of the US stock market was followed by further restrictions on American lending to Europe, thus depriving the latter of what had been a vital factor in its economic recovery. The real impact, however, was experienced in 1931 when the central European banking system was undermined. The crisis began with the collapse of the Austrian bank, Credit Anstalt, and spread to Hungary, Czechoslovakia, Romania, Poland and Germany.

The economic impact was devastating. All the underlying deficiencies already referred to now came to the surface. By the end of 1932, for example, total world industrial production had declined by 30 per cent from 1929 levels and trade in manufactured goods by 42 per cent. During the same period world food output fell by 11 per cent and the extraction of raw materials by 19 per cent. Of the individual countries, Germany was the most seriously affected: her 39 per cent decline in industrial production forced unemployment levels up to over 6 million. Other central European countries were also badly hit, including Austria and Czechoslovakia; the crisis was especially serious in Czechoslovakia's most highly industrialized region, the Sudetenland. Eastern Europe had suffered before the onset of the depression from a drop in agricultural prices, but the depression intensified the misery by destroying the trade in agricultural goods. The Soviet Union was, supposedly, insulated from the mainstream of the world economy because of her self-sufficiency and rigid economic planning. But even here the depression had an impact. The Soviet Union depended for its own industrialization on imports of foreign machinery. These were paid for by exports of Soviet grain, the value of which declined steadily as a result of the fall in agricultural prices. Relatively, therefore, imports became more expensive.

The Great Depression presented a double aspect. In the words of Hughes, the crisis of capitalism also appeared as a crisis of liberalism and democracy. All the remaining parliamentary regimes came under severe strain. Some successfully preserved their political systems. The Scandinavian countries, especially Sweden and Denmark, made effective use of consensus politics to contain the emergency. Britain went through a political upheaval, but confined this to the parliamentary context by substituting a National Government for the usual bipartisan approach. France managed to hang on to democracy through the expedient of broad-based coalitions or Léon Blum's Popular Front of 1936. In most other European countries, however, democracy fell apart. Germany was the classic case. The broad-based coalition government of Müller collapsed in 1929, unable to agree a strategy to deal with the economic crisis. The subsequent shift to the right benefited the Nazis, and made possible the rise to power of Hitler by 1933. In eastern Europe, and in the Balkans and Portugal, there was an almost universal resort to emergency powers to replace already discredited parliamentary governments. The only real exception to this process was Spain, which actually progressed during the depression from dictatorship to the democracy of the Second Republic. This could, however, be seen as a coincidence and, in any case, the depression helped destabilize the republic and laid it open to the eventual counter-attack of the right in 1936.

How did the various governments come to terms with the problems caused by the depression? Several policies were attempted. France refused to devalue its currency and, like Britain and Germany in 1931, relied on cutting government expenditure and carefully balancing the budget. Italy, Portugal and Austria tried variants of corporativism, and Nazi Germany introduced a drive for self-sufficiency, or autarky. The degree of success varied; by 1932 some countries were beginning to pull out of the depression, and most were emerging by 1934. It seemed, therefore, that capitalism had survived the turmoil. The same, however, could not be said of democracy.

In one area economic recovery was delayed. The complex web of international trade was irreparably torn. The main reason for this was the collapse of any real international co-operation and the adoption of essentially national programmes of survival. There was only one compromise: the 1932 Lausanne Conference agreed to cut reparations by 90 per cent. However, the significance of this was overstated at the time, for Hitler proceeded after 1933 to ignore reparations totally. There were to be no other agreements. The World Economic Conference, convened in London in 1933, achieved nothing. All states were imposing high tariffs and drawing up bilateral or regional agreements which effectively destroyed free trade. Examples included the Oslo Group, comprising the Scandinavian countries, and the Ottawa

Agreement of 1932 which covered the British Empire. France made similar arrangements with its colonies, while Germany drew up a series of trade pacts with the Balkan states which had profound political consequences (see Chapter 5).

The failure to provide a common approach to dealing with the world economic crisis also contributed to the rapid deterioration of international relations. The three major powers particularly responsible for this were Japan, Italy and Germany, all of which sought economic solutions in rearmament and aggression. The Italian invasion of Abyssinia, for example, was hastened by the withdrawal of American investments after 1929, which had the dual effect of removing all restraints on Italian foreign policy and encouraging Mussolini to reformulate his entire economic strategy. By far the greatest blow to the international system, however, was dealt by Germany. Hitler's Four Year Plan was intended to prepare Germany for war by 1940, and the increase in military expenditure contributed greatly to the growing confidence and aggression of Hitler's foreign policy during the late 1930s. Dictatorship had finally forged its association with expansionism and militarism, whereas democracy, enervated by the depression, clung desperately to the hope for peace.

Chapter 2

Dictatorship in Russia

LENIN'S REGIME, 1917–24

Russia between 1917 and 1953 experienced two periods of dictatorship. The first was intended by Lenin to be a temporary dictatorship of the proletariat, a phase in the movement towards a communist system. The second was the more permanent and personalized dictatorship imposed by Stalin.

The revolution of October/November 1917

Soviet Russia was born in October/November 1917, when the Bolshevik Party, under Lenin, seized power in Petrograd and Moscow. In doing so it toppled the Provisional Government, mainly identified with the leadership of Alexander Kerensky. This, in turn, had replaced the regime of Tsar Nicholas II in March 1917.

Nicholas II's government had been severely weakened by a combination of military defeat at the hands of the Germans in the First World War, economic collapse and serious misgovernment. In March 1917 it was confronted by a largely spontaneous movement which began as a series of food riots and ended with the desertion of troops and security forces. When Nicholas II eventually abdicated on 15 March, two institutions claimed political authority. One was the Petrograd Soviet, a workers' council which was elected by soldiers and labourers. The other was the Provisional Government which had been set up by a committee of the Duma, a parliament which had been conceded reluctantly by the Tsar in 1905. The question now arising was: which of the two institutions – Soviet or Provisional Government – would provide the future power base?

There was nothing to indicate at this stage that the Bolsheviks would shortly be bidding for the control of Russia. They had played little part in the events of March and had no influence either in the Soviet or in the Provisional Government. The Soviet consisted mainly of Menshevik and Socialist Revolutionary deputies, while the Provisional Government, under Prince Lvov, was dominated by liberals and moderate conservatives – or Constitutional Democrats and Octobrists. Gradually, however, the Bolsheviks made their presence felt. Lenin returned from exile in Switzerland in April 1917 and set about making the Bolshevik Party the major organization of the working class. His intention was to take over the Soviet and use it to destroy the Provisional Government. For a while this seemed an impossible task. The Socialist Revolutionaries and Mensheviks within the Soviet were prepared to form a political partnership with the Provisional Government; this was

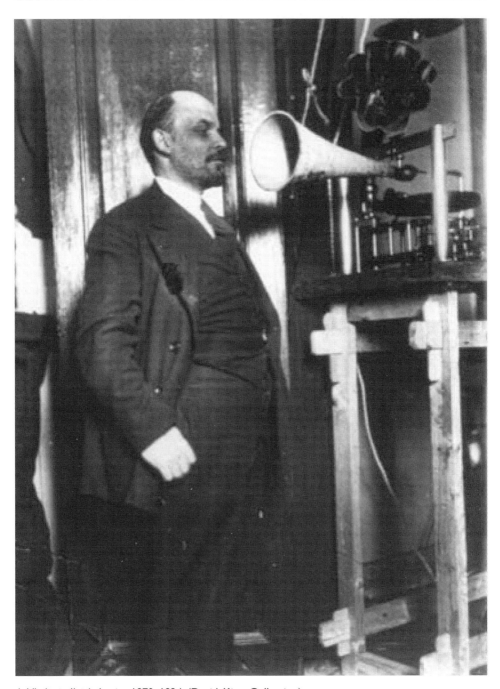

1 Vladimir Ilyich Lenin, 1870–1924 (David King Collection)

cemented in the person of the Socialist Revolutionary Kerensky, who succeeded Lvov as head of the Provisional Government on 20 July. Earlier in the same month Lenin had been seriously embarrassed by an abortive Bolshevik uprising; he had tried to prevent it on the grounds that it was premature. The Provisional Government ordered the raiding of the Bolshevik headquarters and issued warrants for the arrest of the Bolshevik leaders. Lenin escaped this only by going into hiding in Finland. It seemed, therefore, that the Provisional Government had triumphed and that the Bolsheviks had shot their bolt.

Through much of 1917, however, the Provisional Government faced serious difficulties which eventually worked in favour of the Bolsheviks. It maintained Russia's support for the Allies but, in the process, suffered further losses of territory to the Germans from July onwards. The economy, too, was in desperate trouble and the peasantry were openly seizing their landlords' estates in many of the rural areas. Kerensky, hoping to preside over an orderly land transfer, sent troops to deal with peasant violence, thus antagonizing a large part of the population. The Bolsheviks were able to take advantage of this policy and came out openly in support of the peasants. But the real crisis confronting the Provisional Government was the Kornilov Revolt. General Kornilov, Commander-in-Chief of the Russian army, tried in August/September to overthrow the Provisional Government and to substitute for it a military dictatorship that would, he hoped, drive back the German invader and deal with the internal threat of revolution. Kerensky could rely upon the Petrograd Soviet to mobilize support against Kornilov's troops, but he needed additional help if he were to save the Provisional Government. In desperation he turned to Bolshevik units known as Red Guards and agreed to arm them if they joined the defence of Petrograd. This decision saved the capital but placed the Provisional Government in grave peril. The liberals pulled out of the coalition with Kerensky, who was now left with a small fraction of his original support at a time when the Bolsheviks were growing in confidence.

By September the Bolsheviks had also become the most popular alternative to the Provisional Government. They had won majorities in the Petrograd and Moscow soviets, and soon came to dominate most of the provincial soviets as well. From this, Lenin deduced that the time had come to seize the initiative and sweep Kerensky from power. The Petrograd Soviet was used as a front for Bolshevik revolutionary activity. Trotsky, its president, was also the overall co-ordinator of the impending coup, directing the activities of the newly formed Revolutionary Military Committee from his headquarters in the Smolny Institute. On the night of 6/7 November 1917 (Gregorian calendar), the Bolshevik Red Guards seized, with surprising ease and minimal bloodshed, the key installations of Petrograd. These included banks, telephone exchanges, railway stations and bridges. By 8 November the Winter Palace and the Admiralty Buildings, the administrative headquarters of the Provisional Government, had also been stormed. Kerensky had left the city to spend the rest of his life in exile.

Why were the Bolsheviks successful?

Lenin was assisted by three main factors. The first was the social and political situation between March and November, which gradually undermined the Provisional

Government. The second was the growing popularity of the Bolsheviks during the course of 1917, which meant that they were able to harness a powerful undercurrent of revolutionary activism. And the third was the Bolsheviks' organization and strategy, which enabled them to take maximum advantage of the vulnerability of their opponents and the resentment of the urban and rural masses. Each of these has been the subject of controversy among historians, especially since 1991.

The weaknesses of the Provisional Government?

The Provisional Government has traditionally had a reputation for inefficiency and underachievement. This is not entirely just and attempts have been made to rehabilitate it. There was, nevertheless, an underlying problem which undermined its best efforts in the period between March and October 1917. This was the existence of a dual power base, referred to in the previous section. The Provisional Government consisted, at first, of Constitutional Democrats and Octobrists, and stood for the development of a Western type of parliamentary system. Established at the same time, the Petrograd Soviet comprised parties of the left, like the Mensheviks, Socialist Revolutionaries and ultimately the Bolsheviks. There were attempts to achieve collaboration between the two institutions. The Soviet, for example, passed an early resolution to co-operate with the Provisional Government laws in so far as they corresponded to the interests of the proletariat and the broad democratic masses of the people. Members of the Soviet were also drawn into the Provisional Government; Kerensky, a Socialist Revolutionary, was there from the start and several others joined the coalition governments of May and July.

These developments did not, however, guarantee political harmony. On the contrary, the Provisional Government and the Soviet pulled apart on conflicting policies over the continuation of the war and the distribution of land; to make matters worse, there was also dissension within the Provisional Government itself. The liberals pulled out of the government in August over the Kornilov Revolt so that Kerensky was left virtually isolated, presiding over a mere rump separated by an ever widening gulf from the Soviet. The latter was becoming increasingly radical and assertive, under the growing influence of the Bolsheviks, while Kerensky was becoming vulnerable to the accusation that his own claim to power was still untested by parliamentary election. In the words of one historian, it was a 'pre-legitimate regime'.

The Provisional Government was therefore inherently unstable and would have found survival difficult even in favourable circumstances. Its task, however, was rendered impossible by its military commitments. In the summer of 1917 it launched a great offensive against the Germans and Austrians in Galicia. This proved a disastrous failure, and from July onwards the Provisional Government faced the constant spectre of German advance. The Russian army was in imminent danger of collapse which, in itself, caused problems; mass desertions increased the level of instability, while, at the top, officers like Kornilov felt that they had little to lose by taking matters into their own hands. The Provisional Government's commitment to continuing the war was one of the main reasons for its growing rift with the soviets and for the movement of the latter towards the Bolsheviks.

One further issue is worth brief examination. Why did the Socialist Revolutionaries and the Mensheviks in the Petrograd Soviet not take the initiative and set up an alternative to the Provisional Government? The answer is that they were considering this seriously and, but for the Bolshevik initiative in October, may well have done so. They were, however, hampered in taking decisive action by the different types of socialism which they represented; these could not easily have been reconciled. The Menshevik commitment was particularly strange. They were tied to a rigid version of Marxism which believed that the proletariat needed to help bring the bourgeoisie to power and then to wait, possibly for a long period, until capitalism had run its course before expecting the arrival of a socialist system. This justified co-operation with the liberals but hardly found favour with the Petrograd Soviet or with the first and second Congresses of Soviets which convened in June and October. (In his study of Menshevik strategy, A. Ascher asks the pertinent question: 'Had any class ever helped to make a revolution and then voluntarily stepped back to allow another to reap most of the benefits?'[1]) The Bolsheviks were therefore presented with a perfect opportunity to appeal to the radicals in the soviets through a series of promises in Lenin's *April Theses*. The result was a steady increase in Bolshevik influence which coincided with the deterioration of the Provisional Government. In the first Congress of Soviets (June 1917) the Bolsheviks had only 150 representatives to the Mensheviks' 248. By October the situation had been reversed; the Bolsheviks now had 300, the Mensheviks 80 at the most.

An incident at the June meeting of the Congress of Soviets shows the contrasting attitudes to power of the Bolsheviks and other parties of the left. Tsereteli, one of the Menshevik leaders, argued that there was as yet no real alternative to the Provisional Government. He concluded: 'At the present moment there is no political party which would say, "Give the power into our hands, go away, we will take your place." There is no such party in Russia.' Lenin was heard to say from his seat, 'There is.'[2]

The influence of the masses?

It was once thought that the October Revolution was really a coup by a minority group against the real wishes of the population. In this sense, the key influence was the leadership and co-ordination of the Bolshevik Party, which planned and executed the transfer of power from the Provisional Government with military precision. In a sense, the acceptability of the new regime did not matter at first, since between 1918 and 1921 Lenin and Trotsky were able to transform the coup into a revolution.

This view has now been strongly challenged by a new wave of revisionist historians. This is largely because recent historical studies, of other European countries as well as Russia, have fundamentally reconsidered the way in which political power operates. It is now argued that there has been too much emphasis on the idea of power being a process which is exercised downwards, by leaders and organizations over peoples. Instead, there needs to be more recognition that leaders and organizations can be heavily influenced by pressures from below. The practical effect of the new perspective is that the Bolsheviks are now seen as being much more in line with the most immediate wishes of large parts of the population. Instead of forcing the pace of revolution by exploiting popular grievances, they were adapting their policies to enable them to move with a revolutionary current which already existed. The common people therefore had a vital influence on events. Acton's summary of this view is that, 'The driving force behind their intervention, their organizational activity and the shifts in their political allegiance was an essentially autonomous and rational pursuit of their own goals.'[3]

Which groups exerted the most influence on the Bolsheviks? One, which has in the past been greatly underestimated, was the peasantry. They provided a radical impetus, insisting on the return of the land to those who worked it and taking action to ensure that this happened. Peasant petitions also demanded justice through peasant courts, elected local authorities and more extensive education. Although there were frequent revolts, violence was not mindless but aimed at eliminating opposition to such designs. The Bolsheviks would have been unwise not to take note of such pressure. This explains the tactical adjustments to their policy made in the *April Theses* and subsequent pronouncements on land ownership, which were not exactly in line with Marxist collectivism. The urban workers also exerted pressure. The most active were the skilled workers, who tended to dominate the local soviets and factory committees. Like the peasants, they were radicalized by their own aspirations rather than by stimulus from the Bolsheviks. Elements within the army reacted in very much the same way. Their two main demands were for the democratization of the command and an early end to the war. This war weariness was less the result of external agitation, especially from the Bolsheviks, than from a deep welling up of discontent as a result of years of defeat and suffering. The resultant instability within the army was, of course, very widespread and would have led to further upheaval even if the Bolsheviks had not seized control in November 1917.

Rather than being manipulated themselves, therefore, these groups pressurized the Bolsheviks into taking action on their behalf. The Bolsheviks succeeded because they followed the trend rather than established it.

The organizational strengths of the Bolsheviks?

This more recent approach has implications for the whole question of the effectiveness of Bolshevik organization and leadership.

The argument which is now commonly used is that the Bolsheviks did not need to be effectively organized, since they rode to power on a wave of popular resentment. They were in a stronger position than their rivals, the Socialist Revolutionaries and the Mensheviks, who had sacrificed much of their credibility in 1917 by urging support for the policies of the Provisional Government. The Bolshevik Party was more democratic and decentralized than is often realized – precisely because this was the best way of adapting to the goals of the different sectors of society; centralized structures would have been a liability. The coup was carried out by Trotsky and the Military Revolutionary Committee in the name of the Soviet, which had a real influence over the decisions taken by the Bolsheviks against the Provisional Government. Whether or not the Soviet and the workers' committees approved of the seizure of power on 6–7 November, they were certainly not likely to try to prevent it, which meant that the Bolsheviks were given a clear path. It has therefore been argued that the Bolsheviks represented the general revolutionary trend in 1917 more effectively than any of the other parties precisely because they were not, at this stage, a centralized and conspiratorial organization.

Revisionist interpretations are based partly on new research and partly on a new emphasis. They should be considered but do not have to be accepted in full. There is one obstacle to the view that the popularity of the Bolsheviks made effective organization unnecessary. As soon as they had come to power the Bolsheviks arranged for an election of a new Constituent Assembly. Polling took place literally within weeks and the surprising result was that the Bolsheviks lost heavily to the Socialist Revolutionaries. If the Bolsheviks were so successful in 1917 in reflecting public opinion, why did they not achieve a majority so soon after their successful seizure of power? Why, in particular, did they not experience a 'honeymoon period' with the electorate?

This may suggest a partial move back towards the more traditional view that the Bolsheviks *were* centrally focused. Certainly this was the attitude of Lenin himself, who had for many years emphasized the need for a tight party structure with a core of persons engaged in revolution as a profession. He gave the party a double objective in 1917. The first was to use organization on behalf of the masses to accomplish what the masses by themselves could not. The second was to take over the soviets, using them to legitimize the party's revolutionary activities. Lenin observed on 22 October: 'If we seize power today, we seize it not against the soviets but for them.'[4]

Effective organization would have been to no avail without a clear overall strategy. The basic principle of the Bolsheviks was to have a fixed long-term objective but a flexible short-term approach to it. The long-term aim was described in Lenin's *April Theses* as the 'transition from the first stage of the revolution, which gave power to the bourgeoisie . . . to the second stage, which should give the power into the hands of the proletariat and poorest strata of the peasantry'.[5] The short-term approach, however, would avoid any rigid or doctrinaire commitments. Above all, the right degree of force was essential at the right time; Lenin spoke of a judicious alternation between withdrawal and attack, depending on the strengths and weaknesses of the opponent. The Bolsheviks were, of course, fortunate in their leadership. Lenin, from the time of his return to Russia in April 1917, was the overall strategist of the revolution; he also dealt with internal divisions within the party and provided an authoritarian base which promoted a degree of discipline and unity which the other parties lacked. Above all, he was entirely responsible for the timing of the October Revolution. He had realized that the rising of July 1917 was premature and therefore urged restraint on that occasion. But by October he calculated that circumstances had changed sufficiently to warrant immediate action, and he urged: 'We must not wait! We may lose everything!'[6] From this point the initiative passed to Trotsky who used the Revolutionary Military Committee to take over the key installations in the capital.

However, while acknowledging that organization, conspiracy and timing were essential features of the Bolshevik Party, we should not lose sight of the balancing effect of revisionist ideas. A reasonable synthesis might go as follows. The Bolsheviks were not at this stage imposing their will on the people, nor were they shaping the revolution to their own design. Organization was therefore not essential for mobilizing support for revolution. Nevertheless, the situation in 1917 was highly volatile. Although the Bolsheviks had increased their popularity between March and October, it is possible to exaggerate the extent to which the peasantry had been won over. Quite possibly any transfer of allegiance was temporary, motivated by disillusionment with the indecisive policies of the Socialist Revolutionaries. The Bolsheviks would have been well aware of this and would have wanted to take maximum advantage of a situation which was only temporarily in their favour. This meant that they needed organization to take over the reins of power.

The survival of Bolshevik Russia: the Civil War, 1918–22

Seizing power was accomplished with surprising ease, but retaining it was to prove more difficult, as Lenin himself was all too aware. The most immediate threat was war – in two forms. The first was that the Great War, which had already been the catalyst in destroying Tsarism and the Provisional Government, would bring down the Bolsheviks as well. The second was that the regime would be destroyed in a bloody civil war. Lenin might survive one form of conflict, but he could hardly survive both. He resolved, therefore, to end the struggle with which he had never agreed and in 1918 accepted the terms of the Treaty of Brest-Litovsk dictated by the Germans. He justified the enormous loss of territory by pointing to the greater good of saving the regime; hence 'a disgraceful peace is proper, because it is in the interest of the proletarian revolution and the regeneration of Russia'.[7] As a result, he was able to concentrate on dealing with the threats against the Bolsheviks.

Views have changed recently as to just what these were.[8] Traditionally, the Russian Civil War has been seen as a struggle between the Reds and the Whites. The Reds were aiming to save the Bolshevik Revolution and to extend it to all parts of the country, while the Whites sought to bring down the Bolshevik regime and to restore the previous system. The conflict was therefore about saving the October Revolution against attempts at counter-revolution. Revisionist historians now argue that there were actually two civil wars. One was the struggle between different strands of revolutionaries to control the revolution: this has been called the Red–Green civil war. The other – the Red–White civil war – was between one strand of revolution and attempts made to overthrow it.

Using the second approach, we can trace the conflict through three main stages. The first was the Red–Green war between the Bolsheviks and the Socialist Revolutionaries. The latter had set up rival governments to the east of the rather limited confines of Bolshevik rule. These were a real threat to Red control since they had a broad base of popular support. Several, however, were overthrown by military coups in the middle of 1918; the main instigators were such ex-Tsarist officers as Kolchak.

These became part of a broader White offensive against the Reds on all fronts between 1918 and 1920 – the second stage of the Civil War. The earliest attacks, which came from the south, were led by Kornilov, Deniken and Alexeyev. When these were contained in 1918, the southern initiative passed to Deniken alone and then, in 1920, to Wrangel. The eastern front saw extensive engagements with Kolchak's troops, culminating in the capture of Omsk by the Bolsheviks (1919). In the Baltic sector Yudenitch made a lunge for Petrograd but was driven back from the outer suburbs. Meanwhile, foreign expeditionary forces had landed, in support of the Whites, at Archangel and Murmansk in the north, as well as in the Crimea and the Caucasus. The Japanese penetrated far into eastern Siberia, via the port of Vladivostok. By 1920, however, the White armies had been repulsed by Trotsky's newly formed Red Army and the powers had all withdrawn their supporting troops.

This enabled the Bolsheviks to focus on the third and final stage: the revival of the Red–Green conflict between 1920 and 1922, as peasant armies, supported by the Socialist Revolutionaries, sought even at this late stage to remove Lenin's regime.

The reasons for the Civil War?

The three phases of the Civil War had causes which were distinct and yet merged into each other.[9]

The first Red–Green phase (1917–18) was the direct result of rivalry between the Bolsheviks and the other revolutionary groups seeking to control the revolution. The Bolsheviks provoked the other parties by refusing to share power with them. Indeed, Lenin had seized power in October to prevent the formation of a broad-based government. He then rejected conciliatory proposals by the Socialist Revolutionaries, victors in the Constituent Assembly elections, to set up a coalition and instead dissolved the Assembly. The Socialist Revolutionaries and other moderate socialists, such as the Mensheviks, resisted what they regarded as a drift to dictatorship; they tried to convince the workforce that it was now vital to over-throw Bolshevik rule and reconvene the Constituent Assembly. Nor was dis-satisfaction with Bolshevism confined to Petrograd and Moscow. Early in 1918 the Yaroslavl soviets elected Menshevik majorities, while the Right SRs and Mensheviks scored similar successes in Riazan and Kursk. Within weeks there was widespread resistance to the Bolsheviks in the whole Volga region, including Samara and Yaroslavl, and the SRs established a directory at Ufa, which extended as far as the northern region around Archangel. Such widespread opposition was a real danger to the new Bolshevik regime which was, at this stage, by no means certain of survival.

Yet these same regions saw a swift transition from the Red–Green to the Red–White civil war. The links in the chain were a series of military coups conducted by ex-Tsarist officers. An attempt was made in September 1918 in Archangel, which failed; this was followed in November by another, in Omsk, which brought down the Socialist Revolutionary administration there. The new regime, under Admiral Kolchak, became the main focus of the westward offensive against the Bolsheviks. Other White thrusts from the Baltic and from the south emerged from the wreckage of moderate socialist governments. The overall effect was to transform the conflict from competing strands of revolution to a direct confrontation between revolution and counter-revolution. This was given an addi-tional dimension by the intervention of the foreign powers on behalf of the Whites. Why did they do this? Britain, the United States, France, Italy and Japan aimed to return Russia to the war against Germany, an undertaking made by the Whites. In the process they hoped to restore a regime which would acknowledge the debts which Tsarist Russia had incurred from them during the process of industrializa-tion and which would remove the threat of communism from the rest of Europe.

The Red–White civil war was largely over by late 1920. But the Bolsheviks were now confronted with a second Red–Green war. There was extensive upheaval in thirty-six provinces. By April 1921 there were 165 peasant armies in Russia, about 140 of which were connected with the SRs. The Bolsheviks simply referred to outbreaks of hooliganism and banditry, but clearly this was too dismissive. Other reasons are much more likely. For example, tension had now re-emerged between different revolutionary strands, which had been temporarily subsumed into the Red–White conflict. Many of the rebels again demanded an end to one-party dictatorship and a renewal of democratic elections. The slogans of the peasant armies were 'Soviets without Communists'. Unrest was also the result of peasant fears of the food levy, grain requisitioning and early attempts at collective farming; another peasant slogan was 'Down with State Monopoly on Grain Trade'. The Socialist Revolutionaries now tried to co-ordinate initially spontaneous uprisings into a second great effort to wrest control of the revolution from the Bolsheviks.

Despite these threats, the Bolsheviks had established control over the whole of Russia by 1922. The White armies had been forced to withdraw and many of the leaders of the Green enterprises were dead – either summarily shot by Red Army detachments or purged in a series of show trials. Bolshevik survival had therefore been transformed into victory.

Why did the Bolsheviks win the Civil War?

Again, the phases of the Civil War interacted with each other, to the advantage of the Bolshevik regime which, it should be remembered, was very much on the defensive. There is plenty of evidence that the Bolsheviks benefited from external or objective circumstances. At the same time, they also made their own luck at crucial moments. It is rare for success to result without a combination of the two.

Lenin's initial policy to deal with the Green threat was crucial. He acted quickly to remove the German threat in March 1918 by signing the Treaty of Brest-Litovsk with Germany. This withdrew Russia from the First World War and enabled the Bolsheviks to focus on the internal situation. In August 1918 he also concluded a trade agreement, by which the Bolshevik government was to pay 6 billion marks and provide the Germans with one-quarter of the oil production of Baku on the Caspian Sea. In return the Red Army were able to take their focus off the west, especially the Ukraine, and switch their forces eastwards to deal with the rival revolutionary movements in the Volga area. This enabled them to recapture Kazan and Samara. Swain goes so far as to say that, by agreeing to the treaty, 'the Kaiser saved Lenin'.[10] Whether this guaranteed a permanent victory, however, is uncertain. The Socialist Revolutionaries were still securely ensconced in Ufa and the rival revolutionaries appeared evenly matched. Survival did not, at this stage, mean victory.

What made the crucial difference was the series of coups, conducted against the Greens by Kolchak and others in 1918. Again, Swain attributes enormous importance to this: the first phase of the conflict was ended 'not by Bolshevik victory in that war but by the armed action of White generals'.[11] Through their coups against the Socialist Revolutionaries, they 'changed the whole nature of the civil war'. They severely weakened the Green governments, which had been the greatest threat to the Bolsheviks. The Bolsheviks were actually better equipped to fight counter-revolutionaries than they were fellow-revolutionaries. The new war forced many Greens to join with the Reds to deal with the common enemy. The catalyst for this was the Allied intervention on behalf of the Whites, which most Socialist Revolutionaries and Mensheviks found offensive. By December 1918 most areas saw negotiations between the Bolsheviks and other socialist parties; even the Socialist Revolutionaries sank their political differences with the Bolsheviks until victory could be accomplished against the Whites. This, of course, undermined their own chance of resisting the Bolsheviks in the longer term.

During the Red–White phase which followed, the Whites did a great deal to destroy their own bid for power. Their deficiencies were considerable. They were, according to Heretz, 'a large and disjointed agglomeration of forces operating on several fronts in diverse local circumstances'.[12] They had no real political base and even the areas through which they campaigned were not usually controlled by White governments: often they were under conflicting warlords or in the chaotic after-math of disintegrating socialist governments. They also lacked a common strategy and failed to co-ordinate the separate campaigns of Yudenitch, Kolchak, Deniken and Wrangel; nor did the Whites and the supporting powers ever set up an overall war council. They entirely failed to appeal to the masses, particularly the peasantry. According to Kenez, the White generals 'did not systematically summarize their goals and beliefs. They never understood the importance of ideology and did not take ideas seriously. They had no body of doctrine and no overall leader.'[13] The rural populations tended to support the Bolsheviks as the lesser of two evils: they feared that the Whites would restore the powerful landlords and reimpose the former dues and obligations. In any case, the White armies lived off the land during their campaigns and therefore caused immense destruction through their foraging and looting.

Nor were the Whites greatly assisted by foreign intervention. According to Mawdsley, 'Contrary to what is often thought ... the "fourteen power" anti-Bolshevik alliance that was featured in Soviet propaganda was a myth.'[14] Comparatively few Allied troops were sent to Russia and of these none participated in the battles. Keep lays particular stress on this point, attributing Bolshevik survival 'in part to sheer good luck'. Neither the Allies nor the Central powers were willing or able to take decisive action against them. The Bolsheviks 'were saved by the continuation of the war in the West, which held first priority in the thinking of all the protagonists'.[15] The Western powers were always lukewarm about supporting groups of nationalist conservatives who lacked even the pretence of a programme of reform. In addition, each Western government was internally divided as to whether to maintain the intervention after the end of 1918. Some ministers, espe-cially in Britain, were receptive to anti-White public opinion which was being mobilized by trade union movements. Politicians such as Winston Churchill who wanted to continue an anti-Bolshevik crusade were very much in a minority. By 1920 Lloyd George's coalition government had decided to withdraw any remaining British forces – despite Churchill's pleas – while the French government had decided to switch to a more defensive anti-Bolshevik strategy by bolstering up Poland.

Meanwhile, the position of the Bolsheviks was greatly strengthened by several advantages which they possessed and the Whites did not. The Reds controlled all the internal lines of communication: they were therefore able to deal with emer-gencies as they occurred, switching their troops from one front to another. By contrast, the Whites had severe transport difficulties and found that the trans-Siberian railway was clogged through political and military disputes. The Bolsheviks were defending the industrial heartland which contained Russia's major cities, industrial

centres and a rail network, which radiated outwards from Moscow. They also had
the advantage of Trotsky's reorganization of the Red Army. He was able to increase
the number of regular troops available to the Bolsheviks from 550,000 in September
1918 to 5.5 million by 1920; during the equivalent period support for the Whites
drained away so that the White troops were outnumbered by ten to one. Finally,
the Bolsheviks had a clear and systematic ideology and used their control over all
forms of communication to put across their propaganda. This undoubtedly had some
effect on the civilian population.

Once they had dealt with the Whites the Bolsheviks were able to switch their
attention back to the Greens. Although the military threat was more widespread
than in 1918, the Green political and ideological infrastructure had in the meantime broken down. This meant that there could be no concerted anti-Bolshevik
effort based on an alternative revolutionary strategy, as had existed in 1918. The
peasant armies may have been temporarily stiffened by the guerrilla warfare of
peasant leaders such as Antonov, but they were not up to resisting permanently the
Bolshevik forces which had just gained experience from putting down the White
armies. In any case, Lenin took political action to supplement the military campaigns
of the Red Army. A crucial factor in bringing to an end the wave of peasant rebellions was the decision to end food requisitioning and to introduce the New Economic
Policy in 1921. This meant that there was no longer a cause for which the peasantry needed to prolong its resistance.

Bolshevik victory was achieved at enormous cost. The Russian Civil War was,
after the Taiping Rebellion in mid-nineteenth-century China, the most destructive
in human history. The loss of life was far greater than that in the First World War.
At least 900,000 were killed in the Red Army; the various peasant armies lost some
1 million; and no-one has ever managed to come up with a satisfactory estimate
of White casualties. Civilian deaths were about 8.2 million, whether from disease,
military atrocities or terror, the last of these accounting for anything up to 5 million.
Destruction was massive and widespread, caused by deliberate sabotage or wanton
looting. In some areas starvation was so prevalent that normal social structures
completely broke down and cannibalism occurred. The economic impact was catastrophic, as agriculture was set back by several decades and the industrial
developments which had occurred under Tsarism were extensively dislocated. The
ways in which the Bolsheviks mobilized for victory also cast a shadow on the
regime which they created.

Creating the Bolshevik state, 1918–24

The creation of of the Bolshevik state was the result both of the October Revolution
and of the Civil War. How did the two relate to each other in the development of
a new communist regime?

It has generally been argued that the Bolsheviks had come to power as the result
of a limited coup in October 1917 and then proceeded to introduce the real revolution between 1918 and 1921 – as they had always intended. This revolution
consisted of four key components. The first was the organization of Russia's people
and resources to win the Civil War; this was the revolution mobilized. Second, the
Bolsheviks took the decision to move away from a Western democratic system to

a communist one based on the soviets; this was the essence of the political revolution. In the process they used coercion on a massive scale; the third constituent was therefore revolutionary terror. Fourth, the Bolsheviks aimed to introduce a revolutionary economy in the form of War Communism and to transform society through revolutionary egalitarianism. In all of these, the Bolsheviks had underlying ideological objectives and were therefore normally proactive. Not all of their changes succeeded. They were forced to backtrack on economic and social changes from 1921 and to concede that immediate changes were not going to be possible. However, any economic or social concessions were made possible only because the Bolsheviks retained a monopoly of political control throughout the whole period.

An altogether different view is possible – which is the one adopted in the next three sections. This moves away from the assumption that the Bolsheviks were solely designing a new system from above. Rather, they were also responding to pressures from below. This produces a perspective which is almost the mirror image of the first. The real revolution occurred not between 1918 and 1921, but in 1917: as we have already seen, the Bolsheviks had come to power in October by harnessing the full force of popular revolutionary feeling. Between 1918 and 1921, by contrast, they set about closing that revolution down, fearing the reviving popularity of the Socialist Revolutionaries and other moderate socialists. The Bolsheviks therefore resorted to changes which amounted in many respects to a *counter*-revolution. The mobilization of resources was initially intended to defeat the Green strand of popular revolution and to ensure that only the Red regime survived. The abandonment of Western parliamentary institutions, a direct response to the election victory of the Socialist Revolutionaries, was a means of permanently removing all other revolutionary parties. This was reinforced by the use of terror, which became the main device of counter-revolution. Economic policy was geared mainly to undermining other revolutionary influences. In the first Green and White phases this meant War Communism; in the second Green phase it meant the New Economic Policy. Social policies were more genuinely radical, but were partly a response to popular expectations for change and, in any case, were modified after 1921 in line with economic retreat.

The Bolsheviks justified many of their changes after 1918 by referring to ideological principles. Again, the two views differ in their approach to this. The traditional approach takes much of the ideological theory at face value. This assumes that Lenin and Trotsky were implementing from above policies and schemes which had already been planned. It is, however, more likely that they were constantly improvising in response to pressures beyond their immediate control and that ideology was usually a justification of policy introduced for essentially pragmatic reasons.

Political changes and terror

Shortly after the October Revolution one of the Menshevik leaders, Axelrod, said that 'the Bolshevik regime's days and weeks are numbered'.[16] He may have had good grounds for this, but events were to prove that the counterpart to the Bolsheviks' military survival was the consolidation of their internal political power.

The main development was the move away from a mixed democracy, with different types of representative institutions, towards a single or monolithic base.

The first casualty was the Western-type Constituent Assembly. The elections of November 1917 produced a sweeping majority for the Socialist Revolutionaries over the Bolsheviks. In January 1918 Lenin dissolved the Assembly and put an end to the hopes of the other socialist parties that a western democracy would emerge. This was clearly a pragmatic response to popular pressures which threatened to unseat the Bolsheviks, but Lenin justified it by a new layer of ideology. He explained that the Assembly was 'an expression of the old relation of political forces'.[17] In his search for an alternative he turned to the system of soviets, arguing that 'a republic of soviets is a higher form of democratic principle than the customary bourgeois republic with its Constituent Assembly'.[18] This was directly opposed to the policy of the Menshevik leaders, who saw the soviets as a means of expressing popular opinion only in exceptional times; after the end of the crisis, they argued, the soviets would take second place to the more conventional institutions of democracy. But Lenin's priority was to close down, to all but the Bolsheviks, access to the revolution and the power it had generated. This meant that the powers of the soviets had to be carefully controlled. Hence, although their number increased rapidly from 1918, their influence declined steadily. Keep considers that Lenin's intention was quite clear: he 'conceived of the soviets as instruments of rule rather than sovereign bodies'.[19]

The hand which controlled these instruments was the Bolshevik Party, shortly to be renamed the Communist Party. As far back as 1902 Lenin had maintained that the party should be the vanguard of the proletariat, based on the leadership of the few. This was, however, far from being a permanent blueprint: a more relaxed structure was necessary in 1917 to adapt the party to the wishes of the peasantry, workforce and soldiers. By 1918 pressures from below had become more negative and Lenin responded by reinstituting a more rigid structure of authority which led upwards to the Central Committee. This, in turn, had three specialized organs in the form of the Politburo, Orgburo and Secretariat. The party dominated the soviets at all levels to ensure that Socialist Revolutionaries and Mensheviks were denied access. Indeed, according to a party resolution of March 1919, 'the strictest centralism and the most severe discipline are an absolute necessity'.[20] The whole process was described as 'democratic', but not in a Western or bourgeois sense. Instead, Lenin's term 'democratic centralism' came to epitomize the complete subordination of state organs to the party – the main characteristic of the Communist regime within Russia between 1918 and 1991.

How were these changes carried out? Both Lenin and Trotsky believed in the need for force, although this was to be justified in 'the name of the interest of the workers'.[21] Between December 1917 and February 1922 the secret police, or Cheka, hunted down opponents of the regime and, by one calculation, executed over 140,000 people. This compared with an estimated total of 14,000 despatched by the Tsarist secret police, the Okhrana. Trotsky, a hardliner on the use of terror, explained the strategy on the grounds that 'we shall not enter into the kingdom of socialism in white gloves on a polished floor'.[22] Not all Bolsheviks approved. Victor Serge, a French communist, referred to the activities of the Cheka as one of the most impermissible errors that the Bolsheviks committed. He added: 'Was it necessary to resort to the procedures of the Inquisition?'[23] The first group to be dealt with by the Cheka were the anarchists, their views of unfettered political liberty being seen as a threat to the Bolshevik theory of the dictatorship of the proletariat. The moderate socialists – Mensheviks and Socialist Revolutionaries – were expelled from the soviets during the course of 1918, while thirty-four Socialist Revolutionary leaders were put on public trial in 1922. Again, there is a strong suspicion that terror was more about eliminating other revolutionaries than it was about preserving the revolution.

Yet the emergence of the one-party state was not a complete guarantee against dissent and unrest. If anything, the Bolsheviks encountered more extensive opposition as a result of their actions against the other parties. The critical year was 1921, when the Cheka reported no fewer than 118 separate uprisings. One example was the Kronstadt Revolt, which carried demands for soviets without Communists, elections by secret ballot and an end to the belief that the only alternative to a bourgeois regime was the dictatorship of the Communist Party. Although the Kronstadt Revolt was suppressed by Trotsky and Tukhachevskii, the threat was taken seriously by Lenin, who referred to it as 'the biggest . . . internal crisis'[24] of the period. Since the immediate cause had been the appalling economic situation, Lenin's response was to moderate Bolshevik policy in the way examined in the next section. At the same time, however, Lenin maintained his grasp on political power by ensuring that the opposition parties did not re-emerge. He proceeded therefore by trial and error rather than by systematic policy. Only when he was fully satisfied about the security of the Bolshevik position did he end the terror by closing down the Cheka in February 1922.

Other potential threats to Bolshevik control were the aspirations of the various nationalities. Tsarist Russia had contained many captive peoples who had seized the opportunity provided by the First World War and the Bolshevik Revolution to go their own way. Some, like the Poles, Finns and Baltic peoples, achieved complete independence as a result of Russian defeat in the First World War. Others, like the Ukrainians and Georgians, stayed out during the Civil War but were brought back into line after the Bolshevik victories over the Whites. Lenin's whole approach to the nationalities was cautious and pragmatic. Originally he had viewed any form of federation with suspicion. Faced with the practical problems of the period 1918–24, however, he came to the conclusion that the only safe means of allowing for self-determination was through federalism. As a result, the constitutions of 1918 and 1924 established the two largest federations in the world – the Russian Soviet Federated Socialist Republic and the Union of Soviet Socialist Republics. This, however, was only a partial concession, for the total subordination of the organs of each republic to those of the party ensured that federalism did not mean decentralization. The USSR, in other words, was controlled by the Communist Party: national self-determination was cancelled out by 'democratic centralism'.

Just how important the control of the Communist Party was can be seen in the events of 1991. In August Yeltsin banned the operation of the Communist Party within the Russian Federation, to be followed in September by similar measures in other parts of the USSR. By the end of December the Soviet Union had fallen apart.

Economic changes

Bolshevik ideology was based at least in part on the economic principles of Marxism. One of these was that any society consisted of a foundation – or base

– and a superstructure. The former comprised the economic system upon which the society was based, the latter the political and social institutions which were created by the foundation. A change of institutions therefore needed to be accompanied by a transformation of the economy. Lenin probably intended to transform the Russian economy by wiping out all exploitation of man by man and eliminating the division of society into classes. But he found that his hands were tied, first by the need to adjust Bolshevik policies in 1917 to popular demands and, second, by the rapidly changing circumstances between 1918 and 1924. The result was anything but the planned system which Marxism predicated. Rather, it was characterized by trial and error; even Lenin admitted that he had taken 'two steps forward, one step backward'.

In the first step forward, taken between November 1917 and mid-1918, the emphasis was on caution, and nationalization was applied only to banks, foreign trade and armaments works. In particular, Lenin was careful to avoid antagonizing the peasantry and made every effort to coax them away from the party which they had traditionally supported – the Socialist Revolutionaries. Hence, by the 1917 Decree on Land he confirmed the peasant takeover of the nobles' estates, without, however, introducing large-scale socialist collective production.

Then, in mid-1918, came a second step forward, with the introduction of a policy generally known as War Communism. This was basically an attempt to replace the free market with state control over all means of production and distribution. The Decree on Nationalization, for example, covered all large-scale enterprises, while grain requisitioning greatly reduced the food stocks of the peasantry in order to supply the workers in the cities and the troops fighting the Whites. The result was chaos. The monetary economy disintegrated, to be replaced by barter and black marketeering. Grain requisitioning led directly to a drastic decline in production as the peasantry lost all incentive to labour, while the inevitable shortage of food in the cities provoked strikes and riots which shook the very foundations of the Bolshevik regime. Of these the most serious was the Kronstadt Revolt (1921), mentioned in the previous section.

Why was such a policy introduced at all? There are two possible explanations. One is that it was a genuine emergency measure to mobilize the resources of the state in its struggle for survival against counter-revolutionary forces. Lenin later said: 'War Communism was thrust upon us by war and ruin. It was not, nor could it be, a policy that corresponded to the economic tasks of the proletariat. It was a temporary measure.'[25] If so, this is another example of the adjustment of Bolshevik policies to meet immediate exigencies. By taking such drastic action Lenin was now trying to squeeze out of the peasantry the sort of attachment to private property which made the Socialist Revolutionaries an abiding danger to Bolshevik control. He hoped, in other words, to deprive the Socialist Revolutionaries of the keystone of the policy. As it turned out, the policy of War Communism was a fundamental error. R. Medvedev emphasizes that the New Economic Policy, eventually introduced in 1921, should have been applied from the start instead of War Communism and that it must be concluded that Lenin did not at that time arrive at the better solution to the economic problems of the post-revolutionary period.[26]

The year 1921, therefore, saw a step backward. The basic strategy was now to restore to the economy a degree of capitalism and private enterprise. Introducing his New Economic Policy (NEP), Lenin argued that the road to socialism would be longer than originally thought. 'Our poverty and ruin are so great that we cannot at one stroke restore full-scale factory, state, socialist production.'[27] It was also impossible to think only in ideological terms. 'If certain communists were inclined to think it possible in three years to transform the whole economic foundation, to change the very roots of agriculture, they were certainly dreamers.'[28] Thus the peasantry were now permitted to dispose of their surplus produce on payment of a tax, and 91 per cent of industrial enterprises were returned to private ownership or trusts. The early results of the NEP were disappointing, as economic recovery was held up by famine (1921–2) and a financial crisis (1923). But, by 1924, the year of Lenin's death, considerable progress had been made, and by 1926 the economy had regained the 1913 production level.

In the NEP Lenin left an intermediate strategy which contained a long-term problem. Should the mixed economy be retained indefinitely, as Bukharin argued, or should socialism be accelerated – a course urged by Trotsky? As will be seen, this turned into a major dispute which overlapped the manoeuvring in the struggle for the political leadership.

Lenin: an assessment

Lenin was plagued by ill health during the last two years of his life. He suffered a stroke in May 1922 and, although he made a partial recovery, he never again played a full part in political life. His health deteriorated rapidly from March 1923 with the loss of speech and the onset of paralysis. On his death in January 1924 a post-mortem revealed that one of the two hemispheres of his brain had shrunk to the size of a walnut. The new leadership ignored one of his last wishes by having his body embalmed and placed on open display.

What are we to make of the period 1917–24? How should we interpret the dual process of revolution and consolidation? On the one hand, certain positive features are evident. Lenin led a party to electoral victory in the major soviets in Russia by October 1917, replacing the Mensheviks and Socialist Revolutionaries as the real spokesman of the urban workers. He used this new-found popularity to seize power and overturn a temporary regime which had clearly lost its way. He subsequently held the new state together against a series of counter-revolutionary attacks which were extensively backed by the major powers; eventually he expanded the frontiers almost to the previous limits of Tsarist Russia, thereby preventing the sort of disintegration which had already overtaken the Ottoman Empire and Austria-Hungary. Finally, he brought a dramatic change to the lives of the ordinary Russian people. The last social remnants of the Tsarist regime were swept away as the Bolsheviks confirmed the peasantry in possession of the nobles' estates; while measures were taken to end the exploitation of labour in industry by capitalists careless of such essentials as working conditions and health schemes.

There is, however, another picture. The cost of Russia's transformation was greater than she had ever experienced. Over 20 million lives were lost during a period of unprecedented conflict and destruction which affected the country – from the Polish frontier in the west to eastern Siberia, from Archangel in the north to the Caspian Sea in the south. It is possible to absolve Lenin from total responsibility for the ruin caused by the numerous military campaigns, but not from the unnecessary suffering and wastage caused by War Communism. And during the conflict with external enemies Lenin was strengthening the internal apparatus of coercion, establishing a one-party state and dispensing with more moderate forms of socialist democracy. In the process, he demolished one of history's promising what-might-have-beens.

This double-sided view is reflected in the controversies which have arisen over the two components of the period 1917–24: the Leninist revolution and the Leninist state.

At its most fundamental, the conflict of opinion concerns the very nature of the events which occurred in October 1917. The Bolshevik view was that the revolution was inevitable, part of a historical and dialectical process and representing, in Trotsky's words, the 'transfer of power from one class to another'.[29] A superior form of state was emerging; in this sense the revolution was, according to Lenin, a turning point in history, with the Bolsheviks directing and channelling the 'upsurge of the people'. The other contemporary explanation was advanced by Kerensky, a principal victim of Lenin's success. He saw the October coup as a freak occurrence and a 'perversion' of Russia's historical trends. He argued that a series of unfortunate events provided the opportunity for the Bolsheviks to 'break up the Provisional Government and stop the establishment of a democratic system in Russia'. Kornilov's attempt at dictatorship 'opened the door to the dictatorship of Lenin'; in fact, far from responding to any popular surge, Lenin succeeded 'only by way of conspiracy, only by way of treacherous armed struggle'.[30]

Lenin's interpretation was endorsed by official Soviet historiography. All other parties and types of democracy were mere throwbacks to a lower stage of historical development; hence, they could be thrown on the rubbish heap of history. Western historians, not confined to monolithic interpretation, vary in their approach. Some incline towards the conspiracy view of Kerensky. They see the Bolshevik Revolution as a distortion of socialism and Marxism used to construct a dictatorship which was by no means the logical outcome of previous trends. According to Gregor, the conspiracy was self-perpetuating, for 'the conspiratorial party of the revolution became a conspiratorial party of legitimacy'.[31] Others, such as Acton, see the Bolsheviks under Lenin as the only group successfully to tap into the real aspirations of the people. Christopher Hill adopts a Western Marxist position; to him, 'Lenin symbolizes the Russian Revolution as a movement of the poor and oppressed of the earth who have successfully risen against the great and powerful.'[32] This does not, however, harmonize with the revisionist view that Lenin may have been in tune with revolutionary fervour in 1917 but that he proceeded to close the revolution down after coming to power.

Another major controversy concerns the nature of Lenin's regime. One extreme has been put forcefully in Solzhenitsyn's *Gulag Archipelago*, published in 1974. One of the central themes of this book is that the October Revolution and the Bolshevik regime led inexorably to Stalinism, that they were one and the same process. In a review of the *Gulag Archipelago*, however, Mandel puts the reverse case, emphasizing the fundamental difference between the two regimes: the Bolshevik Revolution and the Stalinist counter-revolution.[33]

Some historians incline towards the case for continuity between Lenin and Stalin, although this is a criticism of Lenin rather than a rehabilitation of Stalin. A strong case is established by Leggett, who is convinced that terror was implicit in Leninism. Lenin's Cheka led ultimately to Stalin's NKVD (People's Commissariat for International Affairs – the forerunner of the KGB); consequently, 'it was Lenin who laid the police state foundations which made Stalin's monstrous feats technically possible'.[34] By contrast, E.H. Carr has argued that Lenin was sufficiently different to Stalin to have been likely 'to minimize and mitigate the element of coercion' had he lived to face Stalin's difficulties. Lenin was 'reared in a humane tradition, he enjoyed enormous prestige, great moral authority and powers of persuasion'. By contrast, 'Stalin had no moral authority whatever … He understood nothing but coercion, and from the first employed this openly and brutally.'[35] Mandel points out that whatever terror did exist under Lenin was a direct response to attempts at counter-revolution, to 'the White terror that came first' and the 'invasion of Soviet territory on seven different fronts'. Unlike Stalin, Lenin and Trotsky did not destroy the basis of justice. They did make mistakes in suppressing other parties and banning factions within the Communist Party itself, but these were direct responses to a desperate emergency and were conceived only as temporary measures.[36] Finally, L. Schapiro maintains that, despite being authoritarian in his methods, Lenin never destroyed the basic machinery of the various party organs. Stalin, on the other hand, ceased to use the party as a base of power, depending instead on a personal secretariat. He therefore exploited and abused Lenin's system – but, of course, the system had no inbuilt safeguards to prevent this from happening. Thus 'Stalinism was not a necessary consequence of Leninism, but it was nevertheless a possible result.'[37]

THE SUCCESSION, 1924–9

The struggle for power

During the last months of his effective rule, Lenin seemed increasingly concerned about the problem of his successor. In his *Testament* of December 1922 Lenin provided comments on the leading contenders. He mentioned, but passed over briefly, Kamenev, Zinoviev, Bukharin and Piatakov. He gave more attention to Trotsky, although he considered that he had become too heavily involved in administrative detail. When he came to consider Stalin he expressed real doubts: 'Comrade Stalin, having become General Secretary, has concentrated limitless power in his hands, and I am not certain that he will always be careful enough in his use of this power.' Shortly afterwards, in January 1923, Lenin added a codicil to the *Testament* urging the party to take action to remove Stalin from his post as General Secretary. He should, Lenin concluded, be replaced by 'some other person who is superior to Stalin only in one respect, namely, in being more tolerant, more loyal, more polite and more attentive to comrades'.[38] Before Lenin could do anything to prod the party into action he was incapacitated by his second and third strokes.

When Lenin died in January 1924 the succession was still uncertain. At first Stalin's chances seemed remote, particularly in view of Lenin's *Testament* and its codicil, which were read out at a meeting of the party's Central Committee. But the other party members agreed that Stalin had improved his reputation during the

2 Joseph Stalin, 1879–1953, photo taken in 1927 (David King Collection)

course of 1923 and therefore voted to put aside the recommendations of the codicil. Meanwhile, Kamenev and Zinoviev had come to the conclusion that Trotsky was the main threat to the party's stability, partly because of his forceful personality and partly because of his close association with the army. Hence, they collaborated with Stalin and a power-sharing triumvirate emerged, with Stalin remaining in his post of General Secretary. But the triumvirate was to be only a temporary phase in the succession to Lenin. By 1929 Stalin was in total control, having overcome the challenges of all his possible rivals: Trotsky, Kamenev, Zinoviev and Bukharin. There appear to have been three main phases in this development.

The first was the emergence, between 1923 and 1925, of a major split between the triumvirate (Stalin, Kamenev and Zinoviev) and the isolated figure of Trotsky. This division was expressed in an ideological debate between 'Permanent Revolution' and 'Socialism in One Country'. Trotsky's strategy of Permanent Revolution emphasized rapid industrialization and the abolition of private farming at home. Abroad, Russia would promote the spread of revolution to the rest of Europe which would ensure the survival of Bolshevism. Socialism in One Country, advocated by Stalin, stressed the need to maintain the more moderate economic course of the NEP within Russia and to promote more positive relations with other countries to increase trade and attract foreign investment. Stalin was far less deeply committed to the economic principles of this right-wing strategy than Trotsky was to the left, his motive being the political one of isolating Trotsky. In this he succeeded. At the XIVth Party Congress in 1925 he received overwhelming support (although not from Kamenev and Zinoviev, both of whom opposed further concessions to the peasantry). Trotsky's political days were clearly numbered.

The second stage was the disposal of Kamenev and Zinoviev, which occurred between 1925 and 1927. Never one to share power for long, Stalin aligned himself with the most obvious rightist elements within the party, including Bukharin, Rykov and Tomsky. Between 1926 and 1927 Kamenev and Zinoviev made common cause with Trotsky, but it was too late. The Party Conference of 1927 gave its approval to Socialism in One Country and denounced Permanent Revolution. Trotsky was expelled from the Politburo, along with Kamenev and Zinoviev, and was exiled from Russia in 1929, while both Kamenev and Zinoviev were to perish in the purges of the 1930s.

The third stage was predictable: the elimination of Bukharin and the rest of the right, which was accomplished by 1929. The end of the 1920s also saw a hardening of Stalin's own economic ideas as he began to associate Socialism in One Country with the total transformation of industry at the expense of the peasantry – the programme of Trotsky, in effect, without the insistence on spreading revolution to the rest of Europe. This was strongly opposed by Bukharin, Rykov and Tomsky, who had always supported a moderate policy towards the peasantry. As Stalin gradually introduced measures against the wealthy peasantry, or kulaks, Bukharin, Rykov and Tomsky became more outspoken. Stalin accused them of plotting against the party's agreed strategy and forced them to resign from the Politburo and from their state offices.

By 1929 Stalin dominated the party and, through the party, the state more completely than Lenin had ever done. Ahead lay the sweeping economic changes and the purges. Bukharin compared him to Genghis Khan, adding 'Stalin will strangle us. He is an unprincipled intriguer who subordinates everything to his lust for power.'

Why Stalin?

Stalin was probably the least impressive of all the candidates for the succession. He was totally eclipsed by Trotsky in the October Revolution and never succeeded in winning the friendship and confidence of Lenin. He was even regarded as a plodder; Trotsky referred to him as 'the party's most eminent mediocrity'. This was to prove a serious underestimate. Stalin had skills which were less obvious, but more deadly. He was also able to benefit from a set of objective conditions which favoured mediocrity rather than brilliance.

Beneath Stalin's bland and grey exterior was a singularly ruthless and opportunist character. While posing as a moderate, he waited for the opportunity to attack other candidates for the leadership – first Zinoviev and Kamenev, then Bukharin. Historians have remained in agreement about Stalin's attributes here. McCauley's view is typical: 'He was a very skilful politician who had a superb grasp of tactics, could predict behaviour extremely well and had an unerring eye for personal weaknesses.'[39] In particular, he was able to capitalize on Bukharin's inability to convert his plausible economic theory into a credible programme, on Kamenev's lack of vision and on Zinoviev's organizational weakness. Stalin, by contrast, showed consistent skills in grouping around him an alternative set of allies – men like Kalinin, Kuibyshev, Molotov and Voroshilov.

What made this possible was Stalin's supremacy within the party. His vital appointment was to the post of General Secretary in 1922. Lenin had good reason to be concerned about Stalin's accumulation of power and influence. Stalin controlled the party administration and was responsible for giving out offices: hence, he had the main voice in membership and promotion. Gradually he built up a steady base of support which made it possible for him to manoeuvre so effectively among his political rivals. The process operated as follows. The Communist Party was officially a democratic institution, in which the lowest level – the local parties – elected the Party Congress which, in turn, produced the membership of the Central Committee. The latter then elected the Politburo. The composition of the local parties was determined by the Secretariat, which was under Stalin's control. Over a period of time, therefore, Stalinist supporters moved into the upper levels of the party. There was an added incentive for these men; if Stalin's opponents could be removed from the highest offices then there would be a series of vacancies. It is hardly surprising, therefore, that Stalin's appointees should have been so willing to support him and that other prominent Bolsheviks were not accorded the respect which their experience perhaps deserved.

But even this would have had limited effect if he had not been assisted by objective circumstances, the most important of which was the threat of the impending collapse of Bolshevism into chaos, to which two main factors contributed. The first of these was the failure of revolution abroad. Trotsky's reputation had been closely tied to the spread of communism in Europe. But the opportunities for this had all disappeared by 1919. The Spartacists failed to seize power in Germany, while the Béla Kun regime was overthrown in Hungary in under a hundred days. The benefit to Stalin was enormous. According to Colletti, 'The first rung of the ladder which was to carry Stalin to power was supplied by the Social-Democratic leaders who in January 1919 murdered Rosa Luxemburg and Karl Liebknecht . . . The remaining rungs were supplied by the reactionary wave which subsequently swept Europe.'[40] Against this Stalin could project a solid, traditionally Slavic appeal which was more in keeping with his emphasis on Socialism in One Country.

The second factor favouring Stalin was the insecurity of Bolshevik economic policies. The two strategies proposed for the 1920s appeared to be alarmingly antagonistic. On the one hand was the planned retreat of the NEP – what Lenin described as 'one step forward, two steps backward'. Bukharin interpreted this as meaning that the economy should now progress at the pace of 'the peasant's slowest nag'. On the other hand, Trotsky and the leftists argued for increasing the pace of industrialization to implement socialism. Russia was therefore caught up in a conflict involving a new peasantry, which benefited from a revived capitalism allowed by the NEP, and the urban workers who had more to gain from accelerated socialism. Stalin was actually one of the few leading Bolsheviks who was able to make the necessary adjustments between these extremes, going with the objective conditions of the time. The early 1920s favoured the NEP and the rightists, whereas the procurement crisis of 1927 demonstrated that the NEP was no longer working and so needed a radical rethink. Hence Stalin's struggle against Bukharin, Rykov and Tomsky was seen by many at the time as a balanced reaction to a policy which had failed by all objective criteria. This may or may not have been true, but crucially the majority of the party thought this way. They therefore considered that they had good grounds for supporting the leader to whom many owed their positions. So Stalin confirmed support for his position by reading correctly the signs of the economic times. A recent view is that 'Machine politics alone did not account for Stalin's triumph'; rather, 'the salient political fact' of 1928–9 was 'a growing climate of high party opinion'.[41] Stalin's ability to bend like a reed therefore owed much to the prevailing wind of circumstances.

One final issue needs careful analysis. The rise of Stalin can be seen too much as the calculation of a supremely rational party machine taking advantage of an efficient dictatorship already established by Lenin. What we have already seen might point in this direction. Or the reverse could apply. The revolution had experienced an emergency in the form of the Civil War which had created widespread chaos. Policies and organizations were thrown into the melting pot. Stalin was by normal criteria a mediocre politician but his rather basic skills were enhanced by these circumstances. He succeeded not in producing order overall but in controlling particular pressure points within the chaos. Trotsky was right about Stalin's ability but wrong about the situation which allowed mediocrity to prevail.

Why not Trotsky?

At first sight Trotsky might seem ideally placed to assume the mantle of Lenin. He had been the tactician of Lenin's strategy in October 1917; as President of the Petrograd Soviet he had organized the Revolutionary Military Committee which had seized power. During the chaotic months which followed he created the Red Army and, as Commissar for War, was instrumental in overcoming the threats from the Whites and foreign inverventionists. He has, indeed, been described as the 'dynamo of the militarised Bolshevik state'.[42] At the same time he made fundamental additions to Bolshevik doctrine, the most important of which was his emphasis on Permanent Revolution. He had considerable personal talents. He was unquestionably the greatest orator of the October Revolution, and was renowned for his intellect, statesmanship and administrative ability. Yet, for all these attributes, he found himself out of effective power by 1925, out of the party by 1927 and out of the country by 1929.

Part of the reason has already been provided – Stalin's rapid accumulation of power within the Bolshevik Party which enabled him to outmanoeuvre Trotsky. The rest of the explanation can be found in a number of serious disadvantages which helped turn some of Trotsky's apparent strengths into liabilities. The first was his incompatibility with other leading members of the party. He towered above them intellectually but in a way which brought him suspicion rather than respect. His whole attitude was profoundly influenced by contacts with western Europe. He therefore tended to play down Russian or Slavic achievements in culture and, in particular, in philosophy. After Lenin's death, however, the most influential of the Bolshevik leaders had little experience of the West and were therefore much more sympathetic to Stalin's pro-Slavic line. Hence, in January 1925 a resolution of the party's Central Committee condemned Trotskyism as 'a falsification of communism in the spirit of approximation to "European" patterns of pseudo-Marxism'.[43] As a 'westerner', Trotsky was also regarded as an intruder. He had avoided joining the Bolshevik Party until 1917 and had previously shown more sympathy for the Marxist principles of the Mensheviks. Lenin had found his assistance indispensable and had therefore given him rapid promotion, which was resented by others in the party.

It was therefore crucial for Trotsky to consolidate his own position within the party. This, however, is precisely what he neglected to do. The revolutionary leader and military organizer was unable to adapt to party politics; in Mikoyan's words, Trotsky 'is a man of State, not of the Party'.[44] This made him particularly unpopular with men who had tended to sink their own identities into the party organization. Kamenev, for example, complained that Trotsky entered the party as an individualist, 'who thought, and still thinks, that in the fundamental question of the revolution it is not the party, but he, comrade Trotsky, who is right'.[45] Throughout the period 1917–29 Trotsky persistently underestimated the suspicion in which he was held and took no effective measures to try to dispel it. His capacity for leadership and his ability to persuade were employed *outside* the party; as Carr observed, 'he had no talent for leadership among equals'.[46]

Soviet historians saw Trotsky as an incorrigible opportunist. This, however, is an exaggeration as, in many respects, he was just the opposite. He lacked all the essential components of patience, tact and timing and missed a unique opportunity to make a move against Stalin. He failed, in May 1924, to turn the knife in Stalin and even voted for the suspension of Lenin's codicil which would have removed Stalin from high office. The picture which emerges is of a politician completely out of his element, with no natural political instinct and no real understanding of how to exploit a particular situation.

After being expelled from Russia in 1929 Trotsky launched a series of verbal attacks on Stalin's regime. He criticized the growth of Stalin's personality cult; he was outspoken about Stalin's total failure to comprehend the threat of the Nazis in Germany in the early 1930s; and he wrote extensively on what he saw as Stalin's distortions of Marxism–Leninism. But, lacking a power base, he could be no more than a 'prophet in exile', to use the description of Deutscher.

Learning the wrong lesson from history

The Bolsheviks tended to adopt a determinist approach to history. Marxism weaves patterns into historical development and claims that these patterns are repeatable and therefore predictable. The contemporaries of Stalin and Trotsky were influenced to some extent by an interpretation of the past that shaped their reactions to the two contenders for the succession. A retrospective view suggests that they made the wrong choice because they failed to appreciate that history is unlikely to repeat itself in the same way. If history is a science, it is not based on any deducible formula; rather, it is 'the science of what never happens twice'.

The Bolsheviks were especially mindful of the events of the French Revolution. Between 1793 and 1794 had occurred a radical phase, often known as the Reign of Terror. This had then been sharply reversed by the *coup d'état* of Thermidor, in which the policies and leadership had swung to the right, eventually to be taken over by the military under Napoleon Bonaparte. By 1802 the French republic had been converted into the personalized rule of Napoleon as Emperor. The Bolsheviks drew from this the lesson that the most dangerous threat after 1917 was the emergence of a new Bonapartism. One of the main advantages that Stalin had was that he was seen as a much safer alternative than Trotsky. The latter was associated by many with this Bonapartist threat, largely because of the way in which he had built up the Red Army during the Civil War between 1918 and 1921. Because of this deterministic belief that revolutionary patterns must repeat themselves, Trotsky was feared and isolated. This, ironically, enabled the emergence of Stalin, a dictator far more formidable than any Bonaparte. The lessons of history differ according to the power of those who interpret them. The Bolsheviks, by trying to avoid the repetition of one mistake, merely committed another. Orwell must have been conscious of this in *Animal Farm* when he gave the name Napoleon to the pig representing Stalin, not Trotsky.

STALIN'S RULE TO 1941

What kind of dictator was Stalin?

After establishing himself, Stalin ruthlessly extended his power and pushed ahead with his policies. The result was an extreme totalitarian dictatorship. Stalin went further than Lenin in imposing his own stamp on Russia. He exerted greater personal control over the Communist Party and, to ensure its permanence, he unleashed a flood of coercion and terror which was unprecedented and unparalleled. His use of the NKVD and the purges caused the deaths of many millions of Soviet people. This eliminated any serious threat to his position and enabled him to proceed to major economic changes in the form of forced collectivization and industrialization through three Five Year Plans. He was also responsible for some major social and cultural changes under the collective description of Socialist Realism which, in turn, played a vital role in augmenting Stalin's own personality cult. Foreign policy, too, came under Stalin's direct control; he determined its overall rationale and dictated what course it should take. He was unquestionably one of the most ruthless and most pragmatic of all the statesmen contributing to the international scene between the wars.

This picture of Stalin is easily recognizable and is not really open to dispute. But huge changes have recently occurred in its corollary. It was once thought that

Stalin's very ruthlessness ensured the efficiency of his system, and that the Soviet Union was a far better totalitarian model than, for example, Nazi Germany. Increasingly, however, the Stalinist regime is being seen as inefficient and even ramshackle. Far from managing to control the Soviet Union, he was often pushed by circumstances or by pressures from below. The overall argument for this can be summarized as follows. Although Stalin came to power partly through his own abilities, he was also greatly assisted by circumstance. Lenin's Bolshevik regime had run into the ground by 1921 and had had to resort to the New Economic Policy (NEP) and a general relaxation of the earlier radical socialism. By 1927, however, moderation was failing to deliver results, so that radicalism was revived with renewed energy. This coincided with Stalin's consolidation of power, so that he was able to take the initiative in launching a series of new programmes such as collectivization, the Five Year Plans and political centralization. In this respect, Stalin was reactivating the earlier dynamism of the Bolsheviks and was stealing some of the policies for which he had condemned Trotsky to exile. He was determined to push ahead with this radicalism through economic and social change.

Far from being a model totalitarian dictatorship, however, the Stalinist political system was remarkably defective. The main problem was that there was less power at the centre than is commonly supposed. The core of both the administration and the party had enormous difficulty in exerting controls over local officials and institutions. Although Stalin took the initiative for most of the policies of the period 1929–41, he frequently lost control over their implementation as here the initiative passed to the localities. Usually what happened was that local officials and groups pressed on too enthusiastically in carrying out their orders, creating widespread chaos which then had to be dealt with by the centre applying the brakes. This, in turn, would result in local inertia so that again the centre had to recreate momentum. There were therefore violent swings of the pendulum: local interests sought to interpret central policies in the most favourable way, in response to which the centre had to take corrective action. As a general principle, therefore, Stalin's political power was used initially in a proactive way, but then became increasingly reactive. At times he came dangerously close to losing control altogether.

The purges are particularly open to reinterpretation. The traditional view is that Stalin was entirely responsible for the terror which swept the country during the 1930s and again after 1945. Certainly he initiated it. But it is highly questionable whether he was able to control it and it could well have assumed a momentum far beyond what he had intended. The purges were therefore exacerbated by local forces which interpreted Stalin's orders in their own way, whether on collective farms or in factories. The incidence of terror ebbed and flowed as Stalin sought constantly to regain control.

The second area is the economy, in which a similar picture emerges. Stalin launched a policy of collectivization in 1928, only to find that it was implemented too rapidly and unsystematically. Local party officials and detachments of the NKVD exceeded their quotas, for which they were rebuked by Stalin in 1930. When the brakes were applied, local interests became more defensive so that a second offensive had to be launched and the whole economy became caught up with the purges. In industry, too, local managers had their own reasons for reinterpreting instructions from the centre. As a result, economic changes were inefficiently planned and implemented.

A new angle has also been applied to Stalin's social changes. He did not reverse a radical Bolshevik trend: this is too positive a perception. The situation was that the changes made by the Bolsheviks were already beginning to slow down under the impetus of the NEP after 1921. Stalin attempted to revive the radical policies in relation to the family and education, only to find that these added to the chaos of the early 1930s which was apparent in politics and the economy. For this reason there was a swing back to support for traditional social institutions and a revival of conservative educational policies. This has been seen as part of a deliberate effort to underpin his personal authoritarian status. It could, however, be interpreted as a more instinctive reaction to escape the consequences of a programme which was not working.

None of this reduces the repressiveness of the Stalinist system. Stalin is still seen by most historians as perhaps the most ruthless dictator of the twentieth century, responsible for the deaths of many millions and prepared to make cynical use of terror on a massive scale. It remains extremely difficult to attempt to justify Stalin's actions or to rehabilitate Stalin as a character. But, as the following sections show, the extent of his control was often not in accordance with that of his brutality.

The political system: party, constitution and administration

The period 1929 to 1941 saw an apparently contradictory political development. On the one hand, Stalin gradually squeezed all signs of democracy out of the party, confirming his personal power and eliminating any possible rivals. On the other hand, changes in the Soviet constitution appeared to extend the range of democracy in the electoral system and some of the state institutions.

During the early 1930s the top levels of the party, especially the Central Committee, had taken vital decisions concerning economic planning and had greatly accelerated the collectivization of agriculture. At the same time, the party swelled its numbers and modified its organization to include more members from trade unions and factories. But the high point of the party was reached in 1934. The XVIIth Party Congress was full of euphoria and self-satisfaction at the scope of the party's achievements in industry. The next five years, however, saw drastic changes as Stalin reduced the top membership in systematic purges, as described in the next section; by 1939 none of the original Bolsheviks who had participated in the October Revolution was left. Stalin also restructured the party as a pyramid, with high grades being conferred as a reward for unquestioning loyalty.

Constitutional developments presented a strange contrast. The adoption in 1936 of a more progressive constitution coincided with Stalin's onslaught on the party. As part of the build-up, there was unprecedented preliminary discussion, with millions of people being consulted. A considerable change was introduced into the electoral system. Universal suffrage now applied to all over the age of eighteen, while voting was to be secret, direct and no longer weighted (as it had been in the 1918 and 1924 constitutions) in favour of the urban workers. The soviets, or legislative bodies, were also reformed. The new Supreme Soviet comprised two chambers, the Soviet of the Union, based on electoral districts, and the Soviet of the Nationalities, reflecting the regional and ethnic composition of the country as a whole. Article 30 of the constitution affirmed that collectively these were the supreme organ of state power. The Supreme Soviet elected a series of specialist committees and a thirty-three-man presidium for executive functions. The whole structure was undoubtedly an improvement and remained in existence until the largely insubstantial amendments made in Brezhnev's 1977 constitution.

How can one explain the disparity between developments in the party and the constitution? First, the 1936 constitution was made as progressive as possible in appearance in order to attract a favourable response from the West. The mid-1930s, after all, saw a growing concern within the Soviet Union about the spread of fascism and serious attempts by Stalin to foster popular fronts against it. Second, Stalin used the constitution as a means of diverting attention, internal and external, away from his purges. Hence, at a time when the party was being systematically drained of its top leadership, publicity was given to the constitution. This could well explain the remarkably restrained reaction of the West to events in the Soviet Union in the late 1930s. Third, the 1936 constitution was democratic in theory only. Many of the high-sounding principles were not implemented in practice and the supposed power of the Supreme Soviet remained under the direct supervision of Stalin himself. He therefore aimed to dominate the proceedings of the Soviet as directly as he controlled the party. In theory, there was nothing to stop him, at the centre, from pursuing any administrative policy he wanted.

But did this actually *work*? Revisionist historians have shown that we cannot take for granted a direct connection between totalitarianism and efficiency – whether in Fascist Italy, Nazi Germany or Stalinist Russia. The key point is that although dictatorship may well have been strengthened at the centre, this could not be fully effective unless it was properly implemented at local level, within both the state and the party. Centralized dictatorship had to operate outwards through effective channels or, to use a different metaphor, the influence of the apex had to seep down through all levels of the hierarchy.

There were widespread problems in the link between the central decision-making process and the localities: in the party, the administration, the factories, the collective farms and the army. Policies were issued by the leadership at the centre, but were not sufficiently specific. These were then variously interpreted by officials at different levels within the state and party, all of whom had their own aims and agendas. Local party secretaries defended the interests of their particular sector and interpreted orders from the centre as they saw fit. This, in turn, came in for criticism from the centre, which soon realized that policies were not being strictly adhered to. Stalin made frequent accusations that bureaucrats were impeding policy; in 1930, for example, he complained that local officials had become 'dizzy with success' in exceeding central quotas for collectivization. The centre therefore tried to restore discipline over the lower levels of management. Further waves of chaos followed in the localities as rank and file members now attacked their branch leaders or factory managers or collective farm chairmen. The latter retaliated by identifying troublemakers and dealing with them summarily. The whole decision-making structure was therefore riddled with conflict and dissent. In the ensuing chaos the centre sought to restore a semblance of order, by adjusting, intensifying or ending particular campaigns.

Hence, the centre would eventually react to local influences. According to Arch Getty, 'Campaigns – including purges – could be stalled, sped up, aborted, or implemented in ways which suited local conditions and interests.'[47] Real power lay in local hands and with local party and government machinery. 'Even if one assumes Stalin's personality was the only or main factor in the initiation of policies, one must still explain the obvious disparities between central orders and local outcomes.'[48] The situation was further destabilized by the constant expansion of local officialdom. This made it increasingly difficult for the centre to control local officials without creating more officials, and thereby compounding the problem. Ironically, Stalinism, supposedly confined to the centre, in practice created the ideal conditions for 'little Stalins' in the localities. These were not a threat to the basis of Stalin's power, but they did threaten the effective enforcement of his policies.

This contrast between dictatorship at the centre and still powerful local initiatives has two overall implications. First, Stalin was less completely in control of policy than is generally supposed. He certainly intended to direct the economy and foreign policy through periodic decisions and adjustments, just as he was determined to remove all opposition and democracy within the party. But he frequently lost control of what he had started: the complexity of the administration defeated the attempts of the centre to monitor the changes, with the result that there was as much chaos and anarchy as there was order and direction. And, second, the impetus (as opposed to the inspiration) for change came as much from below as from above. The result could be violent changes, oscillations and swings as the top tried to correct the bottom's attempts to adapt to the direction imposed by the top. Seen in this light, Stalin had to give as much of his time to adjusting as to initiating, and more to reacting than to planning.

The purges

The most spectacular and notorious of all Stalin's policies was his deliberate creation of a state of total terror through a series of purges. The earliest of these affected the captains of industry and plant managers, of whom about 75 per cent were eliminated in the early 1930s. From 1934 onwards the purges became more openly political, with the assassination of Kirov, Stalin's main potential rival. There then followed a series of spectacular show trials to deal with the party's most prominent figures, while below the surface Stalin's NKVD under Yagoda, Ezhov and Beria hunted down numberless unknowns. The first show trial (1936) disposed of Kamenev and Zinoviev; in the second, in 1937, Piatakov and Sokolnikov were accused of being the Anti-Soviet Trotskyist Centre. The third, in 1938, accounted for Bukharin, Rykov and even Yagoda – all on the charge of belonging to a bloc of right-wingers and Trotskyites. The army was also affected. In 1937 Marshal Tukhachevskii, hero of the Civil War years and now Commissar for Defence, was shot. All eleven deputy Commissars for Defence were executed, together with seventy-five out of the eighty members of the Supreme Military Council. The navy lost all eight of its admirals. Meanwhile, throughout the Soviet Union, something like 300,000 people were executed and 7 million put through the labour camps. By 1939 Stalin considered that the terror had run its necessary course and decided to call a halt.

Causes

Although the enormity of Stalin's purges defy a completely logical explanation, a number of motives have been suggested. One is that Stalin had a disastrously flawed personality. Khrushchev, for example, later emphasized his brutality, vindictiveness, pathological distrust and sickly suspicion. More recently, Tucker has maintained that, in addition to serving a political function, the trials also rationalized Stalin's own paranoid tendency.[49]

A second reason for the purges is that Stalin was never one to resort to half measures. He aimed to wipe out the entire generation of Bolsheviks who had assisted Lenin between 1917 and 1924. This alone would guarantee Stalin as the sole heir to Lenin and would secure his position for a lifetime. Most of the threats to his power were latent and would possibly not reveal themselves for several years. They should, nevertheless, be dealt with as soon as possible. Since these latent threats were impossible to identify, a large number of people who would ultimately prove innocent of any form of opposition to Stalin would also have to go. It was only by having such a clean sweep that Stalin could make sure of eradicating those who would be a threat. In contrasting the liquidation programmes of Stalin and Hitler, Ulam points out that, by and large, the latter dealt with individuals and groups clearly identified as enemies of the Nazi regime.[50] Ninety-nine per cent of Stalin's victims, however, were innocent of any opposition to the Soviet system and were loyal Soviet citizens.

A third explanation was economic. The forced pace of industrialization and the implementation of collective farming required a disciplined workforce and a compliant peasantry. Both necessitated, in Stalin's eyes, the use of force. Measures had to be taken against reluctant managers in the factories in 1930 and 1931, while the NKVD operated dekulakization squads to clear the countryside of resistance to collectivization. As the pace of industrialization speeded up in the Second and Third Five Year Plans additional labour was provided by the growth of the Gulag system. Convict labour built the Belomor Canal, opened in 1933, and provided the mainstay of mining in Siberia, especially in the inhospitable Kolyma region. Terror was therefore inseparable from Stalin's vision of modernization.

Some historians have pointed to the importance of Stalin's reaction to external factors. There are two very different variants of this. On the one hand, Stalin was obsessed with the fear that the West would smash the Soviet regime before his industrialization programme was complete. It therefore made sense to adopt a pragmatic approach to foreign policy; Germany, the main threat, could be won over by a temporary policy of co-operation. Stalin found it no more difficult to collaborate with fascism than with any other European system, for he regarded it merely as a variant of Western capitalism. The old-style Bolsheviks, by contrast, were profoundly anti-fascist and saw Hitler as a far more deadly enemy than either France or Britain. According to Tucker and Conquest, Stalin therefore considered it essential to remove the anti-Hitler element to make possible the accommodation with Germany which eventually materialized in August 1939 in the Nazi–Soviet Non-Aggression Pact. Deutscher puts a different case. Stalin's main worry was that his regime would be destroyed from within – by internal revolt. There seemed little chance of this happening in 1936, unless, of course, some major external catastrophe occurred, which could lead to a revival of the scenario of the First World War; military crisis could well bring about a revolution. Stalin's solution was therefore to destroy any elements within Russia which could possibly take advantage of such a situation. The show trials dealt with these potential threats by magnifying the charge against them. They had to die as traitors, as perpetrators of crimes beyond the reach of reason. Only then could Stalin be sure that their execution would provoke no dangerous revulsion.[51]

Varied though these explanations are, they all have one thing in common: Stalin is seen as ruthlessly transforming an authoritarian system, inherited from the Bolsheviks, into a totalitarian one. He used it to cut huge swathes through the population in the pursuit of his economic and political objectives. This is where most previous analyses have stopped. But, until recently, it has never been fully explained why the purges were so complete and all-embracing – and why so many ordinary people played an active part in them. The traditional analysis adopts a monolithic 'top-down' approach and assumes that Stalin remained in control and dictated the momentum of the terror. But did he? Was the Soviet administrative system that efficient? And did the apex of the bureaucracy really succeed in imposing its will on the localities? Some historians now emphasize that there were 'bottom-up' reactions to 'top-down' orders which gave the purges an additional momentum far beyond anything intended by Stalin. In other words, although Stalin introduced the policy centrally, the way in which it was implemented was determined locally.

From the very beginning of collectivization, terror became endemic in the countryside as instructions from the centre were exceeded; measures even had to be taken to control the dekulakization squads. The All-Russian Central Executive Committee, or Council of People's Commissars, issued decrees in 1929 defining precisely who was classified as a kulak and warned that dekulakization should not become an end in itself. This, however, scarcely prevented the wave of terror which followed, so that Stalin had to try to stem the tide in 1930. When the campaign was resumed later that year, and extended between 1932 and 1934, the central government attempted to exert more direct control. In each case, Viola distinguishes between the repressive policy which the state undoubtedly pursued and the methods used by the cadres in the field for actually implementing the policy. The latter were influenced by a 'general political culture of the early 1930s', which was based on 'a mixture of traditional Russian radical fanaticism' and the 'unleashing of years of pent-up class rage and retribution'.[52] This was intensified by shortages created by collectivization and by the development of a siege-like mentality. We could go even further. The repression and persecution at local level were manifestations of the breakdown of central control. Peasant resistance, disobedience and defiance were others. The two extremes fed off each other – resistance to the local terror undermining official policy. Or, in the words of Arch Getty, 'Stalin had initiated a movement with vague instructions and ambiguous targets. As the process unfolded on the ground, though, it degenerated rapidly into chaotic and violent struggles based on local conditions.'[53]

Industry, too, became affected by endemic terror. There was widespread chaos as managers conflicted with the party and the workforce, all in pursuit of different interests. An additional complication was the Stakhanovite movement. Thurston argues that this created tension in factories as young Stakhanovites with personal and political ambitions upset the productivity balance which managers tried desperately to maintain. In turn, the latter became subject to accusations of wrecking and sabotage. 'Whatever its scope, as the terror unfolded the resentments and demands fostered by early Stakhanovism heightened tensions in industry.'[54] Much the same applies to the army. Reese claims that the party organizations within the armed forces experienced upheaval which was well beyond the control of the central administration.[55]

At all levels, therefore, there was a feeling of real involvement in the purges. People everywhere had a variety of motives. Some used the opportunity of informing on others to settle old scores. Many were genuinely convinced that the economy was riddled with 'wreckers' and saboteurs who had to be brought to book. Here an important part was played by the show trials which helped whip up suspicion of and resentment against managers.[56] Peasants provided information and they testified at local *raion* trials (the local counterparts to the show trials). A striking simile has been advanced with 'mice burying the cat';[57] because of the special conditions interacting with longer-term tensions, this happened all over the country. Paranoia spread through all levels of society, helping to maintain the momentum of terror at the lowest levels. Rittersporn maintains that the regime's emphasis on the 'subversive' activities of 'conspirators' interacted with traditional prejudices to produce an 'imagery of omnipresent subversion and conspiracy'.[58] According to Suny, 'The requirement to find enemies, to blame and punish, worked together with self-protection and self-promotion . . . to expand the Purges into a political holocaust.'[59]

Overall, it is quite right to move away from the limited view of Stalin as the sole driving force behind the terror. Whether he was insane or suffering from paranoia is only partly relevant. He inherited a revolution, revived the terror which had gone cold and renewed the turmoil at all social levels. But the sheer scale of the upheaval can only be understood on a national scale, as the intervention of local factors which distorted the central intention. Until further evidence becomes available, a provisional conclusion might be that, although Stalin initiated and maintained the purges, they assumed a momentum which outpaced even his expectations. This reflects the relative inefficiency of the Soviet system and a loss of control by it. The terror becomes even more terrible, since it can no longer be attributed entirely to one man's paranoia, but to the multiple manifestations of human nature.

Effects

The last section concluded that Stalin's terror was less carefully controlled and centralized than has often been thought. The corollary to this is that the effects are also less clear-cut and need partial reinterpretation.

It has been argued that the terror was the chief method by which the party machinery of the Bolshevik state was transformed into the personalized totalitarian dictatorship of Stalin. As a result, Stalinism created a regime which was more consistently ruthless and pervasive even than that of Nazi Germany. This is only partly true. Any capacity for debate about different strategies was certainly squeezed out of the centre of the party with the elimination of Kamenev, Zinoviev, Bukharin, Rykov and others. The chances of persuading Stalin to adopt a course different to what he had in mind, whether in economic or foreign policy, could never seriously arise after 1934. It could also be argued that the terror was a necessary complement to the development of the Stalinist personality cult – the obverse side of the same coin. The terror also made it possible to experiment with more obvious democratic forms in the 1936 constitution, since these were neutralized and therefore never amounted to anything in practice.

This is true: terror did all these things. But it has traditionally been seen as working in one way only – as tightening the political system and therefore enhancing the powers of dictatorship. There is, however, another possibility – that it unleashed chaos into the system which *limited* the extent to which dictatorship could operate effectively. We have already seen how local groups in industry and the country-side interpreted central decisions. Normally such groups would have been cautious, but the terror acted as a stimulus for greatly intensified activity. Hence, the result was more often the descent into chaos, with wild oscillations developing as first the local groups implemented the instructions of the centre in their own way before the centre attempted to restore an approved line. Paradoxically, terror was a democratizing force, although in a negative sense: it created a tyranny *of* the people quite as much as the traditional image of a tyranny *over* the people.

The economic impact of the terror was also paradoxical. It is normally seen as having provided the impetus for the command economy; and the debate has focused on whether such an economy was preferable to a mixed economy which would have allowed a measure of market consumerism. But it can now be argued that terror confused the command network, thereby undermining the whole Stalinist system. Two examples can be given of this. One was the approach to collectivization and dekulakization which, as we have seen, was conducted with excessive zeal by local party officials and the NKVD. The result was one of the greatest mass disobedience campaigns in the history of the twentieth century, aimed not at Stalin but at those who were interpreting his orders more freely than even he wanted. The second example is the impact of the Stakhanovites in industry. Their initiative, which was intended to promote an increase in productivity, helped slow it down. In the climate of terror managers were understandably hostile to anyone who distorted their own implementation of industrial plans. This, in turn, made them targets for denunciation, with the result that the very people most likely to achieve local stability were removed. Far from underpinning the command economy, therefore, terror did much to disrupt its smooth operation.

What of the impact of the Stalinist terror in terms of the amount of suffering caused? No one doubts that Stalin was directly responsible for the deaths of millions. Accurate estimates have, however, always been open to dispute and the opening of the Soviet archives since the onset of glasnost has only served to accentuate this. The total number of deaths has been put by Nove and Wheatcroft at between 4 and 11 million, significantly below Conquest's estimates of 20 million and recent Russian textbook figures of 40 million. Prison populations also vary from Rosefielde (10 million during the late 1930s), to Conquest (up to 8 million in 1938 and 12 million in 1952), to Nove and Wheatcroft (a peak of 5.5 million in 1953). The main problem is distinguishing between those who died as a direct result of a purge and those whose deaths were caused by famine or diseases associated with Stalin's agricultural policies.

There is also growing doubt about the once-held belief that Stalin was widely hated as well as feared – because he was seen as the instigator of the terror. We have seen that the terror was often sustained and intensified at grass-roots level, which meant that huge numbers of people were directly implicated in actions against colleagues or neighbours. Paradoxically, this meant that Stalin, who may well have been held responsible for starting the process, was also seen as the only person who could genuinely transcend and stop it. The people who were most feared and blamed were those who carried out changes locally. The surprising and unpalatable truth is that Stalin remained popular. The real test came when the Germans invaded the Soviet Union in 1941. Those who collaborated with them had a grievance on traditional grounds, not against Stalin himself. Collaborators were found mostly among the minority nationalities who aspired to independence, not among repressed Russians who aspired to freedom. Despite years of terror, there was far greater unity and patriotism in the Second World War than there had been in the First.

This brings us to the impact of the terror on the security of the Soviet Union. The purging of the armed forces cannot but have had a negative effect on Soviet defences. Experience was undoubtedly affected by the wholesale expulsion of officers. The real loss was of experience at the highest level, surely a crippling blow to any impending war effort. The result, it is generally argued, was a humiliating performance against Finland in the Northern War of 1939–40 and a disastrous collapse when the Germans invaded the Soviet Union in 1941. Yet, again, the impact of the terror may have been exaggerated. Most of those purged in 1938 were not arrested but merely expelled from the party. Hence, the impact was more limited than once thought. It was originally estimated that the purges had accounted for between 25 per cent and 50 per cent of army officers. Recent estimates have put the figures at somewhere between 3.7 per cent and 7.7 per cent.[60] There are two main reasons for this disparity. One is a previous underestimate of the size of the officer class in the Red Army, the other the rapidity with which many were rehabilitated. Both of these points have the effect of diluting the impact of the terror on the efficiency of the armed forces. In any case, many military expulsions from the army were not accompanied by loss of military rank. It has now been estimated that 30 per cent of army officers discharged between 1937 and 1939 were reinstated.[61] This was part of the policy of the central authorities to reduce the scale of denunciations. At the XVIIIth Party Congress in March 1939, for example, it was said that 'Political organs and party organizations often expel party members far too light-heartedly. The party commissions of the Political Administration of the Red Army find it necessary to reinstate about 50 per cent of the expelled men because the expulsions were unjustified.'[62] It seems, therefore, that measures were being taken to correct the severity of the purges well before the German invasion.

Overall, we may conclude that the effects of the terror were more blurred than is traditionally supposed – largely because the momentum was less centrally controlled. Effect overlaps into cause, spontaneous momentum into deliberate policy. Hence, on the one hand, the state benefited less from the terror – because it controlled less of it. On the other hand, the state suffered less from the terror's negative side-effects.

The economy under Stalin

Economic change was Stalin's immediate priority once his authority had been confirmed. He intended to transform the Soviet Union into a superpower by equipping it with a huge industrial base. The process began in 1929 and continued, with the interruption of war, until his death in 1953. Lenin's New Economic Policy had allowed limited private enterprise in the agricultural and industrial sectors. The peasantry were permitted to grow grain for the market, under licence, while most of the smaller industrial enterprises were denationalized. By the time of Lenin's death, the NEP had attracted widespread support and its continuation was urged by the 'rightists' within the party, including Bukharin, Rykov and Tomsky. Some, however, considered that a more appropriate strategy would be rapid industrialization and the introduction of collective farming. Trotsky, in particular, favoured this approach as part of his strategy of Permanent Revolution.

At first, Stalin favoured the continuation of the NEP, which he associated with Socialism in One Country. By 1928, however, he had reversed the NEP and associated Socialism in One Country with collectivized agriculture and rapid industrialization. How can we explain this apparent turnabout in economic policy? The following analysis shows that, in both cases, Stalin was at the same time reacting to events beyond his immediate control while trying to push the economy in a new direction. The result was bound to be a large measure of confusion.

Collectivization

Most explanations for Stalin's agricultural changes start with the years 1926–7. These saw a procurement crisis, when only 17 per cent of the grain harvested by the peasants reached the workers in the cities. Stalin felt that it was essential to reintroduce requisitioning, a measure last used during the period of War Communism between 1918 and 1921. This led inexorably to the longer-term policy of collectivization, which was intended to reverse the whole policy of the NEP. How, precisely, did the procurement crisis influence future economic policy? Two quite different interpretations are possible. One is that Stalin used the crisis as an excuse to bring the whole system into line with his own economic preconceptions and political designs. In other words, he dictated the trend from above. The alternative is that Stalin was pushed by the crisis into a series of measures over which he had less control than he would have wanted: pressures came from below.

By the first argument, Stalin was the prime mover of economic change. He saw two possibilities for the future of the Soviet economy, 'There is the capitalist way, which is to enlarge the agricultural units by introducing capitalism in agriculture'; the alternative was 'the socialist way, which is to set up collective and state farms'. The latter was preferable, since it would provide the means for using agriculture as a means of subsidizing industry and developing socialism. The problem was how to persuade an innately conservative part of society to accept the role of being in the forefront of this socialist advancement. It was becoming increasingly unlikely that they could be won over voluntarily since the NEP seemed to be evolving away from communist principles: the movement was very much towards the search for fair prices by the peasant producer. Stalin was convinced that all this needed to change – quickly. He therefore launched a revolution from above to break with the economic trend of the NEP and to herd the peasantry into collectives. He was also determined to tighten his political control over the party: according to Brovkin, his move was therefore 'a pre-emptive strike on the central party–state apparatus'.[63] In essence, Stalin used the procurement crisis as an excuse to destroy an economic system which was working economically in order to gain full political control. It was a deliberate and calculated policy which went against the natural course that Russia was taking. It marked the beginning of the Stalinist revolution.

There is, however, a very different perspective. Stalin was not in control of the changes in agriculture from 1927. He did not impose collectivization as a policy decision: instead, he stumbled into it with neither planning nor forethought. The reason was that the NEP was not working and the attitudes of both peasants and workers forced him into a fundamental change of policy. The procurement crisis occurred because industry was failing to provide the goods for the peasants to buy: hence they held on to their grain. Since it could not satisfy basic consumer needs, the NEP had failed. Stalin therefore had no choice. According to Lewin, 'The market mechanism of NEP, which had worked wonders at the start simply by following its natural course, had in the end led the regime into an impasse.' Hence, when faced with the procurement crisis, Stalin reacted instinctively by operating 'the lever whose use he best understood; he resorted to force'. Nevertheless, 'When he manipulated this particular lever in January 1928, Stalin did not know where the process set in motion by his "emergency measures" would ultimately lead him.'[64] It may even be that Russia was moving away from the NEP anyway – and that Stalin simply went with the momentum. Arch Getty maintains that, although Stalin was officially responsible for collectivization, he was strongly influenced by 'the social, economic and political environment that he did not create'.[65]

These explanations seem to be mutually exclusive. But are they? Both emphasize Stalin's willingness to use force: this could be seen as the common and most important factor in the change of economic direction. The consolidation of personal power was his most important consideration, which meant that political criteria dominated the economic. It is unlikely that he would have had a long-term economic blueprint for implementing socialism. At the same time, he could certainly have developed a socialist strategy as a solution to his immediate political difficulties. In 1927 he faced the prospect of political humiliation caused by the procurement crisis. The alternatives were to make further concessions by continuing the NEP or to take a tougher line by ending it. The latter was more attractive since it would also enable him to cut down his remaining opponents, like Bukharin, who favoured the continuation of the NEP. He therefore took an economic decision for political reasons. It was not systematically planned – but, at the same time, he did not simply drift into it. He reacted to circumstances to enhance his power. Once the power was secure he could convert reactive measures into something resembling projective plans.

These were based on the principle of collectivization. The rationale which Stalin now produced was that the existing organization of agriculture was a major obstacle to the country's overall economic development. Existing grain supplies were inadequate to feed the industrial workers in the cities. The basic reason for this was the pattern of land ownership, which was based on fragmentation into small individual holdings. This led to a capitalist mentality which promoted individual rather than collective values; the procurement crisis could therefore be explained as the result of selfish hoarding. As the reasons were simplified, the solutions could be made clearer. Temporary requisitioning in 1928 led inexorably towards collectivization, officially announced in 1929. Private land was now to be brought within collective farms (*kolkhozy*) or state farms (*sovkhozy*). The end of private property would, in turn, remove the remaining cause of class divisions: this meant that the main target were the kulaks, the landowning peasants who had prospered under the NEP. Finally, and above all, agricultural changes could be used to assist the country's industrial transformation.

Industrialization

As in agriculture, the reasons for Stalin's industrial policies are now open to debate. Did he dictate the process from above or was he pushed by pressures from below? The former model may attribute too much to the decision of one man. As important as the initiatives from above, it is now argued, were pressures from below. Stalin was under considerable social pressure exerted by the industrial working class whose interests were out of line with the more conservative peasantry. The working class wanted readily available food and job security, both of which depended on a compliant peasantry. The latter, however, needed higher commodity prices to enable them to buy more consumer goods. The problem was that consumer goods would not guarantee job security for the workers or state investment in industry. Hence, there was a tension between agriculture and industry, which was bound to affect the decisions taken from above in the name of the various groups. By this analysis, Stalin reacted to the needs of the working class in the cities, just as he had to the dangers posed by the peasantry over the procurement crisis.

This, however, should not obscure the importance of Stalin's own influence on industrialization. By 1927 he had moved towards taking command of an economy which, through the NEP, had been left for a while to take its own course. As we have already seen, this was due partly to Stalin's own accumulation of power, and partly to problems within the economy which required his attention. Stalin therefore developed a series of priorities related to the future security of his own regime. This meant an emphasis on heavy industry and, in particular, on armaments. These decisions were taken by Stalin himself for reasons which were partly political and partly a reaction to the conflicting pressures of sub-groups. Once his position was secure, however, he was able to present a more coherent overall strategy with a clearer underlying logic. Two of his priorities stand out.

The first was Soviet Russia's very survival. Stalin took over Trotsky's emphasis on the threats of capitalist encirclement by the West. He then welded this anti-capitalism to a basic commitment to Russia's self-sufficiency, or Socialism in One Country. In February 1931 he summarized his position as follows: 'We are fifty to a hundred years behind the advanced countries. We must make good this distance in ten years. Either we do it or we shall be crushed. That is what our obligations to the workers and peasants of the USSR dictate to us.'[66] From the start, therefore, Stalin was moving the Soviet economy on to a war footing. This placed the emphasis on heavy industry at the expense of light or consumer industry, since iron, steel and heavy machinery could more easily be converted to armaments production. It could also be adapted to a change in Soviet military strategy which occurred during the 1930s: Stalin came under the influence of military theorists who believed that the Soviet Union should move on the offensive and prepare for a pre-emptive strike at a time of its own choosing. This meant the building and stockpiling of massive amounts of armaments. Through the industrial Five Year Plans Stalin therefore gradually moved the motive from defence against the West to the preparation of an offensive against it.

The other motive was ideological: industrialization was the only fully reliable means of developing a socialist economy. Any genuine intention to ditch the NEP was bound to mean a reorientation from agriculture to industry, since the NEP had been geared to the former. Stalin had come to accept that Socialism in One Country had to enlarge the urban proletariat and that the socialist way of doing this was through state control of industry. Any such development would involve curbing the consumer sector, which tended to strengthen capitalism. If capitalism was to be eradicated from the Soviet Union, action had to be taken against the class most likely to try to preserve it. Hence, Stalin was able to justify using the peasantry to subsidize industrial development and to reduce the emphasis on consumerism. The reorganization of agriculture would therefore make possible accelerated industrialization, thereby bringing the Soviet Union's social structure more into line with the classless society. Stalin was enough of a Marxist to be able to justify pragmatic decisions with retrospective ideology.

The impact of Stalin's agricultural policies

The impact of Stalin's policies needs to be related to several specific questions. How rapidly was collectivization carried through? What effect did this have on productivity? How were the peasantry affected by the changes? Finally, did agriculture *really* subsidize industrial growth?

If one of the purposes of collectivization was to end private property, a key criterion for success was surely the number of units collectivized. The process was implemented with remarkable speed. The proportion of collective holdings increased from 23.6 per cent in 1930 to 52.7 per cent in 1931, 61.5 per cent in 1932, 66.4 per cent in 1933, 71.4 per cent in 1934, 83.2 per cent in 1935, 89.6 per cent in 1936 and, finally, 98 per cent by 1941. Unfortunately, all this occurred too quickly. The process spiralled out of Stalin's control as the centre of administration lost the initiative to the local party officials, local industrial managers and local officials of the secret police, the NKVD. Stalin became so concerned about their frantic activities that he accused them of being 'dizzy with success' and called a halt in 1931. As the local officials fell into line with the new instructions, inertia set in and Stalin had to start the whole process up again. Throughout the period the pendulum swung violently backwards and forwards as the centre launched policies which became distorted in their operation locally. The result was administrative chaos.

All this was bound to affect productivity. Production figures showed collectivization to be a disaster. The grain harvest declined from 73.3 million tons in 1928 (itself a low point) to 71.7 million in 1929. An increase to 83.5 in 1930 was followed by a sharp reversal to 69.5 in 1931 and 69.6 in 1932. The figures for 1934 and 1935 were 67.6 and 75.0, respectively. There were also catastrophic losses in number of livestock: between 1928 and 1932 cattle declined from 70 million to 34 million, sheep and goats from 146 to 42 million and pigs from 26 to 9 million.

The impact on the peasantry was disastrous. It has been argued that this was partly self-induced: the result of deliberate defiance sparked by fear and the threat of massive collective resistance. Alternatively, agricultural production was sacrificed to hunt for kulaks as class enemies. As a result, local conditions became so volatile that it became physically impossible in some areas to fulfil even the normal agricultural processes of sowing, harvesting and breeding. Either way, the result was misery – although the extent of this did vary. Nationally, food consumption dropped between 1928 and 1932: bread from 250 kilos per head to 215 and potatoes from 141 to 125. But these figures do not show that the countryside was far worse off than the cities. Between 1932 and 1933 areas like the Ukraine experienced a major famine. There was also an unprecedented upheaval in Russian society. Peasants were turned against each other, as the kulak minority fell victim to the less affluent, who, in turn, were affected by mass hysteria and panic. This had a knock-on effect on the urban areas as factories, workshops and munitions were overwhelmed by the influx of millions of desperate peasants seeking employment and survival.

Stalin has been credited with using agriculture to subsidize industrial growth; although this caused chaos, it also avoided any dependence on Western loans. This argument has, however, been strongly challenged. In the first place, such a process would have been impossible to administer since there was simply no means of transferring resources efficiently from one sector to the other. Indeed, agricultural changes impeded industrial growth: the transfer of population was too rapid for industry to absorb, which meant huge administrative problems and worsening social conditions. A more specific argument is that capital did not flow from agriculture into industry at all. Either it stayed *within* agriculture or there was a reverse flow from industry into agriculture. Any agricultural recovery in the Second and Third Five Year Plans was due to allowing a partial return to individual initiative on the one hand and the growth of machine tractor stations (MTS) on the other. The former showed capital being retained by agriculture; the latter showed capital being invested in agriculture by industry. In one respect the flow of investment was cut off; in the other the flow was reversed.

It is difficult, therefore, to say anything favourable about Stalin's agricultural policies. The results were simply disastrous. Even the few positive arguments have now been countered. The whole process is now seen to have been out of control and it is no longer believed that the exploitation of the peasantry could at least be said to have subsidized industrial growth. The picture is uniformly bleak.

The impact of Stalin's industrial policies

In 1928 Stalin introduced the First Five Year Plan which was intended to transform the industrial base of the Soviet Union. The organization of this was the responsibility of the State Planning Bureau, or Gosplan. The emphasis was placed on heavy industry rather than on consumer goods, and especially on coal, steel, oil, electricity and armaments. The Second and Third Five Year Plans followed in 1933 and 1937, the last of these being interrupted by the German invasion of the Soviet Union in 1941.

But did they work? Stalin has certainly been credited with the development of heavy industry. He did not, as is sometimes suggested, lay the actual foundations for this. The Tsars had developed a considerable industrial capacity, based on five main centres: Moscow (textiles), Petrograd (heavy industry), the Donetz region (coalfields), Baku (oil) and the Ukraine (iron and steel). Lenin added plans for widespread electrification and for the development of the Urals. Stalin did, however, enhance the scale of heavy industry: he was responsible for the emphasis on 'gigantomania' – the construction of new industrial cities such as Magnitogorsk and the expansion of heavy plant and steel production. The increase was considerable: the First Five Year Plan (1928–32) raised steel production from 3 to 6 million tons, coal from 35 to 64 million and oil from 12 to 21 million; the Second Five Year Plan (1933–7) increased the figures to 18 million tons for steel, 128 million for coal and 26 million for oil. The last complete figures for the Third Five Year Plan before it was interrupted by the 1941 German invasion were 18 million, 150 million and 26 million, respectively.

There was also a positive impact on employment: far higher levels were achieved than had been anticipated at the outset of the First Five Year Plan. Instead of the 3.9 million expected in state industry by 1922–3, the number reached 6.4 million. The pace then slowed to 7.9 million by 1937 and 8.3 million by 1940. The bulk of these were peasants leaving the countryside. Urban populations also increased dramatically by something like 200,000 per month, or by a total of 30 million between 1926 and 1930. Unemployment ceased to be a serious factor since the magnet of industrialization brought in ever increasing numbers from the countryside and enabled more ambitious targets to be established for projects in heavy industry. In the process, Stalin generated the capital and labour necessary for such developments from within the Soviet Union itself. This was the purpose of subordinating agriculture to industrialization. Stalin therefore effectively sealed Russia off from the West and enabled the country to progress amid its hostility. Ultimately, Stalin's industrialization assisted the Soviet Union's survival in the Second World War. According to R. Hutchings, 'One can hardly doubt that if there had been a slower build-up of industry, the attack would have been successful and world history would have evolved quite differently.'[67] In a more direct sense, heavy industrialization had made it possible for the Soviet Union to rearm. In 1933 defence comprised 4 per cent of the industrial budget; by 1937 it had risen to 17 per cent and by 1940 to 33 per cent. Heavy industrialization therefore translated into ultimate survival.

All these points are part of the traditional argument which credits Stalin with the development of Soviet industrial infrastructure through ruthlessly centralized control. Although this is still widely supported, a number of reservations have now been added.

Although Stalin did try to set an overall agenda, based on accelerating heavy industry, the effectiveness of the planning mechanism has been called into question. Recent research has shown that setting targets did not in itself constitute planning. It was one thing for the central administration, including Gosplan, to draw up target figures for the different components of industry, but quite another to develop the mechanism whereby these might be achieved systematically. Hence, the ruthlessness of the Stalinist dictatorship did not necessarily produce efficiency in the promotion of heavy industry. There was, for example, little overall consistency in the pace of the Five Year Plans. This was due largely to the disruption caused by local influences. Local managers had to protect themselves by exaggerating their needs for investment and by hoarding materials to ensure that they had sufficient supplies. This meant shortages elsewhere and a consequent lack of overall balance. There was a lack of harmony between the different sectors of the economy. Soviet industrial development was, in fact, well behind that of the United States. The latter benefited from auxiliary developments which enhanced industrialization, including transport, services and managerial and accounting expertise.[68] Many of these were provided by private enterprise. This was missing in the Soviet Union, which meant that the initiative had to be taken by the state.

The result was a great deal of complexity and not much cohesion. In effect, argues Shearer, there was 'a command-administrative economy' but that it was 'not a planned one'.[69] Although complexity seemed to pass for 'planning', what actually happened was administrative chaos. This had one long-term consequence which proved particularly serious. When the Germans invaded the Soviet Union in 1941, the whole system was taken completely by surprise. Stalin had prepared the country for an offensive war, while the situation in 1941 required a defensive response. All the mechanisms related to the Five Year Plans were geared to this and therefore reacted badly to the crisis. The result was that the planning mechanism actually had to be relaxed to achieve the levels of mobilization required. This is in direct contrast to the argument that Russia defeated Germany because of planning; instead, Russia achieved this *despite* planning.

Less controversial is the severe deprivation which accompanied industrial growth. Russia was unique in European economic history in experiencing an industrial revolution without corresponding improvements in the quality of life of its inhabitants. This produced social upheaval. The pressure on accommodation resulted in serious overcrowding and extensive squalor as huge dormitories were established for workers. Hence, there was an inherent contradiction in the whole process. Collectivization and industrialization, intended to modernize Russia, tore apart its social fabric. The result was the collapse of many accepted codes of behaviour and morality. This made it easier to exploit the population but more difficult to stabilize working patterns. It also meant that there was an undercurrent of fear which contributed enormously to the purges and to political instability.

The final evaluation of the effect of Stalin's industrialization returns to the cause. Starving the consumer sector to develop heavy industry can be seen in two ways: either it was a deliberate strategy to create an industrial superpower with a compliant population or it was the result of inefficient planning worsened by local chaos. If it was the first, then any imbalance was part of a design and the overall result was efficient industrialization bought at a high price. If, however, it was the second, then the process of industrialization was almost as badly flawed as that of agricultural change. This, in turn, raises the possibility that the price was not only too high, but unnecessary.

Society and culture

Major changes occurred in both of these areas. But the way in which they occurred provides a perspective on Stalin's overall rule. The general trend was away from earlier experimentation and relaxed control to a more rigid and authoritarian approach. Stalin placed the emphasis firmly on discipline, imparting a mixture of traditional Russian values and his own interpretation of Marxism.

According to the traditional view, the experimentation had been introduced by the Bolsheviks under Lenin. Radical changes had been intended to transform all areas of society and culture. Unfortunately, these produced chaos and Stalin restored order with a more conservative and traditional social policy. This approach, however, is oversimplified. The Bolsheviks relaxed their own radical measures from 1921, at the same time as the NEP. Stalin at first revived the radical impetus but, when this proved impossible to implement, he retreated into a traditional approach.

The first interpretation assumes that Stalin himself took a 'top-down' initiative, moving deliberately to the construction of a totalitarian state. This involved using Russian traditions to strengthen his own power. Throughout the whole process Stalin was fully in control. The second interpretation, by contrast, shows Stalin being forced to make unplanned adjustments because the policies he initially pursued recoiled on him. He tried to revive flagging radical policies by dictating from the centre. As in the economy, however, the centre lost some of the initiative to local forces. Stalin therefore tried to regain control through more traditional policies. This 'bottom-up' theory works as follows. Stalin found that local officials and educational bodies were over-enthusiastic in applying radical policies: their motive was sheer survival by trying to exceed central diktats. Any attempt by the centre to restore control therefore had to involve the return to more traditional policies, since this made an authoritarian style more feasible.

Of the two explanations for Stalin's change of policy, the second is the focus for the following sections on social, educational and cultural changes. In each case, the effects of his measures are also considered.

Social changes

Perhaps the most basic of all changes concerned egalitarianism. The Bolsheviks had made an absolute virtue of equality by reducing social distinction and wage differentials. They had also undermined military ranks and decorations within the army. Again, Stalin initially went along with, and even intensified, this. But the crisis caused by the extent of the early radicalism meant that Stalin revived distinctions. He had two reasons for this. First, he needed to be more certain of the loyalty of subordinates and officials, which could be best guaranteed by a system of privilege and rewards. Hence he reintroduced all the distinctions in army rank, together with epaulettes, and developed a hierarchy in industry and the party. Second, he came round to the view that trying to implement equality caused chaos which, in turn, impeded economic growth. He therefore ended the practice of 'wage equalization', arguing that it had nothing to do with socialism. Indeed, it was essential to 'abolish wage equalization and draw up scales which would take into account the difference between skilled and unskilled labour'.[70] Hence, the old Marxist principle of 'from each according to his ability, to each according to his needs' was modified. Under Stalin the maxim was 'from each according to his ability, to each according to his work'. This had mixed results. On the one hand, by increasing incentives it did accelerate the momentum for industrial change. On the other hand, such incentives were highly selective. The only real beneficiaries were the Stakhanovites, or workers who exceeded their quotas. As we have already seen, they were a mixed blessing anyway, since they frequently threw into chaos any attempts by local factory managers to work out how to implement their targets.

Women and the family also received Stalin's attention. Official policy between 1917 and 1926 had been to encourage the break-up of traditional institutions associated with the old order, of which the family was typical. In her treatise *The New Morality and the Working Class* (1918) Alexandra Kollontai had stated: 'The old type of family has seen its day.'[71] Divorce was made extremely easy and free love was sanctioned. A decree in Vladimir made every virgin over the age of eighteen state property, but this went beyond official party policy. Stalin swung from one extreme to the other. At first he saw continued social radicalism as the best means of promoting economic change. After all, he did subscribe to the Marxist premise that the family was a bourgeois institution, and he was attempting to eradicate any remaining bourgeois influences within the economy. He therefore intensified measures against the family as part of the drive for collectivization in the late 1920s. But the social backlash was so serious that Stalin had to reverse the policy and seek refuge in traditionalism. He restored the family to its full status within society. In 1935 divorce was made more difficult and expensive for women to obtain and abortion became illegal in 1936. The emphasis also moved away from amorality to an enforcement of the strictest sexual code. Nowhere is the contradiction of Stalinism greater than with the reluctant acceptance of the family.

The effect of Stalin's policies on women and the family was mixed. The radical measures of the Bolsheviks, intially continued by Stalin, did give women more chance to take their own decisions, and the easy availability of divorce and abortion made this a practicality. In Muslim areas women were also protected from traditional customs like polygamy and were able to dispense with the veil. The consequences were, however, damaging in other respects. By 1934 37 per cent of marriages in Moscow ended in divorce and there were 2.7 times as many abortions as live births. There was also a massive increase in juvenile crime and serious social disruption. Particularly worrying to the authorities were the prospects of a long-term population fall. The restoration of the family provided the benefit of greater security for women, although their previous experience of greater freedom was now ended. Many found that a double burden had been imposed upon them by Stalin's changes: their family responsibilities and their integral role within the labour force.

Stalin's policies towards religion followed a more complex pattern. At first he accelerated the campaign for atheism which had started under Lenin. From 1928, for example, any conversions were forbidden, steeples were pulled down by volunteers in the League of Godless, and, during the 1930s, all religious denominations were affected by the purges. Stalin did eventually change this policy, although in this case the reversal was later and less complete than for the family. This time, the rethink was due to expediency, influenced by the pressures of war. During the struggle with Germany the Orthodox Patriarchate, abolished during the radical period, was re-established to provide a focus for Russian patriotism. On the other hand, where he felt that there would be little benefit to the regime the concessions were not forthcoming. There was no let-up for the Jews who, in the circumstances, were hardly likely to support the German invaders, nor for the Muslims, most of whom were outside the German invasion path.

In religion it is easier to see the negative than the positive effects of Stalin's dictatorship. The persecution of minority groups was ruthless and relentless. Jews were equated with capitalism and opposition to communist principles; there were even periodic, although not explicit, revivals of the type of racist anti-Semitism apparent in Tsarist Russia. Islam and Buddhism experienced virtually no direct benefits from a regime which was profoundly suspicious of both. Of 26,000 mosques which had existed in 1921 only 1,312 remained by 1942, while Islamic courts had all been abolished. On the other hand, Islam was never seriously weakened. Its abiding social influence, along with the absence of physical damage caused in central Asia by the war, meant that the population increased more rapidly in the Muslim republics than in the Slavic areas of the Soviet Union. This had enormous implications for the future – Islam outlived not only Stalinism but communism itself.

Education and culture

Education underwent a similar transformation to the social changes outlined above. Under Lenin during the 1920s educational theory had favoured relaxed discipline and group activity in schools based heavily on Marxist ideas. At first Stalin intensified the Leninist approach. In history, for example, the books of Pokrovskii emphasized the negative heritage of the Tsarist and capitalist past. This seemed to harmonize with Stalin's plans to modernize industry and accelerate socialism. By 1934, however, Stalin had completely changed his approach. He reintroduced formal learning, examinations and grades, and the full authority of the teacher. Another example of revived conservatism was the restoration of school uniforms, including compulsory pigtails for girls. History now placed a positive slant on the Tsarist past and created heroic figures out of Ivan the Terrible and Peter the Great. Stalin also reversed the tendency of the 1920s to base access to higher education on social criteria. Thus, instead of favouring applicants from the proletariat, Stalin insisted that the demands of technology would be best served by selecting candidates with the highest academic qualifications. As in other areas, his educational changes were an attempt to wrest the initiative back from the radical dynamic which had spiralled out of control by the end of the 1920s.

Much has now been written about the impact of Stalin's initial radicalism and subsequent conservatism in education. Both phases had advantages and disadvantages. During the 'radical' period, from 1927 to 1931, there were huge increases in institutions and enrolments. The priority of Narkompros (People's Commissariat for Enlightenment) was to create education for the masses. Numerically this seemed to work. Schools increased from 118,558 in 1927–8 to 166,275 by 1933, and pupils from 7.9 to 9.7 million. During the same period 1,466 specialist institutes came into existence in higher education, student numbers increasing from 168,500 to 458,300. Soon, however, the benefits of an expanding base gave way to the problems of declining quality: in 1931, Narkompros was criticized by the party for falling short on educational standards, in particular for general knowledge. The end of the radical phase brought a revival of standards, partly through the restoration of formal content such as the theoretical element of the sciences, and partly through the reintroduction of entrance requirements based on academic success. This meant a change in the social intake of students. Access to higher education once again favoured the more articulate sectors of society and the automatic preference previously given to the proletariat was ended. It seems, therefore, that overall numbers benefited from the radical phase, while improved standards resulted from the return to traditional policies.

The official line intruded also into culture. At first, Stalin was even more radical than the Bolsheviks. Art and literature were used to publicize the Five Year Plans and collectivization. 'Artistic brigades' were set up, under RAPP or the Russian Association of Proletarian Writers. As in other fields, however, complications soon emerged. Works of real merit declined, while local application of artistic criteria allowed mediocrity to flourish in an atmosphere of repressive confusion. Clearly something had to be done to instil order and raise standards. In 1932, therefore, RAPP was replaced by the Union of Writers, which redefined cultural criteria in accordance with 'Socialist Realism'. This laid down direct guidelines so that writers would mobilize the masses and aim consciously to be engineers of the human soul. All literary works must also provide 'a truthful, historically concrete depiction of reality in its revolutionary development'.[72] In 1958, the writer Sholokhov provided a more straightforward description of Socialist Realism as 'that which is written for the Soviet government in simple, comprehensible, artistic language'.[73] Stalin was also susceptible to Russian tradition, showing a liking for Russian stories and folk tunes. His own view of Socialist Realism, therefore, was that it was 'National in form, Socialist in content',[74] in effect a synthesis of socialist change and highlights from the past.

Again, the results were mixed. On the one hand, he reduced all art forms to state subservience, which had obvious implications for quality. Painting was used directly for political propaganda, which meant that most works were stilted or conveyed blatant untruths about collectivization. The most common themes were contented peasants, industrious workers with Stakhanovite aspirations, and the paternalist qualities of Stalin himself. Architecture was even more directly controlled by the state, since plans and designs could rarely be achieved without state funding. Priority was given to prestige projects, which formed an integral part of the regime's obsession with gigantomania. On the other hand, the Soviet Union experienced something akin to a renaissance in music and film. Composers were able to work more successfully under Stalin's constraints than under Hitler's. The output of Prokofiev, Khachaturian, Kabalevsky and, above all, Shostakovich was impressive by any standard, and the Soviet Union had a greater musical output than any other dictatorship of the twentieth century. Film, too, was used more subtly in Russia than in Germany, and Sergei Eisenstein directed *October*, *Battleship Potemkin* and *Ivan the Terrible*, all abiding masterpieces.

Overall, Stalin moved from an early acceleration of Bolshevik radicalism to a revival of past traditions. This has usually been put down to a deliberate policy on his part. It might, however, be more appropriate to see it as a response to initial failure. As the regime appeared increasingly ramshackle he had to abandon radicalism and attempt to restore authoritarianism through more reliable traditions. The later policies were generally more beneficial – or less harmful – than his earlier ones. The fracturing of society by collectivization and enforced industrialization was predominantly negative, while the revival of traditional values provided greater stability for social and cultural developments. Without exception, however, the changes were introduced to bolster an insecure dictatorship. As a result, the main casualty of all Stalin's policies, whether radical or traditional, was the individual.

SOVIET FOREIGN POLICY, 1918–41

The foreign policy of Lenin and Stalin was highly complex, and involved numerous zigzags. At its best, it was skilful, confident and effective; at its worst, it was blundering, uncertain and ruinous. Throughout the period there was an internal conflict between ideological motives on the one hand and, on the other, a pragmatism which bordered on cynicism.

1918–24

The new Bolshevik leaders displayed an intense ideological hostility to the Western powers, believing in the inevitability of their eventual collapse and also in the necessity of this as a precondition for the survival of communism. Trotsky argued that this collapse must be accelerated by Russia: 'Either the Russian Revolution will create a revolutionary movement in Europe, or the European powers will destroy the Russian Revolution.'[75] At the same time, Lenin had to take into account the immediate situation in which he found himself and make policy adjustments as he considered necessary. This meant that he was forced to make agreements with Western powers in a style of diplomacy which was essentially pragmatic. Although he also encouraged foreign revolutionary activity, as ideology seemed to demand, this became a lesser priority.

There were two reasons for this apparent turnabout. The first was the influence of external developments. From the time of the October Revolution until the death of Lenin the Bolsheviks had to adapt to the pressure exerted on Russia by Western powers. This was far more important than that exerted by the Bolsheviks on the West. The second factor was even more important. Throughout the period the Bolsheviks remained vulnerable to internal pressure from the Russian population. This did much to condition their response to the West. Faced with these two inter-related influences, Lenin had to adapt rather than devise: his foreign policy had to be more reactive than projective.

This became apparent almost as soon as the Bolsheviks had seized power. Ideology suggested using the First World War to spread revolution among the working classes of the capitalist powers. Common sense, however, dictated withdrawal from the war as quickly as possible. Russia's continued involvement had already brought down the Tsarist regime and the Provisional Governmnent; why should the Bolsheviks now succeed where these others had failed? The revolutionary impetus would almost certainly continue. Just as the Provisional Government had fallen to the Bolsheviks, so the Bolsheviks were, in turn, vulnerable to the Socialist Revolutionaries who were establishing separatist governments to the east of the areas under Lenin's control. To make matters worse, it was becoming apparent that the bulk of the population was swinging its support behind the Socialist Revolutionaries early in 1918. The Red revolution was therefore in danger of being overtaken by a Green revolution. Marxists – Lenin and Trotsky included – were only too aware of the importance of war as a catalyst for such a change. After all, 'war is the locomotive of history' and, to use a different metaphor, acts as the 'midwife for every old society pregnant with a new one'. While being optimistic that history was on their side, the Bolsheviks were more pessimistic about the indiscriminate impact of war.

As soon as he had come to power, therefore, Lenin issued a decree which called upon 'all warring peoples and their governments to begin negotiations immediately for a just and democratic peace, a peace without annexation and indemnities'. Unfortunately, Russia's negotiations with Germany at Brest-Litovsk at the end of 1917 hit a major snag. The Germans insisted that Russia surrender, as the price for peace, Finland, Lithuania, Poland and the Ukraine. The Russian delegation withdrew from the talks in February 1918 but was forced to return. This was partly because the Germans had renewed their military offensive and partly because the Socialist Revolutionaries were applying increasing pressure in the Urals and the Volga region. In March 1918, therefore, the Bolsheviks conceded, in the Treaty of Brest-Litovsk, to all the German demands. This enabled the Bolsheviks to deal more immediately with their internal opponents, the Greens, and with the growing threat of the Whites and their Western support.

It might be thought that the Civil War gave the Bolsheviks ample reason for permanent hostility to the West. After all, the latter had provided supplies to the Whites through Murmansk, Archangel, the Black Sea, the Caucasus and Vladivostok. Although this intervention failed, there was to be further anti-Bolshevik action, in the form of aid to Poland. In 1920, a Polish invasion conquered much of the Ukraine. The Red Army launched a counter-attack, coming within striking distance of Warsaw, but a second Polish offensive was made possible by extensive reforms carried out by Marshal Piłsudski and French help provided through General Weygand. By the Treaty of Riga (1921) Russia suffered its second territorial amputation in three years. Yet the period after 1921 saw attempts by Lenin's regime to come to terms with the West. There were two main reasons for this.

The first was pressure from within. Although the Whites had been defeated in the Civil War and the Socialist Revolutionaries reduced to a splintered opposition, the Bolsheviks were faced from 1920 with a wave of resentment from the peasantry. There were widespread revolts and peasant wars (see p. 32, largely in reaction to the unpopular policy of War Communism. The introduction of the New Economic Policy in 1921 was a tactical retreat which also required a different attitude to the Western powers. The priority was now the end of Soviet isolation and the acceptance of coexistence with capitalism. This would enable Soviet Russia to concentrate on industrial growth in an attempt to create a balanced economy. It might even be necessary to attract Western investment. According to Kamenev in 1921, 'We can, of course, restore our economy by the heroic effort of the working masses. But we cannot develop it fast enough to prevent the capitalist countries from overtaking us, unless we call in foreign capital.'[76] There was, however, more to it than that. By 1921 the Bolsheviks had come to the conclusion that they could not hope to control the population of Russia *and* engage in an offensive against capitalism.

The second reason for the search for coexistence was the failure of the Bolshevik hope that a revolutionary flame would spread across Europe, consuming Russia's enemies. The year 1919 had brought high expectations but eventual disappointment.

The left-wing socialist regimes of Bavaria and Hungary were overthrown, while the communist uprising in Berlin was put down, in January 1919, with considerable bloodshed. Clearly world revolution was further off than had originally been hoped. There was a powerful irony here. Trotsky and Lenin had believed that Bolshevik organization would be sufficient to activate revolutions against the regimes in the leading capitalist states. In other words, a 'top-down' communist initiative would promote a 'bottom-up' campaign against capitalism. In fact, the reverse occurred. The 'bottom-up' threat came from within Russia, forcing the Bolshevik leadership to take a 'top-down' decision to live with capitalism rather than to try to destroy it.

Between 1921 and 1924 the Bolsheviks therefore reversed the connection between diplomacy and revolution. Marxist theory had previously emphasized revolution as the main strand of foreign policy, with diplomacy a method of adjustment. In the light of experience between 1918 and 1921, however, Lenin focused on diplomacy in practice, although he continued to use revolution as a subordinate theme.

Diplomacy produced some real gains for the Soviet government: in 1921 and 1924, for example, trade agreements were drawn up with Britain. But the real target for Soviet activity was Germany, isolated and resentful after the harsh terms of the Versailles Settlement. As Lenin had stated in his 1920 speech, 'Germany is one of the strongest advanced capitalist countries, it cannot put up with the Versailles Treaty . . . Here is a situation we must utilize.'[77] He did. The Soviet Foreign Minister, Chicherin, conducted secret negotiations with Rathenau, his German counterpart. These reached their climax in Genoa in 1922. Ostensibly, Russia and Germany were themselves objects of discussion among the other powers, but the tables were turned when the Russo-German Treaty of Rapallo was announced. Germany became the first state to extend full diplomatic recognition to Bolshevik Russia; both countries agreed to expand trade, and Germany would provide credits and investment for Russian industry. Rapallo is usually seen as a diplomatic victory and a vindication of Lenin's approach. It succeeded in splitting the Western powers and destroyed any immediate chance of a united Western response to communism.

Meanwhile, Lenin continued to use revolutionary activity and propaganda as a subsidiary device in his foreign policy. In March 1919 he established Comintern (Communist International) to co-ordinate communist movements and to bring them under the overall direction of Moscow. In 1920 Comintern based its whole structure on that of the Soviet Communist Party and declared itself to be 'a single Communist Party having branches in different countries'.[78] Its purpose was to promote radical activity and to weaken anti-Soviet policies pursued by Western governments. At the same time Lenin established relations with 'countries of the East' (a term which has now been replaced by 'Third World') to encourage them to throw off Western influence. It did not matter that most of these countries were themselves anti-communist. The important thing was they were also anti-imperialist; wars of liberation in the colonies could be just as damaging for the Western powers as internal revolution.

The overall impression was that ideology was in practice subordinated to practicality. At the same time, Lenin clearly did not relish what he was doing. He could not, of course, admit that he was being forced in this direction by pressures from within Russia since this would not fit well with Bolshevik claims to be leading the revolution rather than merely reacting to it. Hence, he described his diplomacy with the West as a temporary expedient, a mere diversion until the preferred policy of worldwide revolution could be resumed. The main advantage, as he saw it, was that diplomacy would enable Russia to work on the differences between the various capitalist states. In a speech to Moscow party activists in December 1920, he argued: 'So long as we have not won the whole world, so long as we remain economically and militarily weaker than what is left of the capitalist world, we must stick to the rule: be able to exploit the contradictions and oppositions between the imperialists.'[79] He saw three particularly important areas of discord: in the Pacific between the United States and Japan; the differences between the USA and Europe; and, above all, the gap between the wartime Allies and defeated Germany. One – or more – of these was bound to provide communism with opportunities in the future.

1924–39

Stalin's foreign policy was so complex that it is the subject of considerable controversy. This section will, therefore, provide a brief outline of the main developments and then attempt to interpret their meaning.

At first the Soviet government succeeded in extending its respectability. It gained diplomatic recognition, in 1924, from Britain, France, Italy and Japan. In 1926 a second agreement was drawn up between Russia and Germany; the Berlin Treaty was, in effect, a neutrality pact which also renewed the various agreements made at Rapallo. There were, however, complications in Soviet relations with the West. In 1927, for example, the British government broke off diplomatic relations after ordering the Soviet embassy in London to be raided. By the end of the 1920s Stalin was deliberately playing down friendship with the West. He argued that the Soviet Union no longer needed any form of Western economic assistance and that, in any case, capitalism would be destroyed by an economic crisis. He decided to keep open the contact with Germany by renewing, in 1931, the Treaty of Berlin, but he made no attempt to assist the Weimar Republic to prevent the rise of Nazism between 1931 and 1933 and even restrained the German Communist Party (KPD) under Thalmann from collaborating with the German Social Democrats (SPD). Indeed, Stalin saw the latter as merely another manifestation of that same crisis of capitalism which had increased Hitler's support; hence, social democracy was the 'moderate wing of Fascism'.[80] Stalin's insistence that the SPD were unworthy of power because they were social fascists certainly played a part in destroying any meaningful opposition to the Nazis, who came to power in January 1933.

Between 1933 and 1934 Stalin attempted to maintain close relations between Russia and Germany. In 1935, however, he appeared to change course and to draw up agreements to contain Germany. Two examples are the Soviet–French and Soviet–Czechoslovak Treaties of Mutual Assistance. Meanwhile, Stalin had also secured Russia's entry into the League of Nations and from 1935 he sponsored the growth of popular fronts throughout Europe in which communists, socialists and liberals were encouraged to resist fascism. By 1938, however, Stalin was clearly envisaging further alterations in Soviet foreign policy, while 1939 saw separate negotiations between Russia and, on the one hand, Britain and France and, on the other, Nazi Germany. In August 1939 Stalin eventually settled for Germany and the foreign ministers of the two powers, Molotov and von Ribbentrop, formally signed the Nazi–Soviet Non-Aggression Pact.

This somewhat tortuous route to Soviet security has often puzzled Western observers. It is, however, possible to examine Stalin's motives on two levels. First, what was the underlying aim of his relations with other powers throughout the period as a whole? Second, and arising from this, why did he pursue particular policies at various stages between 1924 and 1939?

The underlying motive seems to have been to provide security from abroad for the construction of communism at home. This would eventually enable the Soviet Union to turn its power outwards. In Stalin's own words, 'Our banner remains, as before, the banner of peace. But if war breaks out, we shall not be able to sit with folded hands – we shall have to make a move, but the move will come last.' Stalin assumed 'hostility from all imperialist powers and, therefore, the need to keep them divided.'[81] Short-term security therefore merged with prospects for long-term offensives. From this basic assumption, three priorities followed logically.

The first was the transformation of Russia into an industrial superpower: this would give the military base necessary for survival. In justifying his policy of Socialism in One Country and the introduction of the planning system Stalin constantly harped on the theme of Soviet insecurity. In February 1931, for example, he said, 'We have lagged fifty to a hundred years behind the leading countries. We must cover this distance in ten years. Either we do that or they crush us.'[82] The second priority was to safeguard the Soviet Union, while this reconstruction was under way, by not precipitating attacks from the West. Stalin therefore opted for Socialism in One Country rather than Permanent Revolution, which might well upset the external situation to Russia's internal disadvantage. The third, and more distant, option was eventual military involvement to defeat the capitalist West: this would both ensure Soviet security and enable the recovery of territory lost by the treaties of Brest-Litovsk (1918) and Riga (1921).

In his approach to foreign policy, therefore, Stalin gave priority to rapid internal growth regulated by a planning mechanism, short- or medium-term external security, and long-term military intervention. This was not a blueprint but a series of fairly general objectives which linked the economy to industrial and military mobilization. It was, however, much more difficult to decide what specific line of foreign policy was most likely to achieve them. This is where historians have disagreed with each other. Broadly, they have followed two lines of argument.

The first is based on the so-called 'Rapallo' approach. Stalin tried to continue the special relationship established with Germany by the Treaty of Rapallo in 1922. This made sense for a number of reasons. Rapallo and its successor the Treaty of Berlin (1926) secured for the Soviet Union investment and military co-operation from Germany. It put pressure on Poland, which had, after all, won the Russo-Polish War of 1920–1. It might even have neutralized the Anglo-French combination. This was an important consideration since Britain and France were always likely to be hostile to Russia. Sooner or later, Russia's special relationship with Germany would pay off, especially if the latter could be enticed into a conflict with the other capitalist powers. In this event, Soviet involvement could be used, in Stalin's words, to 'throw the decisive weight onto the scales, the weight that could be preponderant'.[83]

The other view of Stalin's foreign policy is that he adopted a 'collective security' approach. This involved seeking a more important role in Europe than a mere bilateral relationship with a single power would permit. In any case, Germany was the most likely threat to Soviet security, which meant that Stalin's foreign policy would have to be directed towards maintaining contacts with those countries most likely to constrain Germany. This meant increasing Soviet contacts with France, especially during the period between 1933 and 1938.

Are these two interpretations entirely antagonistic? By one analysis, the Nazi–Soviet Non-Aggression Pact of August 1939 was a logical and direct consequence of a long-term strategy. Stalin's main hope, it is argued, was that Germany and the West would tear each other apart and that Russia would be well placed to pick up the pieces. One of the main reasons for Stalin's willingness to see the Nazis in power in Germany was that they would be much more likely than a democratic regime to attack the West. Another reason was that the alternative – a collaboration between the SPD and KPD – would be highly embarrassing to Stalin. The SPD were pro-Western and were therefore likely to reduce the chance of a split between capitalist powers. Hitler's rise, it would seem, suited Stalin perfectly. Of course, Hitler's policies from 1934 onwards were more forceful than Stalin had anticipated and it was therefore necessary to take steps to contain Germany and to remind Hitler that Germany had no option but to consider an eventual deal with Russia. But the collaboration between the Soviet Union and the Western powers was never more than a temporary expedient, designed to last until Stalin was able to return to his preferred policy. The opportunity came in August 1939 and the Nazi–Soviet Pact represented, in Tucker's words, 'the fruition of Stalin's whole complex conception of the means of Soviet survival in a hostile world and emergence into a commanding international position'.[84] A new war was now inevitable, a war which Stalin could help start. Then, from a position of neutrality, he could watch the combatants exhaust themselves. He could then involve Russia, claim territory and sponsor revolutionary movements to create a ring of socialist states.[85]

All this has a certain logic. But it is stronger in its analysis of the general purpose of Soviet rearmament than it is in explaining the details of Soviet diplomacy. For one thing, it attributes to Stalin the sort of long-term diplomatic objectives which amount almost to a blueprint. The very considerable changes in Stalin's foreign policy are seen as mere tactical deviations in pursuit of a long-term strategy. But might they not actually have been a change of long-term strategy as a result of short-term indecision, uncertainty and awareness of previous errors? Within two years of Hitler's rise to power, Stalin realized that Nazism was far more resilient than he had expected. The only answer was a total change of strategy, to end the connection established with Germany in the 1920s and to seek accommodation with the West and Czechoslovakia. Stalin also ordered communists everywhere to collaborate with socialists, in direct contrast to his previous policy towards the German communists and socialists. The eventual switch back to Germany can be explained by the events of 1938. The Anschluss and the crisis over Czechoslovakia showed the West in the worst possible light. Stalin was forced to the conclusion that the Western powers were unreliable allies. It appeared that they would now allow Germany to rearm and expand without hindrance. In 1939 Stalin had two options open to him. He could maintain the Soviet friendship with France and extend it to Britain – but with more definite and specific military commitments. Or he could seek agreement with Germany and draw up a territorial settlement which would eliminate any possible cause of conflict. During the first half of 1939 Stalin seemed willing to incline towards either alternative but was eventually infuriated by the unwillingness of Chamberlain, the British Prime Minister, to meet his terms. In August 1939, therefore, he informed the Politburo of his decision to do a deal with Hitler. In this perspective, the Nazi–Soviet Non-Aggression Pact can be seen as one of two last-minute alternatives, rather than as the logical outcome of all Stalin's previous policies.

This line reveals a very different Stalin. Had he been as consistent as Tucker maintains, he would have had to transcend not only Chamberlain and Daladier – admittedly not too difficult – but even Hitler, whose forward planning has now been called into question by a whole battery of historians. Stalin was no better as a diplomat than his contemporaries. Perhaps he was worse. Indeed, his whole commitment to foreign policy has been open to dispute. According to Haslam, he 'took only a sporadic interest' in this area; 'on the whole, Stalin abstained from direct intervention and contented himself with merely reviewing and approving . . . Even the process of review was occasionally delegated to others.'[86] We could go further down the road opened by Haslam. The zigzag in policy shows the impact of subordinates, upon whom Stalin relied to extract him from previous errors. For example, Soviet agreements with France in 1935, together with the promotion of broad anti-fascist fronts all over Europe, owed much to Foreign Minister Litvinov, who sought to improve Soviet relations with the West through involvement in the League of Nations. When, by 1938, it had become apparent that collective security had not worked, Stalin switched to another track. He blamed Litvinov for moving the Soviet Union too closely to France and replaced him with Molotov, who was known to favour a more pro-German line. In each case, therefore, Stalin was influenced by his advisers quite as much as he directed them – until things went wrong and Stalin needed a scapegoat.

By this approach, the rapid changes in foreign policy were similar to what happened in domestic policy: far from being *in* control, Stalin had to pull back after an earlier policy had run *out of* control. He was fundamentally pragmatic, adjusting his policies according to immediate needs rather than to long-term preconceptions. He had the power and authority to make sudden changes and explain away previous errors of judgement in a way which would have been much more difficult in a democracy. All this gives an illusion, rather than the substance, of control.

The Nazi–Soviet Pact and the period 1939–41

The terms of the pact may be summarized as follows. Germany and Russia undertook 'to desist from any act of violence, any aggressive action, and any attack on each other, either individually or jointly with other Powers'. Should either become involved in any conflict, the other would remain strictly neutral. Neither would 'participate in any grouping of Powers whatsoever that is directly or indirectly aimed at the other party'.[87] Accompanying the Non-Aggression Pact was a secret additional protocol which provided for the demarcation of spheres of influence in eastern Europe, including Poland. The two countries proceeded almost immediately to implement this. Stalin invaded Poland on 17 September 1939, two weeks after the start of the German Blitzkrieg from the west. The Red Army encountered comparatively little resistance, for the Polish airforce had been obliterated by the Luftwaffe and the Polish cavalry had destroyed itself in heroic but futile attacks against German tank divisions. A further agreement followed between the two powers, partitioning Poland for the fourth time in that unhappy country's history. The Soviet Union regained the Belorussian and Ukrainian areas lost to Poland in the war of 1920–1. From this point Russia and Germany shared a common frontier and maintained an uncomfortable coexistence – until Hitler broke this by launching an invasion in June 1941.

The Non-Aggression Pact and its accompanying protocol put into perspective every other initiative taken since Stalin's assumption of full control in 1929. Not surprisingly, two very different interpretations can be advanced about whether it was a success. These depend on whether the pact was the outcome of a long-term plan or whether it was put together at the last minute to compensate for all the frustrations and difficulties which had occurred during the 1930s.

Tucker contends that it was always Stalin's long-term intention to come to terms with Germany. If so, then the agreement can be seen as the fulfilment of a difficult and, at times, frustrating policy. The pact itself was undoubtedly the best means of promoting discord between Germany and the Western powers: Hitler could feel confident in invading Poland which would, in turn, provoke France and Britain. The accompanying secret protocol enabled the Soviet Union to regain the areas lost to Poland in 1921 in the Treaty of Riga – but without the risk of action against Russia. Since Stalin was, in effect, reoccupying territories beyond the original frontier of Poland, Britain and France would be unlikely to declare war on Russia; Hitler, on the other hand, was clearly violating the Polish state itself. In addition, the pact would enable Russia to maintain the economic link with Germany which had been started at Rapallo and then resumed, after interruptions, in 1939. Overall, the agreement was a stunning coup. Germany would now weaken itself in a war with the West while Russia could recover lost territory and continue to benefit from German industrial credits. Stalin even had the option of intervening decisively in the now inevitable European conflict. It was the culmination of everything he had planned.

The alternative, and more likely, interpretation is more negative. If the whole process was *not* planned, then there must have been a violent swing of the pendulum which Stalin was unable to control. As we have already seen, the 1930s saw a series of disasters in Soviet policy. This started with Stalin's blunder in helping put Hitler into power. He had to compensate for this by trying to reactivate collective security in conjunction with France, only to be buffeted back towards Germany by the Anglo-French policy of appeasement. As in domestic policy, therefore, Stalin was rarely in control of the situation and was well aware of the threat of impending chaos. The Non-Aggression Pact was a lifeline which he seized without realizing its full implications. The Polish dimension has been especially misinterpreted. There was no specific agreement to partition Poland between Germany and Russia. Rather, the protocol focused more generally on spheres of influence in eastern Europe. Roberts therefore argues, 'The partition of Poland in September 1939 was the direct result not of the Nazi–Soviet pact but of the unforeseen rapidity of the Polish military collapse.'[88] There is an element of desperation here, too. Stalin was forced to occupy eastern Poland to limit the extent of German advance, the speed of which took him completely by surprise. Hence, any territorial advantages of the pact to Russia were entirely unplanned and were the result of a reaction to events as they occurred.

So far we have assessed the Nazi–Soviet Pact in relation to what Stalin intended. There is, of course, another criterion for success. Irrespective of whether it was the logical outcome of Stalin's earlier policies, just how necessary was the pact for Russia? Again, two cases have been put. One is that the measure was fully justified. Soviet historians argued that 'subsequent events revealed that this step was the only correct one under the circumstances. By taking it, the USSR was able to continue peaceful construction for nearly two years and to strengthen its defences.'[89] It has also been stated that between 1939 and 1941 Stalin was able to build up a buffer zone in eastern Europe, which absorbed some of the impact of the German invasion in 1941. Where would Russia have been without this?

But this view is simplistic. The alternative is that the pact was not necessary for Russia. Laqueur argues that it should not be assumed that without the pact Germany would have attacked Russia in 1939. Hitler was too preoccupied with Poland, Britain and France to draw off divisions for yet another campaign. More telling is the observation that even if Hitler had moved immediately, the Soviet Union would have been better off. By 1941 German military production had grown, proportionately, more rapidly than Russia's, enabling Hitler to launch, in Operation Barbarossa, the sort of offensive which would have been impossible in 1939.[90] In addition, it could be argued that Russia lost any strategic advantage with the fall of France to Germany in June 1940 and the inability of Britain to launch an attack on the continent. This more than cancelled out any advantage from Soviet territorial gains from the pact.

Supposing that a respite was provided by the Nazi–Soviet Pact (and this is by no means certain), it could further be argued that Stalin failed to make proper use of it. At the end of 1939, for example, he precipitated a war with Finland. He did not intend to try to reverse the Treaty of Brest-Litovsk and force Finland back into Russia but he did mean to extend the boundary back from the outer suburbs of Leningrad and to gain facilities for a Soviet naval base near the mouth of the Gulf of Finland. The Finnish government had, since 1938, rejected all proposals for exchanges of territory or Soviet leases. There were those in Helsinki who thought that the Russian requests were reasonable, but Stalin's ruthless policy towards Poland stiffened Finnish determination not to compromise. On 30 November 1939 twenty Soviet divisions were launched against Finland's fifteen, opening what soon came to be known as the Winter War. The task proved far more difficult than Stalin had envisaged and the Red Army experienced a number of humiliating reverses before the Soviet Union extracted the desired territory from Finland in February 1940. The Winter War had important results. It showed up Russia's military deficiencies and bankrupted her diplomatic reputation to the extent that she was thrown out of the League of Nations for aggression. In all probability these failings convinced Hitler that he could afford to attack the Soviet Union sooner rather than later. The way in which Stalin used any respite from the Non-Aggression Pact therefore actually jeopardized that respite.

During the rest of 1940 and the first half of 1941 relations between the Soviet Union and Germany deteriorated rapidly. The Germans regarded Stalin's Winter

War as entirely unnecessary and they openly expressed their sympathy for the Finns, with whom, indeed, they eventually allied. Stalin, for his part, was openly dissatisfied with the amount of territory in eastern Europe which had come under Soviet influence and was putting pressure on Hitler to make further concessions, especially in the Balkans. There were also diplomatic complications. In September 1940 Germany, Japan and Italy concluded a Three Power Pact, which Stalin was invited to join. When Molotov, the Soviet Foreign Minister, visited Berlin in November 1940, he refused to adhere to this pact until the remaining Soviet demands in eastern Europe had been met. According to Grey, this meeting probably confirmed Hitler's decision to invade Russia in 1941.[91]

Stalin's policy during this period seems to have based on a total misreading of Hitler's intentions. He considered that Russia was safe from Germany, at least for the foreseeable future, and that it was therefore safe to apply his own pressure. He assumed – wrongly – that the more Russia demanded, the more pliable Germany would become. But, as Roberts points out, 'Moscow's pursuit of this objective resulted not in the further development of the Nazi–Soviet alliance but the beginning of a fateful crisis in Soviet–German relations which was to end in war.'[92] What Stalin did not realize was that Soviet demands depended on Germany's *existing* tolerance: it was not likely to *increase* that tolerance. All Stalin was doing by insisting on further concessions in the Balkans was to increase Hitler's determination to settle the Russian issue once and for all. And, of course, the problems encountered by the Red Army in Finland encouraged Hitler to reduce the timescale for doing this.

Worse was to follow. Even when it became clear that Soviet relations with Germany were deteriorating rapidly, Stalin showed little awareness of any imminent threat. Indeed, it could be argued that he lost control over the whole situation. This can be shown in three ways. First, he failed to make any use of possible contacts with Britain. He considered that this might run the risk of diverting the Nazi war machine eastwards, which would play into Churchill's hands by releasing the pressure on Britain. This subsequently proved to be a mistake, since Hitler was already planning to throw the weight of the German armies against Russia. Through his inaction here Stalin therefore lost the initiative. Instead – in a second error – Stalin assumed that any war with Germany would be preceded automatically by warning signals from Germany as part of a clearly visible deterioration in relations; Stalin was confident that, in such circumstances, Hitler would issue an ultimatum before hostilities ensued. In that event Russia would have time to respond by making the diplomatic adjustments necessary to prevent the outbreak of war. This meant that Stalin committed a third blunder by ignoring all the warnings he received about an impending German invasion. These came from intelligence reports from Soviet agents as well as details about German troop movements provided by the British government. These will be dealt with in further detail in the next section. Consequently, according to Churchill, Stalin and his advisers proved at this stage to be 'the most completely outwitted bunglers of the Second World War'.

THE GREAT FATHERLAND WAR, 1941–5

Defeat: 1941–2

Operation Barbarossa was launched by Hitler on the Soviet Union on 22 June 1941. Other states soon followed in declaring war on Russia, especially Romania, Italy, Slovakia, Finland and Hungary. The invasion force totalled 3 million men, the greatest in the whole of human history to that date. The objective was no less than the complete destruction of the USSR.

At first, German troops were remarkably successful. Their advance divided into three prongs – against Leningrad in the north, Moscow in the centre and Kiev in the south. By the end of 1941 the whole of the Baltic coastline had been conquered, Leningrad was almost surrounded and the Germans were within 25 kilometres of Moscow. Although the attempt to take the capital failed, most of the Ukraine was occupied, including Kiev, Kharkov, Odessa and the Crimea. When the offensive was resumed in the spring and summer of 1942 the main advances came in the south with the crossing of the Don and the capture of the oilfields and agricultural areas of the Caucasus. By August 1942 the Germans had reached the Volga and Stalingrad. During the early phases of this advance the Soviet armies folded like cardboard. German tanks, for example, advanced an unprecedented 250 kilometres within the first three days and, within the first few months, killed 1 million Russians and took 1 million prisoners. Hitler had told his generals at the outset: 'We have only to kick in the door and the whole rotten structure will come crashing down.'[93] Initial events seemed to justify his confidence.

Soviet historians have explained this sensational collapse by the numerical superiority of German armaments in 1941. This simply will not do. Soviet forces outnumbered the Germans and, at the time of the German invasion, the Soviet Union possessed 24,000 tanks – most of the world's supply. Western historians have tended to focus on the element of surprise and Stalin's defective leadership in the opening months of the invasion. This is nearer the mark, but now needs to be considered within the context of recent research into the specific way in which Russia had prepared for the war. This suggests four closely related factors. First, during the 1930s Soviet military infrastructure had been prepared for one type of war. But, second, because of his inappropriate diplomacy between 1939 and 1941, Stalin blundered into an altogether different war. Third, in these circumstances the infrastructure came close to collapse. This meant, fourth, that there was little to stop the already well-tried German strategy of Blitzkrieg.

Recent studies have shown that the main aim of the first three Five Year Plans had been to mobilize the Soviet Union for total war. Stalin had been influenced by a new strategy of warfare developed by military theoreticians such as Varfolomeev and Triandafilov. They suggested abandoning defensive warfare, Russia's traditional response to invasion, largely because it had not worked between 1914 and 1917. Instead, they argued that the Soviet Union should in future prepare to deliver a swift and crushing blow through 'the conduct of operations of annihilation'.[94] To do this, the Soviet Union would need to deploy all its forces as soon as war broke out to deliver a sudden and decisive blow. Hence, the priority of the Five Year Plans was rearmament – in preparation for an offensive war – and throughout the

1930s tanks, artillery pieces, aircraft and small weapons were produced and stockpiled on a massive scale. Mobilization was no longer geared for defence but for a pre-emptive strike at a time of Stalin's own choosing.

This, of course, did not happen. Instead, Stalin's actions obliged Soviet forces to fight a defensive war against a pre-emptive strike from Germany. The timing of the hostilities was chosen by Hitler, not Stalin; the latter tried everything possible to avoid war until he was ready. In the process, Stalin more than misjudged the situation: he committed colossal blunders. The most basic was a misinterpretation of what Hitler intended. Stalin had initially assumed that Nazism was an unstable form of radicalism, which would soon give way to communism. When this failed to happen he decided instead that Hitler was primarily a pragmatist. He therefore took it for granted that Hitler was logical in his objectives and that he would not want Germany to fight a war on two fronts. Since Hitler would try to avoid this, Stalin could expect plenty of warning of a deterioration in relations, which he could then try to repair through well-timed concessions to Germany. The real danger, as Stalin saw it, was any action which might provoke Hitler.

It was this attitude which delivered up Russia to Hitler's attack. Stalin was totally unreceptive to warnings, from British intelligence in April 1941, of German troop concentrations near the Soviet border. Stalin's reasoning – not illogical – was that Churchill was trying to provoke a conflict between Germany and Russia which would open up a war on two fronts, to the benefit of Britain. But he also ignored intelligence reports from his own agents. On 20 March, for example, General Golikov, the head of military intelligence, forwarded to Stalin information he had received about the build-up of German troops in the border areas. Similarly, in May, Admiral Kuznetsov quoted the Soviet naval attaché in Berlin that war was imminent, but the warning was thought to have been planted. Vital information was also received from the pro-Soviet German agent in Japan, Richard Sorge, as well as from the Soviet Embassy in Berlin. Both gave the precise date of the intended attack – 22 June 1941. Stalin chose to ignore these because they did not fit into the way in which he had rationalized Hitler's intentions. In trying to keep his diplomatic options open he had therefore closed off his military options and laid his country wide open to a devastating German assault. As German armies moved up to and across the frontier, Stalin even ordered the withdrawal of Soviet units to avoid border provocations and conflict, in the belief that there could still be a negotiated settlement between Germany and Russia. Soviet defences were further hamstrung by orders from Stalin against the mobilization of reserves or the conduct of normal military manoeuvres, in case these should provoke Hitler. Historians generally agree that 'The causes of this disastrous behaviour lay in Moscow, with Stalin.'[95]

Not surprisingly, Stalin was devastated by the turn of events. He experienced a breakdown and confined himself to his flat in the Kremlin for the first week of the invasion. Through his blunders, he had produced a situation in which a defensive war was the only option. But, as we have already seen, this was precisely the course for which he had not prepared Russia. Everything now depended on whether the overall strategy could, at this late stage, be changed from offensive to defensive. Stalin's personal recovery was swift, but could he save his country?

The problem was that any such change would have to be rapidly orchestrated. In the circumstances it could not be done in time to stop the German advance.

Long-term preparations for offensive war now prevented short-term orderly retreat. The result was a rout on all fronts. Yet even at this stage the leadership failed to adjust its strategic thinking. With the Germans in sight of Moscow and Leningrad, propaganda maintained the fiction that there had been no reverses – and that any references to them was 'defeatism'. This delayed the possibility of tactical retreat until it was too late. There were also longer-term reasons for the military paralysis in 1941, going beyond immediate decisions and back into the layers of confusion which had accumulated in the 1930s. The purges had decapitated the Red Army's leadership, thereby reducing the amount of practical military experience. Even more important was a massive increase in political interference. According to Konstantin Simonov, any 'military illiterate felt free to meddle with the business of the military'.[96] All this was symptomatic of the chaos which had existed within Stalin's dictatorship throughout the 1930s. Stalin had adopted a strategy, which he had implemented in the planning system. But others had interpreted this in their own way. They were 'political illiterates', spawned by the purges, who had become accustomed to interfering with the military decisions of the army. Beneath Stalin's own blunders there was therefore a vast sum of lesser incompetents, suddenly exposed by the emergency of the German invasion.

It would be no exaggeration to say that the Soviet Union faced physical disintegration. In addition to the military and administrative crisis, there was the potential for the eruption of mass discontent. This might occur for two reasons. One was economic and social, the accumulated resentment of millions of peasants subjected throughout the 1930s to the rigours of enforced collectivization. Even more serious was the nationalist resistance to Soviet control. The Germans were initially welcomed as liberators by millions of Belorussians, Ukrainians and Georgians, as well as by people of the Baltic states. According to G. Fischer up to 2 million Soviets defected to and fought for the German armies.[97] How could the Soviet state possibly hope to survive such centrifugal forces?

In this situation Hitler held the military initiative. He could take full advantage of Stalin's negative leadership and the lethargy imparted by the Stalinist system. The German strategy of Blitzkrieg made full use of Soviet military indecision. The Wehrmacht attacked in strength at specific points across a broad front. Armoured panzer divisions advanced at great speed, as they had already done against Poland in 1939 and against the Low Countries and France in 1940. Hitler's forces, which comprised 5,500,000 troops, 4,950 aircraft, 47,260 pieces of artillery and 2,800 tanks, were sufficient to cut through the Soviet forces and to sustain the momentum of the advance in the three sectors of Leningrad, Moscow and Kiev, and to extend conquests further to the Volga and Stalingrad in 1942. Blitzkrieg made possible the capture of an area which extended 600 kilometres eastwards and 1,500 kilometres from north to south. The element of surprise explains the shattering impact: 56.7 per cent of all Soviet losses in the war were incurred in the initial campaign of 1941–2, and 17,500 of the 24,000 Soviet tanks were destroyed. Because of the enormous area occupied by the Germans, the Soviet workforce initially fell from 66 million to 35 million. The German conquests also threatened to wipe out all the major centres of industrial production which had been developed by the Five Year Plans.

In summary, although Stalin had been mobilizing the Soviet Union for total war to be followed by swift victory, what Russia suffered was swift defeat followed by total war. The German invasion came as a profound shock to the whole military strategy of the Soviet Union, as the diplomacy of Stalin destroyed any initiative that Russia might have had. The Soviet Union was forced back into the more traditional expedient of defensive warfare – for which, however, it had not prepared. The situation was desperate.

Revival and victory: 1943–5

The furthest extent of the German advance was reached towards the end of 1942. From this stage onwards the occupying forces were slowly but steadily driven back by the unremitting counter-offensive of the Red Army, made possible by a remarkable national revival.

The first major Soviet achievement was the successful defence of Moscow by Marshal Zhukov. This was made possible by the withdrawal of Soviet troops from the Far East to strengthen the capital. (It seems that this time Stalin decided to believe the news of the Soviet agent in Tokyo, Richard Sorge, that Japan was about to launch an attack on the United States, not on Russia.) The Battle for Moscow tested the German army to its utmost and, although the German advance continued in 1942, it was directed against the south, not against the capital. Stalin decided to focus the Soviet counter-attack on the city of Stalingrad, which was eventually captured by Zhukov early in 1943. This was undoubtedly the turning-point of the war and was followed in July 1943 by a Soviet victory in the tank battle at Kursk. From this time onwards the Soviet advance proved irresistible. Kiev was liberated by November 1943 and Leningrad early in 1944. During the first half of 1944 the Germans were finally forced out of Russian territory while, in the second half, the Red Army advanced into the Nazi-occupied states of eastern Europe. Most of Poland was captured, although virtually no assistance was provided by Stalin to the Warsaw revolt against the Germans, which was eventually put down with great brutality. Romania was forced to surrender in August and Bulgaria in September, while in October the Yugoslav resistance forces under Tito were assisted by the Russians to liberate Belgrade from German occupation. A final effort from the north-east resulted, in January 1945, in the fall of Warsaw and the conquest of the rest of Poland. From February 1945 Zhukov concentrated on the advance on Berlin. The capital was besieged and heavily bombarded, eventually falling in April after savage street-to-street fighting.

In view of the extent of the initial collapse in 1941 and 1942, the extent of Soviet military recovery was nothing short of remarkable. Most explanations have focused on the reversal between 1943 and 1945 of the negative factors which had contributed to the defeat of the Soviet Union in 1941–2. Hence, credit is given, first, to Stalin's own recovery and his ability to co-ordinate military revival and make full use of the climate and size of Russia. Second, despite its earlier loss of territory, the Soviet Union also managed to outproduce Germany in war *matériel*, the direct result of the Five Year Plans of the 1930s. Finally, the Soviet war effort was greatly assisted by the errors made by Hitler during this period. These explanations are broadly correct, but in the light of recent research they need some refining. This applies especially to explanations based on the mobilization of the Soviet economy. Overall, a combination of factors existed in delicate balance, and there are a few surprising twists to long-held assumptions.

Stalin's own recovery of the leadership was crucial to the implementation of a more appropriate strategy. He probably reached the peak of his administrative efficiency during the war years and was able to make the structural changes which could enable the Soviet Union to take full advantage of other factors. The method was new. Rather than attempting to pull together the previous components of Stalinism, he decided instead to dismantle them as a more effective way of meeting the emergency. Two new institutions were established specifically for this situation: one was Stavka, the general headquarters, the other the State Defence Committee, or GOKO. The latter, which was given powers to conduct all aspects of the war, comprised Molotov, Voroshilov, Malenkov and Beria. Under the ultimate authority of Stalin as People's Commissar for Defence, it replaced the usual party channels of communication. The emergency of war therefore did much to reduce the administrative confusion which had been seen at all levels during the 1930s and made possible a more rational approach to economic and military planning as well.

This brought a more effective adjustment and mobilization of Russian resources. The usual argument is that the Five Year Plans of the 1930s had geared the economy to total war and could produce more armaments than the more limited Blitzkrieg-based German economy. There had also been a long-term shift of resources into Siberia which meant that the Soviet Union had greatly increased its industrial capacity to the east of the European centres: some 20 per cent of the total by 1941. This meant that the Soviet Union could recover from initial defeat by continuing weapons production, a process enhanced by the transfer of factories eastwards to escape the German invasion.

While this is sound enough, the conclusion usually drawn from it is not. It has been assumed that Soviet recovery was due to the full implementation of Stalin's command economy: more armaments were produced after 1942 because the planning system was stepped up a gear. Historians such as Sapir have now shown that the reverse happened. Although the Five Year Plans had developed a mobilized economy, this was inefficient, with tension between central and local decision-making. The emergency of war brought a much more efficient approach. Interference from the centre with the local bodies was reduced and more local initiative allowed in meeting central armaments orders. From 1943 onwards, local production was based on individual decisions about supply of raw materials and on the most effective methods of using the labour force. Market forces therefore became more significant than central administrative constraints. This led to the paradox that the earlier '"mobilisation economy" had to be at least partially "demobilised" to achieve war mobilisation'.[98] But it worked. The process was possible because the types of weapons and components were kept deliberately unsophisticated, which meant that they were quick to build, easy to maintain and inexpensive to replace.

The partial demobilization of the command economy delivered overwhelming numbers of tanks, aircraft, artillery pieces and small weapons to wherever on the front they were required. These enabled Soviet forces to overwhelm the German Wehrmacht. Among the most important of these were the Katyusha rocket-launchers, the SUS (self-propelled artillery), heavy mortars, and the T-34 tank, which was admitted by one of the German commanders, General Guderian, to be superior to anything in the panzer divisions. German vehicles were not equipped for winter conditions and did not even have antifreeze (something that the Soviet vehicles did not need as they ran on diesel). The initial German superiority in the air was soon reversed as the Soviet airforce was provided with fourteen new types of aircraft, including the Il-2, nicknamed the 'Golden Plane' by Soviet pilots and the 'Black Death' by the Germans.[99]

Soviet military recovery was, therefore, due to more appropriate styles of leadership and more efficient use of economic resources. These were accompanied by a new strategy which departed from the unqualified emphasis on 'offensive' warfare developed during the 1930s. Instead, it was now considered more appropriate to combine the more traditional defensive approach with a devastating counter-attack whenever this became possible. Zhukov's advice to Stalin in April 1943 showed this line of thought: 'I consider it inadvisable for our forces to go over to the offensive in the very first days of the campaign . . . It would be better to make the enemy first exhaust himself against our defences, and knock out his tanks and then, bringing up fresh reserves, to go over to a general offensive which would finally finish off his main force.'[100] The result was a close co-ordination between partisan warfare and the massive thrusts of the Soviet forces at Kursk in 1943, followed by the invasion of Poland and the Balkans in 1944. This meant the end of Blitzkrieg for the Germans and the beginning of the type of Soviet offensive which had been anticipated in the 1930s. Clearly, the army had to be given more initiative to implement these military changes. This was another example of the partial reversal of an interwar policy – in this instance the politicization of the army was abandoned. After the catastrophe of 1941 and 1942 Stalin allowed a much greater degree of military initiative. He promoted to supreme command able officers like Zhukov, Tolbukhin, Konev, Malinovsky, Vatutin and Rossakovsky. He also allowed crucial military decisions to be taken at the front. Hitler, by contrast, allowed the destruction of the German army at Stalingrad by refusing to let von Paulus conduct an orderly withdrawal.

Stalin and Soviet historians always maintained that the Soviet Union liberated itself and that any economic and military assistance given from outside provided the slightest of contributions to Soviet victory. Western historians have traditionally tended to agree with this. Recently, however, external help has come to be seen as crucial. The economy, for example, was served by US and British aid under the Lend-Lease programme. The provision of back-up equipment and transport facilities, such as trucks, jeeps and heavy rolling stock, meant that the Soviet factories could concentrate on producing armaments. By filling gaps in Soviet infrastructure, the Allies therefore made it possible for the Soviet Union to move more quickly than it could otherwise have done from the defensive to the offensive. Much the same applies to military developments. Stalin frequently complained that Britain and the United States were using up Russian lives by not opening a second front in France. But the process of diverting Hitler had already started with the British campaigns in North Africa against Rommel in 1942 and 1943. These drew off divisions which were vitally needed by the Wehrmacht for the Russian front. It is therefore no coincidence that the victory of the Soviet resistance at Stalingrad occurred at the same time as the British victory at El Alamein. The interaction between events on different fronts is now increasingly recognized and Soviet victory is seen within the context of other sectors of the Second World War.[101]

The patriotic response was also crucial to Soviet success; indeed, this has been upgraded as a factor by recent historians. But the connection between the 'people's war' and Stalin's policies is being reassessed. To some extent, patriotism was manufactured from above as a response to the threat to external invasion. Somehow, Stalin's propaganda had to penetrate all levels of the population. He had to remove pockets of latent opposition which remained, despite the purges. He had to overcome ethnic forces which might welcome the break up of the Soviet Union. Measures were therefore taken by Stavka and GOKO to unite a population which had been stirred up and confused, first by the traumas of the 1930s, then by the experience of military defeat. They eliminated as many collaborators as possible through the forcible resettlement of Balkars, Chechens, Karachais, Meskhetians, Crimean Tartars, Balts, Ukrainians and Cossacks. Even though huge numbers of non-Russian civilians still managed to defect, any core which might have organized mass rebellions was removed. Soviet citizens were also targeted by propaganda which stressed the connections with the Russian past – especially with the defeat of the French in 1812. Hence the description of the 'Great Fatherland War' against Hitler was a replica of the 'Great Patriotic War' against Napoleon. There was, however, a considerable degree of patriotism from below, which far transcended Stalin's measures. To claim that Stalin's coercion and propaganda – in other words the outward manifestations of his leadership – were mainly responsible for the resurgence of Soviet patriotism would do less than justice to some of the most remarkable instances of mass heroism of the whole of the Second World War. The self-sacrifice of the citizens of Leningrad in the face of the German siege, or of the Soviet troops at Stalingrad and in the Battle of Kursk, or in the resistance of the partisans behind enemy lines, were all unprecedented in their scale, even in Russian history.

Soviet recovery from defeat was paralleled by the German collapse from victory. The Nazis contributed much to their own demise, in three ways. First, Hitler's military strategy proved inappropriate. The impetus of the German attack was sustainable only in the short term. Once the surprise had worn off, the German numerical inferiority began to count, especially in crucial areas such as Moscow in the autumn of 1941 and Stalingrad from the summer of 1942. Hitler was unable to learn from military errors in Russia; nor would he accept advice from experienced commanders like Guderian. Second, atrocities committed against the civilian populations of the captured territories undermined any goodwill which the Germans might originally have encountered. Indeed, Hitler's measures acted as a catalyst for a Soviet patriotic revival. In not allowing regional autonomy in the conquered territories, Hitler missed the opportunity of enlisting a massive wave of anti-Soviet ethnic support. Instead, his appalling misrule, borne of extreme racial arrogance, put Stalin's earlier policies and blunders into perspective. Although brutal, Stalin's measures had no equivalent to the deliberate extermination carried out by Hitler's SS units and Einsatzkommandos. Third, the German economy had not been fully geared to such a major undertaking as the destruction of the Soviet Union. Whereas the Soviet economy had been mobilized for total war in the 1930s, the Nazi economy had been mobilized only for partial war. Hitler's solution was a series of rapid victories followed by the absorption of the vanquished countries' infrastructures. Hence German Blitzkrieg was as much an economic as a military policy. The problem was that it was difficult to extend it to make it function more completely. By contrast, the Soviet economy could be made more effective through relaxing some of its constraints. Germany moved to a total war economy only in 1943; the Soviet Union, on the other hand, was already there.

Relations with the West: 1941–5

When Germany attacked Russia in June 1941 Stalin's whole attitude to Hitler underwent a profound change. He hastened to seek the co-operation of those Western countries which he had previously suspected. Hence, in 1941, the Anglo-Soviet Mutual Assistance Pact was drawn up, followed in 1942 by the twenty-year Anglo-Soviet Treaty of Alliance. Stalin also concluded a Lend-Lease agreement with the United States worth $11 billion. When the United States entered the war against Germany, the Grand Alliance was formed (although no document was actually signed), aimed at bringing down the Nazi regime. However, collaboration was never complete. Throughout the war there existed an undercurrent of distrust which grew stronger as the need for unity receded. This distrust went back as far as the foundation of the Bolshevik state and was largely ideological: Trotsky, for instance, had once referred to Lenin and Wilson as the 'apocalyptic antipodes of our time'. But there were also specific irritants throughout the period 1941–5 which were particularly apparent at the major wartime conferences – at Tehran (November to December 1943), Yalta (February 1945) and Potsdam (July to August 1945).

The first of these irritants was military. Stalin wanted an active alliance and no repetition of the 'sitskrieg' which had been the West's response to Hitler's Blitzkrieg against Poland in August 1939. He considered it vitally important for the Western Allies to open up a second front in France to draw off between forty and sixty German divisions from the Russian sector. He made his first request for this to Churchill in July 1941. In August 1942 Churchill visited Moscow to disclose his plans for Operation Torch – to be opened up, however, in North Africa. Stalin's reaction was bitter disillusionment: 'All is clear', he told his associates. 'They want us to bleed white in order to dictate to us their terms later on.'[102] The Anglo-American landings in North Africa did help matters but Stalin did not regard them as a justifiable substitute for an attack on France. This finally came in June 1944, although by this stage Stalin was accusing the Anglo-American forces of advancing into Germany as quickly as possible in order to minimize Soviet conquests in central and eastern Europe.

The second main breach concerned the frontiers and regimes of eastern Europe. The most significant of these was Poland. Britain and the United States were prepared, at Yalta and Potsdam, to concede the Curzon Line as Poland's frontier, thus allowing the USSR to retain all the Polish territory conquered in 1939. But at the same time they were profoundly unhappy about the possibility of permanent Soviet control over Polish institutions; hence their insistence on the Yalta Declaration on Liberated Europe, by which the powers undertook to assist the liberated states to create democratic institutions of their own choice. This, of course, produced an inevitable difference of interpretation between the Western powers, who hoped for the installation of liberal democracies, and the Soviet Union, which had always intended to promote revolutionary communist regimes. Above all, Stalin was determined to develop a buffer zone between Russia and the West, or a glacis of friendly socialist states. Clearly this would be a major post-war issue.

The outcome of the war, and of the disagreements with the Western Allies, was clearly in Russia's favour. Stalin had, by the middle of 1945, every reason to feel satisfied with the Soviet position in Europe. Nazi Germany had been smashed and partially dismembered by the principle of zoning agreed at Yalta and Potsdam. All the gains made by Russia as a result of the Nazi–Soviet Pact of 1939 were retained, namely eastern Poland, the Baltic states and part of Romania. Indeed, Soviet expansion went beyond the 1939 limits, also encompassing parts of East Prussia and Czechoslovakia. In the Far East, Russia had gained, in return for minimal participation in the war against Japan, Sakhalin and the Kurile Islands, which had been ceded by Tsarist Russia in 1905 and 1875, respectively. The sphere of Soviet control extended far beyond these enlarged frontiers. Moscow now dominated a huge socialist arc comprising Poland, Czechoslovakia, Hungary, Romania and Bulgaria, together with the Soviet zone of Germany. At last the USSR seemed to have both security and the means to spread communism into the heart of Europe. Many of Stalin's expectations had therefore been realized. The capitalist states had come into conflict with each other and the end result had been the strengthening of the Soviet Union and the opportunity to spread Soviet influence.

The cost

It was not until 1956 that the full extent of Soviet losses in the Second World War were revealed. It is now known that they are the heaviest suffered by any country in history as the result of an invasion by another power.

The most devastating impact was on the population, both military and civilian: 5.7 million Russian soldiers surrendered to the Germans, of whom 3.3 million subsequently died in captivity. The German High Command bore direct responsibility for the appalling conditions faced by Russian prisoners-of-war; an order stated that the Bolshevik soldier lost all claims to treatment as an honourable opponent in accordance with the Geneva Convention. The occupying forces also treated Russian civilians with extreme brutality. The Slavs were seen as a subhuman race and the Reichsleiter of the east, Rosenberg, aimed at no less than the national disintegration of the USSR. Overall, the Soviet Union lost 23 million dead, compared with 375,000 Britons, 405,000 Americans and 600,000 Frenchmen. The total looks even worse when placed in the context of previous losses. Ellenstein's figures have been tabulated as follows:

1913–21	(First World War, Civil War and epidemics)	13.5 million
1930–9	(Famine and purges)	7.0 million
1941–5	(Second World War)	23.0 million
Total 1913–45		43.5 million

To this total can be added the shortfall in births, an estimated 45 million. By 1945, therefore, the population was about 90 million less than it should have been.[103]

Destruction of property was also on a massive scale. Details were released as early as 1947. According to Molotov, the Germans destroyed 1,710 towns and 70,000 villages, 31,850 industrial enterprises and 98,000 collective farms. The sufferings of two Soviet cities are particularly well known. Leningrad experienced a siege which lasted for 900 days and the eventual casualty figure for this one city was greater than that of all the Western Allies combined. The suffering was the direct result of starvation, dystrophy and scurvy, as well as German bombing and bombardment. Stalingrad, meanwhile, was totally devastated. Russian and German troops fought over each street, and then in the ruins and rubble. An official Soviet description reads as follows:

> In the trenches carved out in the steep banks of the Volga, in gullies and the shells of ruined houses, in the cellars of bombed buildings the Soviet soldiers fought to the last to defend the city. The German forces launched 700 attacks and every step forward cost them tremendous losses. . . . Between 500 and 1,200 splinters of bombs, shells and grenades per square metre were found on the slopes of Mamai Hill, one of the main centres of the fighting, after the Battle of Stalingrad had at last come to an end.[104]

Hutchings has placed Soviet sufferings in perspective by comparing the losses inflicted in the two World Wars. Population losses in the Second World War were 50 per cent larger, but the population of 1941 was much greater than that of 1913. Russia during the Second World War experienced greater economic destruction than in the First, but substantially less disruption, largely because the industrial base of 1941 was much greater than that of 1913. There was a significant contrast in the pattern of destruction; in the First World War industry suffered more severely than agriculture, while the reverse was true in the Second. Indeed, after 1945, agriculture remained a serious problem long after factories and houses had been rebuilt. A key question was how Stalin would adapt his policies to deal with this specific problem.

As it turned out in the longer term, the extent of destruction was to be an issue for the very survival of the Soviet Union. Just as the Civil War had helped shape Bolshevism into a repressive communist bureaucracy, so the experience of the Second World War proved to be a major factor in its inability to change. Stalin won the war – but could he survive the peace?

1945–53: MATURE DICTATORSHIP?

The regime and the man behind it, 1945–53

Stalin was unique among the dictators covered in this book in that he emerged as a victor in 1945. Others, like Hitler, had committed suicide in the face of defeat or, like Franco and Salazar, had kept their countries out of the conflict. In theory Stalin's position should have been unassailable.

Until recently, this is precisely what historians argued. For the next eight years, until his death in 1953, Stalin's ascendancy was total. During this period he launched a campaign of reconstruction and finally achieved his original objective of making the Soviet Union a superpower. He also extended Russian control, for the first time, over most of eastern Europe and established a series of satellite states. Meanwhile, he took measures to consolidate his authority which meant that the Stalinist dictatorship was actually more severe than it had been between 1941 and 1945. The war was therefore the means by which the totalitarian measures of the 1930s reached

3 Joseph Stalin, late in life, c. 1952 (David King Collection)

their logical completion in the late 1940s. This was the fulfilment of Stalinism in mature dictatorship. The man behind the system grew in power and used this power to intensify the totalitarian nature of the regime. There were even forebodings in the West that this type of dictatorship might provide a general pattern for the future: Orwell's *Nineteen Eighty-Four* was actually a forward projection of his understanding of Stalinism in 1948: ruthless, effective and totally in control.

Although this approach is still popular, a more convincing alternative has now emerged. This throws an entirely different light on Stalin's post-war regime. The period 1945–53 was *not* one of dictatorship fulfilled. All the problems which had confronted Stalin before 1941 now returned in full measure so that, far from being settled into 'mature dictatorship', he was as insecure as ever. It is true that Stalin remained arbitrary and despotic. But this was not because he was now so secure that he could do whatever he wanted. His increasingly irrational behaviour was the response to threats to his system and a real fear that it might break up. Age and the war had also taken their toll and it was clear that he was now deteriorating physically and mentally. Hence, in Ward's view, 'This was no self-confident tyrant in charge of a smoothly functioning totalitarian machine, but a sickly old man; unpredictable, dangerous, lied to by terrified subordinates, presiding over a ramshackly bureaucracy.'[105]

If anything, victory increased Stalin's difficulties. His personal ascendancy, far from reaching a new peak after 1945, was more seriously challenged than at any time since 1929. The paradox, pointed out by Ward, is that 'whilst the Russo-German conflict strengthened the regime and legitimized the Generalissimo as a symbol of the will to victory, Stalin's personal power was threatened'.[106] The success of the Red Army raised the spectre which Stalin had always feared – that the regime would be militarized. It was for this reason that he had considered Trotsky, the organizer of Bolshevik military victory in the Civil War, a powerful opponent who had to be destroyed. Now, after 1945, he had to neutralize the military again, this time by demoting Zhukov. This was a particularly delicate operation since Soviet security remained a constant priority with the onset of the Cold War. But in a way this made the re-establishment of political control essential, since Stalin was now increasingly vulnerable to the possibility of an internal coup generated by an external crisis. This explains why he wound up the State Defence Committee (GOKO) which had played such a vital administrative role during the war. He also reverted to the inter-war policy of rarely consulting the core of the party – the Politburo and the Central Committee – again for fear that a rival might emerge from within its ranks to challenge his supremacy.

Neutralizing the army and the party in this way might well upset the balance of tensions upon which Stalin relied to maintain his personal power. Hence, he was forced into a new round of purges. But these were for defensive reasons. They were initiated from a position of weakness rather than from one of strength: Stalin used them to recover rather than to sublimate his power. His targets showed the extent of his insecurity. He sought to re-establish his control over the party in the 'Leningrad Affair'. This resulted in the trial and execution of party leaders and war heroes, such as Voznesensky, who had done what they could to organize resistance to the German siege. He also tried to restore his grip on society at large through the 1946 Zhdanov decrees. These tightened working practices and reimposed upon the arts the full force of Socialist Realism, which had been temporarily relaxed during the war. Underlying the whole system was the revival of the terror. The NKVD continued to take its toll, under the direction of Beria. It is also clear that another purge was about to be implemented in 1953; it was prevented only by Stalin's death. It seems, therefore, that Stalin was having to manoeuvre for power and control, very much as he had done during the 1930s. Indeed, he was now experiencing even greater difficulty than in the 1930s in retaining the initiative. Certain individuals became relatively more powerful after the war than they had been before it. Beria was a particular threat as he was establishing himself as one of the candidates for the succession.

Stalin's post-war economic policies

Stalin's main priority after 1945 was the reconstruction of Soviet industries and agriculture after the appalling destruction caused by the war with Germany. He decided in 1945 to return to his economic strategies of the 1930s, including central planning and collectivization. The Fourth and Fifth Five Year Plans (1946–50 and 1950–5) again placed the emphasis on collective farming and the development of heavy industry at the expense of consumer goods. Such measures are usually explained as an intensification of the command economy as the most effective means of reconstruction. This, however, fails to take into account that many of Stalin's measures after 1945 were retrogressive. The inefficiencies of the 1930s were all revived in the formal planning system. Despite its failings in the 1930s, collectivization was not only revived but intensified: the *kolkhozy* increased in size and their number was reduced from 252,000 to 76,000. The recentralization of industrial planning was also a step backward, especially after the success of the partial demobilization of the economy during the war. In effect, Stalin missed the opportunity to continue the more progressive wartime policies and thereby abandon the more blatant failures of formal planning.

There were some positive achievements, however. As during the 1930s, Stalin pushed the Soviet Union further in the direction of the status of a superpower. Considerable investment was also channelled into the nuclear industry, again for military reasons. By 1949 the Soviet Union possessed the atomic bomb and, by 1951, the hydrogen bomb. By 1950 it was also announced that all the targets of the Fourth Five Year Plan had been exceeded and that the overall industrial base was now substantially larger than it had been in 1940. But the deficiencies were as obvious as they had been during the 1930s. The emphasis on heavy industry meant the continuing neglect of the Soviet consumer. The conditions of the workforce were also very harsh. The forty-eight-hour week was regarded as a minimum; workers were unable to choose their jobs or to move to other areas; industrial discipline remained especially severe; and wages were based on piece work. But the Achilles' heel of the Soviet economy was undoubtedly agriculture. The 1946 harvest, for example, produced only 40 per cent of the crop of 1913. The problem was aggravated by low investment, as agriculture received only 7.3 per cent of the total available in the Fourth Five Year Plan. There was also widespread discontent with the *kolkhozy*, with their artificially low prices for agricultural produce and a lack of incentives.

Although recovery did occur between 1945 and 1953, it was much slower than that accomplished by West Germany or Japan. In a real sense the infrastructural damage inflicted by the Second World War was permanent because it was dealt with by the inappropriate measures from the 1930s rather than new measures anticipating the 1950s. The emphasis was very much on restoration rather than renewal. As we have seen, however, this was in line with Stalin's political perspectives.

Stalin's post-war foreign policy

The last years of Stalin's rule were dominated by the Cold War. The traditional explanation for this is that Stalin sought to maintain his control over eastern Europe for strategic and ideological reasons, both of which incurred growing hostility from the West. Stalin's suspicions of the West went back to the 1930s. These were intensified by rival claims at the wartime conferences at Teheran, Yalta and Potsdam. From 1945 onwards Stalin was determined to spread Soviet influence wherever possible, but especially to those areas liberated by the Red Army from Nazi rule. He enforced and institutionalized Soviet hegemony by four main methods. The first was the establishment in 1947 of the Communist Information Bureau (Cominform). This was intended to ensure Moscow's complete control over international communism and especially to guarantee conformity to Stalinism in eastern Europe. The second was the takeover of the governments of the eastern European states. Originally these had been broad fronts, consisting of Communist and non-Communist parties. Stalin, however, tightened the control of the former and ensured total Communist domination from 1948. The third means of achieving Soviet control was the formation in 1949 of the Council for Mutual Economic Assistance (Comecon). This was designed to co-ordinate the economies of eastern Europe and to direct Czech, Polish and Hungarian trade towards the Soviet Union, thereby creating an almost self-sufficient commercial bloc. The fourth method was military dominance; the number of Soviet troops in eastern Europe stood at 5.5 million during the early 1950s. It fell, however, to Stalin's successor to create a multilateral military alliance in the form of the Warsaw Pact (1955).

The result was a steady increase in tension between the Soviet Union and the West. The ideological confrontation was now more intense than at any time since the creation of the Bolshevik state. In a major speech on 9 February 1946 Stalin announced that he would abide by the basic principles of Marxism–Leninism, and proceeded to attack the capitalist powers as instigators of the Second World War. In the following month Churchill openly criticized Stalin's policy in eastern Europe. His speech, delivered in Fulton, Missouri, contained the famous sentence: 'From Stettin in the Baltic to Trieste in the Adriatic an iron curtain has descended across the continent.' The Cold War was subsequently hardened by two open declarations of policy. One was the Truman Doctrine (1947) which promised military or economic aid to Greece and Turkey and 'support for peoples who are resisting attempted subjugation by armed minorities or by outside pressures'.[107] The promise of economic aid was subsequently implemented by the Marshall Plan. Stalin's response was the so-called Zhdanov Line. In a speech in 1947 Zhdanov warned of the new threat of the capitalist West: 'The cardinal purpose of the imperialist camp is to strengthen imperialism, to hatch a new imperialist war, to combat socialism and democracy, and to support reactionary and anti-democratic pro-Fascist regimes and movements everywhere.'[108] The only answer, he concluded, was to tighten Soviet control – in the ways already outlined.

Tension between the Soviet Union and the West was also apparent in areas beyond eastern Europe. One of the earliest confrontations was the Iranian crisis (1945–6), in which the continued Soviet occupation of the northern part of Iran was challenged by the United States and Britain. The threat of armed conflict was eventually averted when, in 1946, Soviet troops were withdrawn in return for oil concessions. Back in Europe, the Cold War entered a particularly dangerous phase in 1948 with the Berlin Crisis. Stalin attempted to squeeze out the Western presence from Berlin by closing off the supply routes which connected West Berlin to the Western zones of occupied Germany. This policy, however, backfired. The British and Americans airlifted sufficient quantities of food and fuel to supply West Berlin, and Stalin was unable to prevent this for fear of American nuclear retaliation. The Berlin blockade had another undesirable side-effect for Stalin. It convinced the West of the need for a more systematic defence pact against Soviet aggression in Europe: hence the formation of the North Atlantic Treaty Organization (NATO). Soviet involvement in the Far East met with mixed success, especially over the Korean War (1950–3). When Soviet-backed North Korea invaded the South, the latter was assisted by United Nations forces, comprising mainly Americans. Stalin was forced to watch while the newly established communist regime in China came to the rescue of North Korea. From now on the Soviet Union had a major rival in the communist world.

This traditional analysis of the motives behind Stalin's post-war foreign policy focuses on his response to external pressure on the Soviet Union. Stalin was determining his policy from a position of power within a political system that he once again completely dominated. The key events of the Cold War were therefore activated from above. This now needs to be supplemented by another perspective. It is true that Stalin did take key decisions which led to the events outlined. But the political system within which he operated was, as we have seen, badly flawed. There were, as a result, internal pressures within the Soviet Union which helped shape Stalin's responses to the West. As on other occasions, these sometimes came from below.

Stalin found the Soviet Union affected in two contrasting ways by the Second World War. In one way the war had exerted a centripetal effect. It had pulled the country together, partly through the massive patriotic response to the emergency of the German invasion, and partly because the military success had prevented it from disintegrating again once the emergency was over. On the other hand, there were also centrifugal influences. Military victory had threatened Stalin's personal ascendancy and created alternative role models which threatened a weakening of central power. As the wartime emergency gradually wore off, there was also a revived threat of ethnic disintegration.

To maintain the centripetal effect, and to offset the centrifugal, Stalin restored political coercion and the command economy of the 1930s. These measures were given a new justification: they were needed to confront the revived and enhanced menace from the West. Direct comparisons can therefore be made with Stalin's measures in the 1930s. In 1929 and 1931, he had used the threat from the West to justify forced collectivization and rapid industrialization. The Cold War could now be used to justify the renewal of such measures. Stalin depended on the new conflict with the West to maintain his system internally. This explains why domestic crises were so often related to the external threat and given the language of the Cold War. He could also use the newly conquered glacis of eastern Europe as an additional form of security. In tightening Soviet control over the satellite states, he could put further pressure on ethnic groups within the Soviet Union itself. Hence, his subjection of Poles, Czechs and Hungarians was an added guarantee of his control over Ukrainians, Belarussians and Tartars.

Did Stalin succeed in his foreign policy and in his manipulation of the Cold War? There are both positive and negative arguments here.

On the positive side, the Soviet Union seemed to have achieved the security which both Lenin and Stalin had sought. After 1945 it was a superpower with the world's largest standing army. It had achieved direct control over East Germany, Poland, Czechoslovakia, Hungary, Bulgaria and Romania, thereby increasing the security of Soviet territorial gains in the Baltic and the Ukraine. The Cold War had also been the means whereby defeating an enemy had been converted into the spread of ideology. Stalin had proved Trotsky wrong: communism was spread not by Soviet-inspired revolution but by direct Soviet conquest. In this respect Stalin's Cold War policies were the logical means of maintaining and extending the fruits of victory of the Great Fatherland War. From 1949 and 1951, the extension of Soviet influence was given greater permanence by the protection of nuclear weapons. Thus, compared with Soviet insecurity in 1931, huge steps had been taken by the year of Stalin's death in 1953.

Or had they? Stalin's use of the Cold War to increase internal security generated its own problems, which increased the vulnerability of the Soviet Union to outside pressures. For example, the spread of Soviet influence in eastern Europe provoked a Western response which was far more concerted than anything which had happened in the inter-war period. This included the Truman Doctrine and Marshall Plan (1948) and the establishment of NATO in 1949. In addition, Stalin was obliged to back down over the Berlin blockade in 1948–9. As Kennedy-Pipe maintains, 'The Cold War was not a competition of equals: rather, it was an unequal struggle between one strong regime, the United States, and one fragile regime, the Soviet Union.'[109] In addition, having to maintain very high levels of defence expenditure meant that there was never any real possibility of lightening the burden on the Soviet consumer. The contrast in living standards between the Soviet bloc and the West became even greater than it had been during the 1930s: this was to create a huge problem for the future. Finally, Soviet control over eastern Europe was to provide a constant concern about the possible impact of protest movements there upon the Soviet Union itself. This was both a cause and an effect of the return to persecutions and purges.

The death of a dictator

All this brings us back full-circle to Stalin's vulnerability. By 1953 Stalin had become more insecure than ever; in Ward's phrase, he was 'raging, like Lear, against failure and mortality'.[110] This made him more dangerous than ever, especially to his subordinates, who feared a revival of the great fear of 1938. In fact,

Stalin was was about to launch a new purge, but this was prevented by his death in March 1953. He was staying at his country dacha in Kuntsevo, where he suffered a stroke. When he did not make an appearance on 1 March, none of his staff dared find out the reason. As Stalin's absence lengthened into days, the officer on duty contacted Stalin's senior associates – Beria, Malenkov, Khrushchev and Bulganin. They came quickly to the residence to find Stalin lying on his bedroom floor at the very point of death. Stalin's body was embalmed and placed next to Lenin's in the mausoleum. There it remained until 1961 when, on the orders of Khrushchev, it was cremated and buried in the Kremlin Wall.

Stalin's death had obvious implications for his system. Would this die with him? This was the case with almost every other dictator covered in this book. Or would his – alone – outlive the founder?

REFLECTIONS ON STALIN'S DICTATORSHIP

This chapter has considered the merits and defects of Stalin's individual policies before 1941, during the Great Fatherland War, and after 1945. This final section will provide some overall views of Stalin's rule, concentrating on three questions.

What was the basis of Stalin's power?

We have seen that Stalin rose to power through his control over the party and sought to maintain it by means of social discipline and purges. Throughout his rule, however, there were four factors which gave Stalinism its distinctive character: ideology, historical tradition, personality cult and, of course, terror.

Stalin was not originally renowned as a philosopher, but he aimed to establish himself as an authority on Marxism and to adapt Marxism to the needs of an industrializing society. He wrote four major works: *Marxism and the National Question* (1913), *Foundations of Leninism* (1924), *Marxism and Linguistics* (1950) and *Economic Problems of Socialism in the USSR* (1952). He always prefaced any major policy statements with ideological references, even in his speeches to the people during the Second World War. He succeeded in turning Marxist principles upside down in order to justify his enormous personal powers. As a result, Stalin has been disowned by most Marxists, who denounce his use of their ideology to construct a totalitarian state.

Stalin did not, however, base his power entirely on ideology. Most of the early Bolsheviks, especially Lenin, Trotsky, Bukharin, Kamenev and Zinoviev, had been Westernized Russians who had turned against their Slavic inheritance – political, social and cultural. Stalin, by contrast, was profoundly Slavic and quite deliberately revived an interest in an earlier phase of Russian history. He was particularly fascinated by Ivan the Terrible (1533–84), with whom he seemed in many ways to identify. Ivan had been confronted by opposition from the landed nobility, or boyars, under their spokesman Prince Andrei Kurbsky; this paralleled Stalin's problems with dissidents within the party, led by Trotsky. Ivan tackled the problem by initiating a series of purges carried out by the *oprichniki* (horsemen who carried, as the emblem of their special authority, brooms and dogs' heads attached to their saddles).

This may well have been one influence behind Stalin's purges and the activities of the NKVD. Stalin insisted on the official rehabilitation of this most unpopular of tsars and ordered Eisenstein to produce an epic biographical film. He also restored pride in other periods of the Russian past and, during the Second World War, patriotism was deliberately linked to ideology. In the words of Tucker, 'Stalin merged Marx with Ivan the Terrible.'[111] He also developed an almost tsarist attitude to power, but with his version of Marxism taking the place of Divine Right.

This brings us to the personal basis of Stalin's power. During the period 1929–53 Stalin constructed the most elaborate personality cult in history. An extract from an official history read:

> Stalin is the brilliant leader and teacher of the Party, the great strategist of the Socialist revolution, military commander and guide of the Soviet state. With the name of Stalin in their hearts, the collective farmers toiled devotedly in the fields to supply the Red Army and the cities with food, and industry with raw materials. Stalin's name is cherished by the boys and girls of the Socialist land.

On Stalin's seventieth birthday so many letters of congratulations and greetings were sent to *Pravda* that it took three years to publish them. The Soviet Union was filled with Stalin statues and busts, and numerous cities and towns were named after him.

In part this cult of personality was developed to cover Stalin's personal deficiencies and lack of charisma. Mediocrity and facelessness had assisted his rise to power, as his contemporaries had not seen Stalin as a danger until it was too late. But mediocrity bred insecurity, and insecurity was certainly a factor in Stalin's campaign to eliminate the entire 1917 crop of Bolsheviks and to project himself as the only true successor to Lenin – the best Leninist.[112] Ulam provides another explanation for the cult: 'Stalin was a butcher, who had sent tens and hundreds of thousands of men, women and children to be tortured and shot on the strength of a diseased imagination. The cult acted as a safeguard or a barrier keeping him from stepping over into actual insanity.'[113] He needed, it could be argued, to be reassured by overwhelming acclamation that he was pursuing the right policies after all. In effect, therefore, Stalin practised the ultimate in self-delusion, and indoctrinated himself.

How effective was Stalin's power?

Stalin's search for power was therefore total and the methods he used were more extreme than those of his contemporaries – Hitler and Mussolini included. For decades historians and students in the West have seen an automatic connection between method and result. Stalin, it has been assumed, was both ruthless in his pursuit of power and efficient in his use of it, with the first point leading directly to the second. Ruthlessness and efficiency combined to create a form of totalitarianism which was more complete than that of Nazi Germany. Stalin was fully in control of internal developments. He created an industrial infrastructure through an effective planning system; he cut down possible opposition by directly instigating purges; he changed the people's cultural and social perceptions; and he pursued a foreign policy which, with occasional changes in tactics, had an overall strategy.

Because of these developments, and despite the suffering inflicted, the Soviet Union was able to inflict defeat on Nazi Germany. This followed a disastrous initial response, in which Stalin completely misinterpreted Hitler's intentions. But Stalin's subsequent recovery interacted with the long-term economic and military preparation, and with the centralization already instilled, to overcome the much more limited military and economic base of Nazi Germany. Victory also strengthened Stalin's position after 1945. He restored the power and the planning system which he had employed during the 1930s and ensured compliance through a new set of purges. He also spread Soviet influence across eastern Europe and set the pace in the development of the Cold War. In all respects, this was the period of 'mature dictatorship'.

Almost all parts of this chapter on Russia have put forward a different approach, one which has gained ground rapidly since 1991. By this interpretation, Stalin's regime was ruthless but not, as a direct consequence, efficient. Totalitarianism was fundamentally flawed: this was especially apparent during the 1930s and in domestic policy. As we have seen, Stalin sought to centralize a political and economic system which kept falling to local initiatives. As a result, central correctives had to be applied, which meant that Stalin's policies were as much reactive as they were planned. Similarly, his foreign policy had to be put on to corrected courses, partly because of earlier errors of judgement and partly because of circumstances beyond his control. The war with Germany initially paralysed the whole system. The economic planning of the 1930s had been geared to mobilizing Russia for an offensive campaign, whereas Stalin's inappropriate diplomacy necessitated a defensive response which could not immediately be delivered. Major changes were, however, introduced to transform the situation. Soviet production was made more efficient, paradoxically, by partially demobilizing the economic structure to enhance military mobilization. The Soviet Union defeated Germany because it was able to transcend the limits of Stalinism from the 1930s.

After 1945, however, Stalin's position was vulnerable to the very forces which had been responsible for military victory. He therefore had to reinstitute the sort of control which had existed during the 1930s but which had been relaxed during the war. But this was an expression of insecurity rather than 'mature dictatorship'. There was also an element of desperation about Soviet expansion in Europe. In part, it was a response to circumstances, in part a means of justifying internal policies, a rerun of the interaction between foreign and domestic policy during the early 1930s. As had always been the case, ruthlessness did not necessarily engender efficiency; as often as not, it was itself a reaction to inefficiency. As a system, Stalinist totalitarianism tended to use up more than it created.

Was Stalin necessary?

The most recent verdict on Stalin is therefore largely unfavourable. This was not, however, always the case.

Among Western writers, the most ardent defender of Stalin was Ian Grey, who deliberately set out to redress what he considered a long-standing bias against Stalin. Many historians, he argued, have been influenced by Trotsky's vilification of Stalin. In reality, Stalin may have had defects, but he also possessed a 'great and highly disciplined intelligence' together with 'single-mindedness' and 'implacable will'. He was totally dedicated to 'the two causes of Russia and Marxism–Leninism', in the service of which 'no sacrifice was too great'. His ruthless measures were therefore applied for a higher objective. Throughout the purges Stalin 'showed an extraordinary self-control and did not lose sight of his purpose'. In the last analysis, Stalin could claim that 'Soviet Russia had become stronger as a result of his grandiose campaigns of industrialization, collectivization and social transformation.'[114]

Before 1991 most Western historians followed a more ambivalent approach. Their argument was that Stalin constructed the most brutal dictatorship and used appalling methods, but his achievement was considerable. His industrialization drive, in particular, made possible eventual victory against fascism and the subsequent development of the Soviet Union into one of the two superpowers. McCauley argued:

> One may dismiss Stalin as a tyrant, as an evil man whom the USSR could have done without. On the other hand, it is possible to argue that he rendered the Soviet people a service which may eventually be seen as his greatest achievement. It is quite probable that had the USSR not gone through the forced industrialisation of the 1930s she would have succumbed to the German onslaught of 1941.[115]

E.H. Carr believed that Stalin was necessary, in that he was 'an agent of history', produced by the circumstances following the Bolshevik Revolution. If Stalin had not set in motion the process of industrialization, someone else would have done. In this respect, Stalin was 'the great executor of revolutionary policy'. He was, however, a man of opposites. He combined immense achievements with utter brutality: he was, in Carr's words 'an emancipator and a tyrant'.

The main dissenting voice against this line was Ulam, who chose to lay much more stress on Stalin's deficiencies, believing that Russia would have been much better off without him. He refuted the argument that Stalin's industrialization programme dragged Russia into the twentieth century; on the contrary, much faster progress would have been made by an alternative regime – possibly even by Tsarist Russia. It is also inappropriate to argue that Stalin paved the way for victory in the Second World War; if anything, he impeded it by his earlier liquidation of vast numbers of people who would have been useful to the war effort.

This approach anticipated the most recent analysis which has emerged since the collapse of the Soviet Union at the end of 1991. Previous views that Stalin was necessary were based on the assumption that he developed and controlled a system which worked; disagreement focused on the cost of this system. Revisionist historians have, however, shown that the system did not necessarily work and that Stalin was not always in control. Perhaps the most telling argument is that the Soviet Union was able to defeat Nazi Germany only by dismantling the planning system which had been developed during the 1930s – the very system which has always been considered to have been Stalin's main contribution to the victory over Nazism. If this argument is true, then the whole essence of Stalin's achievement is undermined. It is possible to pursue the argument further. Stalin's Five Year Plans were based on the premise of a future offensive by the Soviet Union. This conditioned Stalin's diplomacy and delivered up to Hitler the opportunity for a surprise attack in 1941. Stalin's system would have collapsed but for the dismantling of that system and the reversion to a more traditional form of warfare.

Such an argument would make Stalin redundant in the history of Soviet survival, let alone that of Soviet development. Yet the answer is not that simple. The question which must also be considered is whether the Soviet Union could have produced sufficient war *matériel* as a result of the dismantling of the Five Year Plans if the Five Year Plans had never existed in the first place. In other words, it is possible to criticize Stalin's methods while acknowledging that he had a vital role to play in preparing the Soviet Union for war. The result may have been the wrong war but at least the infrastructure was there. It may have been the wrong infrastructure for the particular war, but the infrastructure could be modified to bring about a different type of war. In other words, Stalin's system was unpicked by him in the face of emergency to produce a new and less dogmatic method, which helped produce victory. This appears not only to vindicate Stalin, but to make him crucial for the very survival of the Soviet Union.

Until, that is, we consider the impact of Stalinism on the future. We now have the advantage of a longer perspective. Previously the ultimate criterion for success or failure was victory or defeat in the Second World War: this was bound to vindicate Stalin ultimately. But we are now aware of the ultimate paradox of Soviet history: that the regime which survived Hitler died of old age in 1991. This, too, was Stalin's legacy.

It used to be thought that Stalin's victory in the war had created a hardened system which was fully in control of a totalitarian dictatorship within and which pursued the Cold War outside. Stalin was predominant: small wonder, therefore, that he should have been criticized by his successor, Khrushchev, who felt that he was in the shadow of Stalin's monolith. The destalinization campaign which was launched in 1956 was therefore an attempt to escape from the shadow and restore the light of Lenin's legitimate succession. The problem was that Stalinism kept reappearing as the forceful strand of Soviet development. When Khrushchev was overthrown in 1964, for the failures of agricultural reforms and for his action in the Cuban Missile Crisis, Stalinism made a partial return in the policies of Brezhnev; from 1964 and 1981, the Soviet Union re-established its military and nuclear credibility. Between 1985 and 1991 Gorbachev sought to end the Cold War and reorganize the Soviet economy, only to face attempted overthrow by neo-Stalinists under Yaneyev. The post-Soviet regime of Yeltsin also experienced opposition from groups nostalgic for the Stalinist past – and the association which it still enjoyed with power and efficiency.

There is now an altogether different perspective. Stalin reached his peak during the war *despite* his system. When he attempted to restore his system after the war, he fell into a decline which led to a crumbling of his regime. Stalin was not a posthumous threat to Khrushchev because of his strength, but because of his weakness. And that weakness was the way in which Stalin had personally distorted the communist system, which had somehow survived in spite of him. Khrushchev therefore removed Stalin from history not to destroy an entrenched system but to clear away its wreckage. Perhaps Khrushchev was the first to realize that the Soviet Union had survived *despite* Stalinism, not *because of* it. As events turned out, the negative legacy of Stalinism proved stronger than the positive. Khrushchev fell in

1964 at least partly because of his experiments to rehabilitate agriculture. Brezhnev and Kosygin failed on the same ground, while Gorbachev failed in his efforts to Westernize the economy through perestroika largely because of the inflexibility of the Stalinist system. The ultimate failure of Stalin, therefore, was to create a system which could not survive in peace as well as in war.

Chapter 3

Dictatorship in Italy

Italy was the first of the major European states to seek salvation in the policies of the radical right, and Mussolini was the first of a succession of fascist dictators. Yet there has always been a puzzling element about Mussolini's rule. Although his influence was profound, he is often derided as a buffoon. In 1919, for example, the socialist Giacinto Serrati described him as 'a rabbit; a phenomenal rabbit; he roars. Observers who do not know him mistake him for a lion.'[1] More recently A.J.P. Taylor called him 'a vain, blundering boaster without either ideas or aims'.[2] 'Fascism', he added 'was a façade. There was nothing behind it but show and empty rhetoric.'[3] There have also been references to Mussolini as a 'sawdust Caesar'.

With views like this it has often been difficult to take Mussolini and Italian Fascism seriously. Yet this is precisely what we have to do if we are to avoid trivializing a topic which has as much historical significance as Stalin's Russia or Hitler's Germany. The key to understanding the Italian dictatorship is not to assume that it was simple but, rather, to accept that it was complex. By avoiding the simplistic, recent analyses have provided plenty of lines which can be pursued. This chapter aims to look at some of them.

THE RISE OF MUSSOLINI TO 1922: AN OUTLINE

From the beginning of his stormy career in journalism and politics until he became Prime Minister in 1922, Mussolini underwent a series of major shifts in the direction of his beliefs and tactics.

His original radicalism was of the left, not of the right. He leaned towards revolutionary socialism, thought in terms of class struggle and uncompromisingly condemned nationalism and imperialism, particularly Italy's conquest of Tripoli in 1912. He was a member of the PSI (Italian Socialist Party) and in 1912 was appointed editor of the newspaper *Avanti* by the party's militants. Through *Avanti* he aimed to promote popular revolutionary fervour, while at the same time attempting to enter Italian politics legally; he failed, however, to win a parliamentary seat in the 1913 elections. Throughout 1914 he devoted his energies to putting the case against Italian involvement in the First World War.

Then occurred the first of Mussolini's changes. By 1915 he was pressing openly for Italy to join the fighting; clearly his ideological views were built on shifting sands. He was promptly deprived of his editorship of *Avanti* and was expelled from the PSI. He succeeded, however, in acquiring his own paper, *Il Popolo d'Italia*, in which he wedded war with revolutionary fervour, using slogans like 'Who has steel has bread' and 'Revolution is an idea which has found bayonets'. His own personal contribution to the Italian war effort was a spell of loyal but undistinguished military service, ended in 1917 by wounds received after a grenade exploded in his trench.

In March 1919 Mussolini presided over a meeting in Milan which gave birth to the Fascio di Combattimento. The Fasci soon spread to some seventy other cities and towns, where they established themselves as local political movements with local programmes. At the national level, the Fascio di Combattimento identified as its enemies a surprisingly large number of groups: organized labour (especially the trade unions and the PSI), capitalism and big business, the monarchy and even the Church. Not surprisingly, the Fascists failed to win a single parliamentary seat in the 1919 elections, and the Socialists mocked Mussolini by burying an effigy of Fascism in Milan.

These developments induced Mussolini to undergo, in 1921, a second change. This time he was prepared to abandon his revolutionary inclination and prepare Fascism for a parliamentary struggle. Hence, he set up a political party (the PFI or Partito Nazionale Fascista) and appealed to as wide a cross-section of society as he could by targeting the enemies to socialism and the threat of red revolution. This strategy was more successful, and in 1921 the Fascist Party won thirty-five parliamentary seats.

But broadening the appeal and abandoning open revolution did not mean less violence. On the contrary, black-shirted Fascist squads launched numerous attacks on the left. They were given their opportunity by a wave of strikes organized in the cities by the trade unions and the PSI, as well as by action taken in rural areas by peasant leagues against landowners. Throughout 1920 and 1921 militant workers and peasants were intimidated into submission, through beatings and being forced to consume castor oil and live toads. All over Italy Fascist activities were directed by local leaders (or *ras*). One of the most successful of these was Balbo, who captured Ferrara and much of Romagna from the Socialists in May 1922. The Socialists responded in August with an appeal for a general strike as a protest against Fascist violence, but this played further into Mussolini's hands. It took the Fascists only one day to smash the threat and thus to emerge as the main safeguard against industrial disruption.

Meanwhile, the post-war Italian governments had become increasingly unstable and unpopular. A succession of prime ministers sought to contain what they saw as a threat from the left and, in the process, came to depend on the parliamentary support of the Fascist Party. Even so, Mussolini had nowhere near sufficient electoral backing to establish an alternative government; the best he could reasonably have expected was an invitation to play a minor role in Prime Minister Facta's cabinet. Yet 1922 saw a spectacular political development: the replacement of Facta by Mussolini.

This occurred as the result of a threat of force from Mussolini and a reaction of near panic from the government. On his way to the Fascist Party Congress in Naples in October 1922, Mussolini stopped off in Rome to demand at least five cabinet ministries. In Naples he made preparations for a Fascist march on Rome to seize power if his conditions were not met. Facta urged King Victor Emanuel III to declare martial law so that the threat could be countered by force. The King refused and, mindful of the Fascist contingents gathering outside Rome, invited Mussolini to join a coalition government. Sensing the possibility of total capitulation, Mussolini declined. On 29 October Mussolini, then in Milan, received a request from the King to form his own government. This was followed shortly afterwards by the much heralded March on Rome as Mussolini, now Prime Minister, paraded his henchmen through the streets and announced the beginning of a new era.

THE RISE OF MUSSOLINI TO 1922: AN EXPLANATION

Four reasons can be given for Mussolini's success by the end of 1922. First, Italy itself had undergone a prolonged crisis before 1914, and again more acutely from 1919, in which conventional political and economic solutions no longer worked. Second, during the same period, a new ideology had grown out of this crisis, providing Mussolini with an alternative route to power. Third, this new movement attracted the support of a cross-section of a society thoroughly disillusioned with the existing establishment. And fourth, Mussolini's leadership and strategy gave to this movement a versatility and vitality which contrasted all too obviously with a tired and dull government.

Underlying instability, 1861–1922

Italy had been united as a liberal parliamentary regime but, in the era between Cavour and Mussolini, lacked political stability. There was a rapid succession of ministries: 22 between 1860 and 1900 (an average of 1.8 years each), 9 between 1900 and 1914 (1.6 years each) and 7 between 1914 and 1922 (1.1 years each). At first, parties were not clearly defined and government depended on a consensus reached between the different political groups, a process known as *trasformismo*. Unfortunately, this could be maintained only by the distribution of favours and offices, a corrupt system which kept political power in the hands of the very few.

There were several attempts to achieve political stability before 1914. During a period of political crisis in the 1890s a conservative politician, Crispi, tried to convert the state into a more authoritarian regime, based on that of Bismarck's Germany. Although this failed at the time, the potential was not lost on future politicians. For the moment, however, a more liberal line was followed in the decade before 1914 as Giolitti (Prime Minister 1903–5, 1906–9 and 1911–14) tried to reform the whole process by seeking the co-operation of the Catholic Church and the Socialists, and by introducing near-universal manhood suffrage in 1912. Giolitti's critics, however, argued that his efforts were already in trouble by 1914 and that Italian politics had not been able to adjust to mass participation. These experiences were to be enormously important in the early 1920s. Pollard maintains that 'Fascism was to be the agent of reaction on behalf of the grouping of forces which had been at work in the End of the Century Crisis.'[4] In this respect, the roots of Mussolini's solution to the crisis of Italian constitutionalism can be seen in the 1890s. Giolitti, in the meantime, failed to build up a system to prevent this development: 'It is no exaggeration to say that Giolitti's failure to launch Italy on the path of a representative, mass democracy in the pre-war years helped open the way for Mussolini and Fascism in the post-war period.'[5]

Two contrasting traditions had therefore appeared within the Italian political system. One was the liberal experience of power, which was moderate but also corrupt and uncertain. The other was the authoritarian backlash which seemed to offer something more substantial and secure – if, that is, it could ever be achieved. Clearly a major upheaval was needed to turn prospect into reality.

This was provided by the First World War; in the words of De Grand, it 'marked a rupture in the course of Italian political development'.[6] In effect, it pushed Italy from instability into crisis. The traditional governing groups were split in their attitude to the war. Giolitti remained consistently opposed, while the wartime prime ministers, Salandra, Boselli and Orlando, could neither co-operate with him nor do without him. The result was a paralysis of parliamentary government, which was worsened by Italy's military defeat at the hands of the Austrians at Caporetto in 1917. The regime was reprieved only by the Italian victory in 1918 at Vittorio Veneto against an Austria which was falling to pieces internally. Governments were also under pressure from the threat of economic collapse and social disruption. The total cost of the war was 148,000 million lire, over twice the total expenditure of all Italian governments between 1861 and 1913.[7] The economic base was weakened by huge budget deficits and by unbalanced trade and industrial production. It has been estimated that, by 1919, exports covered only 36 per cent of Italy's imports. Furthermore, the growth of industrial production between 1915 and 1918 had been geared so directly to the war effort that it could not be maintained by the requirements of the post-war home market. Unemployment soared, with demobilization mainly responsible for the total of 2 million by the end of 1919. Inflation had also become a fact of life, with the cost of living in 1919 about four times that of 1913.

With this gloomy economic background, it appeared that Italy had emerged from the war with all the potential for violent confrontation. On the one hand, the urban and rural working classes were desperate to prevent any further decline in their standard of living. On the other, the industrialists and landowners feared that demands for increased wages and employment protection would raise costs and threaten productivity and profits. The situation was further complicated by the impoverishment of a large part of the lower middle class which became radical and assertive, distrusting labour and capital alike. The crucial issue from 1919 was whether the post-war governments could salvage the liberal approach and pull these conflicting forces back together for the collective national good.

Giolitti, Prime Minister between June 1920 and July 1921, made some attempt but found that all hope of consensus politics had now been dashed. The Socialist Party (PSI) and the majority of the unions were militant in their demands, the lower middle classes were no longer dependable as moderate voters, and the whole political scene was further complicated by the emergence of the Italian Popular Party (PPI), a large Catholic grouping. The only real hope for stability was a coalition which included Italy's two largest parties, the Socialists and the PPI. However, the gap between them was unbridgeable. Giolitti and his successors, Bonomi (1921–2) and Facta (1922) therefore operated in a political vacuum. Increasingly, they came to depend on the Fascists – but in a way which was underhand, unparliamentary and ultimately suicidal. Unable to resolve the growing crisis between labour and capital, and ever conscious of the threat of revolution, the governments tacitly allowed the Fascists to take direct and often brutal action against unions and peasant leagues. This was the last resort of a government which seemed to have lost the will to govern.

Even so, the crisis of liberal government does not fully explain the ease with which the handover was made to Mussolini and authoritarianism in 1922. After all, Mussolini was appointed Prime Minister with a parliamentary base of only 35 seats out of 535. The reason seems to be that 1922 was a low point in government stability, with both the Prime Minister and the King contemplating disaster. Facta was in a caretaker role and was clearly hoping that Giolitti would be able to resume power. His immediate concern was to try to prevent Mussolini from pre-empting this changeover, which is why he was prepared to confront him with the threat of martial law. The King, however, had different concerns. In the event of a confrontation between the Fascists and the army, the latter might desert or there could be a civil war. In either event, he could well be forced to abdicate. To him, therefore, Mussolini seemed a safer alternative to Giolitti.

There is one final point. The fact that Mussolini had only 7 per cent of the seats in parliament did not matter too much. Such a proportion was not unprecedented, as a number of previous governments had been built on similarly insubstantial foundations. The assumption was that a coalition would be quickly added around the core – perhaps the usual combination of Liberals and Popolari. Only this time, the core would prove stronger because it was more authoritarian. Perhaps this is what the King had in mind: giving more energy to a failing liberal system while restraining the authoritarian alternative.

Or perhaps there was no such calculation and Mussolini and the Fascist movement were simply the beneficiaries of collective government indecision. Either way, the influence of both Mussolini and Fascism must have increased phenomenally over a short period for such decisions to have been made.

The emergence of a Fascist movement

Fascism did not, as is sometimes suggested, spontaneously ignite in post-war Italy. It had a longer history than that and the ingredients which made it so combustible had been a long time in the mixing. Nor was Fascism simply a superficial set of slogans designed to give an appearance of an ideology to the personal pretensions of Mussolini. Instead, Fascism and Mussolini were separate identities, although they came together in a symbiotic relationship.[8]

Normally the far left and the far right are seen as the two poles on the political spectrum, separated from each other by all the other political positions. Fascism was uniquely the result of what happened when the far left and far right came together, bypassing the more moderate sectors. This conjunction occurred first in France and then spread to Italy through a series of cultural and political channels. The result was a system which seemed to offer a radical alternative to failing liberalism.

The argument that fascism originated in France was pursued by Sternhell in a series of works during the 1970s and 1980s.[9] As we have seen in Chapter 1, this was part of a general disillusionment with rationalism which sought an outlet in revolution – although not of the Marxist variant. In France a crucial step was taken when the syndicalist left, under Georges Sorel, discovered a common identity with the ultra-nationalist right, under Charles Maurras. Sorelian syndicalism aimed to overthrow bourgeois society by means of organized trade union activism. Although originally a Marxist, Sorel moved away from the rest of the revolutionary left in that he considered that revolution should be accomplished without political parties. A new society would be created in which existing corruption would be eliminated and the West's effete culture and civilization would be helped to die. A new and more decentralized community would emerge, based on the earlier and purer form of socialism advocated by Proudhon.

Meanwhile, opposition was also developing from the far right under Maurras. He, too, believed that France should return to an earlier condition, again with a complete absence of political parties. Instead, the people would be loyal to a locality, to family and to tradition. The values of the republic were all wrong and were therefore an aberration. The alternative was decentralization, stronger local government and a dynastic monarchy. The two strands of Sorel and Maurras came together as their supporters wrote for the same journal, *Les Cahiers du Cercle Proudhon*. According to Sternhell, this provided the synthesis of socialism and nationalism by 1912. The appeal was increasingly widespread, initially among university students and then among the working classes.

The next stage was the spread of these ideas, via parallel channels, to Italy. This was possible because Italy had traditionally been strongly influenced by France, from the intellectual elite to the organizations of the working class.

Syndicalism gained ground in Italy in the first decade of the century, acting as an alternative to Marxism on the far left. From 1908, however, the movement developed a split: in 1911 one wing supported Italy's imperial expansion into Libya, justifying this as gaining experience in class violence. The remaining syndicalists, under Mussolini, opposed such campaigns. This issue enabled Mussolini to develop his reputation and influence: by 1912 he was editing *Avanti* as a revolutionary paper well known for its attacks on the liberal-style policies of Giolitti.

The Italian equivalent to the far right in France emerged under the leadership of Gabriele D'Annunzio. He reflected the widespread disappointment in the way Italy had been united: the process seemed incomplete, lacking in poetry and action. Hence the far right had strongly theatrical inclinations. D'Annunzio himself spent much of his time in France, whence ideas from Maurras filtered into Italy. The right was all too aware that Italian aspirations were not being taken seriously in Europe. This provoked a power cult connected with ancient Rome and the establishment in 1910 of the Italian National Organization, a parallel organization to Action française.

As in France, the left and right converged. The catalyst was the involvement of Italy in the First World War. Mussolini, now converted to the idea of Italian intervention, resigned from *Avanti* and founded *Il Popolo d'Italia*. He therefore allied with the far right, although he retained his attachment to the key ideas of syndicalism. D'Annunzio was also strongly in favour of Italian participation in the war. He focused on the prospects of empire and imperialism, while at the same time meeting the syndicalism of the left as a means of achieving a more radical economic organization.

If the war brought the convergence of left and right, the peace which followed helped make the result more dynamic. Italy emerged disillusioned and heavily indebted to the Allies. Political instability worsened and in the ensuing chaos the two strands now intertwined to produce the characteristic components of Fascism. Mussolini concentrated on organization, instituting the Fascio di Combattimento for activists of the far left and far right. When this failed to develop properly he turned to a second wave of organization at a local level in the form of the *ras*, before finally opting for the level of a political party. By this time, Mussolini had adapted his syndicalist origins to the realities of the Italian political situation. Meanwhile, D'Annunzio was adding the theatrical elements to Fascism. His involvement in the Fiume escapade immediately after the war produced the uniforms, slogans and rituals which were soon to become an integral part of Fascism. Those who returned from Fiume also became prominent in the *ras* squads.

Thus Mussolini benefited partly from the failure of traditional Italian politics and partly from the emergence of Fascism as an alternative. The next question which needs to be answered is: why did Fascism increase in popularity during the crucial years of Italy's political instability?

Support for Fascism

The emblem eventually adopted for the Fascist Party was the fasces, a bundle of rods with a protruding axe-head, carried by magistrates in ancient Rome. These rods came to symbolize the various groups supporting Fascism, individually weak but deriving a collective strength from being bound together. Certainly Fascism appealed to a wide cross-section of society at a time when the prevailing atmosphere was one of political instability and economic insecurity. To many people, Fascism offered an alternative to a narrowly based and discredited government on the one hand and, on the other, the upheaval of a socialist revolution.

The original support for Fascism came from war veterans – young, aggressive and, according to Gregor, 'irretrievably lost to organized socialism and ill-disposed toward the commonplaces of the traditional parties'.[10] Most of them were fiercely patriotic; they denounced the mutilated peace of the Paris Settlement and their ardour was fired by the occupation of Fiume in 1919–20 by D'Annunzio. The Italian army was generally sympathetic towards the Fascists, although two attitudes tended to prevail: the lower levels participated enthusiastically in Fascist rallies and diverted a considerable amount of military equipment and arms, while the officer corps tried to keep discipline within the army without actually attacking Fascism. On the civilian scene, the *carabinieri* which, as the constabulary, was the main force of law and order, openly sympathized with Fascism and stood aside when attacks were directed at trade unionists.

The backbone of Fascism has long been considered to have been the lower middle class, especially small shopkeepers, artisans and clerical workers.[11] This normally moderate sector of society had been destabilized by the process of industrialization and by the economic difficulties caused by the war. They were the casualties of changes occurring all over central Europe, and the sociologist Seymour Lipset has called them the 'displaced masses'. They were caught between the rival forces of labour and capital and spurned the solutions of the socialist left, for these would involve a further depression of their status and their being levelled down into the working class. Hence, in De Grand's words, they saw the Fascist movement as 'the long sought instrument of bourgeois resurgence'[12] since it promised an end to industrial disruption and revolutionary socialism on the one hand while, on the other, it seemed ready to curb the power of big business. De Felice goes even further: for him, 'Fascism as a movement was the idealisation, the desire of an emerging middle class.'[13]

In terms of its sheer influence, however, the agrarian sector has until recently been underestimated. At first most of the support came from the landlords and estate owners. Their contacts with Fascism emerged from fear of the left. In the 1920 elections the PSI won control over many of the cities, including Milan and Bologna, along with 25 provincial councils and 2,200 district councils. In these circumstances the traditional ruling elites lost their predominance. At the same time they were also facing pressures from the labour markets and the peasant leagues. This meant that the traditional groups were greatly assisted by the Fascist attacks on peasant strikers. During the first half of 1921 Fascist squads destroyed 119 labour chambers, 107 co-operatives and 83 peasant league offices.

Yet there is evidence that even more substantial numbers of the peasantry were won over. These were mainly the smaller-scale peasant proprietors who were alienated by the undertaking of the PSI to collectivize the land. Some 500,000 people had managed to acquire ownership of land since 1918 and, even if the amount was meagre, they were determined not to lose it to socialism. There was therefore an active preference for the later Fascist policy of small land grants given to individual cultivators rather than the socialist alternatives.[14] Thus Fascism appealed to the cravings of two separate sectors of the landed interest. The fact that these two sectors opposed each other was one example of the inherent contradiction within Fascist support. Mussolini was even surprised by the extent of peasant support, as he had originally seen Fascism as an urban phenomenon.[15] The rural situation is highly complex and is an area where further research is particularly needed.

Industry produced the most dramatic class rupture in post-war Italy and it is scarcely surprising that the great industrialists should have backed Fascism. Because Mussolini's followers battered the unions into submission, the industrialists were willing to provide large donations; two examples were Alberto Pirelli, the tyre magnate, and Giovanni Agnelli of Fiat. Then, during the course of 1921, a number of workers joined the Fascist movement. The main reason for this was the growing crisis of socialism. The PSI split in 1921 and a separate Communist Party was established under the influence of Gramsci. The organization of the socialist movement became even more decentralized and provincial, which meant that the attacks of the Fascists rarely met co-ordinated resistance. Those workers who defected from what they saw as a sinking ship were also attracted by the emergence of alternatives to the unions – the Fascist syndicates.

Finally, there were sectors who assisted Fascism indirectly: although they could not bring themselves to support Fascism openly they were at least prepared to tolerate it in a way which would have been out of the question with, for example, socialism. One of these groups was the political establishment, whose attitude has already been examined. Another was the aristocratic class, who were appeased by Mussolini's willingness to end his attacks on the monarchy: he said in Udine in

September 1922, 'Now I really believe that the regime can be profoundly altered without touching the monarchy . . . Therefore, we shall not make the monarchy part of our campaign.'[16] The Queen Mother, Margherita, and the King's cousin, the Duke of Aosta, rapidly became admirers of Fascism. A third sector was the Catholic Church. This was won over by the moderation in Mussolini's stance by June 1921, when he was asserting in parliament: 'Fascism neither practises nor preaches anti-clericalism.'[17] The Church also took its cue from Pope Pius XI who, from the time of his election in 1922, remained on good terms with Mussolini. The Church undoubtedly considered a communist revolution to be the main threat. Mussolini, by contrast, had abandoned atheism and had come to accept that 'the Latin and Imperial traditions of Rome are today represented by Catholicism'.[18]

The role of Mussolini himself

A distinction has already been drawn between Italian Fascism and Mussolini. The former possessed considerable independent momentum, as was shown by the widespread local support gained in 1920 and 1921. But Fascism was also diffuse and incoherent, likely to dissipate unless given a national structure and identity. This is what Mussolini provided.

His first contribution to Fascism was its organization. It is true that he had an enormous struggle to achieve any sort of centralization in 1921 and that local activism would continue, undisciplined, for several years to come. He did, however, give Fascism its vital foothold in parliament, and the PFI gained respectability and political credibility which transcended purely local interests. He was also able to establish links between local activist groups, so that Fascism could claim to be a national movement as well as a national party. In the process, he provided a much needed synthesis between different parts. Augusto De Marsanich observed in 1922 that the party was often 'revealed as a mosaic' and that in such circumstances 'only the intellect and will of Mussolini can still control and direct us.'[19]

Second, Mussolini showed the importance of opportunism and action rather than a fixed ideology. Admittedly, he sometimes hesitated: Balbo, for example, is supposed to have prodded him into action over the March on Rome by telling him: 'We are going, either with you or without you. Make up your mind.'[20] He was also strongly inclined to intuitive behaviour and he lacked a policy or a programme. He did, however, succeed in projecting himself as a flexible pragmatist and he managed to cover up any erratic or inconsistent views. He once explained: 'Only maniacs never change. New facts can call for new positions.'[21] He claimed that his was a doctrine of action, and he saw his strength as having neither an overall system nor, after 1919, an ideological straitjacket. This pragmatism enabled him to make full use of the chaotic conditions in post-war Italy. He could use the largely spontaneous Fascist campaigns of pressure and violence in order to satisfy the popular craving for positive action; at the same time, he could pretend that Fascism was moderate in parliament, so winning the grudging approval of the government.

This brings us to Mussolini's personal leadership. His career has been presented as one of bluster and bluff – in huge proportions. But then the early 1920s were a period in which outrageous bluff had a better than usual chance of success. Mussolini applied all his journalistic skills and tricks to attract popular attention

4 Benito Mussolini, photo taken in 1923 (Popperfoto)

and support. He also learned, from D'Annunzio during the Fiume escapade, how to create a sense of power among his followers, even incorporating into the Fascist movement the war-cry of the Arditi: 'Ayah, ayah, alala!'. His personal attributes, according to Hibbert, included 'a physical stance not yet devitalised by illness, a style of oratory, staccato, tautophonic and responsive, not yet ridiculed by caricature and a personal charm not yet atrophied by adulation'.[22] With this presence, he was able to act his way into power.

For this is what happened. He played upon the post-war crisis, making it appear that Fascism really did have the strength to smash socialism and remould society, and that it could disrupt the functioning of parliamentary politics. No chances were taken by the politicians, and Mussolini was given more respect than his strength perhaps deserved; this would explain the capitulation of Facta and Victor Emmanuel when they were put under threat in October 1922. The counterpart to Mussolini the destroyer was the constructive statesman who, alone, could reconcile, rally and unite; under his leadership 'Fascism would draw its sword to cut the many Gordian Knots which enmesh and strangle Italian life.'[23] This personification of power had inherent dangers as, eventually, the bluff turned inwards and, as Mack Smith argues, Mussolini fell victim to his own delusions.[24]

MUSSOLINI'S DICTATORSHIP, 1922–43

Between 1922 and 1943 Mussolini established, at least in theory, all the institutions and devices associated with the totalitarian state. The foundation was the Fascist ideology, upon which was set a one-party system and all the paraphernalia of the personality cult. Popular support was guaranteed by indoctrination and, where necessary, coercion, while the economy was brought under a corporative system and geared to the needs of war. This section will examine the attempts to develop a dictatorship, the extent to which these actually changed Italy, and whether they worked in practice. Below the surface there are indications that the totalitarian state was extremely precarious. Fascist ideology was a makeshift alliance of different interests, the political institutions retained a surprisingly large number of non-Fascist influences, and the processes of indoctrination, coercion and corporativism were never completed. Above all, foreign policy eventually destabilized the whole system.

The stages in Mussolini's dictatorship

Although the individual components of Mussolini's dictatorship are complex, there is a discernible chronological trend to which they all at least partly relate.

The period between October 1922 and January 1925 saw Mussolini coming to terms with his appointment as Prime Minister and his attempts to make that power more substantial and permanent without, however, making radical changes based on ideology. Then, between 1925 and 1929, he aimed more consciously to step up the process of creating a Fascist regime, in the process using the term 'totalitarian' for the first time at the annual congress of the PNF in June 1925. A degree of stability seemed to have been achieved by 1930, in both domestic and foreign policies.

This was, however, subsequently threatened by the economic pressures of the Great Depression. During the early 1930s, therefore, Mussolini moved more definitely towards a concept of the 'corporate state' and tried to integrate the various forms of totalitarian control. The problem was that the regime needed a more obvious appearance of success. Mussolini sought this in a more active foreign policy, which involved his dictatorship in a series of wars. This meant another round of radical changes in the late 1930s; these were the result partly of domestic pressures and partly of influences from Nazi Germany. The result was, in Morgan's words, that 'Between 1936 and 1940 the regime consciously stepped up and intensified its attempts to "fascistise" Italian society.'[25] This broke the earlier balance and consensus within Italy and meant the intensification of repression on the one hand and of opposition on the other.

Meanwhile, Italy's economic infrastructure, seriously weakened between 1936 and 1939 by constant exposure to war, was tested to the point of collapse by

5 Benito Mussolini, 1883–1945 (Popperfoto)

Mussolini's disastrous decision to enter the Second World War. Although Mussolini attempted between 1943 and 1945 to recreate something of the original dynamism of Fascism, by this time he had become no more than a Nazi puppet within a small part of northern Italy.

The ideology of Fascism

In 1932 Mussolini defined the basic ideas of the movement, clearly and emphatically, in his *Political and Social Doctrine of Fascism*. Fascism, he said, was anti-communist, anti-socialist and strongly opposed to an economic conception of history. He denied that class war can be the preponderant force in the transformation of society. Fascism was also anti-democratic, denouncing the whole complex system of democratic ideology. It was certainly authoritarian: 'The foundation of Fascism is the conception of the State. Fascism conceives of the State as an absolute.' Finally, it promoted territorial expansion as an 'essential manifestation of vitality'.[26]

On the negative side, this definition was a hotchpotch of the ideas of conflicting sub-movements and sub-ideologies, of which De Grand has identified no fewer than five.[27] The first was national syndicalism which, in its emphasis on creating syndicates of workers and managers, was initially republican, anticlerical and vaguely socialistic. The second was rural fascism, which was anti-urban, anti-modern and anti-industrial. The third was technocratic fascism; because it accepted industrialization, and all the implications of modernization, it differed markedly from rural fascism. The fourth was conservative fascism; with its industrial, agrarian, monarchist and Catholic connections, it was basically traditional, pragmatic and non-ideological. The fifth was nationalist fascism, perhaps the most coherent version with an emphasis on an aggressive foreign policy and an authoritarian political system.

In addition to this five-way division between the strategies of these groups, there were other gaps. National syndicalism and technocratic fascism were both radical. They regarded themselves as the logical outcome of western Europe's revolutionary heritage, although they restored the emphasis on order and social harmony rather than individualism and liberal democracy. By contrast, conservative and nationalist fascism rejected Europe's revolutionary tradition altogether; their purpose was not to rationalize the French Revolution but to do away with it. This wide range of attitudes may originally have helped Fascism to gain popular support but, once the Fascist regime had been established, it proved a source of weakness. The Fascist state lacked the sort of monolithic base which Stalin's version of Marxism–Leninism gave to the Soviet Union.

Fascism was therefore an eclectic ideology, or one in which diverse components were loosely stuck together. This was perceived even at the time. De Marsanich observed in 1922 that 'our party is revealed as a mosaic' and that there was 'a multiplicity of interpretations made by Fascists themselves so that each individual believes in his own type of Fascism'.[28] This was partly because of the different strands which contributed to the emergence of the ideology. We have already seen the broad convergence of the radical right and radical left. Within this broad framework came the more specific views of a number of individuals bringing with them the wreckage of their previous attachments. Hence, radicals of the left included

Arpinati, an anarchist, and Bianchi and Rossoni, both revolutionary anarchists. To the right flocked radicals influenced by D'Annunzio, followed by Catholics, conservatives and monarchists. Mussolini was always conscious that Fascism had never been able to develop the sort of synthesis normally attributed to Marxism–Leninism. He gave reasons for this in 1932, as an introduction to the attempts to define Fascism: 'The years which preceded the March on Rome were ones in which the overriding need for action did not allow us the possibility of profound philosophical enquiries or complete doctrinal elaborations.'[29]

From these puzzling observations we may draw several conclusions. First, because Fascism was so eclectic, support was the most important issue. This meant that the leadership was always influenced by views and developments from below. As a result, the real issue was mobilization of support rather than purity or correctness of belief. But this had further consequences. Mobilization at the expense of ideology meant depoliticization. The contraction of ideology left a gap. This had to be filled by leadership as a pragmatic attraction rather than as an ideological principle. As will be seen, this meant that a tension was to develop between the ideology and the leader who purported to represent it.

Political power and institutions

Mussolini had come to power in extraordinary circumstances. From the end of 1922 he was therefore in charge of an emergency government. In fact, he presided over two coalitions. One was the multi-party cabinet, in which he was now Prime Minister; the other comprised the different strands of the Fascist movement, of which he was the Duce, or Leader. From this not very promising beginning, Mussolini gradually converted a semi-liberal regime to a one-party dictatorship.

The process was complex and often confused. Between 1922 and 1925 Mussolini settled for modifying the constitution to enhance his position in government. Then, following the Matteotti Crisis, Mussolini set up from 1925 onwards a different type of regime, in which two priorities emerged. One was to squeeze any remnants of democracy out of Italy's constitutional system through the advancement of Fascism. But the other was to adapt Fascism to Italy's traditions by wringing much of the radicalism out of the Fascist Party.

The regime therefore developed a dual momentum. In one sense, it has been seen as revolutionary, with an acceleration into the institutions of dictatorship. At the same time, the wilder nature of Fascism was being tamed: its momentum was being slowed to make it more acceptable to Italian traditions. The result of this was political confusion as the processes of change and continuity frequently tripped each other up, so that Mussolini himself became the only figure able to reconcile the contradiction. This explains his enormously enhanced position and the extent of his personality cult.

Initial coexistence with the liberal regime

In 1922 Mussolini headed a cabinet in which there were four Fascists and ten non-Fascists. Since his party had only 7 per cent of the seats in the lower chamber of parliament, Mussolini had, at first, to be cautious and conciliatory. He lulled the other deputies into a sense of security by promising that he would defend, not destroy, the constitution. The former governing parties seemed to have given up completely. Nitti, an ex-Prime Minister, was convinced that 'The Fascist experiment must be carried out without interference: there should be no opposition from our side.'[30] The King, meanwhile, was prepared to grant Mussolini emergency powers for one year. As a result, Mussolini gradually built up his credibility. This was shown when, in 1923, the Fascist Party (PNF), absorbed the Italian Nationalist Association (ANI) and one of the latter's leaders, Federzoni, joined Mussolini's government.

The problem for Mussolini with this early constitutional arrangement was, of course, that he could always be removed. The only thing that could prevent him from suffering the same fate as Orlando or Giolitti was to establish a secure Fascist majority in the chamber. This would then provide opportunities for the establishment of a permanent dictatorship in the future. Mussolini managed to persuade the chamber that his intention was constructive, not revolutionary. In a mood of revulsion against Italy's habit of producing brief and unstable ministries, the chamber passed the Acerbo electoral law in 1923. This stated that the party, or bloc, with a 25 per cent poll would automatically have a two-thirds majority in the parliament and would therefore form the government. The Italian electorate confirmed Mussolini's power in the election of April 1924 by giving the Fascists 4.5 million votes (64 per cent of those who voted) and control over 404 seats. The combined vote for the opposition was about 2.5 million. From this time onwards Mussolini could claim a genuine electoral mandate and therefore pursue more radical policies with fewer inhibitions.

In view of the previous electoral performance of the Fascists, this was a colossal victory. The main reason for this success has been put down to Fascism's 'Big List'. This involved the defection of candidates from other parties – thirteen from the Popolari and eighty from the liberals and conservatives. The support of major candidates like Orlando was especially important. Such defectors were crucial in bringing electoral support which Mussolini would not otherwise have had. In addition, Fascist intimidation had a considerable impact on the election process, putting off much of the potential opposition vote. A divided left was another crucial factor: in 1924 there were three parties, the original PSI, the reformist PSU under Matteotti and the PCI under Gramsci. The working class was still an undecided constituency, but it was not mobilized against Fascism. According to Pollard, 'United, the working-class parties might have robbed Mussolini of his victory.'[31]

The election result was a sensation. Mussolini was jubilant and could afford to disregard the claims of the PSU leader, Matteotti, that the election was invalid because of the extent of Fascist violence and intimidation. He could not, however, ignore what happened next.

The turning-point: the Matteotti Crisis

In June 1924 Matteotti was seized outside his house, bundled into a Lancia and stabbed to death. His body was discovered two months later in a shallow grave on the outskirts of Rome. It soon became evident that the crime had been committed by over-zealous Fascists. The impact of this was enormous: Payne considers it 'the most serious crisis Mussolini would experience before World War II'.[32] The media turned against Mussolini, and many of the recent converts to Fascism now hastened to desert. The murder was seen as a direct blow at the Italian constitution by the Fascist Party, especially since the car was traced back to Mussolini's private office. More significantly, the support built up in the 1924 election now threatened to unravel: Mussolini's two-thirds majority had represented the decision of only one-third of the electorate – and many of their votes had been delivered to the PFI via the defections of the normal recipients of their votes. The Matteotti affair threatened a major revival of the opposition, as Mussolini was criticized by Giolitti, Orlando, Salandra, and others who, for the previous three years, had been either supportive or mute.

Mussolini's recovery, however, was rapid and his subsequent actions illustrate his opportunism. The Socialist deputies withdrew from parliament, as a protest, in what came to be known as the Aventine Secession. Their intention was to show that parliamentary democracy was dead and to force the King to dismiss a discredited government. In fact, this proved to be the wrong strategy. The Aventine Secession undercut the position of Giolitti, who remained within parliament, and allowed Mussolini the opportunity to seize the initiative and defend the integrity of the chamber against pressures from outside. It also gave the King a reason to wait on events rather than to make an immediate decision.

If the crisis was the worst Mussolini faced in peacetime, his recovery from it was certainly the most pronounced. He reshaped his government by removing compromised Fascists such as Finzi and De Bono; he attacked the Socialist deputies for reneging on their parliamentary responsibilities; and he held out an olive branch to the parties which were on the brink of deserting their alliance with Fascism. Probably the most influential speech of his career was made to parliament on 3 January 1925: 'Very well,' he said, ' I now declare before this assembly and before the entire Italian people that I assume, I alone, moral and historical responsibility for all that has happened.' He brought everything, however, within the broad scope of the Fascist movement, losing the specific incident within the general: 'If Fascism has been nothing more than castor oil and the truncheon, instead of being a proud passion of the best part of Italian youth, then I am to blame.'[33] By confessing to everything – and therefore to nothing – Mussolini regained the initiative. He emerged as a statesman prepared to take on burdens rather than as a politician confronted by a crime. The opposition, meanwhile, appeared to have given up. Mussolini proceeded to hammer home his advantage by refusing to allow the Aventine Secessionists to return to their places within the chamber.

The significance of the Matteotti Crisis was enormous: indeed, it is often seen as a turning-point in the development of the Fascist regime. Once Mussolini had recovered his confidence and control, he clearly had to do something more permanent to stabilize the political situation. In a series of measures usually described as a 'second wave', he resorted to a programme which has been seen as both revolutionary and conservative, which broke with the past while retaining some of its traditions.

Political 'revolution'

From January 1925 onwards, Mussolini accelerated towards the establishment of a dictatorship. This involved the destruction of the Italian liberal state which had been in continuous existence since 1861. It is not surprising that this process is sometimes considered to be a 'Fascist revolution'.

The first component of the 'revolution' was the destruction of parliamentary sovereignty. This meant the swift dismantling of the opposition. The Secessionists were prevented by force from resuming their seats in parliament, while in 1926 other anti-Fascists were told that their electoral mandate was no longer valid. Many of the leaders went into exile, including the Liberal Nitti and the PCI member Togliatti. Gramsci was jailed and died in 1936. The one-party state was formalized in May 1928 by the introduction of a new electoral law; this ensured that all parliamentary candidates would be selected by the Fascist Grand Council from lists submitted by confederations of employers and employees. The final list had to be voted for as a whole by the electorate. In effect, parliamentary elections had been replaced by a plebiscitary dictatorship. The process was completed when, in 1938, the Chamber of Deputies was abolished and replaced by the Chamber of Fasces and Corporations.

A second purpose of the political 'revolution' was to strengthen the executive powers and to free them from any dependence on the legislature. Instead, the executive had considerable freedom of action. This meant the massive consolidation of Mussolini's personal powers. A fundamental law, passed in 1925, altered the constitution to make him responsible to the King rather than the legislature. Then, in January 1926, he was empowered to govern by decree, a process which was to be used over 100,000 times by 1943. During the late 1920s he also accumulated offices on an unprecedented scale. In 1929, for example, he was personally responsible for eight key ministries: foreign affairs, the interior, war, navy, aviation, colonies, corporations and public works. This authority was accompanied by the deliberate inflation of Mussolini's own image in the creation of the cult of the Duce (this is examined further on p. 119).

A third component of radical political change was the reorganization of the Fascist Party to enable it to meet the responsibilities of dictatorship. Originally it had been localized in its composition, and there was a faction which demanded a permanently decentralized organization and a limited membership. Eventually, however, the centralist viewpoint prevailed. The radicals of the party, led by Farinacci, wanted a carefully organized machine to ensure that the policies of Fascism could be uniformly implemented. The first step was the establishment in 1922 of the Fascist Grand Council, under the control of Mussolini himself. Then, during the Matteotti Crisis, the original party bosses at local level were purged and a new structure came into being, based on the principles of centralized direction and widespread party membership. In 1928 the Fascist Party Grand Council was made 'the supreme organ that coordinates all activities of the regime'.[34] Meanwhile, in 1926 a Special Tribunal for the Defence of the State was set up to deal with suspected anti-Fascists – another blow against the liberal tradition of political and ideological diversity.

The late 1920s saw a fourth example of radical Fascism. Mussolini had always been strongly influenced by revolutionary syndicalism and, once his power was secure against any opposition, he proceeded to implement it. In September 1926 he laid the foundation of the corporate state in the form of twelve national syndicates, under a Ministry of Corporations that was also established. The process was completed in 1934 when the syndicates were replaced by national corporations. The corporate state was merged into the political system by the replacement of a directly elected parliament by a corporative chamber; this, in turn, was reorganized as the Chamber of Fasces and Corporations.

There were, finally, developments in ideology. Attempts were made in the early 1930s to stabilize and define the Fascist revolution by giving its ideas a more dynamic appearance. An article, written in 1932, for the *Enciclopedia Italiana* hailed the 'Fascist century', attempted a 'sacralization of politics' and anticipated the wave of imperial expansion. We are left, therefore, with a picture of an ideological dictatorship operated, with immense executive authority, through a one-party system. All this seems to have been constructed on the ruins of the liberal state: it must, therefore, have been a 'revolution'.

Political continuity

A closer look, however, reveals some surprising inconsistencies in this picture. There is evidence that Fascism conceded at least as much to tradition as it managed to change it. Mussolini left a considerable part of the previous political structure intact. After all, he had said in August 1921: 'For me fascism is not an end in itself. It is the means to re-establish national equilibrium.'[35] This stopped the Fascist 'revolution' from attacking some of the traditional bases of Italy – the monarchy, the Church and the army. In order to prevent these from being openly threatened, Mussolini took as many measures to constrain the Fascist Party as he did to advance it. Indeed, the constitution of the party (1929) explicitly provided for the subordination of the party to the state. Although Fascist ministers were prominent in government departments, in each case they were under the ultimate authority of Mussolini himself.

At local level the submission of party officials to the traditional authorities, the prefects, was even more pronounced. Mussolini's circular to prefects of 5 January 1927, read:

> I solemnly affirm that the prefect is the highest authority of the state in the province. He is the direct representative of the central executive power. All citizens, and in particular those having the great privilege and supreme honour of supporting fascism, owe respect and obedience to the highest political representative of the fascist regime and must work under him to make his task easier.[36]

Mussolini even referred to the need to deal with any violent actions by the *squadristi*: 'The prefects must prevent this happening by using all means at their disposal, I repeat by using all means at their disposal.'[37] Other major local officials, such as the mayors, tended to be agrarian notables rather than Fascist activists – and the latter were again expected to follow orders.

The party was therefore controlled at all levels. According to Payne, 'One of the most striking features of the regime was that the political dictatorship also became a dictatorship over the party rather than of the party.'[38] To make this possible, radicalism was removed from the party. Some 60,000 of the more violent members were removed from its ranks, and new members were only admitted from the youth movements: this ensured their loyalty and obedience. The party increased in size from 300,000 in 1921 to over 5 million by 1943, in which middle-class membership predominated. The core of the party was also constrained. In theory the Grand Fascist Council was the supreme co-ordinating body; in practice it operated under the direct control of Mussolini himself, whose priority was to ensure that it did not replace the traditional state institutions

Several historians have deduced from these developments that there was an overall party depoliticization. 'Beginning in the late 1920s,' Tannenbaum argues, 'the party became the servant of the State rather than its ruler.'[39] This, according to Payne, means that 'There was no "Fascist revolution", save at the top.' Indeed, 'State administration changed comparatively little.'[40] If there was 'not a revolution', then what happened must have been 'an authoritarian compromise'.[41]

Political chaos and the cult of the Duce

Revolution or continuity? The two approaches can be seen as entirely different interpretations of how Mussolini consolidated his power, each complete in itself. Or they may have been two different strategies used by Mussolini as circumstances allowed or dictated. The latter is more likely, since common sense suggests that there were elements of both political revolution and political continuity between 1922 and 1939.

Assuming that revolution and continuity could develop together, logic would next suggest an uneasy and contradictory relationship between the two. Yet, on the surface, Mussolini appeared to have achieved a one-party state, based on an overriding ideology, without eradicating Italy's traditional institutions. In an illusion of order and harmony, Mussolini had managed to avoid a direct confrontation between party and state by injecting revolutionary dynamism into traditional institutions. The trouble with this interpretation is that it underestimates the turbulent impact of one upon the other. On the surface, there may well have been order and collaboration between Fascism and traditional Italy, but beneath the surface there was seething unrest as numerous members of the Fascist Party and the *squadristi* came into direct confrontation with the equivalent layers of state officialdom. Especially important was the conflict between local Fascist leaders on the one hand and the prefects and mayors on the other. Numerous complaints reached Mussolini about the way in which state authorities and the Church were flouting Fascist ideology. Mussolini must have been aware that the harmony between the party and the traditional institutions was only superficial. Indeed, after 1930, he became increasingly disillusioned with the most important of these, the monarchy. Why, therefore, was he prepared to tolerate such an unsatisfactory situation?

One view is that the conflict was deliberately created. Mussolini was able to construct an overall relationship between the party and the state which ensured the survival of both. At the same time, he aimed to create conflict and discord below the surface in order to promote his own position and to make himself indispensable. Lyttelton, for example, maintains that Mussolini 'deliberately fostered untidiness and illogicality in the structure of government'.[42] This was because he intended to rule by balancing the different elements which made up the state and the party. His basic fear was that one or more of these elements might eventually challenge his authority, and the greatest immediate threat seemed to come from the Fascist Party itself. Hence, he took the drastic but logical step of depoliticizing the regime. The result was a strange paradox: the strength of Fascism depended on the weakness of Fascist organizations. Or, to put it another way, a movement which was famed for its activism was encouraged by its leader to show inactivity. Mussolini was deliberately creating a vacuum in the political and administrative structure where one would normally expect to find a ruling class or elite. The explanation of this was that Mussolini was opposed to the emergence of any group which was likely to compete with him for power and public support. The gap was filled by the cult of the Duce,[43] or Mussolinianism, and Fascism was restrained so that this could predominate. The cult of the Duce was not an essential part of the Fascist programme, but rather an elaborate superstructure imposed on top of it. As far as Mussolini was concerned, however, it was the whole point of his rule; after all, he had once said, 'If Fascism does not follow me, no one can make me follow Fascism.'[44]

There is much to be said for this approach. It gives more meaning to the cult of the Duce than does the view of Taylor that Mussolini was a 'vain, blustering boaster'. It also separates Mussolinianism from Fascism and shows that the former did not arise from the latter but, in fact, lived in tension with it. On the other hand, it assumes that Mussolini's dictatorship was dictated from above – that the cult of the Duce forced itself into the political vacuum contrived by Mussolini himself.

It is difficult to imagine a personality cult being sustained entirely on a created need. It is more likely to be the deliberate intensification of a need which was already there. An additional dimension was therefore necessary. Mussolinianism was as much the response to pressures from below as it was to calculations from above. The cult of the Duce met a deep psychological need and therefore responded to public demand rather than creating it. In their situation the population found hero worship an essential antidote to fear since it provided hope and as near as they were likely to get to certainty. Ideology needed to be personified so that the irrational could be rationalized and projections turned into realities. The personality cult could succeed only if the projection of the personality was accepted by the people. In a very real sense, therefore, Mussolini was a reflection of popular aspirations. Mussolinianism was an extension of his skills of oratory: he adjusted to the crowd in order to sway it.

Mussolini's position was therefore doubly strong, but simultaneously doubly precarious. During the 1920s and 1930s he could exist through a combination of radicalism and conservatism, smoothing over conflict on the surface while allowing it to seethe underneath. He could do this because he was sustained by popular adulation, which he strengthened through speeches, role-modelling and sloganizing. Of the three major dictators he was at one moment the most acclaimed and at another the most reviled (his eventual fate, at the hands of the system and the people, is dealt with on pp. 150–1).

Indoctrination and culture

While altering the base of political power, Mussolini also sought to establish a new national identity for the Italian people. This followed broadly the same pattern as the political developments within Italy. In the first three years the changes were relatively slow, followed by a more adventurous approach between 1925 and 1929, but as yet without any radical ideological input: this was increased as a result of the Great Depression between 1930 and 1934. The most significant developments in indoctrination occurred after 1935, with the invasion of Ethiopia and the growing influence of Nazi Germany. The main emphasis throughout was on the personality cult, the political implications of which were dealt with in the previous section. All allegiance was to be focused on the Duce himself. Mussolini's short stature and partial baldness were disguised by a ramrod-straight stance and shaven head, both of which were intended to give him a Roman appearance. His demagoguery remained impressive, based on the unsubtle belief that 'The crowd loves strong men.' He was also portrayed as an expert rider, fencer, racing driver and violinist. The public were constantly assailed by slogans like 'Mussolini is always right!' and 'Believe! Obey! Fight!'. During the 1930s Mussolini extended the scope of Italianization to include the creation of the 'new Fascist man' who would live in the 'century of Fascism'.

It might be thought that education would play a crucial role in the new order, but changes were slow at first and subject to subsequent modification. In 1923 the Education Minister, Gentile, introduced a structure specifically intended to create a new elite: technical education was separated from the classical courses which became the passport to university education, and a rigid examination system was applied. This, however, came under universal criticism from parents and was so difficult to operate that Fedele, Gentile's successor, had to modify it from 1925 onwards. After 1929 there was more of an effort to Fascistize schools under the Ministry of National Education, which replaced the earlier Ministry of Public Instruction. The process was accelerated by Bottai in 1936. Textbooks became a state monopoly; the number of approved history texts, for instance, was reduced from 317 to 1, while a junior Italian reader informed solemn eight-year-olds that 'the eyes of the Duce are on every one of you'. From 1938 racism was openly practised and taught in the classroom, while 1939 saw the introduction of the Fascist School Charter. By and large, however, education was not one of the more successful examples of indoctrination. There were too many loopholes and evasions and, in the universities, underground resistance to and contempt for so-called Fascist values.

Hence, the regime came to place more emphasis on the organization of youth groups outside the school sector. Again, the pace gradually intensified. Initially the whole process was very haphazard. From 1926, however, the youth organizations were grouped into the Opera Nazionale Balilla (ONB). During the 1930s the stages of these became more clearly defined. At the age of four, boys became Sons of the She-Wolf; at eight they joined the Balilla, before moving to the Avanguardisti at fourteen and finally the Fascist Levy at eighteen. The creed of the Balilla blatantly superimposed a doctored version of Italian history on a twisted religious format:

> I believe in Rome the Eternal, the mother of my country, and in Italy, her eldest daughter, who was born in her virginal bosom by the grace of God; who suffered through the barbarian invasions, was crucified and buried, who descended to the grave, and was raised from the dead in the nineteenth century, who ascended into heaven in her glory in 1918 and 1922 and who is seated on the right hand

of her mother Rome; who for this reason shall come to judge the living and the dead. I believe in the genius of Mussolini, in our Holy Father Fascism, in the communion of the martyrs, in the conversion of Italians and in the resurrection of the Empire.[45]

This was principally part of the more radical wave which occurred after 1936. The organization was further tightened as all sections of youth were brought under the collective Gioventu del Littorio (GIL) in 1937, membership of which was made compulsory in 1939.

How effective were these organizations? It is true that a large proportion of Italy's youth responded enthusiastically to Fascism. They were, for example, given opportunities for outdoor recreation which had previously been lacking. On the other hand, membership of these paramilitary organizations was by no means universal, as some 40 per cent of the age group between eight and eighteen managed to avoid joining them. The proportion was much higher among girls, many of whom were not given a sufficiently fulfilling role to compensate for the subservience which Fascism expected of them in society. Recent research has also shown that the youth groups were more influential in the urban than in the rural areas, in the north and centre rather than in the south, and in the middle classes rather than in the peasantry or working classes.

Fascism also tried to organize the population at large, through the OND or Dopolavoro. Although set up in 1925, this really came into its own during the Great Depression as a means of ensuring the total commitment of the workforce. It co-ordinated the various different work schemes and clubs, and promoted library, radio, sports and recreation facilities. The next stage was the emergence of the OND as a full ministry in 1935, with the intention of providing for a more fully co-ordinated use of the mass media for the purpose of indoctrination. This is another example of the increased radicalization from the mid-1930s, but did not develop into anything like the more sophisticated systems of the KdF and SdA in Germany.

That Mussolini considered the control of the press to be a major priority was hardly surprising, in view of his own experience as a newspaper editor. Early measures included the suppression of many papers by the exceptional decrees of 1926 and, in 1928, the compulsory registration of all journalists with the Fascist Journalist Association. The press office under Rossi controlled news and censorship. The process was extended in the early 1930s when the press office came under the control of Polverelli. He increased the control over individual journalists and was responsible for the development of the cult of the Duce in the press. He managed to exert effective control over what was published; in difficult cases the government called upon the local prefects to enforce its decisions. Further changes were made when Ciano established the Ministry for Press and Propaganda – another example of radicalization for the purpose of presenting the Ethiopian campaign in the most positive way. By and large, Mussolini's regime of journalism was more successful than most other elements of the totalitarian state. There was, however, a price: constant distortion of the facts about Italy's record in her three wars led eventually to the entire government being misinformed. Mussolini, in particular, lost all contact with reality, even though – or because – he spent several hours each day reading the newspapers.

Cultural output was, on the whole, more diverse in Italy than in either Germany or the Soviet Union. There was less attempt to create a grand style and there was more receptiveness to outside influences. According to Pollard, 'There was no such thing as a "Fascist culture", even less a cultural revolution in Italy. What Fascist Italy lacked was a clear cultural programme and strategy.'[46] This began to change, however, from 1935 onwards when Mussolini expressed increasing concern about the preoccupation of Italians with art for art's sake. Instead, he insisted, it was now necessary to develop a more utilitarian approach which would help reinforce Italy's expansionist and martial roles.[47] Attempts were later made to institutionalize the control of culture through two bodies set up in the 1930s. The first was the Propaganda Ministry (1935), with the Ministry of Popular Culture following in 1937. The latter tried to regulate music, literature, art and the cinema. But it was never as efficient as the measures used by Goebbels to Nazify German art and literature or the Socialist Realism of Stalin.

One of the more popular forms of culture was the cinema which, according to Mussolini, was 'the strongest weapon'. This provides a more detailed example of the incomplete nature of Fascist control. On the one hand, there was an increase in institutions and regulations. A film institute was set up in 1925, followed, in 1934, by the Office for Cinematography. The government insisted on quotas (100 films were to be made in 1937) and tried to dictate the themes of major epics. On the other hand, such controls were far from total. Most films were produced by private enterprise and were not geared to the state's propaganda requirements. Indeed, Fascism's lack of cultural awareness alienated the younger generation of film directors, like De Santis and Visconti, who aimed at realism rather than distortion. Thus, ultimately, Mussolini's 'strongest weapon . . . was turned against Fascism itself'.[48]

The overall impression, therefore, must be that the Fascist state failed to exert the type of control over ideas which is normally associated with totalitarianism. The traditional liberal culture proved impossible to eradicate, even through the more radical impulses of the 1930s. The negative result was that Mussolini was able to attract less total popular commitment than either Hitler or Stalin through culture. The positive side was that there was less to expunge after the end of the Fascist regime. Bosworth, for one, has shown that there is more continuity in Italian culture, before and after 1945, than is commonly realized.[49]

Coercion

Indoctrination is invariably linked to coercion. The use of force had been implicit in the Fascist movement from the beginning and a system of repression was gradually constructed. The Law on the Defence of the State was established in 1926. This provided for terms of imprisonment for anyone attempting to reconstitute an opposition party, or attempting to propagate 'doctrines, opinions or methods' of such organizations.[50] These offences would be tried by a Special Tribunal for the Defence of the State. The following year saw the formation of a secret police, or OVRA (Opera Voluntaria per la Repressione Antifascista). Those who experienced the full pressure of these organs were mainly ex-politicians and dissidents who refused to take the oath of loyalty to the regime, although, from the late 1930s, the apparatus was also used to enforce a policy of anti-Semitism.

How effective was this system? On the one hand, it was clearly part of the paraphernalia to exert control over the population and to eliminate alternative ideas. Historians accept that the intention was to facilitate subjection. According to Morgan, 'the police's preventive and repressive powers were now so extensive and pervasive as to create a real climate of fear and repression'.[51] The Fascist regime operated on the joint principles of conversion and coercion. Support for the system was therefore engendered in a repressive atmosphere which was intended to remove any element of choice. Ultimately the effectiveness of the conversion depended partly on the strength of the propaganda and indoctrination but partly on the fear of the consequences of evasion. During the 1930s about 20,000 actions were taken by the police every week, many of these being initiated on the basis of information received from people known to the accused. This meant that repression was assisted by the people themselves within a general and widespread fear of recrimination.

The scope of repression was therefore considerable. But the degree of terror it employed was not. OVRA was not equivalent to the SS in Germany or the NKVD in the Soviet Union. Nor was there any fundamental change in criminal justice to correspond with the creation of the People's Court in Germany: within Italy the legal system continued to operate much as it had always done, despite the so-called Fascistization of the regime. The death penalty was used only nine times between 1927 and 1940 while, of the 4,805 cases actually brought to court, 3,904 ended in acquittal. During the entire Fascist period 5,000 people were given prison sentences for political reasons and 10,000 sent into political exile.[52]

There is, not surprisingly, a broad consensus about the Fascist police state which has been unaffected by any other interpretations concerning Mussolini. During the 1990s, Payne argued that 'In Italy the Mussolini regime was brutal and repressive, but not murderous and bloodthirsty';[53] according to Whittam, the 'threat posed by this mysterious organisation [OVRA] . . . was more important than its actual activities',[54] while Pollard maintained that 'Though life was no joke for dissidents in Fascist Italy, it was eminently preferable to their fate in the other two totalitarian states.'[55] Such views only reinforce the earlier conclusion of Cassels that 'The Fascist regime used terror, but was not in any real sense based on terror.'

Anti-Semitism and racism

Nowhere is there a greater contrast in the earlier and later policies of Mussolini than in the treatment of Italy's Jewish population.

During the1920s anti-Semitism was hardly an issue. There were, it is true, some anti-Semitic influences from France – and especially from Maurras. A few Fascists, such as Preziosi and Farinacci, tried to propagate them, but they did not translate easily into practice. Italy had always been less affected than other parts of Europe by anti-Semitism, largely because Jews had never amounted to more than one in a thousand of the total population. Individual Jews had joined the Fascist Party in the early 1920s: ironically the proportion of their membership was well above the overall national average. Mussolini had seen no problem with this. His approach to Fascism had been on the left-wing, syndicalist strand, which meant that he had no instinct for the anti-Semitism of the right. Indeed, he had originally denounced Nazi racism as 'unscientific and absurd',[56] going so far as to ensure full legal status for Italian Jews in 1932 and, from 1933, to give sanctuary to 9,000 Jewish exiles from Germany.

Then came a dramatic reversal of attitudes and policy. In July 1938 a Manifesto on Race was drawn up by Mussolini and ten professors as a scientific exposition of Fascist racial doctrine. It proclaimed that 'the population of Italy is of Aryan origins and its civilization is Aryan', that 'there now exists a pure Italian race and that Jews do not belong to the Italian race'.[57] It was followed by decrees banning intermarriage between Jews and non-Jews and removing Jews from prominent positions in finance, education and politics. Property restrictions were also imposed and any Jews who had entered Italy since 1919 were to be repatriated.

These changes took Italy by surprise and were immediately associated with growing influences from Nazi Germany. Some historians still agree with this. De Felice maintains that Mussolini 'introduced state antisemitism in Italy . . . because of his basic conviction that, to render the Italian–German alliance iron-hard, it was necessary to eliminate every strident contrast between the two regimes'.[58] It would be pointless to deny this external channel of influence. By 1938 Mussolini needed Hitler's support in Europe and the Rome–Berlin Axis was moving steadily towards a military alliance. It therefore made sense to bring Fascist ideology more into line with Nazi racism. Even if, as Pollard maintains, there is no evidence that Hitler put pressure on Mussolini to make this change, it is possible that Mussolini felt 'out of step with almost every other Fascist movement'.[59] It was no coincidence that Hungary and Romania also introduced anti-Semitic legislation in 1938.

But there is a tendency to go too far in this direction and to assume that anti-Semitism was entirely an external transplant into Italy. There was, on the contrary, a powerful influence within Italy for the change of policy – the conquest of Ethiopia between 1935 and 1937. This made race a more important public issue and resulted in direct access to anti-Semitism. Admittedly, 'one can argue equally logically that Italy had already ruled an empire (Eritrea, Somalia and Libya) for fifty years before the invasion of Ethiopia without developing any discernible anti-Semitic tendencies'.[60] On the other hand, the circumstances of the conquest of Ethiopia carried extreme connotations of racial 'inferiority'. The whole process was unusually brutal, involving the use of mustard gas, and there were also fears of miscegenation between the considerable number of Italian troops and the indigenous population. Racism therefore became ingrained in the later phase of Fascist ideology. Mussolini needed to prepare the Italian people for a role of future domination over 'inferior' peoples, in very much the same way that Aryan domination was being projected for eastern Europe.

Italian anti-Semitism was an extension of this vision. The connection was, of course, suggested by developments within Germany. This does not, however, remove the indigenous origins. Given the changing situation in foreign and imperial policy during the second half of the 1930s, Mussolini had his own reasons for revising his views about the Jews. This was partly because a small number of Jews were beginning to draw attention to themselves – thereby creating unintended pressure from below. Two issues proved especially important. The first was the opposition of Italian Zionists to Mussolini's proposals to take over the Palestinian mandate from Britain. The second, and more important, was the courageous criticism by Jewish intellectuals of the Italian campaign in Ethiopia. Mussolini promptly resorted to the traditional

European response of using an identifiable target as a scapegoat. The stance on Palestine and Ethiopia must indicate a Jewish 'conspiracy', which was behind the decision of the League of Nations to impose sanctions against Italy. It was the 'conspiracy' theory rather than direct pressure from Germany which brought Fascist Italy into the mainstream of anti-Semitism – another traditional European response.

The policy was, however, intensified by competition with Germany. Mussolini felt under increasing pressure to compete with Hitler for seniority within the partnership between Italy and Germany. This involved creating an Italian counterpart to the German master race, and Mussolini's special ingredient was racial purity. Hence, 'While the racial composition of the other European nations has altered considerably even in recent periods, the grand lines of racial composition have remained essentially the same in Italy during the last thousand years.'[61] The only blot on this record were the Jews, who comprised non-European racial elements and had never been assimilated in Italy.

Mussolini's anti-Semitism was never the focal point of Fascist ideology; nor did it become the heart of consuming obsession. Policies against the Jews were therefore perceived as being out of place in Italy. Such actions were neither popular nor accepted: they were widely resented. In asking 'Why, unfortunately, did Italy have to go and imitate Germany?'[62] Pope Pius XI was voicing both the Catholic conscience and the secular misgivings of those who saw the creeping influence of Nazism in Italy. In the event, the racial decrees were never applied effectively, another illustration of the incomplete nature of the totalitarian state. During the Second World War there were no large-scale shipments of Italian Jews to Nazi camps until the Germans occupied northern Italy in 1943; elsewhere anti-Semitic legislation gradually lapsed, especially after the fall of Mussolini.

Mussolini's attitude to racism and anti-Semitism can, in the final analysis, be seen as a barometer of the pressures on Fascism. During his rise to power, anti-Semitism was one of the right-wing strands of Fascist ideology which he could entirely ignore. Nor, during the 1920s, was there any reason to target the Jews: they were entirely outside his attempts to carry through a Fascist revolution while keeping traditional institutions intact. As the regime entered economic difficulties during the Great Depression there was still no search for a Jewish scapegoat, the reverse of the situation in Germany. It was the conquest of Ethiopia, itself a radical response to growing internal pressures, which produced a powerful current of racism. The anti-Semitic channel developed with the aforementioned Jewish criticism of Mussolini's objectives. The diplomatic link with Hitler suggested what measures should be applied in Italy – but these were part of an overall intensification of Fascism in Italy in the period leading up to the Second World War. As Whittam argues, 'Mussolini sought to reinvigorate the regime by his racial programme and his foreign policy.'[63]

This, however, carried the risk of upsetting the earlier consensus and creating more resentment. Radicalism would lead to further war and Mussolini was gambling on military victory as a universal panacea. As it turned out, the regime fell into the vortex of defeat but, according to Morgan, it was the contemporary perceptions of anti-Semitism in Italy that 'shaped the Italian people's response to the Fascist regime in the late 1930s'.[64] This, in turn, has been seen as the 'triumph of old humanitarian values over new Fascist principles'.[65]

Relations between Church and state

There was no natural affinity between the Church and Fascism. After all, Mussolini had once been a strident atheist and very few of the Fascist leaders were practising Catholics. Both sides, however, had much to gain from ending the deep rift between Church and state which went far back to the era of Italian unification. Mussolini claimed the credit for this reconciliation, arguing that the 'serenity of relations' was 'a tribute to the Fascist regime'.[66] In fact, the healing was started by Orlando, Prime Minister between 1917 and 1919. It could, however, be argued that the process was greatly accelerated by the Fascist government.

The highlights were the three agreements of 1929. The Lateran Treaty settled the question of the Pope's temporal power by restoring the Vatican City to his sovereignty. The Concordat defined more carefully the role of the Church in the Fascist state. Catholicism was to be the sole religion of the state, religious instruction would return to schools, and Church marriages would be given full validity. In a third agreement the papacy was compensated for financial losses, incurred in the nineteenth century, by the payment of 750 million lire in cash and 1,000 million in state bonds.

Why was this arrangement reached – and what was hoped to develop from it? Each side had its own, somewhat contrasting, view. The Pope hoped that Fascism would provide a better medium than the former liberal state for the revival of Catholic influence over the secular power. Mussolini hoped that the support of the Church would provide more security and stability for Fascism. Although he was acknowledging that Fascism was not now going to replace traditional Catholic virtues, the agreement meant that Mussolini could concentrate on those areas in which Fascism could be more actively extended – the economy, education and foreign policy.

Two views have recently been advanced as to the wisdom of the Lateran treaties. The first, very much in line with the traditional perspective, is Morgan's argument that 'the Conciliation was probably the most important contribution to the consolidation of the Fascist government in power on a wider basis of support and consent'.[67] The alternative approach is that Mussolini was to some extent duped. Bosworth, for example, comments that the 'uneasy relationship between Fascism and Catholicism' was 'a meeting between a long-sighted Church and a short-sighted regime'.[68] There are elements of truth in both. On the one hand, Mussolini was able to use the agreement to considerable political advantage. On the other, he also found himself in conflict with an institution which had no intention of yielding the essential pressure points of its power.

Mussolini's gains are readily apparent. He had, after all, succeeded in gaining the support of a power which had been hostile to successive governments for a period of fifty years. Pius XI claimed that the Lateran Accords 'brought God to Italy and Italy to God'.[69] The Vatican was therefore willing to urge the electorate to vote for the Fascist list in 1929 and 1934. There was also strong support for Mussolini's policies on population increase, the family and divorce. Above all, there was a considerable overlap of interest between the government and the papacy in foreign policy.[70] Cardinal Shuster, for example, compared the invasion of Ethiopia with the Crusades, while Pius XI openly justified Mussolini's participation in the

Spanish Civil War on the grounds that he was helping contain the main enemy of Christianity: 'The first, the greatest and now the general peril is certainly Communism in all its forms and degrees.'[71] This attitude met with the overwhelming approval of the upper levels in the Church's hierarchy.

On the other hand, Mussolini never succeeded in subordinating the Church to the full control of the state; it could even be said that the Church emerged strengthened from the relationship and came eventually to threaten the Fascist state. Three issues proved especially contentious. In the first place, Mussolini's insistence on controlling the minds of the young was bound to lead to conflict. In 1931 the Pope protested in his encyclical *Non abbiamo bisogno* against Fascist attempts to close down youth clubs and to monopolize education. The Church won a number of concessions in the form of the 1931 Accords which allowed involvement in specifically religious activities for youth groups. Second, the Pope reacted with hostility to that part of Mussolini's racial legislation in 1938 which forbade intermarriage between Italians and Jews: this was on the grounds that Jews could no longer be converted to Catholicism. In the process, the Church found itself in harmony with Italian public opinion which opposed racism for more general reasons. Finally, there were underlying tensions throughout the period between the Pope's vision of an Italy reconverted to Catholicism and Mussolini's vision of a sacralized Rome – an eternal secular Italy based on the principles of ancient Rome. Again, the survival of the Church in the 1930s meant that the papacy could restore its claim to represent the conscience of Italians – once the regime was threatened with the spectre of defeat.

The extent to which Catholicism helped to undermine the Fascist regime in its critical period is examined on page 134. Key roles were played by Catholic Action, an organization of laymen which had been established by the Pope in 1922, by the FUCI (Federazione Universitari Cattolici Italiani), a university-based movement of Catholic students and intellectuals, and the Mouvimento Laurienti. It has to be said that, if Mussolini's deal with the Church consolidated Fascism in the 1930s, it also enabled Catholicism to gather its own strength against Fascism in the early 1940s.

Economic policies

The overall trend in economic policy was from initial free enterprise to state intervention and control. The process was complex. In summary, the regime's approach to the economy was, until 1925, a continuation of earlier liberal policies. An attempt was then made to increase state control without going the whole way to establishing a socialist base. Mussolini's solution was a compromise: a partnership between the state and private economic enterprise in the form of 'corporativism'. The corporate state was gradually set up between 1926 and 1934 and was widely publicized. It was not, however, particularly effective. Instead of using it as a means of harmonizing economic policy, Mussolini increased government control outside the scope of corporativism. The result was a confusion of institutions and often a conflict of aims.

The main development between 1926 and 1934 was the emergence of the corporate state. The idea of corporativism was not new; it was based partly on medieval guilds and corporations and partly on the revolutionary syndicalism of Georges

Sorel, an early influence on Mussolini (see p. 105). The basic intention was to replace the old sectional interests (such as trade unions and employers' organizations) which so often produced conflicts between labour and capital. Instead, the Rocco Law of 1926 recognized seven branches of economic activity: industry, agriculture, internal transport, merchant marine, banking, commerce and intellectual work. These were formed into syndicates, under the control of the Ministry of Corporations, also established in 1926. The system was further refined by the creation in 1930 of the National Council of Corporations and the organization of economic activity into twenty-two more specialized corporations by 1934. By 1938 this process was brought into the political system with the creation of the Chamber of Fasces and Corporations in place of the old Chamber of Deputies.

In theory, corporativism was the Fascist alternative to socialism on the left and undiluted capitalism on the right. The so-called 'third way' would increase state control over the economy without destroying private enterprise and it could be adapted to the new Fascist institutions. In particular, it was a means by which Italy could be helped to tackle the pressures of the Great Depression. In practice, however, the whole system proved inefficient and cumbersome. It failed to provide any sort of consensus between employers and workers and was almost entirely excluded from any real decision-making on the economy. Historians have always been critical of its practical applications. Cassels remarks that 'the corporative state was a true child of Mussolini: the great poseur brought forth an organism which was a travesty of what it purported to be'.[72] According to Pollard, 'In reality, in the corporations and other new government agencies Fascism had created a vast, largely useless apparatus.'[73] The corporate state has been seen largely as a means of sharing power between Fascism and the economic interests of the landowners and industrialists. It was more about creating a subservient labour force than about providing a structure capable of undertaking genuine economic change. Hence, in the words of Tannenbaum, 'Fascist Italy had complete control over the labour force and very little control over the nation's economic structure.'[74]

Increasingly, the whole structure of corporativism was ignored and policies pursued outside its scope. In terms of finance, industry and agriculture, the government pursued separate lines. In each case these originated in the 1920s and were intensified during the 1930s. They managed, however, to remain largely beyond the gravitational pull of corporativism.

Between 1922 and 1925 Finance Minister De Stefani followed a traditional course of balanced budgets, avoided price fixing and subsidies, and withdrew government involvement in industry. From the mid-1920s, however, the views of Mussolini became more influential. These were based as much on the dictates of national prestige as on sound economic thought. He was obsessed, in particular, with the value of the Italian currency, declaring: 'I shall defend the Italian lira to my last breath.' In 1929 the lira was reflated to the level of 90 to the pound sterling, a decision which seriously undermined Italy's competitiveness as an exporter and which probably brought on recession even before the impact of the Great Depression. During the 1930s the government imposed increasingly tight financial controls which, from 1936, became an integral part of the policy of autarky (self-sufficiency) necessitated by war. This was the most radical phase of Mussolini's economic policy, corresponding with the acceleration of changes in other areas. The impetus for such decisions was certainly not a corporate one: it came from Mussolini's priorities in foreign policy and from pressures from heavy industry.

Fascism always favoured heavy industry as the expense of light (or consumer) industry, because of the former's close association with armaments. At first the emphasis was on encouraging private enterprise and leaving untouched private concerns like Fiat, Montecatini Chemicals and Pirelli Rubber. With the onset of the Great Depression, however, the government became more heavily involved by introducing schemes for job-sharing and for rescuing those industries in difficulty. In 1933 it set up the IRI (Istituto per la Recostruzione Industriale) to channel state investment into those industries which were considered most vital. The policy of autarky brought more rigid controls and centralization. By 1939, according to De Grand, the IRI controlled 77 per cent of pig-iron production, 45 per cent of steel production, 80 per cent of naval construction and 90 per cent of shipping.[75] Morgan points to the separation between these developments and the corporate state. The organization of the IRI was parallel to corporativism, rather than integrated into it, and therefore 'resembled a "consortial" rather a "corporate" state'.[76]

In some respects, industry recovered reasonably well from the impact of the Great Depression. Between 1936 and 1940 it overtook agriculture for the first time in Italian history as the largest single contributor to the GNP (34 per cent as opposed to 29 per cent).[77] Imports had dropped considerably by 1939 when compared with the levels of 1928: raw materials by 12 per cent, semi-finished articles by 40 per cent and finished articles by 48 per cent. Meanwhile, industrial production as a whole had risen by 9 per cent. These figures were offset, however, by the persistence of serious weaknesses in the Italian industrial sector. Mussolini's policies failed to remove the huge disparity between north and south, while Italy remained affected by low productivity, high costs and a decline in domestic consumption. Overall, Italy's recovery from the effects of depression was slower than that of any other European power. What made the situation intolerable, however, was the exposure of an inadequate industrial infrastructure to the constant pressures of military conflict – in the form of the invasion of Ethiopia (1935–6), involvement in the Spanish Civil War (1936–9) and the invasion and occupation of Albania (1939). It is hardly surprising that Italy was defeated so rapidly during the Second World War: the country had already been brought to the point of exhaustion by policies which undermined any reconstruction which had been managed. It has to be said that neither the policies nor the reconstruction had much to do with the corporate state.

The most important development in agriculture was the drive for self-sufficiency in grain which was intended to improve Italy's balance of trade with the rest of Europe and with North America. Characteristically, Mussolini introduced the 1925 campaign as the Battle for Grain and, amid massive publicity, was photographed reaping, or driving tractors. The battle succeeded in increasing grain production by 50 per cent between 1922 and 1930 and by 100 per cent between 1922 and 1939. This was, however, largely at the expense of other crops like fruit and olives which would have been more suited to the additional land given over to grain.

Mussolini also sought to create extra arable land, through reclamation schemes, and extra people, through a higher birth rate. The former was accomplished by schemes like the draining of the Pontine Marshes. The latter was attempted by the Battle for Births, the aim of which was to double Italy's population within a generation. The reasoning behind such a dramatic demographic change was that a static population reflects a decay of national vitality and that a larger population would be essential for the empire which Mussolini was in the process of creating. The incentives for larger families included the payment of benefits for children, the imposition of extra taxation on single people and giving priority in employment to fathers. The whole scheme, however, failed in its objective: between 1921 and 1925 there had been 29.9 births per 1,000 people, whereas between 1936 and 1940 this had declined to 23.1 per 1,000, due partly to the mobilization of men to fight in Mussolini's foreign wars.

It is difficult to avoid a negative overall assessment of Fascist economic policy. The 'third way' of corporativism was attractive in theory but irrelevant in practice. The economy was taken forward instead by a process of mobilization, based on increasingly direct government intervention. The result was a confusion of two strategies which had implications also for social policies.

The social consequences of Mussolini's regime

Before 1922 Mussolini claimed that Fascism represented the interests of all classes. By 1939, however, it was evident that any real benefits had accrued only to a small minority – the great industrialists, the estate owners and those members of the middle class serving in the Fascist bureaucracy. For the majority of Italians, by contrast, the quality of life deteriorated.

The industrialists were able to depend on a permanent alliance with the government. The 1925 Vidoni Pact and the Charter of Labour (1927) greatly increased their powers while destroying the capacity of the trade unions to resist. The corporate state, too, was loaded in favour of employers, who continued to be represented by their traditional spokesmen, while the workforce had to depend on government lackeys. Thus all forms of industry, from mass production to small-scale sweatshops, were free from official regulations. Of course, parts of industry were adversely affected by the Great Depression, but they were given top priority by the government after 1933, either through investment from the IRI or through official approval of the spread of cartels. The latter effectively reduced competition between the industrial giants, making life easier at the top but also preventing any substantial modernization.

The landed gentry also maintained their status despite the depression. They were helped by government policies which were intended to maintain a large rural labour pool. In 1930, for example, the movement of rural workers to cities was allowed only by permission of local prefects, while in 1935 special workbooks (*libretto di lavoro*) were introduced. Also, despite Mussolini's original belief that Italy was a country of small landholders, the large estates were maintained undiminished. By 1930 the large landowners, who accounted for 0.5 per cent of the population, owned nearly 42 per cent of the land; the small landholders, 87 per cent of the rural population, owned a mere 13 per cent.

The lower middle class experienced mixed fortunes. Those in private enterprise were adversely affected by the economic circumstances of the 1930s, but those who entered state service did reasonably well for themselves. The complexity of the administration and the growth of the corporate state produced large numbers of civil service jobs. On the whole, wages were reasonably high and the fringe benefits considerable.

The rest of Italian society suffered severely, mainly for the same reasons that the upper classes benefited. The urban workers were tied down by the regulations introduced by the industrialists with government approval, and were also intimidated by the fact of high unemployment (about 2 million by 1932). The peasantry and agricultural workers were so badly affected that many defied government edicts and moved to the cities (particularly Rome, Milan and Turin) to swell the slum population. They were driven to this by a reduction in agricultural wages of up to 40 per cent during the 1930s. The working masses as a whole experienced a comparable decline in living standards; it has been estimated that the index of real wages fell between 1925 and 1938 by 11 per cent. Food became more expensive because, although retail prices moved downwards, they did not correspond to the reduction in wages. Moreover, Mussolini's obsession with the Battle for Grain meant the neglect of other foodstuffs and the wasteful use of marginal land. Hence, a whole range of essentials and luxury items like meat, fruit, vegetables, butter, sugar, wine and coffee became too expensive for many urban and rural workers. Mussolini recognized this development; he also justified it and, in the process, turned his back on his original guarantee of material well-being for all. 'We must', he said in 1936, 'rid our minds of the idea that what we have called the days of prosperity may return.'[78]

The impact of the Fascist regime on women is more complex. The usual view is that their status was deliberately and systematically depressed. Mussolini's Battle for Births placed women firmly in the roles of childbearing, family management and the homemaking sciences. This was underpinned by the Rocco Criminal Law of 1932 which banned contraception, sterilization and abortion, as well as enhancing the husband's authority over his wife in both financial and legal terms. During the 1930s a spate of edicts also restricted the participation of women in most branches of employment. By 1938 women were permitted to take up no more than 10 per cent of the total jobs available. Mussolini used this trend to control the levels of unemployment among men, but his justification was offensive and contemptuous: 'naturally a woman must not be a slave, but . . . in our state women must not count'.[79]

The impact of Fascism on women was therefore fundamentally negative. But two further factors need to be considered. One is that Fascist treatment of women was not particularly radical in a society which was already patriarchal and anti-feminist: almost all of Mussolini's laws on women had the full backing of the Catholic Church. What Mussolini did was not revolutionary, but rather an intensification of existing trends. The second point is that the impact of Fascism was uneven at the best of times. This was because the policies relating to women were constantly contradicted by other demands. For example, the population policy demanded an emphasis on the maternal role, while the crisis in the standard of living, which affected many Italians, made smaller families more sensible. Hence, according to De Grazia, 'Fascism spoke of the family as the pillar of the state, but family survival strategies in the face of terrible economic want accentuated the antistatist tendencies of Italian civil society.'[80] Another paradox was that the attempts to remove women from employment had to be reversed towards the end of the 1930s as the mobilization of men for war brought increased pressures on industry.

Did Fascism confer any real social benefits upon Italy? Some have, indeed, been identified. According to Gregor,[81] Fascist social welfare legislation compared favourably with the more advanced European nations and in some respects was more progressive. To take some examples, old-age pensions and unemployment benefits were both increased and medical care improved to the point that there was an appreciable decline in infant mortality and tuberculosis. Pollard maintains that the emphasis on increasing the birth rate led to 'the first attempt in Italian history to provide a universal and comprehensive antenatal care system and was thus one of the first steps in the establishment of an Italian National Health Service'.[82] Welfare expenditure also rose impressively – from 7 per cent of the budget in 1930 to 20 per cent in 1940, while the state spent 400 million lire on school-building between 1922 and 1942, compared with a mere 60 million spent between 1862 and 1922. Finally, the party provided welfare agencies known as EOAs (*ente opere assistenziali*) which co-ordinated relief funds for the unemployed, especially during the winter months. This has been seen as a 'capillary' structure which enhanced the general flow of relief to where it was most needed.[83]

On the other hand, state benefits, valuable though they were, could not in themselves make up for the heavy loss in earning power. In any case, many Italians dropped through any safety nets spread by the state. About 400,000 people lived in hovels made of mud and sticks, while others lived ten to a room. Poverty remained deeply rooted throughout the rural south where, in any case, other forms of control remained intact. Duggan's work has shown that Fascism made comparatively little impact on the Mafia. Although the regime claimed to have eradicated this criminal organization, all that happened was the development of a dual system. 'What was distinctive about Sicily in the 1930s was not that the mafia had been destroyed, but that the authorities could not use the word to describe the chaos.'[84] Hence, Fascism was unable to release this highly traditionalist brake on its few attempts at modernization.

Was it entirely the fault of the Fascist regime that so many Italians faced impoverishment? After all, the Italian economy had always been vulnerable and during the 1930s other industrial nations also suffered severely as a result of the Great Depression. While allowing for this, it is still possible to attribute many of Italy's problems directly to Fascist policy. The policies of the 1920s, especially the revaluation of the lira, pushed Italy into recession before the depression, and possible recovery in the 1930s was slowed down by preparation for war. It could be argued that even the population policy contributed directly to the falling standard of living. When the United States cut its annual quota of Italian immigrants to 4,000 in 1924, Mussolini did everything possible to promote migration from the United States to Italy. This reduced the remittances sent to Italy by workers in the United States by something like 90 per cent: from 5 billion lire per annum to 500 million. Given this ambivalent relationship between what Fascism inherited and what it did, we need to turn now to the attitudes of the people who were affected.

Attitudes to Mussolini's regime

Recent research on Germany and Russia has shown that the populations of these two countries were more involved in the actions of the regimes than was originally thought. Conversely, there was also more opposition. Much less research has been done on this in Italy, but it would be surprising if the same overall trend had not applied there as well. De Felice anticipated the first part of the argument when he maintained in 1974 that Mussolini had extensive support within Italy, especially during the 1930s. What is more difficult to accept, however, is that the support remained constant. Indeed, it now seems that Mussolini's regime was more subject to fluctuations than those of Hitler or Stalin and that there were more obvious peaks and troughs.

The first of the peaks was the 1924 election, which showed popular confidence that Mussolini could provide a political stability which had eluded the liberal governments. The second was the 1929 election in which some 90 per cent of Italian voters supported the regime. Even allowing for the absence of any real electoral alternative, this was not entirely a distortion of public political opinion. By 1929 many Italians had concluded that Fascism was offering a real chance of economic recovery as well as becoming more moderate by coming to terms with the Catholic Church; Mussolini appeared to be achieving a balance between totalitarian rule and respect for traditional institutions. The third peak in Mussolini's popularity came with the Italian conquest of Ethiopia between 1935 and 1936 which provided military victory, enhanced Italian nationalist aspirations and offered the prospects of increased international status.

Between these high points in the regime there were, however, alarming dips in public confidence. The first of these occurred in 1924 over the Matteotti Crisis: the turn of events so shocked the parliament and the press that the public response appeared to endanger the very base of Mussolini's government. The second trough, between 1932 and 1935, was caused by growing economic problems; these probably had a direct impact on Mussolini's decision to invade Ethiopia (see p. 140). The euphoria after military success was followed by a third downturn as a result of the increasing commitments to Hitler and the introduction of unpopular anti-Semitic policies. Mussolini never succeeded in regaining his former credibility and the disastrous involvement in the Second World War from 1940 onwards resulted in demands for his dismissal in 1943.

Beneath this zigzag response to Mussolini's leadership and policies there was a more consistent underlying attitude. As we saw in the previous section, estate owners had every reason to support Fascism whatever the aberrations of the moment, as did the leading industrialists and the clerical sections of the middle class. Other groups, such as the industrial and agricultural working classes, were more ambivalent, some joining the adulation in the peak periods, others remaining loyal to outlawed political groups such as the Socialists or Communists. The latter were to experience a sudden resurgence from 1943. Much of the population also managed to evade full participation in the activities sponsored by the regime even though it professed loyalty. This applied, for example, to 40 per cent of young people managing to keep out of 'compulsory' Fascist youth movements, as well as to lay Catholics who chipped away at the secularizing influence of Fascism in the schools. Mussolini's regime, therefore, was never as deeply rooted as those of Hitler and Stalin.

The attitudes of two groups are worth a more detailed examination: women and Catholics. These accounted for a substantial majority of the population.

The previous section considered how women were affected by Fascist social policies. How they reacted is more problematic. The reason for this is that Fascism was continuing and accentuating a traditional undercurrent within Italian society while, at the same time, also encountering cross-currents. The attitudes to women differed in the north and the south, the former coming more into line with liberalizing movements in Britain, France and the United States, the latter remaining more traditionalist. Hence, the changes brought by Fascism were more obvious in Milan and Turin than in Naples and Palermo. Women would also have had a wide variety of attitudes, which can be stereotyped only to a certain degree. Many in the middle classes would have strongly resented the impediments placed upon their professional development; others, however, would have been won over by the renewed emphasis on the family. The majority would have been unconvinced by the new twist given by Fascism to the traditional message of anti-feminism but would have resigned themselves to the inevitable, especially during the period of the depression. For most, the key factor was the impact of Fascist policies on the family, which meant a growing concern about the expenditure on armaments at the expense of consumerism. Above all, the hectic foreign policy pursued by Mussolini from 1935 onwards proved thoroughly disruptive to family life. This more than offset any appeal that Fascism might originally have had as a guarantor of family cohesion, whereas in Germany Nazism proved less disruptive, at least until 1939.

Catholic attitudes to Mussolini were also ambivalent. At first the Church hierarchy was won over by the Lateran agreements of 1929 and largely approved of what Mussolini did until the late 1930s. The Catholic laity, however, showed a lack of enthusiasm for the compromise between Church and state. The main ground of conflict was education. Catholic organizations, especially the youth wing of Catholic Action, continued to compete with the Balilla. This meant initially a division between the upper levels of the hierarchy and the rest of the Church. The leadership eventually came more into line with the laity in 1938 as a result of the introduction of the racial laws and the closer diplomatic relationship between Mussolini and Hitler.

But throughout the period it was Catholic Action, an organization for laymen, which took on the government. The main area of contention was the type of education intended for Italy's youth. An agreement was reached in 1931 whereby Catholic Action would confine its recreational and educational activities to a purely religious content and would not try to undermine Fascist ideology. By 1939, however, Catholic Action had developed a number of institutions for youth which drew membership away from the Fascist paramilitary organizations and which directly competed with official social and cultural groups. It seemed that while approving Mussolini's fight against alien beliefs abroad, within Italy the Church competed aggressively with Fascism for the soul of the people.

There were also political implications. Two other organizations sprang up in the 1930s – the FUCI, for university students and staff, and the Movimento Laureati which aimed, quite deliberately, to foster a new order. Together with Catholic Action, these proved to be a potential opposition. Indeed, according to a police report in Milan in 1935, Movimento Laureati could form 'in a few hours, the strongest and most important political party in Italy'.[85] As the Fascist regime entered a period of crisis after 1939, Catholic leaders began to take a direct initiative. Aldo Moro, for example, revitalized the FUCI, and what was almost an alternative government formed around De Gasperi in 1943. Bitterly disillusioned by military defeat,

Italians eventually shook off Fascism and returned in part to the traditional left, in part to Catholic politics – this time in the form of the Christian Democratic Party.

Overall, the attitude of the Italian mass of the population was still tacitly loyal to the regime in 1939, despite the hardships faced. From 1941, however, discontent grew rapidly as opposition turned into resistance and disobedience into insurrection and civil war. This was the result of Italy's catastrophic involvement in the Second World War – the culmination of an adventurist foreign policy, to which we now turn.

MUSSOLINI'S FOREIGN POLICY, 1922–40

Did Mussolini have a foreign policy?

In his first speech as Prime Minister to the Chamber of Deputies (1922), Mussolini proclaimed that 'Foreign policy is the area which especially preoccupies us.' His intention, he said on another occasion, was simple: 'I want to make Italy great, respected and feared.' He undertook to end Italy's traditional backstage role in European diplomacy; instead of picking up the scraps left by other powers in their rivalries with each other, Italy would seize the diplomatic initiative. As a result, she would be able to secure a revision of the post-First World War settlement – that 'mutilated victory' – and extensive territory in the Mediterranean and Africa.

Historians have not, however, been inclined to take Mussolini particularly seriously. At a very early stage in post-war historiography, he was attacked for being inconsistent and a dupe to Hitler. Salvemini wrote in 1953 that he was 'an irresponsible improviser, half madman, half criminal, gifted only – but to the highest degree – in the arts of "propaganda" and mystification'.[86] This view was more or less duplicated by A.J.P. Taylor in 1961:

> Everything about Fascism was a fraud. The social peril from which it saved Italy was a fraud; the revolution by which it seized power was a fraud; the ability and policy of Mussolini were fraudulent. Fascist rule was corrupt, incompetent, empty; Mussolini himself was a vain, blundering boaster without either ideas or aims.[87]

From the late 1960s historians responded to the opening of the Italian archives by providing more complex interpretations but, even so, there has been nothing like the sort of debate which has been caused by the foreign policies of Hitler and Stalin.

This section will, therefore, attempt an overall perspective on Mussolini's foreign policy which uses some of the themes applied to Germany and Russia. Mussolini is as entitled as any other leader to be considered a serious player on the European scene. Like Hitler, he combined traditional objectives with a new radical vision of the future. Like both Hitler and Stalin, he was an opportunist who took advantage of situations as they arose while, on occasions, seeking to force the pace through more projective action. Like them, he scored successes and made mistakes, although, in his case, the latter were more predominant. In addition, there was in Italy, as in

Germany and Russia, a close interconnection between foreign policy and domestic issues.

In outline, Fascist foreign policy was an amalgam of three main components. The first was a continuation of Italy's traditional objectives, which had been apparent before the First World War. The liberal state, established in 1861 and completed in 1870, had sought to increase its influence in Europe in a variety of ways. Diplomatically, it had allied with Germany and Austria-Hungary in 1882 and had also sought to expand Italy's influence within the Mediterranean and in the Balkans. An empire had been formed in Eritrea and Tripoli, and an attempt had been made to conquer Ethiopia, which failed on the plains of Adowa in 1896. By 1914 Italy was still unfulfilled as a major power and its involvement in the First World War was due to a calculated gamble, in the Treaty of London, that it was more likely to achieve its objectives on the side of Britain and France. Several of the objectives constantly referred to by Mussolini were therefore pre-Fascist. Italy already had expansionist aspirations in its immediate vicinity – conscious that it alone had not benefited here from the collapse of the Ottoman Empire in Europe. Italy was already a state with imperialist ambitions which were given more urgency by the 'martyrs' of Adowa. And Italy was already conscious of its importance in European diplomacy, with any decision to change sides being likely to affect the overall balance of power. Hence, there was nothing new about Mussolini's focus on the Balkans and the Mediterranean, his talk of conquest in Ethiopia, and his policies of 'equidistance' and side-changing in Europe.

The second element was a strong sense of disillusionment which followed the Paris Peace Settlement of 1919. Italy's gains by the Treaty of St Germain had been confined to South Tyrol and Trentino. This meant that Italy's share of territory from the collapsed Austria-Hungary was less than that received by Poland, Romania or Yugoslavia. There was no compensation in Istria, despite strong Italian representation for this at the Paris Conference, and nothing at all was forthcoming from the Turkish islands in the Aegean. Italy was, therefore, already a revisionist state. Nationalist and liberal parties attacked the settlement in parliament and post-war governments were half embarrassed, half pleased by the antics of D'Annunzio in Fiume. On coming to power in 1922 Mussolini therefore inherited an immediate agenda as well as longer-term aspirations.

What, therefore, did Mussolini provide? This was the third component, a Fascist vision for the future, based on the past – both recent and distant. The recent past had produced a united Italy, a country and a people seeking an identity based upon the modern nation state. This priority is often referred to as 'etatism', or directing the focus to the state itself. The distant past, however, provided traditions of power based on the Roman Empire. Mussolini sought to revive this heritage by giving Italy another base: the 'imperium' or empire. The ultimate aim was to transcend etatism by restoring the imperium; in essence, Fascism would bring the reincarnation of the Roman Empire into Italy.

These three influences between them point to a combination of continuity and radicalism in the policies pursued by Mussolini between 1922 and 1940. The ways in which these policies developed are considered below. The speed with which they unfolded varied considerably, depending on the influence of domestic factors (covered on pp. 143–4) and the international situation.

The development of Mussolini's foreign policy, 1922–40

Between 1922 and 1929 Mussolini was tempted by the longer-term aims of Italian statesmen and hoped to revise the Treaty of St Germain. He was, however, constrained by the growth of collective security abroad and by the need to play himself into power at home. The result was a period in which nothing much happened, apart from pinpointed aggression against Corfu and Fiume, unsuccessful anti-French diplomacy in eastern Europe and an unwilling participation in the Locarno Pact of 1925. By the end of the period his international standing was, nevertheless, high.

Between 1929 and 1934 the scope for a more active involvement began to increase, largely as a result of the Great Depression. This undermined international co-operation within Europe and helped bring Hitler to power in Germany. Mussolini seized the opportunity to pursue a policy of 'equidistance' between France and Britain on the one side and Germany on the other. Increasingly, however, Germany's intentions against Austria forced Mussolini over to collaboration with Britain and France, which culminated in the Stresa Front in 1935. Mussolini assumed from this that he could take the initiative and enter a more radical phase, something which was also being influenced by internal developments.

Between 1935 and 1940 Mussolini dispensed with all his earlier constraints. He brought Ethiopia into the Italian Empire between 1935 and 1936, assisted the Nationalists in the Spanish Civil War (1936–9) and invaded Albania in 1939. These developments interacted with the attempted mobilization of the economy and a radicalization of domestic policies. It also meant a swing away from equidistance to a closer connection with Germany: this started with the Rome–Berlin Axis in 1936 and culminated in the Pact of Steel in 1939 and Italy's entry into the Second World War in 1940. As will be seen later (pp. 142–3), Italy and Germany collectively unleashed chaos in Europe, into which were sucked all of Italy's aspirations in foreign policy, whether traditional or Fascist.

1922–9

During the 1920s Mussolini's foreign policy appeared somewhat erratic, alternating between aggression and conciliation. This, it would seem, was because he was constantly seeking to put pressure on the diplomatic fabric to see where it would yield. He aimed to be pragmatic and opportunist but sometimes became irrational, unable to resist the chance of swift glory cheaply bought. Where no such chance existed he had to moderate his activities.

The first instance of aggression was the Corfu Incident. On 21 August 1923 General Tellini and four other Italians were assassinated by terrorists while working for a boundary commission which was marking the border between Greece and Albania. Mussolini seized the opportunity to browbeat Greece, demanding compensation of 50 million lire and an official apology. When these did not materialize, he ordered the occupation of the Greek island of Corfu, clearly his original intention. Greece, however, appealed to the League of Nations which, in turn, referred the whole matter to arbitration by the Conference of Ambassadors. The outcome was a compromise which Mussolini accepted, with extreme reluctance, under strong British diplomatic pressure. Italian marines were pulled out of Corfu on 27 September and the Greek government paid the 50 million lire, but did not apologize. Within two weeks of the settlement of the Corfu Crisis, Mussolini tried again, this time more successfully. He installed an Italian commandant in Fiume, a city whose status was in dispute as it was claimed by both Italy and Yugoslavia. In this instance, Yugoslavia had no alternative but to agree to the Italian occupation as her main ally, France, was militarily involved in the Ruhr. Mussolini's victory was formalized in 1924 by the Pact of Rome.

By 1925, however, Mussolini was showing a more reasonable face – this time to the European powers. Stresemann, Briand and Austen Chamberlain, foreign ministers of Germany, France and Britain, were committed to international co-operation and the construction of a system of collective security. Mussolini was at first reluctant to involve Italy in any specific scheme, as it would limit his chances of a future diplomatic coup. Increasingly, however, he came under pressure from two directions. Externally, he was persuaded by French and British diplomats and was courted by Chamberlain, who particularly wanted Mussolini's participation. Internally, the more traditional and non-Fascist career diplomats of the Italian Foreign Ministry brought all their persuasiveness to bear.[88] The result was Mussolini's signature on the Locarno Pact. Partly as a result of this concession, British opinion of Mussolini became more favourable. Over Corfu he had shown a petulant outburst which seemed to go against the pragmatic trend of Italian diplomacy; Locarno seemed to indicate that he had at last moved to a more moderate and sensible course – in the tradition of Cavour.[89]

Or had he? Elsewhere in Europe Mussolini was doing what he could to destabilize the international scene. It could be argued that he was trying to make up for his lack of influence in western Europe by pressing particularly hard for advantages in the Balkans. He was resolutely hostile to French efforts to influence eastern Europe through a series of alliances. More fundamentally, Mussolini had conceived a deep dislike for France. This was partly ideological, as France harboured most of Italy's anti-Fascist exiles. It was also partly strategic, as France seemed to block the way to Italy's expansion in the Mediterranean and Africa. Hence, he tried to destroy the French system in eastern Europe and, in the process, to penetrate the Balkans. His main target was the French-sponsored Little Entente of Yugoslavia, Romania and Czechoslovakia. At first it appeared that he might break this by peaceful means. In 1924 he drew up a commercial agreement with Czechoslovakia and a treaty of friendship with Yugoslavia. But then he overreached himself in a sudden lunge for territory and glory. He became involved in the Albanian Civil War, supporting the rebel Noli against Yugoslavia's protégé, Zogu. Although Italy came to establish a virtual protectorate over Albania, Mussolini lost the chance to detach Yugoslavia from the French system. Indeed, the Little Entente tightened and Mussolini felt obliged to attempt to sponsor a counter-bloc consisting of Albania, Hungary and Bulgaria.

How successful had Mussolini been by 1929? On the one hand, his policies had been confined to the achievement of the possible: Mussolini's objectives were based at this stage on a limited étatist base and seemed to lack the broader sweep of the imperium. He was clearly frustrated by the restrictions imposed upon him by Italy's limited infrastructure but had not yet developed the confidence (or recklessness) to try to break through these. The positive side was that he was highly rated by British leaders. Churchill called him 'Roman genius in person' and Austen Chamberlain said, 'I trust his word when given and think we might easily go far before finding an Italian with whom it would be as easy for the British Government to work.'[90] On the other hand, there was still much unfinished business. Italy remained outflanked by French influence in the Balkans and there were times when the Locarno Pact seemed a major disadvantage; in helping guarantee the Rhine, Mussolini had freed French and German attention, which could now wander to central Europe, and Austria.

1930–5

The European situation changed between 1929 and 1934 as a result of the Great Depression. Multilateral co-operation through international institutions began to give way to bilateral agreements and rivalries. This situation clearly benefited Mussolini, since it gave him more room within which to manoeuvre.

Between 1930 and 1935 Mussolini aimed to make a more definite mark on European diplomacy by a more consistent and less random policy. In this way he would emerge, as he had always intended, as Europe's senior statesman and arbiter. It has been argued that, at this stage, Mussolini was capable of a shrewd and real-istic assessment of the European scene. His new device was to promote rival blocs, with Italy acting as mediator and maintaining a calculated equidistance between the powers involved. On one side would be France and Britain. On the other would be Germany, increasingly revisionist and determined to undermine the Versailles Settlement. Mussolini would commit Italy to neither; instead, he would create tensions or, alternatively, promote détente in such a way that Italy would always be the beneficiary. He may even have thought that Britain and France would become so dependent on Italian co-operation in containing Germany that they would have to grant major concessions in the Mediterranean and Africa. Should they ever take Italy for granted, Mussolini could always exert diplomatic pressure on them by producing the German card, or backing German revisionist claims. Either way, etatism would eventually expand into the imperium.

Before long, however, Mussolini found this card unplayable, for Germany came to pose an even greater threat to Italian interests than had France. The source of the trouble was Austria. It was well known that the German right had long favoured the absorption of this rump of the former Austro-Hungarian Empire, a danger which increased with Hitler's appointment as Chancellor in January 1933. Mussolini was desperately anxious to avoid this Anschluss, since he regarded Austria as an Italian client state and as a military buffer zone. A crisis occurred in 1934 when the Austrian Nazi Party was involved in the assassination of the Austrian Chancellor, Dollfuss. Fearing that Hitler would use the chaos within Austria as an excuse to annex it, Mussolini sent Italian troops to the frontier. Meanwhile, he was forced to swallow his previous prejudices and seek closer ties with France – who also dreaded the prospect of an enlarged Germany. He therefore dropped his designs on the Balkans, and in January 1935 formed an accord with France. This was followed, in April, by the Stresa Front in which Mussolini joined Britain and France in condemning German rearmament, announced by Hitler in the previous month.

Could this be the answer? Although forced by events in Austria to give up his preferred strategy of equidistance, Mussolini seemed, nevertheless, to have recovered a degree of diplomatic security. Could he now seize the initiative which had so long eluded him? Mussolini seized the opportunity offered by discussions with the French Foreign Minister, Laval, in January 1935. From these emerged an unwritten agreement that Laval would tolerate a free hand in Ethiopia for Italy in return for Mussolini's undertaking that he would back France in future against German expansion into Austria.

Mussolini was now ready to abandon equidistance in Europe, with its etatist base, in favour of expansionism in Africa, with the more direct pursuit of the imperium. This was to be the turning-point of his career and of Italy's stability in Europe.

1935–40

From 1935 Italy entered a period of hectic activity, behaving in every way like an expansionist power (see Map 3). In the process, however, Mussolini committed Italy irrevocably and disastrously to an alliance with Germany.

The first step was the Italian conquest of Ethiopia (1935–6). The motives were partly internal; as is shown in the next section, the cult of the Duce required a boost which only a successful war could provide. But there was also a powerful ideological impetus: a Fascist yearning for expansion and conquest which accentuated the traditional Italian commitment to colonies. The diplomatic scene seemed to favour a swift and decisive stroke. Britain had acknowledged an Italian role in the Horn of Africa ever since 1906 and the French appeared willing in 1935 to grant a carte blanche. As far as the German threat was concerned, an Italian victory in Africa would deter Hitler from any further action over Austria and could be accomplished sufficiently rapidly to restore an Italian military presence in the Danube area.

The Ethiopian War was sparked by the Wal Wal Incident. In December 1934 a party of Italians was fired upon at an oasis on the Ethiopian side of the border with Italian Somaliland. An immediate apology was demanded from Ethiopia, since Italy claimed the right to use Wal Wal. The matter was, however, referred to the League of Nations, while Italy prepared, over the next ten months, for a full-scale invasion of Ethiopia. All seemed well for Mussolini, particularly since Britain and France were unwilling to condemn his attitude. When the League eventually refused to apportion blame for the Wal Wal Incident, Mussolini decided to go ahead with the invasion; this commenced, from Eritrea, in October 1935, under the leadership of Graziani and De Bono. Italian troops won a major victory at Adowa, erasing the humiliating memory of defeat there in 1896. In November, however, a sinister development occurred with Badoglio's use of poison gas against Ethiopian troops and civilians. This time the League responded more decisively by applying, from October, economic sanctions against Italy. Unfortunately, these were largely ineffectual since they excluded vital materials like oil, coal, iron and steel. It also appeared that Britain and France were willing to connive at Mussolini's conquests. The Hoare–Laval Pact of December 1935 would have given Italy northern and southern Ethiopia, leaving an independent state in the centre. This scheme was leaked to the press and eventually howled down by public opinion. Nevertheless, nothing was done to prevent the Italian advance on Addis Ababa, which fell in May 1936.

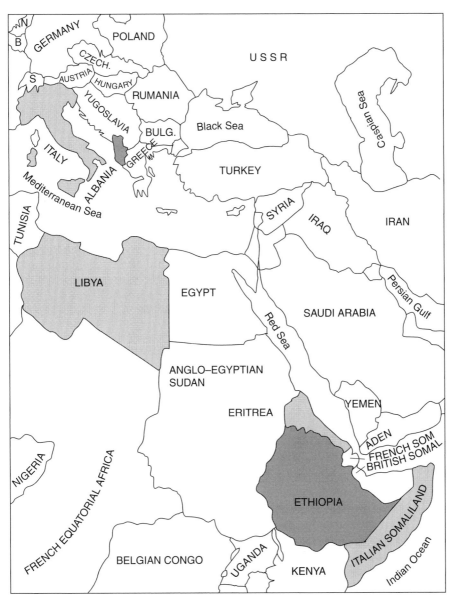

Possessions before 1930

Acquisitions during the 1930s

Map 3 The Italian overseas empire by 1939

The Ethiopian War had momentous results. For example, it narrowed the range of Mussolini's future diplomatic options. Britain and France were alienated by the method of conquest and were never to trust Mussolini again. Germany was considerably strengthened, as Hitler used Mussolini's involvement in Africa, together with the diversion this caused to Britain and France, to remilitarize the Rhineland in 1936. Mussolini had seriously miscalculated; Hitler had reacted far more rapidly than he had expected and, to make matters worse, Austria was more vulnerable than ever before. From 1936 Germany exerted a profound influence on Italy, based on growing diplomatic confidence and military strength. Within Italy this influence took the form of a racial programme, while externally Mussolini was hoping to synchronize his own ideology with Hitler's Nazism to produce a century of Fascism.

From 1936 a policy of consolidation would have made most sense, giving Italy the chance to replace losses caused by the Ethiopian War. Yet even before this conflict had ended Mussolini had made another commitment – this time to assisting Franco's National Front against the Spanish Republic. Involvement in the Spanish Civil War was motivated partly by an obsessive hatred of left-wing popular-front governments. The future, he wanted to proclaim, lay with Fascism, nationalism and right-wing militarism. It might well be possible to establish Italian influence over a series of fascist or semi-fascist states in the Mediterranean; influence over Spain, for example, could well lead to control over Salazar's Portugal. In strategic terms, this would weaken Britain's naval position in the western Mediterranean and make Gibraltar extremely vulnerable. It would mean that the Soviet Union would lose Spain as a potential ally and that France would be outflanked by three hostile states – Spain, Italy and Germany. There was also a military motive for involvement, as Italy could test the efficiency of her armed forces in a different theatre of war. Italian contributions to the Nationalist cause were considerable. By 1937 50,000 Italian troops were active in Spain and the total death-toll had reached 6,000. Mussolini also provided 763 aircraft and 1,672 tons of bombs, 950 tanks and 7,663 motor vehicles, 1,930 cannon and 240,747 small arms, and the use of 91 warships – all at a total cost of 14 billion lire.[91] Admittedly, other governments became involved; Hitler also supplied Franco, and Stalin assisted the Republic. There is no doubt, however, that Italy's sacrifices were by far the largest.

To what effect? Italy's involvement can be seen as a major blunder. Certainly Mussolini was unable to make up the loss of equipment before the outbreak of the Second World War. This was to prove very serious. Both Britain and France, convinced that Italy was now irrevocably hostile, began from 1937 to rearm at a pace which Italy, with her smaller industrial base, could not match. While all the other major powers were stronger in 1939 than they had been in 1936, Italy was undeniably weaker. The full extent of her vulnerability was not yet known, but clues were provided by the humiliation of the Italians by Spanish Republican forces at Guadalajara. Nor was there any real gratitude from Franco, who would agree only to guarantee Spanish neutrality in any conflict between Italy and another power. More than ever, Mussolini had to depend on Germany. He tried to ignore the uncomfortable truth that war, and the policy of autarky which accompanied it, had disrupted Italian trade and allowed Germany to penetrate Italy's markets in the Balkans. He therefore had to swallow his personal dislike of Hitler and give Italy up to what F.W.D. Deakin has termed the 'Brutal Friendship'.

This connection between Italy and Germany was formalized by the Rome–Berlin Axis, a term first used by Mussolini in a speech delivered in Milan on 1 November 1936. This followed a visit by the Italian Foreign Minister, Ciano, to Berlin and Berchtesgaden to secure an agreement on joint intervention in Spain. Both Germany and Italy were well satisfied. Germany had succeeded in pulling Italy into her corner. As von Hassell, German ambassador in Rome, had observed, the Spanish Civil War was reinforcing the lesson of the Ethiopian War and Italy was realizing 'the advisability of confronting the western powers shoulder-to-shoulder with Germany'.[92] The Axis was further tightened by the signing of the Anti-Comintern Pact with Germany and Japan in November 1937 and the Pact of Steel (May 1939) which committed Germany and Italy to mutual support in any offensive or defensive war. Italy, for her part, was momentarily enjoying the sensation of power. In 1937 Ciano exulted: 'The situation of 1935 has been transformed. Italy has broken out of her isolation: she is in the centre of the most formidable political and military combination which has ever existed.'[93]

Unfortunately for Mussolini, Germany's seniority in the Rome–Berlin Axis soon became obvious. Hitler forced the pace, and some of his actions showed open contempt for Mussolini. In March 1938, for example, he gave Rome only a few hours' notice before sending German troops into Austria. This has been seen as the beginning of the end of Fascist Italy as 'the shadow of the predatory and overwhelming force of pan-Germanism'[94] fell over her. It is true that Mussolini managed to regain some of his stature as a mediator at the Munich Conference in September 1938, but this was because it suited Hitler to cast Mussolini temporarily in this role, before returning to his customary offhand manner. On two occasions in 1939 Mussolini was given virtually no advance notice of German intentions: the occupation of Bohemia in March and the conclusion of the Nazi–Soviet Pact in August. Yet, amazingly, Mussolini's government failed to monitor the wording of the Pact of Steel which bound Italy militarily to Germany; instead, Ciano virtually gave a blank cheque to his German counterpart, von Ribbentrop. Mussolini was also deceived over Hitler's timetable. He had assumed in May 1939 that Germany was not intending to fight a war before 1943 at the earliest. When Germany invaded Poland in September 1939, Mussolini was severely embarrassed by Italy's total inadequacy to meet the commitments of the Pact of Steel. Ciano had to submit to Berlin a list of strategic *matériel* urgently needed by Italy. When Germany offered only a small quantity, Mussolini had no option but to seek from Hitler a temporary release from his military obligations. Part of the problem was that Italy's resources had been overextended by Mussolini's attack on Albania in April; he could not afford now to rush into a conflict with France and Britain which Hitler had so inconveniently provoked. Even so, for a man with such a huge ego, this peace was a humiliation, to be reversed at the earliest opportunity.

The interconnection between foreign policy and domestic issues

It has become increasingly common in historical writing to point out the close links between foreign and domestic policies. Much has been made of the attempts made by rulers like Napoleon III and Wilhelm II to mobilize popular support and maintain domestic harmony through the deliberate use of aggressive diplomacy, territorial expansion and war. Most observers see the same tendency in Mussolini's policy and would agree with Morgan's assessment that the 'customary separation of foreign and domestic matters' can be 'artificial and distorting'. Instead, 'Internal and external policies were explicitly linked and interacted in a synchronised way.'[95]

There is, however, some difference over the extent of his calculation, especially over the decision to invade Ethiopia. Perhaps the grandest conception has been put forward by De Felice, who sees Fascism as a 'revolutionary phenomenon' which aimed at the 'mobilization of the masses and the creation of a new kind of man'.[96] This had not been accomplished during the 1920s by domestic policies and clearly a new impetus was needed. This would be external expansion; hence 'the Ethiopian question was not only one of waging war, but also principally of creating the new Fascism after the conquest of the empire'.[97] In terms of generating a new spirit and mobilizing support behind the Duce, the Ethiopian War was Mussolini's political masterpiece and his greatest success.

Another Italian writer, Carocci, emphasizes the search for an instant remedy rather than the achievement of a grand design. By 1935, he argues, the situation at home was potentially dangerous: 'People all over the country felt indifferent to the regime, detached from it. In order to overcome these feelings, in order to galvanise the masses and try to break the vicious circle of economic crisis, more drastic and more attractive measures were needed.'[98] De Grand partly disagrees with this – but in terms of the timing rather than the principle. He maintains that the decision was not born of desperation; there were 'no compelling economic imperatives in Italy for expansion in 1934 and 1935. The worst crisis of the depression had been overcome.'[99] Nevertheless, he adds, the decision for the invasion was made at the peak of the economic crisis in 1932. Mack Smith argues that the purpose of Mussolini's foreign policy was to bolster his prestige, which by the mid-1930s had been affected by economic strain. The device used was propaganda on a massive scale; indeed, 'any history of Mussolini's foreign policy has to be . . . a history of propaganda'.[100] The whole process created an addiction; the addiction led to self-delusion. Increasingly Mussolini was misled by his own pronouncements, pursued erratic policies and ignored basic facts. Such an argument was also adopted by contemporaries of Mussolini. Salvemini, an exile from Fascist Italy, identified Mussolini as 'a buffoon, a sawdust Caesar', living hand-to-mouth in a desperate effort to make his foreign exploits rally support for his domestic measures and to stabilize the base of his regime.

Some historians remain unconvinced by this type of argument. Knox,[101] for one, sees in Mussolini's expansionism a genuine vision – equivalent to Hitler's quest for Lebensraum. Foreign policy did not proceed from 'internal social or political pressures'. Indeed, what happened in the 1930s was the opposite of 'social imperialism'. To extend this line of reasoning, it might be said that Fascism was an ebullient ideology which had to turn outwards in order to seek sublimation in struggle, militarism and conquest. This approach would reduce the emphasis on domestic problems in the mid-1930s. It could be argued that Mussolini's personality cult had already won the battle for popular acceptance and support; it now had to be justified by action. After all, Italians had been led to believe, it was better to live 'one day as a lion than a thousand years as a lamb'.

WAR AND COLLAPSE, 1940–5

Italy in the Second World War

Italy's neutrality, announced by Mussolini on 3 September 1939, came to an end with his declaration of war on Britain and France on 10 June 1940. Why did he change his mind?

During the intervening months the situation in Europe had been transformed. Hitler's Blitzkrieg had crushed Poland within four weeks and his offensive in the west had brought the collapse of Norway, Holland and Belgium. Mussolini, therefore, felt that he had little to fear. Italy would not be committing herself to a prolonged struggle, as France was on the point of defeat and it was only a matter of time before Britain fell. Hence, there was a chance for Mussolini to erase the humiliating memory of non-belligerence by joining Hitler as an equal partner in a great Axis offensive. He envisaged a short conflict, lasting perhaps only a few weeks, and followed by a conference at which Italy would receive the spoils due to a victorious power.

These expectations were not fulfilled. Italian troops made slow progress in the Alpine War against a severely weakened France, managing to win only a few square miles of territory. The main disappointment was that Hitler was unwilling to hand France's North African colonies to Italy, preferring to leave them and the French Mediterranean fleet under the puppet Vichy regime to ensure the latter's permanent collaboration with Germany. Nor could Mussolini expect easy compensation in the form of British territory in Africa: the Royal Navy was still active in the Mediterranean and the long-awaited German invasion of Britain had not materialized. Once again there was the danger that Italy would play a totally subordinate role to Germany – unless, of course, Mussolini could regain the initiative.

He attempted to do so in the 'parallel war'. The intention was to develop an Italian sphere of influence in the Balkans and North Africa, leaving Germany to dominate northern Europe. Hence, in September 1940, he launched an Italian invasion of British Egypt from Libya and, in October, attacked Greece. But his hopes of a new Roman Empire covering most of the eastern Mediterranean were swiftly shattered. The Greeks repulsed the Italian attack and Hitler had to mount an extensive rescue operation in the Balkans in 1941; when, eventually, Greece and Yugoslavia did fall, it was to the Germans not the Italians. The British, meanwhile, counter-attacked from Egypt, achieving major successes under Wavell early in 1941. Again, the Germans had to take over and Mussolini was partly relieved, partly humiliated by the successful campaigns of Rommel. No rescue was possible, however, in the Horn of Africa where, during the course of 1941, Italy lost to British Empire troops her prized colonies of Somaliland, Eritrea and Ethiopia.

Floundering badly in the sort of prolonged war which he had not anticipated, Mussolini became increasingly desperate and irrational. He proved entirely willing to go along with Hitler in widening the scope of the war. In 1941, for example, he pressed on Hitler a total of 61,000 Italian troops to assist the German invasion of the Soviet Union. In the same year he declared war on the United States in the naïve belief that America was a degenerate power which could never adapt a consumer-based economy to military needs. He placed increasing emphasis on ideology, envisaging an ultimate Fascist triumph over the forces and theories of Bolshevism and liberal democracy. Yet, despite his attempts to retain at least some influence over the Axis alliance, the reality was that Italy's dependence on Germany was now total.

The trouble was that Germany was now beginning to lose ground. From late 1942 German forces in North Africa and on the eastern front were heavily assailed by Montgomery, Eisenhower and Zhukov. Hitler's priority was the Russian campaign, which involved drawing off German troops and supplies from North Africa. This sealed Italy's fate. The Western Allies won back North Africa early in 1943 and, at the Casablanca Conference, agreed that the first attacks on Axis-controlled Europe should be directed against Italy as its 'soft underbelly'. Consequently, British and American troops landed in Sicily in July 1943. Even before they crossed over to mainland Italy, Mussolini had been removed from power. On 8 September the new Italian government officially surrendered to the Allies. The Germans, however, occupied northern Italy, delaying final victory for the next eighteen months.

Reasons for the Italian defeat

One of the main factors in the Italian defeat was the series of disastrous decisions taken by Mussolini himself, often against the advice of his ministers. The first of these was to commence hostilities in June 1940 with the full knowledge that the Italian Commission on War Production had warned that Italy could not sustain a single year of warfare until 1949. The second was to initiate a 'parallel war' when it seemed unlikely that Germany would co-operate with Italian designs on French colonies; Mussolini's invasion of Greece in October 1940 was a botched attempt to gain territory in the other direction to compensate for this disappointment. The third error was to commit Italy so lightly and with so little thought of the consequences against the world's two industrial and military giants, the United States and the Soviet Union. The former played a vital part in rolling back the Axis occupation of North Africa, while the latter drained off the Axis troops needed to prevent this. Of the three mistakes, the first was the most catastrophic, as it made Italy entirely dependent on German military success. Hitler destroyed Mussolini's chances of swift victory by broadening his own objectives to fit into his own visionary scheme, and the invasion of Russia doomed Fascist Italy long before it brought about the collapse of the Third Reich.

Italy's armed forces were inadequate to the demands placed upon them by Mussolini. Earlier losses incurred in the Ethiopian War (1935–6) and the Spanish Civil War (1936–9) had not been made up and there was, by 1940, a hollow ring to Mussolini's boast that Italy could mobilize 8 million men within hours. In fact, the Italian army in 1940 comprised a total of 3 million men, who were inadequately supplied with 1.3 million rifles (of 1891 design); the most reliable weapons proved to be those captured from the Austrians at the end of the First World War. The army had only 42,000 vehicles, including obsolete tanks and armoured cars which could be pierced by rifle fire. Ignorant of these deficiencies, Mussolini gambled everything on a lightning war – or *guerra lampo* – the equivalent to Hitler's Blitzkrieg. In practice this strategy was inoperable, partly because Italy had no equivalent to Germany's panzer divisions and partly because Italian generals were intensely suspicious of such methods; they regarded the tank as having little practical application to the demands of warfare either in Europe or in North Africa. The army was also poorly organized and the mobilization of August 1939 was so inept that it is doubtful whether Italy could have entered the war at that stage even if Mussolini had decided to do so. There was virtually no co-operation with either the German government or the German High Command, in complete contrast to the joint planning undertaken by the Western Allies in their conquest of North Africa and France.

Of the other two services, the navy was the better equipped and had actually been admired by Hitler in the mid-1930s. Yet here, too, there were serious deficiencies. Italian warships were designed essentially for speed, which meant that their heavy fuel consumption limited their effective range to 6,500 miles. No aircraft carriers were built, as Mussolini believed that Italy was herself a 'natural aircraft carrier'. Although eight battleships were under construction in 1939, the incredible fact remains that not one of them hit an enemy ship with its shells. Italy did possess the world's largest fleet of submarines but they were notoriously slow to submerge and losses amounted to 10 per cent within the first weeks of war. Italy's airforce was also defective. Mussolini had once boasted that he could make the skies black with Italian aircraft, but in reality Italian production was far below that of the other Axis powers, Germany and Japan. The quality was also suspect, and the RAF had comparatively little difficulty in knocking out the Fiat CR 42, the Fiat G 50 and the Macchi MC 200. Matters were made even worse by the refusal of the airforce leadership to co-ordinate its plans with the army and navy. Unlike the Luftwaffe and the RAF, the Italian airforce always demanded, and received, special autonomy. This was part of a long-term rivalry between the three services, which made combined operations virtually impossible. Hence, according to Whittam, 'Military weakness had been built into the regime from the very start.'[102]

Underlying Italy's military weakness was a severely limited economic and industrial base. Mussolini's policy of self-sufficiency had failed to solve the problem of the shortage of strategic *matériel* and, as we have seen, Germany was slow to respond to Ciano's appeals for help in August 1939. Italy went against the overall trend for industrial nations by experiencing between 1940 and 1943 a decrease in production of 35 per cent in industry and 25 per cent in agriculture. The figure which most effectively conveys Italy's limitations as an industrial power is that for steel production: 2.4 million tons in 1939, compared with Britain's 13.4 million and Germany's 22.5 million. This meant that Italy had serious problems in converting her limited industrial infrastructure to sustained warfare. Kennedy estimates that Italy's 'war potential' in 1937 was only 2.5 per cent of the combined total of all the great powers, compared with Germany's 14.4 per cent, Britain's 10.2 per cent and the Soviet Union's 14.0 per cent.[103] Between 1940 and 1941 Italy's expenditure on armaments rose from $0.75 billion to $1.0 billion: the comparable figures for Britain over the same period were $3.5 billion and $6 billion.[104]

The problem was, of course, partly historic, as Italy had industrialized at a later stage than her competitors. But the responsibility rests also with the policies of Fascism, as Italy was less prepared for war in 1940 even than she had been in 1915. Germany was able to increase its levels of production from 1941 onwards by converting to 'Total War' (see pp. 231–3); Italy, however, was already in economic overdrive by 1940. It is often thought that Germany had to help Mussolini by shoring up Italy from then onwards. This certainly applied militarily, but there is more doubt concerning economic contributions. Indeed, the overall balance may even have worked against Italy; according to Morgan, 'Germany began to extract more from Italy than she gave.'[105] For example, Germany made use of 350,000 Italian workers, many of whom were skilled specialists. This was partly responsible for the growing internal resentment which brought about the collapse of Mussolini's regime in 1943.

The fall of Mussolini

Military disaster provoked a wave of disillusionment with Mussolini's regime. Taken in by his own propaganda, the Duce was totally unaware of the dangers; as Mack Smith observes, 'he had got used to living in cloud-cuckoo land'.[106] There was increasingly widespread opposition to German ideological and military influence; in March and April 1943 there were extensive strikes and protests, which the police were powerless to prevent.[107] There was also resentment at the rapid fall in living conditions: Italians had to put up with some of the worst hardships suffered by civilians anywhere in Europe. There was, finally, pressure for peace from those traditional groups which had once collaborated with Fascism – the industrialists and military leaders like Badoglio and Caviglia. Even the Church tried to disentangle itself from the regime, and now swung its support behind the King rather than Mussolini. The Fascist Party proved incapable of rallying the population to face adversity and was itself demoralized by the internal convulsions brought about by Mussolini himself.

Indeed, Mussolini set in motion the chain reaction of events which led to his collapse. In February 1943 he sacked Grandi, Bottai and others from high office within the Fascist Party. This provoked a set of conspiracies in which De Grand has identified two main elements. The first involved the traditionalist pre-Fascist politicians and military leaders, the second the moderate Fascists who hoped to dump Mussolini and replace him with Caviglia. With the Allied landings in Sicily, the conspirators decided on drastic measures. At a session of the Fascist Grand Council in July 1943 Mussolini was attacked by Grandi, Bottai and Ciano for his conduct of the war. They called for the full restoration of the legal organs of the state and the dismissal of Mussolini himself. This motion was eventually carried by nineteen votes to seven and Grandi explained the decision to the bewildered Duce: 'You believe you have the devotion of the people . . . You lost it the day you tied Italy to Germany.'[108] The following day Mussolini was dismissed by King Victor Emmanuel and imprisoned at the Gran Sasso. Marshal Badoglio was appointed as the new Prime Minister.

Why was Mussolini so powerless to prevent this startling turn of events? The answer lies in the delicate balance between the different powers and institutions within Italy, which Mussolini had been so careful to maintain. Under the strain of war this balance was destroyed and Mussolini was left without any political protection. During the 1930s he had missed the opportunity of giving the Fascist Party greater unity and had deliberately encouraged the growth of cliques in order to pursue a policy of divide and rule. This recoiled on him in 1943; he could rely on only a single group led by Farinacci, while the majority of the Fascist leaders turned against him, charging him with having deliberately distorted the Fascist movement. This meant, in Pollard's description, that 'The overthrow of Fascism when it came was essentially a "palace revolution".'[109]

Mussolini's vulnerability was intensified by the existence of an alternative form of leadership in Italy. Unlike Hitler, Mussolini had never assumed all the powers of head of state. The monarchy, which had been left intact, became a rallying point for the Italian army in 1943, while the coup against Mussolini was backed by Victor Emmanuel himself. In addition, Mussolini never placed his personal stamp on the Italian army. The oath of allegiance, for example, was still to the state and not to the Duce in person. Nor had he managed to create an entirely loyal military elite like Hitler's Waffen SS. He had also been less careful than Hitler in anticipating trouble from his generals, and had not taken the trouble to shuffle their positions to prevent plotting or the build-up of opposition. Even his intelligence service was defective, for he was taken completely by surprise by the July coup. Despite his known contempt for Mussolini, Hitler was astounded by the suddenness of the Duce's fall and asked: 'What is this sort of Fascism which melts like snow before the sun?'

The Italian Social Republic, 1943–5: a return to the beginning?

Mussolini was rescued from the mountain stronghold of Gran Sasso on 12 September 1943 by a German glider-borne expedition. He was taken to Germany, where plans were made for the formation of a new Fascist state in that part of Italy which had not yet been occupied by the Allies. The headquarters of the regime were at Lake Garda, while the leadership was provided by three main types of Fascist. There were pro-Nazis like Pavolini, Ricci, Farinacci and Preziosi; opportunists like Graziani, who had no military future under the royal government in Rome; and those like Pini who remained devoted to Mussolini himself.

It has been said that the new Repubblica Sociale Italiana (RSI), the Italian Social Republic, alternatively known as the Salo Republic, represents a return to the beginning of the Fascist movement. The plot of 25 July showed Mussolini how treacherous the monarchy and the old establishment could be. Shorn of his alliance with those traditional institutions, the argument continues, Mussolini was free to revive his early ideological preferences. Once again, he became anti-monarchist and displayed the kind of radicalism which had been absent from Fascism for many years. He also returned to a type of socialism which once again attacked capitalism. Instead of allying with industrialists, he now intended to 'annihilate the parasitic plutocracies and . . . make labour the object of our economy and the indestructible foundation of the state'.[110] A new programme was devised at Verona in November 1943, followed by the socialization law of February 1944. Key industries were to be nationalized, workers were to participate in factory and business management, land reform was to be initiated and there were to be wage and price controls. Overall, he hoped to rebuild the original connection between radical nationalists, syndicalist workers and activist Fascist squads.

From the start, however, the Italian Social Republic proved a pale imitation, even a mockery, of the early Fascist movement. For one thing, it had lost all control over its own destiny, as Mussolini was now heavily dependent on Germany. All decisions made by the Republic had to go through German Ambassador Rahn or SS General Wolff, while eight north-eastern provinces in South Tyrol, Venetia and the Adriatic were removed from the republic and placed under direct German administration. Pollard points out the similarity between the Salo Republic and other puppet regimes such as Vichy France, Tiso's Slovakia and Pavelić's Croatia.[111] In addition, the republic held few of the former attractions for the various sectors of the population. Workers and peasants, who had once deserted the left for Fascism, now abandoned Fascism to return to the socialist and communist left. They took part in strikes and demonstrations and joined the Italian resistance movement. Industrialists saw no advantages in Mussolini's new radicalism and did everything in their power to prevent the implementation of the 1944 Decree Law. By 1945, therefore, only a few dozen enterprises had been nationalized. Finally, the mainstay of Fascism, the lower middle class, became resentful at the decline in living standards caused by prolonging the war against the Allies. They, too, switched their allegiance and once more craved parliamentary politics. It seemed that Italy had been jolted back into its pre-Fascist course and that the Social Republic had become totally inappropriate.

What occurred between 1943 and 1945, therefore, was a major internal upheaval. Three struggles have been analysed. One was a patriotic resistance by Italians to the German occupation. The second was a civil war between Fascists and anti-Fascists, each side numbering about 150,000. The third is a class war in which the most organized section of the resistance, the partisans, was dominated by communists. Some historians have concluded from this that the communist offensive in the north was the key factor in the struggle against both the Germans and the Italian Fascists. In one respect this can be seen in a positive light – as communism played the leading role in northern Italy's liberation. Alternatively, it can be viewed as a crude ideological conflict with Fascism, with the majority of ordinary Italians trapped between the two extremes; this is very much the view of De Felice. Most historians, however, see the communists as part of a broader spectrum. Procacci, for instance, maintains that the resistance 'was above all a very wide political movement. It had been the achievement not only of the workers who had sabotaged and the men of the military formations who had fought, but also of the peasants who had fed them and the priests who had hidden them'.[112] Hence, the anti-Fascists also comprised Catholics, Christian Democrats and some liberal monarchists.

The end

The collapse of the Italian Social Republic, although delayed by eighteen months, was inevitable. It was rent with dissension as extremists like Farinacci and Pavolini hunted down the traitors of 25 July, to the alarm of the moderates. The republic seemed to focus on revenge rather than unity; at Verona, for example, Ciano and several others were found guilty of treason and executed. Mussolini himself became bitterly disillusioned and cursed the Italian people for their soft character and dislike of vigorous action. He came to the conclusion that Italy was not, after all, the historical heir to ancient Rome, but a nation of serfs. As for his government, it was almost entirely in foreign hands. Northern Italy had been divided into two sectors

– one under direct German administration, the other under German influence. In the latter, which included the republic, the German army introduced a set of institutions which ran parallel to those of Mussolini and also controlled the entire network of communications between Mussolini's ministries.

Mussolini's survival now depended entirely on German military fortunes. In April 1945, however, German resistance collapsed as the Allies broke through the Commacchio Line and the Argento Gap. After the surrender of General Wolff to the Allies, Mussolini fled from Milan with his mistress, Clara Petacci. They were picked up by partisans on the Lake Como road and, on 28 April, were shot against the gates of a villa. The final indignity was the public exhibition of the mutilated corpses, along with those of Farinacci and other leading Fascists, in the Piazzale Loreto in Milan. By a cruel irony, Mussolini had once said (referring to the martial spirit of Fascism) that 'Everybody dies the death that corresponds to his character.'[113]

Chapter 4

Dictatorship in Germany

Adolf Hitler was appointed Chancellor on 30 January 1933. His rise to power and the decline of the Weimar Republic are sufficiently complex to justify a preliminary section relating the main developments up to that date before proceeding to look at explanations.

THE WEIMAR REPUBLIC AND THE RISE OF HITLER, 1918–33

The formation and development of the Weimar Republic, 1918–29

The Weimar Republic was born of military defeat and revolution at the end of the First World War. Under the threat of military collapse the Kaiser's Second Reich was transformed into the Weimar Republic during what has come to be known as the 'German Revolution'.[1]

This occurred in two phases. The first was a revolution from above as, early in October 1918, the military establishment handed over power to a civilian cabinet. The High Command, under Ludendorff and Hindenburg, sensed the inevitability of defeat and tried to ease the way towards an armistice with the Allies by advising Kaiser Wilhelm II to appoint Prince Max of Baden as Chancellor. A powerful underlying motive was the army's desire to avoid any direct blame for Germany's surrender, when it came. The Allied response, however, was unfavourable; President Wilson argued that the German power structure was still intact and that he could deal only with a genuine democracy. Prince Max now prevailed upon the Kaiser to dismiss Ludendorff from his command and it seemed that, despite the Allies' reservations, the Second Reich had the most genuinely representative government since its formation in 1871.

The second phase was a revolution from below which brought down the Second Reich altogether. In late October and early November the sailors of the German fleet mutinied in Kiel and Wilhelmshaven, while military discipline was also subverted in Hamburg and Cologne. Similarly dramatic events occurred in the south, as Kurt Eisner declared Bavaria an independent republic. Prince Max, fearing the complete disintegration of Germany, resigned on 9 November, to be replaced as Chancellor by the leader of the Social Democrats, Friedrich Ebert. On the same day the Kaiser and the lesser German rulers abdicated, and a republic was proclaimed by another Social Democrat, Philipp Scheidemann, from the balcony of the Reichstag building in Berlin. Scheidemann's concluding words were: 'The old and rotten – the monarchy – has broken down. Long live the new! Long live the German Republic.'[2] Two days later, on 11 November, Germany signed an armistice with the Allies.

But the German Revolution was not yet complete. The country now experienced a brief period of civil war as rival groups of the left competed for power. The main contenders were the Social Democrats (SPD) and two more radical groups, the Independent Socialists (USPD) and the Spartacists. At first a Provisional Government was established, comprising both the SPD and the USPD. The former, however, were afraid that Germany might follow the example of Russia the year before, and that the Provisional Government would be destroyed by a coup from the radical left, perhaps from the Spartacists. To prevent this, Chancellor Ebert made a controversial deal with the army commander, General Groener, to put down any Bolshevik-style revolution which might occur. The test was not long in coming. In December the Independent Socialists withdrew from the government, while the Spartacists (who now called themselves Communists) demanded the 'sovietization' of Germany and the continuation of the revolution. The SPD put down subsequent Spartacist demonstrations in January 1919, and in the violence and bloodshed the two Communist leaders, Karl Liebknecht and Rosa Luxemburg, were killed. A second Spartacist uprising was suppressed, with much greater bloodshed, in March, while, in April, troops were sent to overthrow the Republic of Soviets which had just been proclaimed in Bavaria. Moderate socialism now appeared safe from the far left, but the latter neither forgot nor forgave the experience of 1919.

During this crisis a move was made towards establishing permanent institutions. Elections were held in January 1919 and a Constituent Assembly convened in Weimar, away from the street violence of Berlin. Three of the moderate parties formed a coalition government: the Centre Party (Z), the Democratic Party (DDP) and the Social Democrats (SPD). In opposition to the coalition were the parties of the right – the Nationalists (DNVP) and the People's Party (DVP) – as well as the Independent Socialists (USPD) of the far left. The Communists (KPD) did not contest this election. Ebert now became the first President of the Republic, with Scheidemann his Chancellor until June 1919.

Meanwhile, a constitution was being drafted by a special committee under the jurist Hugo Preuss. Eventually promulgated in August 1919, this embodied many advanced principles of democracy and borrowed freely from the experience of England, France and the United States. The main terms were as follows. The head of state was to be the President, elected every seven years by universal suffrage. He was given, by Article 48 of the constitution, emergency powers: 'In the event that the public order and security are seriously disturbed or endangered, the Reich President may take the measures necessary for their restoration.'[3] The head of the government was to be the Chancellor, appointed by the President and needing the support of the majority of the legislature, or Reichstag. The Reichstag, elected by universal suffrage by means of proportional representation, would be able to deal with legislation, defence, foreign policy, trade, finance and security. The last section of the constitution carefully itemized the various 'rights and duties of the Germans'.[4]

By the end of 1919, therefore, the republic had overcome pressures from the far left and had acquired a legal framework. The question now arising was: could it survive? The next fourteen years saw, in succession, a period of instability and severe problems (1919–23), a remarkable recovery and a period of consolidation (1923–9) and, finally, the crisis which eventually destroyed the republic (1929–33).

The most serious obstacle to the new government in 1919 was the signing of the Treaty of Versailles with the victorious Allies. The German delegation was horrified by the harshness of the terms but the Allies were determined not to make major modifications. In June, Scheidemann resigned as Chancellor in protest but his successor, Bauer, eventually agreed to accept the treaty. Versailles was to prove a millstone around the neck of the republic, and had much to do with the second problem of this early period: inflation. The devaluation of the mark started during the war but was aggravated by demobilization and by the stiff reparations imposed, under a provision in the Treaty of Versailles, in 1921. Speculation, massive overprinting of paper money and the French occupation of the Ruhr in 1923 all completed the collapse of the mark in November 1923 to 16,000 million to the pound. Savings were wiped out overnight and, for a few weeks, barter unofficially replaced the use of coinage. During the same years, political challenges compounded the difficulties of the republic. One example was the Kapp Putsch (1920), an unsuccessful but frightening attempt by the far right to seize power in Berlin; another putsch was tried by Hitler in Munich (1923) in circumstances described in the next section.

Nevertheless, the period 1923–9 saw a remarkable recovery and greater stability. This is generally known as the 'Stresemann era' because of the profound influence exerted by this leader of the DVP, first as Chancellor in 1923 and then as Foreign Minister until 1929. Vital economic developments included the stabilization of the currency in the form of the Rentenmark and an agreement on reparations with the Allies in 1924 known as the Dawes Plan. Massive investment followed, mostly from the United States, which enabled German industry to recover almost to 1913 levels, despite the loss of resources and land in 1919. At the same time, Stresemann stabilized Germany's relations with the rest of Europe. He followed the 1922 treaty with Russia with another in 1926, participated in a collective defence pact with four other countries at Locarno in 1925, and took Germany into the League of Nations in 1926. Underlying these achievements was a period of relative political stability as coalition governments functioned more or less effectively, lubricated by the political diplomacy of Stresemann himself.

These halcyon years did not last. Stresemann died in 1929, a year in which Germany was suddenly confronted by economic catastrophe. Meanwhile, lurking in the background, and preparing to take advantage of any such change of fortune, were Hitler and the Nazis.

The early years of the Nazi movement, 1918–29

Many Germans were bitterly opposed to the revolution of 1918, blaming Jews, socialists, liberals and Catholics for the fall of the Second Reich and military defeat. Particularly resentful were the *völkisch* groups which sprang up all over the country and issued racialist and anti-liberal propaganda.

One of these was the German Workers' Party (DAP), formed by Anton Drexler in Munich in January 1919. It was joined, in September 1919, by an Austrian with unfulfilled artistic pretensions who had fought in a Bavarian regiment in the German army throughout the First World War. Hitler blamed the republic for Germany's surrender and openly expressed his 'hatred for the originators of this dastardly crime'.[5] He rose rapidly to the position of the party's theorist and chief propaganda officer, and his talent as a public speaker was apparent even at this early stage. In February 1920 he headed a committee which devised the party's twenty-five-point programme, consisting of a variety of nationalist, socialist, corporativist and racialist principles. Meanwhile, the name was extended to 'National Socialist German Workers' Party' (NSDAP), commonly abbreviated to 'Nazi'. Branches were organized beyond Munich and support came from disbanded soldiers and from some elements of the army, or Reichswehr. The mouthpiece of the NSDAP was the *People's Observer* (*Völkischer Beobachter*), acquired in 1920. The next stage was Hitler's rise to the leadership of the party. By mid-1921 he was in dispute with the committee under Drexler over the question of organization and strategy. Eventually he outmanoeuvred Drexler and was elected Party Chairman in July. He immediately decided to demonstrate that the NSDAP was radically different from all traditional 'bourgeois' parties and to centralize everything, especially propaganda, on Munich. The movement was given teeth by the formation, in July 1921, of the Sturmabteilung (SA), a violent paramilitary organization intended, in the words of the newly named *Völkischer Beobachter* 'to develop in the hearts of our young supporters a tremendous desire for action'.[6] The SA proceeded to intimidate opponents, disrupt other parties' meetings and engage in bloody clashes in the streets. Hitler developed a sense of irresistible power and overwhelming confidence, and was prepared to prove the *Beobachter*'s maxim that 'history does not make men, but men history'.

Mussolini, it seemed, had demonstrated this in his March on Rome in 1922. Could Hitler do the same in 1923? The republic was experiencing a many-sided crisis at least as serious as that confronted by the Italian monarchy. Hitler hoped to march on Berlin with the support of the right-wing Commissioner of Bavaria, Gustav von Kahr, and the Bavarian armed forces; the majority of the Reichswehr would then be won over. In November 1923, 600 SA men, under Hitler's command, took over a meeting being addressed by Kahr in the Bürgerbräu Keller, one of Munich's largest beer halls. Kahr, even at gunpoint, refused to support the putsch and an SA street demonstration the following morning was dispersed by the Bavarian police. Hitler's attempt at power therefore ended in ignominious failure and he was put on trial for treason. He was, however, treated leniently by sympathetic judges, and was sentenced to five years' imprisonment in Landsberg Castle. He served just over one year, in comfortable conditions which enabled him to write the first volume of *Mein Kampf* (*My Struggle*). On his emergence from captivity in December 1924 he found the NSDAP in total disarray; in his absence it had disintegrated into warring factions. Hitler was not displeased with this, as it guaranteed his own indispensability and meant that he was well placed to resume control.

When he refounded the NSDAP in February 1925, Hitler emphasized the need for a change in strategy. The failure of the Munich Putsch had shown that violence alone was unlikely to succeed; the best course, therefore, would be to participate in regular politics. This did not mean a fundamental conversion to the principles of constitutional democracy; on the contrary, parliamentary politics would be the means, not the end. On the surface, therefore, the NSDAP assumed the role of a parliamentary party, aiming at gaining electoral support at the expense of its rivals. At a deeper level, however, the NSDAP remained a mass movement. Hitler still hoped to emulate Mussolini, given the right circumstances, and concentrated in the late 1920s on taking over the key cities. The party therefore had a Jekyll and Hyde appearance which Hitler made no attempt to conceal.

Despite this new approach, the period 1925–9 proved exceptionally difficult for the Nazi Party and the movement. In the first place, Hitler was confronted by opposition from north German leaders, especially Gregor Strasser, who considered that the party's ideology should place heavier stress on socialism and the nationalization of key industries. Hitler eventually gained unquestioned ascendancy over the northern units of the party at the Bamberg Conference (February 1926) in which he out-argued Strasser and, by the force of his rhetoric, won over one of his arch critics, Josef Goebbels. (The latter had, only a short time before, demanded the expulsion of the 'petty bourgeois Adolf Hitler'!) The overall result of this victory was that Hitler tightened his control and established the monolithic structure he had always sought. In the subsequent reorganization, cadres of dedicated activists were set up in the basic party units, the *Gau*, under the control of the officials, or *Gauleiters*, who were appointed by Hitler himself.

The second and more intractable problem of this period was the stability of the republic and the poor electoral performance of the NSDAP. In the Reichstag election of December 1924, for example, the NSDAP acquired only fourteen seats, making it the least significant of the national parties in terms of electoral support; its performance in 1928 was even poorer, resulting in only twelve seats. Yet the party was nothing if not resilient. It showed a remarkable capacity to survive these hard times and switched its campaign from the cities to the rural areas, which agricultural depression had made more volatile. The *Völkischer Beobachter* observed in May 1928: 'The election results from the rural areas in particular have proved that with a smaller expenditure of energy, money and time, better results can be achieved there than in the big cities.'[7] The party therefore developed an electoral base which expanded rapidly as Germany came under the grip of economic recession.

The years of crisis, 1929–33

The origins of the Great Depression are dealt with in Chapter 1. Of all the industrial states, Germany was undoubtedly the most vulnerable to a sudden downturn in economic conditions. Her industry was heavily dependent on foreign investment to the tune of 5 billion marks per annum by 1928. Her banking system was geared to the use of short-term loans for long-term enterprises and, as a result, was potentially very vulnerable. As the depression deepened, foreign loans were withdrawn and the banking system eventually collapsed in 1931. Meanwhile, industrial output had to be cut back through lack of investment and the contraction of overseas markets. The boom years of the late 1920s came to an abrupt end with a dramatic rise in the number of bankruptcies. The inevitable result was a rapid increase in unemployment, from 2 million in 1929 to 3.5 million in 1930, 4.4 million in 1931 and over 6 million in 1932.

The depression dealt a devastating blow to democracy in Germany. Chancellor Müller's coalition fell apart on 27 March 1930 over the question of cutting dole payments. Since the power of the Chancellor depended on the support of the Reichstag and the economic crisis had made collaboration between political parties more difficult, the initiative now passed to the President. The republic's second President, elected in 1925, was Field Marshal Hindenburg. Very much a product of the old establishment of the Second Reich, he had an authoritarian approach to politics. During the stable years he had had no option but to play an inactive role in the manoeuvring for power between the various parties. From 1930, however, he was able to fill the vacuum left by the sudden death of consensus politics. Under the influence of one of his main advisers, General Schleicher, Hindenburg appointed the Centre Party leader, Brüning, as Chancellor. When Brüning tried to introduce a deflationary budget it was rejected by the Reichstag. Hindenburg sought to enforce it by presidential decree, under Article 48 of the constitution. The Reichstag objected to this course, with the result that Hindenburg agreed to Brüning's request for an election in September 1930. The results proved disappointing to Brüning and he was forced to carry on without the support of the Reichstag. He resorted increasingly to the use of presidential decrees so that, by the time of his fall in May 1932, parliamentary democracy had virtually disappeared.

Meanwhile, the NSDAP was rapidly expanding the base of its support. It was geared to take full advantage of the republic's crisis, as Hitler arranged mass rallies, travelling speakers and a flood of material from the propaganda department. Below the surface the violence and intimidation intensified, although Hitler sometimes considered that the activities of the SA were too extreme. The Reichstag election of 1930 was a triumph for the NSDAP, which secured 6.5 million votes and increased its representation from 12 to 107 seats, thus becoming the second largest party in the Reichstag. Hitler capitalized on this success by cultivating connections with the traditional right, including the Nationalists (DNVP), the army, industrialists like Thyssen, and agriculturalists; this alliance was formalized in the Harzburg Front of October 1931, directed against the republic's policies and record. In January 1932 Hitler made a direct appeal to German industrialists in his Düsseldorf speech, denouncing parliamentary democracy and highlighting the 'Bolshevik threat'. He was carefully establishing his credentials as an anti-revolutionary and providing the sort of reassurance which cancelled out the reservations caused by the obscene violence of the SA.

Hitler's self-confidence was now at its peak and he challenged Hindenburg for the presidency. The 1932 election ran to two ballots. On the first, Hindenburg obtained 18.7 million votes (49.6 per cent of the total), Hitler 11.3 million (30.1 per cent) and Thälmann, the Communist leader, 5 million (13 per cent). On the second ballot Hindenburg secured an overall majority with 19.4 million (53 per cent) to Hitler's 13.4 million (26.8 per cent) and Thälmann's 3.8 million (10.2 per cent). This result was a disappointment to Hitler, who had expended a massive effort to no avail. The only other possibility was now to try for the second most important office – the chancellorship.

In this he was to prove more successful, and ultimately he came to power by the back-door methods of diplomacy and intrigue rather than over the threshold of electoral support. The process was highly complex, involving President Hindenburg, General Schleicher and an aristocrat, Franz von Papen.

6 Paul Hindenburg, 1847–1934 (Popperfoto)

The first stage was the collapse of Brüning's government in May 1932, largely because it had lost the support of those who mattered, namely the President and his retinue. Schleicher had been alienated by Brüning's decision to ban Hitler's SA, and Hindenburg by a proposal to take over bankrupt Junker estates for use by landless peasants. Hindenburg therefore pushed Brüning into resignation and Papen was installed as the new Chancellor, the first in the history of the republic not to have the basis of party support. Hitler agreed not to oppose the new government in exchange for the removal of the ban on the SA and new Reichstag elections. The latter, held in July 1932, showed another sensational swing to the NSDAP, which now became easily the largest party, with 230 seats and 37.3 per cent of the popular vote. When Hitler was invited by Papen to join his cabinet he demanded, instead, the chancellorship. This was refused, however, by President Hindenburg. Papen then tried to weaken the position of the NSDAP by calling yet another Reichstag election in November 1932. This time the NSDAP lost electoral support, declining to 196 seats in the Reichstag and 33.1 per cent of the vote. Clearly Hitler's popularity had peaked and it would have come as no great surprise if the Nazi phenomenon had faded to its semi-obscurity of the late 1920s.

Then events swung back in Hitler's favour. Papen proved incapable of holding power for very long and the chancellorship went to Schleicher, who had managed to convince Hindenburg that he could broaden the base of his support by detaching members of the NSDAP from their support for Hitler. In this he failed dismally; the only Nazi who seemed interested in his offer was Strasser, who was promptly thrown out of the party. Meanwhile, Papen felt sufficiently slighted by Schleicher to intrigue against him with Hitler. In January 1933 Papen persuaded Hindenburg to appoint Hitler as Chancellor in a coalition government which would contain only three Nazis and which would be carefully monitored by Papen as Hitler's deputy. Schleicher had tried to keep his own government afloat by asking for further emergency powers. These Hindenburg was not prepared to grant, since he now had an alternative. On 30 January 1933 he confirmed Hitler's appointment, believing that sufficient precautions had been taken to tame the radicalism of the NSDAP. In fact, Hitler proceeded to destroy the Weimar Republic within weeks of his coming to power. Only one more election was to be held before Germany was subsumed into the Third Reich.

EXPLANATIONS OF THE RISE OF HITLER

The rise of Hitler involved distinct processes which, although connected, did not lead inevitably from one to the other. One was the collapse of democracy within the Weimar Republic and the development after 1930 of an authoritarian regime which was hostile to the whole basis of the republic. Another was the emergence of an entirely new form of right-wing movement which, under Hitler, eventually replaced this authoritarian system with a totalitarian regime. The latter could not have occurred without the former: Hitler's rise was accomplished through the collapse of the republic. But this collapse was not necessarily tied to a historical trend leading inevitably to Nazism; it could have been followed by an alternative system.

7 Adolf Hitler, 1889–1945, at Berchtesgaden (Popperfoto)

An explanation as to why Hitler became Chancellor can be advanced in three stages. First, the Weimar Republic became increasingly destabilized with the disintegration of effective democracy. Second, Nazism emerged as a dynamic movement which was capable of gaining support from a substantial part of an electorate which had become disillusioned with the republic. And third, the conservative right provided a channel which enabled this new dynamic to penetrate and force open the flawed structure. The whole picture is complex, and it is necessary to avoid any one-sided or oversimplified view.

The vulnerability of Weimar democracy

The bedrock of any democracy is its constitution. As we have seen, the constitution of the Weimar Republic had certain advanced democratic features, including the enfranchisement of all men and women at twenty, and a form of proportional representation which guaranteed one seat in the Reichstag for every 60,000 votes cast. It also made it necessary for the Chancellor and his cabinet to have the support of a majority in the Reichstag, thus ensuring that the executive would at all times be responsible to the legislature. Yet several problems soon emerged to negate these positive features, making the constitution extremely difficult to operate.

One was the tendency of proportional representation to encourage the proliferation of parties. When this was associated with the need for majority government, it became evident that everything would depend on the assembling of coalitions. At first this seemed theoretically simple. The three parties most responsible for the formation of the republic – the SPD, the Centre and the DDP – earned in the 1919 elections 76 per cent of the vote, which translated into 78 per cent of the seats. But in the election of 1920 their support dropped to only 48 per cent of the vote, which meant that government became dependent on other parties as well. The eventual solution was the support of Stresemann, who brought in part of the DVP. Unfortunately, this was offset between 1923 and 1928 by the withdrawal of the SPD into opposition. It even became necessary to bring into two cabinets several right-wing politicians from the DNVP. This, of course, meant that the base of the government was broadening all the time, which made more difficult any concerted decision-making. Serious enough in the favourable economic climate between 1924 and 1928, this became an intolerable handicap when Germany was struck by the Great Depression. The result was the collapse of the normal process of democracy as, under Brüning and his successors, the government no longer sought the regular mandate of the Reichstag. This led, between 1930 and 1933, to the authoritarian phase of the Weimar Republic, which, in turn, provided the opportunity for Hitler in 1932 and 1933.

Some historians and recent German politicians have identified an undercurrent of anti-democratic feeling which severely damaged the fabric of the republic. According to L. Snyder, the new regime was seen as a 'stopgap' and 'from the days of its origin the Weimar Republic was unwanted and unloved'. Theodor Heuss, the first President of West Germany, maintained that 'Germany never conquered democracy for herself.'[8] It could certainly be argued that democracy was handed down from above in 1918, without any serious attempt to change the existing civil service or the judicial and military elites. Below the surface of a democratic constitution, therefore, was a profoundly conservative base, with no commitment – emotional or intellectual – to a republic. Certain sections of the community could have become permanently reconciled to the new system – for example, the proletariat and the middle classes. These, however, were severely affected by the impact of the 1923 and 1929 economic crises. Much of the population was highly vulnerable to right-wing ideas and organizations. A strong tradition of anti-Western and anti-democratic thought was maintained by writers and activists like Moeller, van den Bruck and Junger, who induced widespread nostalgia for the Second Reich and anticipation of a Third. The response of much of the population was to criticize the Weimar politicians for their facelessness and to turn to more authoritarian figures like Hindenburg and, ultimately, Hitler. Throughout the period 1918–33, therefore, the onus was always upon democracy to show that it was a better system than the authoritarian models of the past. Many people remained highly sceptical.

Unfortunately, the image of democracy was not strengthened by the performance of the political parties. According to Fraenkel, these failed to fulfil 'the functions which devolve upon them in a constitutional pluralistic Parliamentary democracy'.[9] The traditional right – the DNVP – maintained a consistent hostility to the republic. They attacked it at every opportunity and eventually welcomed its demise. Indeed, in collaborating openly with Hitler's NSDAP, they provided the channel for his appointment (see p. 167).

The more moderate Centre Party did manage to keep a respectable level of support, attracting over 50 per cent of the Catholic vote. It had, however, little appeal to Protestants, despite professing to be primarily a 'Christian' party. But the most damaging impact of the Centre Party was its swing to the right. This occurred in two stages. In 1928 Monsignor Kaas took over from Wilhelm Marx as party leader, emphasizing the party's clerical attachments and undermining its ability to reconcile the moderate parties on secular issues. Then, after 1930, the Centre displayed an unfortunate willingness to adapt to presidential dictatorship. Once Müller had withdrawn the SPD from government, Brüning was content to rely upon President Hindenburg to issue emergency decrees under Article 48 of the constitution. Thus, after playing a key role in upholding democracy, the Centre delivered the first blows against it.

The liberal part of the political spectrum was also badly flawed. Germany had developed the unique phenomenon of two varieties of liberalism. To the left of centre, the DDP represented the political and social freedoms which made their way into the constitution, while the DVP, on the right, merged liberal economic theory with nationalism and authority. The two parties rarely collaborated, except during the period of Stresemann's ascendancy, and neither was able to maintain the support of the middle classes, which should have been their natural constituency. In part, this was because they were never able to appeal to the 'diverse social and economic interests' which constituted the 'material base' of the middle classes.[10] The result was to be a devastating change in voting behaviour as, after 1928, the DDP and DVP lost almost all their electoral support to the Nazis. This defection was the greatest single factor in converting the latter from a fringe to a mass party. In a very real sense, therefore, fascism emerged from the ruins of liberalism.

It might be thought that the best chance of upholding the republic came from the left wing. After all, the parties of the left had fairly consistent support, ranging from 45.5 per cent of the vote in 1919 to 36.9 per cent in November 1932. Unfortunately, the left was also fragmented into two segments (three for the brief period 1919–23). The bitter rivalry between the SPD and the KPD was the legacy of the German Revolution of 1918–19. The KPD never forgot the bloodshed of January 1919 and regarded the SPD, who had put down their attempted coup, as class enemies. There was also a profound ideological gap. Thalmann, the KPD leader, was influenced by Stalin's belief that social democracy was not essentially different to fascism and that they were both manifestations of capitalism. He argued, indeed, that the greatest threat to German communism lay in the SPD, 'in the social democracy which gains the trust of the masses through fraud and treachery'.[11] He believed that the depression would act as a great catalyst for changes in the voting pattern and that the KPD would pull in the working-class vote in much the same way as the NSDAP was benefiting from the support of the middle classes. (The KPD did make certain inroads; for example, in July 1932 it reduced the SPD's share of the vote to 21.6 per cent and boosted its own to 14.3 per cent. But it never became a mass party to rival the NSDAP.) Thalmann also hoped that, if Hitler were to achieve power, he would soon be overthrown by a proletarian revolution organized by the KPD; in this sense, a fascist regime would be a 'temporary intermediate development'. As far as Thalmann was concerned, therefore, there was no reason to co-operate with the other parties in preventing the accession of Hitler.

If the SPD so distrusted the KPD, could it not have made more of its links with other groups? Herein lies the SPD's greatest failing. Although by far the most important influence behind the formation of the republic, it never quite managed to sustain a role in government proportionate to its size in the Reichstag. In the words of Hiden, 'They failed to make of their early association with the bourgeois parties, or so-called "democratic middle" of DDP, Centre and DVP, a lasting and constructive partnership.'[12] They refused, for example, to be involved in the government of the republic during the crucial period between 1923 and 1928. The SPD remained during the period of the Weimar Republic essentially a party of the working class and made very few inroads into the middle classes. This was in contrast to the British Labour Party which sought greater middle-class support as it became the main alternative to the Conservatives. Part of the problem for the SPD at this stage was that it was limited by attachments to its trade union movement and was concerned that any attempt at a more concerted appeal to the middle classes would lose it votes to the Communists.

Chapter 1 referred to the importance of a catalyst in the breakdown of parliamentary systems. This was particularly important in the case of Germany, where economic crisis destabilized the whole social structure, with serious side-effects for the political system. Two stages were involved in the process – inflation and depression. General Morgan of the Disarmament Commission said of the former: 'Inflation has destroyed the equipoise of society. It has ruined the middle classes and impoverished the workers . . . Inflation has undermined the political basis of the Republic and concentrated all real power in the hands of a few, namely the great industrialists.' In fact, a period of recovery followed this perhaps premature diagnosis. But the real significance of inflation was that any future economic crisis would be bound to have a doubly serious impact. Hence, from 1929 the depression radicalized sections of the population which inflation had already rendered unstable, turning them either to the extreme right or to the far left. It also destroyed any possibility of political consensus and, as we have seen, returned Germany to the practice of authoritarian government.

The strength and appeal of the Nazis

The rise of Hitler was also due to a number of positive factors. To be examined in this section are the role of propaganda and organization, Hitler's strategy and identification of key issues, and the importance of his own personality and influence.

Also of vital importance is the support given to the NSDAP by different sections of the population.

The success of the Nazi movement is inevitably associated with the highly skilled use of propaganda and the development of an efficient organization. In these respects it was far ahead of all the other German parties, including the KPD. The importance which Hitler attached to propaganda and organization can be seen clearly in several extracts from *Mein Kampf*: 'The function of propaganda', he argued, 'is to attract supporters, the function of organization is to win members.' He continued: 'Propaganda works on the general public from the standpoint of an idea and makes them ripe for the victory of this idea, while the organization achieves victory by the persistent, organic, and militant union of those supporters who seem willing and able to carry on the fight for victory.' Or, to put it another way, 'The first task of propaganda is to win people for subsequent organization; the first task of organization is to win men for the continuation of propaganda. The second task of propaganda is the disruption of the existing state of affairs and the permeation of this state of affairs with the new doctrine, while the second task of organization must be the struggle for power, thus to achieve the final success of the doctrine.'[13]

The manifestations of propaganda were numerous. Albert Speer later asserted that 'Hitler was one of the first to be able to avail himself of the means of modern technology'. Admittedly, he was unable to make effective use of radio until after coming to power and establishing a monopoly over this medium, but he did use numerous other means, including loudspeakers, provocative posters and bands. Above all, he depended on the power of the spoken word, which he always considered more important than written material. He had a profound insight into the collective emotions of crowds and believed that his message to them had to be kept simple, striking and memorable: 'The receptivity of the great masses is very limited, their intelligence is small, but their power of forgetting is enormous.' Hence, propaganda 'must be limited to a very few points',[14] which must be constantly repeated to establish them as incontrovertible facts. It was also vital to make the individual feel important only in the context of the crowd and to establish stereotyped enemies and targets by means, if necessary, of 'the big lie'. Organization, of course, was essential for the maintenance of mass commitment: hence the vast number of marches and rallies, the uniforms and paramilitary drill, and the street fights with Communists and Social Democrats. The whole process was intended to prepare the movement to seize power when the opportunity arose.

The identification of this opportunity depended on Hitler's strategy and timing. His first bid for power was defective, based, as it was, on the mistaken belief that he could imitate Mussolini's successful March on Rome. But the failure of the Munich Putsch in 1923 was followed by a more skilful adaptation to a dual role of legality in party politics which drew attention away from the radicalism of his mass movement. This course lulled the suspicions of the republican government, which considered the KPD as a more serious threat and, as a result, underestimated the revolutionary potential of the Nazis. It also enabled Hitler to appear as a more moderate politician to those sectors of society who had previously been put off by the gutter politics of the early years of the movement. Along with this overall change in strategy, Hitler aimed constantly to reformulate the party programme so as to appeal to different parts of the population as they became alienated from the republic. In 1927 he told his economic adviser, Keppler, that the economic goals of the original programme were now 'unusable'. He considered that some of the details of the 1920 document were too doctrinaire and he was more prepared than some of the more orthodox Nazi leaders to be flexible and pragmatic in the presentation of a party image. He went so far as to establish a section within the organization to identify the reasons for different types of public discontent and to develop specific remedies which would appeal to different social groups. As Stachura has put it, the 'NSDAP revealed itself to be perhaps the most tactically flexible and opportunistic political movement in the Republic'.[15]

In developing a broad appeal for the Nazi movement, Hitler relied on the projection of general issues for the consumption of the population as a whole, and specific issues for the different classes. An example of the former was his attack on the republic's foreign policy. Taking advantage of the unpopularity of the Versailles Settlement, Hitler was able to implant upon the national consciousness terms like 'November Criminals' and the 'stab in the back'. He also slammed the policy of détente pursued by Stresemann: 'our people must be delivered from the hopeless confusion of international convictions and educated consciously and systematically to fanatical Nationalism'. Another mainline policy, guaranteed to be taken seriously across most of the political spectrum, was anti-communism; this is seen by Hamilton[16] as one of the most important of all Hitler's appeals. Finally, he made effective use of the deep undercurrent of anti-Semitism in Germany, making the Jews scapegoats for all of Germany's evils, whether in the form of callous capitalism or revolutionary communism. Above all, he made a permanent and intentionally damaging connection between the regime and the detested minority, developing the concept of the 'Jew Republic'.

What was the importance of the personal role of Hitler in the rise of the Nazi movement? Emphasis is usually placed on his charismatic leadership and an almost demoniac willpower. Trevor-Roper, for example, maintains that 'His own firm belief in his messianic mission was perhaps the most important element in the extraordinary power of his personality.'[17] He also possessed, according to Bullock, a 'sense of opportunity and timing'. This was the right combination of characteristics to take advantage of the troubles of the Weimar Republic since Hitler was at his best when destroying a system by exploiting its crises. He later experienced much greater difficulty when he had to defend his own system which, in turn, came under threat in the second phase of the Second World War. At this stage, Hitler's personality was to become a major liability to the Nazi movement and to Germany's military survival.

The final issue which needs to be examined is the basis of support for National Socialism. Much research has been carried out on the defection to the NSDAP during the late 1920s and early 1930s. It was once thought that Nazism appealed mainly to the middle classes, with substantial additions from the working class and from the upper levels of society who were, nevertheless, more reluctant to shift from their original political allegiances. Now, however, the tendency is to assume more general and widespread support for Hitler.

It is still possible to say that the middle classes made up the largest single proportion of Nazi support, and that their defection from their traditional parties was vitally important in converting Nazism into a mass movement. During the 1920s they had voted in large numbers for the DDP and the DVP, although some also supported the DNVP and, if they were Catholic, the Centre. Some historians, like Childers, have argued that the basis for the middle-class movement towards the NSDAP had been established during the late 1920s, even before the onset of depression from 1929.[18] Others maintain that the flow occurred only after 1929, making it a direct result of the Great Depression. The middle classes found unbearable the impact of a second economic crisis which destroyed the apparent recovery from the first. The psychological blow was so profound that they made an uncharacteristic move away from the moderate centre to the radical right. These two interpretations can be harmonized. The older section of the middle class, comprising artisans, small retailers and peasant farmers, formed the core of the support for Hitler and were showing support for him before the depression: theirs was a disillusionment with the structure and policies of the republic itself. To these was subsequently added the weight of much of the new middle class – the non-manual employees, civil servants and teachers – who aligned themselves with Nazism as a direct result of the depression. It is possible that they were moving in this direction anyway. But the simple fact is that the NSDAP secured only twelve seats in the Reichstag election of 1928; it therefore took the depression to convert a trickle of middle-class support into a flood.

There is a further controversy over the connection between Nazism and the working class. It was once strongly argued that the working class remained largely loyal to the parties of the left which, in any case, had a distinctively proletarian appeal. The KPD was especially class-based and its support increased during the Reichstag elections of 1930 and 1932. Although the SPD lost seats, it came nowhere near the collapse suffered by the parties of the centre, clearly indicating that it retained the bulk of its support. By this analysis, the proletariat was less drawn to Nazism because in the words of Stachura, 'The Party was unable to establish a significant working-class constituency because it did not develop a coherent interpretation of "German Socialism".' This was partly because Hitler's 'innate contempt and distrust of the proletariat remained paramount'.[19] Other historians, such as Mühlberger, are not convinced by the 'middle-class thesis' of Nazism.[20] Recent research has tended to support the view that working-class input was substantial. Studies of Nazi membership records show something like 40 per cent of the membership coming from the working class, while 60 per cent of the SA were of the same origins. Parallel research on electoral trends has, through computer analysis of statistical data, produced very similar voting results. According to Fischer, 'a good 40 per cent of the NSDAP's voters were working class, remarkably similar to the proportion of workers in the party itself'.[21] Again, there is a possible synthesis between two interpretations. On the one hand, the working class never came to provide the largest body of support for Nazism: in that respect, the original views seem correct. On the other hand, it is possible to overestimate the continued loyalty of the working class to the parties of the left. After 1928 substantial shifts did occur: the growth of the Communists was more than offset by the decline of the SPD. The latter shrank by between a quarter and a third: these lost votes almost certainly went straight to the Nazis. Thus, although the NSDAP was not primarily a working-class party and the majority of workers remained with the parties of the left, the inflow of working-class support for Nazism was still a vital factor in the conversion of Nazism into a mass movement.

The attitudes of the upper classes to Nazism were largely pragmatic. Landowners, businessmen and industrialists saw in Hitler the prospect of safety from the threats of communism and socialism on the left. Arguably, they saw beyond this and looked to Nazism to deliver over to them a disciplined and constrained workforce. They looked to Hitler to undo the pro-trade union and welfare policies of most of the governments of the Weimar Republic. Even those who distrusted the violence and vulgarities of the Nazi movement were still likely to be supporting it indirectly. It was unlikely that the affluent sectors of German society after 1929 voted in signifi-cant numbers for any party to the left of the DNVP, and the DNVP itself was in close collaboration with the NSDAP after Hugenberg assumed the leadership. Hence, the Nazis benefited considerably from the respectability, publicity and funding brought by a relatively narrow but highly influential sector of society.

To some extent, the appeal of Nazism transcended class barriers altogether. The three more general categories usually considered most important are religious denomination, gender and age. There is no doubt that the Protestants were more likely than Catholics to vote Nazi. They had no existing party base, whereas the Centre Party held the Catholic vote even at the height of the economic and polit-ical crisis. Many were also profoundly suspicious of the Weimar Republic, which, as we have seen, they identified mainly with Catholic and working-class values. On the whole, they had far more affection for the memory of the Kaiser's rule and were not, therefore, averse to another change of regime. As far as gender is concerned, the Nazis managed to make up for an early imbalance in their support. Before 1930 the majority of women were more right wing in their voting behav-iour than men; yet the majority of Nazi votes came from men rather than women. By 1933 there was a more even split as many women became convinced that Hitler was the best prospect for bolstering the institution of the family in troubled times; this probably counteracted the earlier and well-founded suspicion that Nazism was profoundly anti-feminist. Finally, the Nazi movement had a powerful generational impact. It appealed directly to youth, partly through its dynamism and attack on traditional ideas and institutions, partly through the oversimplified solutions to the problem of unemployment. Young men, more than any other section of the commu-nity, were prepared to submerge their identity and to respond to Hitler's appeal to the crowd instinct.

It is difficult to escape the conclusion that during the later period of the Weimar Republic the NSDAP was the most heterogeneous party in Germany. It included people from the complete range of social backgrounds, even though the precise proportion of these may be open to debate and controversy. Hitler alone managed to create a radical movement with which he could transform into fanaticism the desperation of a profoundly disturbed people.

The channel to power provided by the conservative right

After 1928, therefore, Hitler succeeded in collecting for the NSDAP much of the electorate which had become disillusioned with the republic's manifest deficiencies. This was essential for Hitler's rise to prominence but it does not fully explain his rise to *power*. A further step was needed – a means of forcing a way in through the republic's fissures. This was greatly assisted by the drift to authoritarian rule within the Republic after 1929, in which democracy was systematically undermined by the conservative right. This, in turn, led to an opportunist alliance between the conservative right and the Nazis as the former tried to use the latter to sweep away democracy and strengthen the conservative–authoritarian base.

Ironically, the initial drift to authoritarianism was made possible by the constitution itself which, in Article 48, allowed the President to assume emergency powers should he consider these necessary. The first President, Ebert, had used Article 48 constructively to maintain the stability of the new democracy. But his successor, Hindenburg, was a very different proposition. His election in 1925 has been seen as a major disaster for the republic: he was an authoritarian and military figure, with a considerable suspicion of the whole parliamentary process. Eyck comments that 'No matter how Hindenburg might comport himself in the immediate future his election as president of Germany was a triumph of nationalism and militarism and a heavy defeat for the Republic and parliamentary government.'[22] Hindenburg brushed aside the problem of finding a parliamentary majority by exercising presidential decree powers allowed by Article 48. According to Boldt,[23] the use of decree laws increased from 5 in 1930 to 44 in 1931 and 60 in 1932, while sittings of the Reichstag declined from 94 in 1930 to 41 in 1931 and a mere 13 in 1932. This trend effectively ended the role of party politics. The situation deteriorated further after the fall of Brüning in 1932 as Papen and Schleicher were both determined to avoid any return to parliamentary sovereignty.

But why were the conservative right willing to allow Hitler and the radical right to benefit from this? The explanation seems to be that the conservative right (which included the DNVP, some of the army command, President Hindenburg and Chancellors Papen and Schleicher) intended to use Nazism for their own purpose. They believed that the republic had outlived its usefulness and that any return to the party politics of the 1920s was impossible. Instead, conservative constitutional theorists argued in *Unsere Partei* that the party system would eventually fracture and be replaced by a broad front. For this reason, the DNVP therefore aimed to create a broad 'movement' of the right which would also include the NSDAP. The latter could be used for its radical impetus. It had the capacity to destroy the republic, but once that was achieved it would be brought into line with the more conservative objectives of the DNVP. The collaboration between the Nazis and the DNVP was crucial; Hiden goes so far as to say that it 'played handmaiden to Adolf Hitler and his movement at the close of the 1920s'.[24] This strategy, which eventually proved to be fatally flawed, provided Hitler with access to power. His appointment as Chancellor was due to a fortuitous circumstance – the personal rivalry between the last two Chancellors, Papen and Schleicher. The latter faced a political crisis when, in January 1933, the Reichstag challenged his use of Article 48. The constitution provided a loophole in that the President could dissolve the Reichstag and call an election. But, having already done this twice in 1932, Hindenburg preferred to find an alternative Chancellor. This explains his receptiveness to Papen's recommendation that Hitler should be appointed, with himself given a watching brief as Vice-Chancellor.

Hence, Hitler came to power largely through a conspiracy. Yet this does not mean that the Nazis did little themselves to achieve it. The conservative right would not have been so willing to collaborate with a weak fringe group. It was evident to them that the NSDAP had managed more effectively than any other party to mobilize popular discontent against the republic. Hitler appeared to them an elemental force whom they intended to use in their own way. But there is a final irony. Hitler came to power as the support for the Nazis was starting to ebb: after all the vote for the Nazis fell back slightly in the second election of 1932 and it seemed a reasonable assumption that Hitler's popularity with the electorate had peaked. This, the conservative politicians calculated, would make Hitler easier to manipulate. Nazism appeared sufficiently strong to be directed against parliamentary democracy but not strong enough to challenge the authoritarian conservatives. It was a flaring flame which would destroy the republic and then die back into the traditional authoritarianism which would be all that was left.

The politicians who gave Hitler power in this way made the most ghastly political blunder in the whole of Germany's history.

THE THIRD REICH, 1933–45

Dictatorship established, 1933–4

When he was appointed Chancellor on 30 January 1933, Hitler's power was by no means absolute. He had only three Nazis in his cabinet and he was constrained by Papen who, in his position as Vice-Chancellor, had to be involved in any contacts between the Chancellor and President. Another problem was that Hitler had no emergency powers beyond those which Hindenburg was prepared, under Article 48 of the constitution, to grant him. It seemed, therefore, that Papen was fully justified in believing that Hitler could be tamed. Within two months, Papen argued, 'we will have pushed Hitler so far into a corner that he'll squeak'.[25] Yet, within six months, all constraints had been eliminated. Hitler was able to kick away the ladder by which he had ascended to power and establish a dictatorship based in effect on a permanent state of emergency.

Hitler's first priority was to strengthen the position of the NSDAP in the Reichstag so that he could use the latter to force through measures to change the constitution. He intended, in other words, to use the democratic process to destroy democracy. He therefore demanded immediate elections, and the Reichstag was dissolved on 1 February, two days after his appointment as Chancellor. In the election campaign which followed, Hitler had two major advantages over the other parties. First, he had more direct access to the media, especially radio; this he used more effectively than any previous politician, thereby enhancing the electoral appeal of the NSDAP. Second, he was able to use emergency powers to weaken the position of some of his opponents. For example, the decree of 4 February made it possible to control the meetings of other parties. It also enabled Goering to draft a special police order in Prussia to the effect that the 'activities of subversive organizations are . . . to be combated with the most drastic measures'. Indeed, 'failure to act is more serious than errors committed in acting'.[26] Even more extreme measures were allowed by the decree of 28 February which suspended many personal liberties 'until further notice'. The pretext for this was a much publicized attempt to burn down the Reichstag building on 27 February. It used to be thought that this was a deliberate ploy by the Nazis to cast the blame on the Communists and SPD. It is now generally believed that the fire was the work of a single individual, van der Lubbe, and not part of an organized plot. Whatever the truth, however, the event was exploited by Hitler to the utmost. He was empowered to suspend various articles of the constitution and to take over the power of the state governments if necessary.

The election results were announced on 5 March. They showed considerable gains for the NSDAP when compared with the results of the elections of November 1932. The Nazi vote increased from 11.7 million to 17.2 million and its percentage of the total from 33.1 to 43.9. Hitler's partners, the DNVP, gained 200,000 votes and an extra seat. The Centre Party made marginal increases and the SPD remained about the same. Real losses were experienced by the DVP and other middle-class parties, and also by the Communists.

Three reasons can be given for Hitler's gains. The first is that his tactic in calling an immediate election completely unsettled his opponents. Most of the non-Nazis in his first cabinet had meekly submitted to this demand for a dissolution and, according to Broszat, 'were guilty of the first fateful blow against the concept of containing Hitler'. Second, there appears to have been a degree of resignation in the Reichstag itself as the deputies failed to use the Committee for the Protection of Parliamentary Rights effectively; this might have challenged Hitler's demand for an election as being too hasty. And third, the Nazi monopoly of the state media and extensive use of emergency decrees cut away much of the opposition's capacity to present an effective case against Hitler.

But the process of establishing a dictatorship was not yet complete, for the NSDAP still lacked an overall majority in the Reichstag. What happened next was a new offensive as the constitution was stormed from below, at the level of local government, and from above, within the Reichstag itself.

Recent historical studies have drawn attention to the importance of Nazi pressure in the individual states or *Länder*, in many cases amounting to a 'terrorist, revolutionary movement'.[27] In March 1933 SA and SS squads went into action, taking over town halls, police headquarters and newspapers. The resulting chaos was usually so serious that the central government had to intervene via the Minister of the Interior, Wilhelm Frick. Nazis were appointed to the local office of Police Commissioner and, on 7 April, a new law allowed for the installation of special Reich governors in all states. In effect, therefore, Nazi rule was imposed at the local level throughout Germany even before dictatorship had been completed at the centre. Nevertheless, Hitler was conscious of the need to restrain some of the wilder Nazi activists in case they should impede the revolution from above – which was now well under way.

The Reichstag reconvened on 21 March 1933. Hitler now intended to secure the passage of an Enabling Act which would radically reduce the Reichstag's powers. Such a major constitutional change, however, needed a two-thirds-majority vote, which the NSDAP and their allies, the DNVP, did not between them possess. Hitler's solution was ingenious. First, he used the emergency decree of 28 February to expel from the Reichstag all Communist deputies. He then negotiated with the Centre Party an agreement whereby the latter would vote for the Enabling Act in return for special guarantees for the Churches. Hitler was very reassuring on this point. He saw in Christianity 'the most important factors for the maintenance of our society' and would therefore 'permit and guarantee to the Christian denominations the enjoyment of their due influence in schools and education'.[28] On 23 March 1933 the Enabling Act secured its required majority, with only the SPD voting against it. Its terms virtually destroyed parliamentary powers by allowing the Chancellor to issue laws without consulting the Reichstag.

The changes now gathered momentum as the new power was used to eliminate other political parties. Between March and July all parties apart from the NSDAP were forced to wind themselves up. The whole process culminated in the law of 14 July 1933 'Against the Establishment of Parties' which declared it a criminal offence to organize any political grouping outside the NSDAP. Another election was held in November 1933, in which a single party list was put to the electorate for its approval. The result was that the NSDAP took all the seats in the Reichstag. Germany was officially a one-party state.

Why did the opposition give up? The most obvious reason is that it had no choice. The parties of the left were smashed by the government's emergency powers. The Communists, for example, were prevented from taking their seats in the Reichstag, and the SPD were banned outright in June. The Centre Party gave up any pretence at political opposition in return for a guarantee of religious freedom; it liquidated itself voluntarily. Even the DNVP was unable to keep itself afloat as its leaders found it increasingly obvious that they no longer had any hold on the political monster they had helped create. President Hindenburg, no admirer of the party system, made no attempt to interfere with Hitler's assault on the opposition, for fear of provoking a more violent and radical constitutional upheaval.

By the middle of 1933 Hitler was still not completely secure. His position could be upset either by the radical wing of his party or by the army. The most likely threat was that undisciplined action by the former could provoke a counter-blow from the latter.

The destructive capacity of the Nazi radicals had been evident in March 1933 when the rank and file had brought about at local level changes which were far more sweeping than Hitler had intended. The SA were especially violent and the party leadership regretted its earlier failure to tame them. By the middle of 1933 there were also demands for a new Nazi revolution. Ernst Röhm, for example, wanted to extend the scope of the SA so that the German army would be absorbed into it. Röhm expressed the disillusionment of the radical Nazis with Hitler's apparent caution: 'A tremendous victory has been won,' he argued, 'but not absolute victory.' He added: 'The SA and SS will not tolerate the German revolution going to sleep.'[29] Hitler was unimpressed by such views. He was particularly anxious to keep the support of those very interests under attack by Röhm. He was also opposed to radicalism for its own sake: 'Revolution is not a permanent condition . . . The stream of revolution once released must be guided into the secure bed of evolution.'[30] Further provocative activities were therefore to stop. Accordingly, Frick's circular of 6 October 1933 instructed the activists that 'These infringements and excesses must now cease once and for all.'[31]

What made Hitler particularly wary of antagonizing the army was that he hoped shortly to become President. Hindenburg was approaching death and the army, if threatened by the Nazis, might prevail upon him to nominate a successor.

Alternatively, the army might attempt a coup against Hitler, with or without Hindenburg's approval. Hitler would be able to counter this coup with the help of the SA, but this would make him a virtual prisoner of the radicals. He could, however, adopt another course: he could crush the SA with the support of the army and, over a period, establish the same influence over the military commanders as he had over the politicians. There would be more chance of total penetration and control if Nazification was slow and cautious. The army had good reason to co-operate with Hitler: it hated the programme of the SA and was particularly averse to Röhm's aim to see 'the grey rock' of the Reichswehr submerged in the 'brown flood' of the SA. The dislike was mutual: the SA despised the aristocratic connections of the army officers, while the army regarded the SA leadership as uncouth upstarts. The Reichswehr commanders saw Hitler as the moderate who would seek to preserve at least some of the traditional values. They were therefore prepared to do a deal with Hitler; they would stand back while Hitler took whatever measures he considered necessary against his own delinquents. They would even intervene to save Hitler from the SA if necessary.

As events turned out, their help was not required. By the beginning of July 1934, the SA leadership had been cut down by Hitler's elite corps, the SS. The 'Night of the Long Knives' claimed the lives of Röhm, Strasser and many other Nazis who were considered disruptive. A grateful army was now prepared to concede to Hitler the office of head of state. When Hindenburg died five weeks later, Hitler succeeded him as Reich President, adding the title of Führer for good measure. The army took an oath of personal allegiance: 'I swear before God to give my unconditional obedience to Adolf Hitler, Führer of the Reich and of the German People, Supreme Commander.'[32]

A legal revolution?

The political changes accomplished between 1933 and 1934 have often been referred to as a 'legal revolution'. Part of the process was accomplished, technically at least, within the ambit of the constitution: this is considered to have made it legal. The results, however, were so devastating that they amounted to a 'revolution'. There is much to support the use of this term as a description of Hitler's overall approach in the opening years of his regime. He had already followed a strategy of legality after the failure of the Munich Putsch in 1923, achieving power constitutionally with the intention of subsequently introducing a 'revolution from above'. This 'revolution' was now accomplished, step by step, within the literal terms of the constitution of the Weimar Republic.

There are several examples of this process. The Enabling Act, passed on 24 March, contained as part of its preamble the words 'The requirements of legal Constitutional change having been met.'[33] This was a clear reference to the achievement of the two-thirds majority required within the Reichstag for such an important amendment. The Enabling Act, in turn, became the vehicle by which the Chancellor used executive powers to modify the whole range of political functions within the Reich. The bureaucracy was brought into line with the new relationship between executive and legislature by the law of 7 April 'for the restoration of the professional civil service' which purged the bureaucracy of potential opponents and non-Aryans. The system of state government was reorganized by law of 31 March 'for the co-ordination of the *Länder* of the Reich'. The whole concept of *Gleichschaltung* ('co-ordination') was therefore slipped through with at least a pretence at a legal basis. The NSDAP were given the monopoly of political power through the law against the new formation of parties, passed on 14 July 1933. Finally, the chancellorship and the presidency were combined on 1 August 1934, following the death of Hindenburg.

At first sight the extent of the constitutional changes introduced scarcely warrants the description 'revolution', especially by contrast with the changes brought by the Bolsheviks in Russia. After all, the Reichstag and the Reichsrat remained intact as legislative institutions. Lenin had, by contrast, taken the decision to remove any remaining connection with Western-style constituent assemblies and to substitute a legislative system based upon soviets. In Germany all of the previous ministries were retained. Indeed, the lists of official positions within Hitler's cabinet were remarkably similar to those within the Weimar Republic: these included the Foreign Minister, Interior Minister, Finance Minister and ministers for Economics, Justice, Defence, Food, Posts, Labour and Transport. By this analysis the Nazification of the institutions of the Weimar Republic occurred in such a way as to minimize the chance of a sudden climactic break which might generate resistance. The process was done step by step, each depending on the one before. There was therefore a certain inexorable logic.

From another viewpoint, the concept of 'legal revolution' is paradoxical at the best of times. When applied to the development of Nazi dictatorship the paradox becomes perverse. The whole emphasis was on using the legal powers of the Weimar constitution to destroy its political authority, not to amend it. Throughout the period there was at best a very thinly disguised use of legality and, at worst, a blatant disregard for it.

The observance of the constitution was strictly limited: the letter of the law may have been kept, but the spirit of the law was not. Hitler's objective was nothing less than the destruction of the Weimar Republic, which he achieved on three counts. First, he converted emergency powers from a precautionary to a regular process. The Enabling Act turned Article 48 on its head by making permanent what had originally been conceived as a temporary power. This completely destroyed the original aim. Article 48 had been included to preserve democracy against future enemies, whereas the Enabling Act was clearly based on the premise that democracy itself was the enemy. A second principle to be shredded was the autonomous power of the *Länder*. Laws issued under the Enabling Act abolished the rights of the *Länder* legislatures and subordinated the state Ministers-President to the Ministry of the Interior in Berlin. This undermined the entire federal system which had been a crucial part of the Weimar constitution. Third, the law against the new formation of parties wiped out the multi-party system, a vital ingredient of the Weimar Republic. Without the element of choice, the purpose of voting was nullified and with it the extension of the franchise to men and women over twenty. Proportional representation, too, ceased to have any meaning. The notion of legality was therefore a mockery. A democratic constitution was imploded by anti-democrats who targeted its emergency charges inwards.

It is not even certain that the Nazis observed the *letter* of the constitution. Hitler's 'legal' changes were accompanied by a considerable degree of mobilized pressure

– of the very type that the constitution was originally conceived to prevent. Article 48 was intended for presidential use to put down mass activism, not to unleash it against selected constitutional targets. Hildebrand, refers to 'Nazi terrorist tactics'[34] and maintains that 'it was often difficult to distinguish terroristic from legal measures'.[35] There are two examples to support this view. First, the Nazi control over the Ministry of the Interior and other key organs of state gave them control over the police apparatus. Goering used this to create an auxiliary police force, the Gestapo, which comprised members of both the SA and the SS. The result was paradoxical: a rampage of law and order directed against political enemies of the Nazi movement – in other words, an officially sanctioned continuation of previously illegal methods. The same involvement of the violent men of the SA can be seen in the intimidation of Social Democrat deputies during the Reichstag vote on the Enabling Bill in March 1933. By the whole range of legal principles, from constitutional law to natural equity, such a gross interference would normally be seen to have invalidated the outcome.

The Nazi revolution included also the element of the mass movement which was entirely incompatible with the principle of legality. This was apparent even during the course of the so-called period of legality, especially in the town hall revolutions, by which the SA purged local governments, and by the boycotting of Jewish stores from 1 April 1933. It might, of course, be argued that the real revolutionaries were the leaders of the SA and that Hitler took emergency measures against these in the Night of the Long Knives. On the other hand, Hitler halted the second revolution not through a preference for legality, but rather for reasons of safety. If he was to remain in power Hitler had to avoid the possibility of a military coup launched by conservatives, something which might be triggered by premature expressions of radicalism. Thus caution had more to do with common sense and pragmatism than with legality – which, in any case, can hardly be used to describe the method by which the leaders of the SA were eliminated.

Finally, the Nazi apparatus came to be dominated by a body which was as far from the constitutional apparatus of the Weimar Republic as it is possible to conceive. The SS/Gestapo/SD complex came to dominate the whole regime. According to Schoenbaum, 'in one form or another the SS made foreign policy, military policy and agricultural policy. It administered occupied territories as a kind of self-contained Ministry of the Interior and maintained itself economically with autonomous enterprises.' This was a revolution in the political structure of Germany which transcended all notions of legality.

Party, government and leadership

By the end of 1934 Hitler had, to all intents and purposes, destroyed the Weimar Republic. The constitution of 1919 was never formally abrogated but all opposition parties had been eliminated, individual rights withdrawn, the Reichstag's control over the government ended, and all the major offices of state concentrated into the hands of one man. Democracy had been superseded by dictatorship and institutionalized terror. The traditional view is that this was efficient and tightly organized, with Hitler in total control. This view has, however, undergone modification. It is now argued that the German dictatorship was far less orderly than used to be supposed; indeed, there were elements of chaos. Basically, there existed in the Third Reich two competing trends. One was the revolutionary activism of the Nazi movement, the other the persistence of traditional institutions and structures. The result was duplication, overlapping and conflict, evidence of which can be seen at the levels both of central and local governments.

Despite the so-called 'Nazi revolution', central government experienced a surprising degree of continuity. All the former ministries were retained, and their powers were even increased by the Enabling Act. The civil service continued to function; in the words of Noakes and Pridham, it was a 'bureaucracy of high competence and long traditions'.[36] There was certainly no attempt to destroy existing institutions and to replace them with new NSDAP organs. Hitler was never over-enthusiastic about the idea of undiluted party rule, but preferred to develop parallel institutions, which generally competed with each other. There were several examples of this process. One was the appointment of Special Deputies who were outside the government ministries but fulfilled similar functions to ministers. Hence, Todt, as General Inspector for German Roads, overlapped and came into conflict with the Minister of Transport, while the Youth Leader of the Reich had powers which impinged on those of the Minister of Education.[37]

The confusion was compounded by the development of a third layer of personnel, who were outside the scope both of the normal ministers and of the parallel party functionaries. These included the office of the Deputy Führer, the Four Year Plan Office (along, confusingly, with its six ministries), and the SS/Gestapo/SD complex under the authority of Himmler. All this resulted in widespread inefficiency. The main problems were the duplication of functions between agencies and growing conflict between officials. On numerous occasions appeals were made to the Führer himself to arbitrate in disputes between them. His response was to distance himself from routine disputes and to rely upon Hess as a mediator. Faced with this sort of problem, it is hardly surprising that there was a threat of creeping inertia among subordinates as officials at all levels shied away from taking responsibility through fear of making a mistake – not of policy but of jurisdiction.

Untidiness and overlapping were also apparent in local government, where two main types of authority jostled for power. The first type comprised the traditional authorities, under the Minister-President of each state. This office was retained even when the Reich was reconstructed in January 1934 and the federal system weakened. The Minister-President was regarded as a useful post in the Nazi regime and was subordinated to the central government's Ministry of the Interior. Meanwhile, a second type of official had emerged – one which was based more directly on the party. Hitler decided to appoint ten Reich Governors from among the most prominent of the Party *Gauleiters*; their purpose was to enforce the Führer's edicts and orders. What happened was open competition and conflict between the Ministers-President and the Governors, each complaining regularly to central government about the activities of the other.

What was the reason for this curious state of affairs? Two broad explanations have been advanced by historians. One is that Hitler did all this on purpose. The 'intentionalists' argue that Hitler deliberately set his institutions and officials against each other in order to maintain his own position as the only one who could manoeuvre between them. Bracher, for example, maintains that Hitler remained detached from the struggles between officials: 'the antagonisms of power were only resolved in the key position of the omnipotent Führer'; indeed 'the dictator held a key position precisely because of the confusion of conflicting power groups'.[38] Similarly, Hildebrand believes that 'The confusion of functions among a multitude of mutually hostile authorities made it necessary and possible for the Führer to take decisions in every case of dispute, and can be regarded as a foundation of his power.'[39]

An alternative position is taken by historians usually categorized as 'structuralists' or 'functionalists'. They stress that any chaos was entirely unintended and that it resulted from confusion and neglect. Far from deliberately distancing himself from competing officials in order to maintain his position, Hitler was simply showing incompetence and administrative weakness. According to Broszat, 'The authoritative Führer's will was expressed only irregularly, unsystematically and incoherently.'[40] Mommsen maintains that 'Instead of functioning as a balancing element in the government, Hitler disrupted the conduct of affairs by continually acting on sudden impulses, each one different, and partly by delaying decisions on current matters.'[41]

Which of these is the more likely scenario? As is often the case in historical interpretation, a judicious combination of the two schools is possible. There is no doubt that Hitler did whatever he could to fragment potential opposition: indeed, he had already welcomed the partial collapse of the party while he was in Landsberg prison. It is not, therefore, beyond the realms of possibility that he welcomed discordance within the state in order to regulate his subordinates and prevent the emergence of 'overmighty' barons. The 'intentionalists' therefore have a point. On the other hand, it is difficult to imagine this being planned. The deliberate projection of chaos carries enormous risks which may seem justifiable in retrospect but which can hardly have been chanced at the time. In any case, if the original 'legal revolution' had been 'planned' on the basis of the simplest and most direct route to dictatorship, what would have been the logic in complicating the process by deliberately creating overlapping bureaucratic layers? The balance of credibility therefore switches here to the 'structuralists'. But only when considering the origins of the chaos; once we focus on its continuation, Bracher's perspective makes more sense. Conceding that the chaos was unintended, what possible motive could Hitler have had for tolerating it unless it was in his interests to do so? Would it be too much to assume that, having adjusted his approach to taking power by 1933 and to consolidating it by 1934, Hitler would have been unable to correct any aberrations thrown up in the process? It is more likely that it suited Hitler to live with the chaos which had emerged despite his efforts because this was an effective way of cancelling out trouble-makers within the party. Broszat therefore convincingly explains the origins of the Nazi administrative chaos, with Bracher providing the vital reason for its continuation.

The apparatus of coercion and terror

Changes in the political system were accompanied and reinforced by the transformation of the institutions of justice and of law and order. The basic principles of the law were radically altered while, at the same time, there developed an enormously powerful apparatus of coercion and terror. In effect, the Third Reich was under a perpetual state of emergency.

The legal system was profoundly altered, in both theory and practice. Hitler disliked the 'liberal' and 'formalistic' elements of legal theory. Instead, he insisted that the basis of law should be 'healthy popular feeling' and 'welfare of the national community'.[42] In other words, more attention was to be given to social influences. Naturally these were to be directed by the party and expressed as 'the will of the Führer'. In practice, the 'legal revolution' brought government control over the whole judiciary. Judges were appointed on the basis of loyalty and part of their training 'must include a serious study of National Socialism and its ideological foundations'.[43] For a while the process of Nazification was incomplete. The Minister of Justice, Gürtner, was not himself a Nazi. On his death in 1941, however, he was succeeded by Thierack, and the whole judicial system slid under the control of the SS.

The SS comprised a complex set of institutions collectively known as the SS/Gestapo/SD complex, which, according to Noakes and Pridham, was 'a separate organizational framework for the enforcement of the will of the regime'.[44] The complex grew from three separate strands to form a network which covered all areas of policing and security. The SS (Schutzstaffeln), originated in 1925 as the elite within the SA and came under the leadership of Himmler in 1929. The SD (Sicherheitsdienst) was set up in 1931 as the NSDAP's internal police force. The Gestapo (Geheime Staatspolizei) was established in Prussia by Goering in April 1933 and was initially accountable to the Ministry of the Interior. Gradually these three strands came together under SS control. In November 1934 Himmler became the effective head of the Gestapo, to which he added the position of Reichsführer SS. The process was officially recognized in Hitler's decree of 17 June 1936 'to unify the control of police duties in the Reich'. From this stage onwards the SS expanded even further. It penetrated the army by means of the SS Special Service Troops (SS-Verfugungstruppe – SS VT); from this was created the Waffen SS, the vanguard divisions which were at the forefront of every military campaign. Finally, the SS took took over from the SA the organization of the concentration camps, manning them with the Death's Head Formations (SS-Totenkopfverbände – SS-TV), while the genocide programme from 1941 came under the control of the Reich Security Main Office (Reichssicherheitshauptamt, or RSHA). The SS were therefore directly involved in the mass extermination programme and in working to death 'anti-social elements' such as 'Jews, gypsies, Russians and Ukrainians, Poles with sentences of more than three years, Czechs and Germans with sentences of more than eight years'.[45]

These developments altered the whole balance of the Nazi state. At first the regime was a compromise between party influences on the one hand and, on the other, the traditional forces in the administration, army and business. In 1933 and 1934, the period of the so-called 'legal revolution', the SS played a subordinate role. Increasingly, however, it became independent of both the party and the state. During the war the SS organized the whole network of conquered territories as well as the programmes for slave labour and extermination. This has led some historians to believe that by 1941 the Nazi state had been transformed into an SS state. In the process, the SS had become the agent of radicalization. In some respects, Himmler went even further than Hitler, especially in his attitude to Christianity. In 1937 he argued that 'It is part of the mission of the SS to give the German people over the next fifty years the non-Christian ideological foundations for a way of life appropriate to their character.' The SS also maintained the racial emphasis of the Volksgemeinschaft far more completely than did any of the state institutions, which tended to follow a more pragmatic course. It could be argued that Himmler and Goebbels, much as they disliked each other personally, were complementary in real-izing the racial mission of Nazism. The difference was that Goebbels hoped to achieve it within the institutional structure of the state, while Himmler sought to transcend the state altogether.

Yet, for all its influence, there were fundamental flaws within the SS/Gestapo/SD complex. The strongest criticism has been made by Höhne, who believes that

> the SS world was a bizarre nonsensical affair, devoid of all logic . . . history shows that the SS was anything but an organization constructed and directed on some diabolically efficient system: it was the product of accident and automa-tism. The real history of the SS is a story of idealists and criminals, of place-seekers and romantics: it is the history of the most fantastic association of men imaginable.[46]

This probably goes too far: after all, might the last point not apply to the story of Nazism generally? But given that the 'fantastic' *did* occur, the SS should rather be seen as a vital structural part in its realization. This makes more sense than seeing it as a fantastic part of the Nazi system. The identification of deficiencies therefore needs to be more specific. One was the perpetual conflict between Himmler and other Nazi leaders such as Goering, Frank and Bormann. Another was the growing difference, within the SS itself, between Himmler and Heydrich, the former drawn to racial 'idealism', the latter being more opportunistic and pragmatic. More funda-mentally, the SS structure was enormously complex, constantly changing shape and generating increasing subdivisions.

Historians have also questioned the extent to which these substructures within the SS complex were fully competent. The most recent target has been the Gestapo. Along with the Soviet KGB, the Gestapo became the twentieth-century's epitome of the effective and all-embracing totalitarian police force affecting the entire popu-lation. But how true is this picture?

On the one hand, the Gestapo has been seen as a success story. Crankshaw, for example, considered it a 'highly professional corps'.[47] According to Schultz, 'scarcely a politically significant initiative against the National Socialist regime went undetected'.[48] Delarue maintains, 'Never before, in no other land and at no other time, had an organisation attained such a comprehensive penetration of society, possessed such power.'[49]

Recent views, by contrast, have stressed that the reputation of the Gestapo is a myth which derives from its own propaganda. Mallman and Paul argue that the Gestapo was insufficiently equipped to carry out its directives and that it had to rely on information volunteered by members of the public. Recent local studies show that 'the Gestapo at local level was hardly an imposing detective organiza-tion, but rather an under-staffed, under-bureaucratized agency, limping along behind the permanent inflation of its tasks'.[50] This applied to Gestapo headquarters in Stettin, Koslin, Hannover, Bremen, Dortmund, Düsseldorf, Würzburg and other areas. The outbreak of war aggravated the problem with a further decline in the number of staff. Inexperienced officials replaced those who had been conscripted into the army. The total membership of the Gestapo was little more than 32,000, of which only half were fully concerned with the task of political policing.[51] In the circumstances it could function only through the enormous number of denunciations which came from a generally compliant population.

It is indeed quite possible that the effectiveness of the Gestapo was superseded by the East German police force, the Stasi, itself directly influenced by the Soviet NKVD and KGB. This is a clear indication that the totalitarian policing methods of Stalin's Russia were more effective than those of Hitler's Germany. But the Soviet Union had no equivalent to the SS, the most completely totalitarian part of the Nazi regime. Certainly Himmler came closer than the official administration to giving effect to the incoherent ramblings of Hitler's *Mein Kampf.*

Indoctrination and propaganda

Goebbels said at a press conference on 15 March 1933: 'It is not enough for people to be more or less reconciled to our regime, to be persuaded to adopt a neutral attitude towards us; rather we want to work on people until they have capitulated to us, until they grasp ideologically that what is happening in Germany today not only *must* be accepted but also *can* be accepted.'[52] In a speech at a Nazi Party Congress in Nuremberg on 7 September 1934 he emphasized the importance of propaganda: 'Among the arts with which one rules a people, it ranks in first place ... There exists no sector of public life which can escape its influence.'[53]

An administrative infrastructure was clearly needed to co-ordinate the transmission of ideology. This was developed by two changes. The first increased the power of the Ministry of Education over the states, or *Länder,* to remove the possible threat of local particularism to the achievement of educational conformity. The second established a new Ministry for People's Enlightenment and Propaganda in 1933. Under the overall control of Goebbels, this eventually comprised a series of chambers for press, radio, theatre, music, creative arts and film. In theory the regime now had the power to apply negative censorship in whatever form it considered necessary and, more constructively, to shape the development of culture at all levels.

How effectively did these institutions carry out the regime's intentions? Any assessment needs to make a distinction between 'propaganda' and 'indoctrination'. It is true that the two were connected in that indoctrination of the population involved regular exposure to official propaganda. There were, however, separate features. Indoctrination was a process carried out largely in education, the youth movements, the workplace and the armed forces. Propaganda made more direct use of channels such as radio, cinema and the press. Indoctrination was a continuous, long-term process, whereas propaganda provided the highlights.

Indoctrination, education and youth movements

The methods used to indoctrinate Germany's youth were nothing if not thorough. The main intention was to indoctrinate, to implant fixed ideas and doctrines, rather than to open minds. Hence, Hitler once said, 'When an opponent declares "I will

not come over to your side", I calmly say, "Your child belongs to us already."'
The subjects primarily affected were history, which emphasized Nordic, Nazi and
military themes; science, based strongly on Nazi race theories; and literature, which
was virulently anti-Semitic. The school curriculum also received the additions of
race study and eugenics, used as vehicles for Nazi ideology. Teachers were recruited
and kept for their ideological conformity, their main obligation being 'to defend
without reservation the National Socialist state'.[54] To guarantee this degree of
loyalty, membership of the Nationalsozialistische Lehrerbund (NSLB), or Nazi
Teachers' Association, was compulsory. The impact of these measures was considerable, creating among the young an emotional commitment to the regime which
was often absent in the adult population. The universities were also the target of a
regime which both despised and feared the academic world. Again the emphasis
was on ideological conformity. The Minister of Culture told the universities in 1933:
'From now on, it will not be your job to determine whether something is true, but
whether it is in the spirit of the National Socialist revolution.'[55] To enforce this
new approach to higher learning, the government deprived university senates of
their authority and assumed control of the appointment of rectors.

In many ways, however, the educational process was flawed. Changes were held
up by constant argument between administrative and party organs. For example,
the Ministry of Education continued to use the guidelines of the Weimar Republic
largely because it could not agree with the party headquarters the shape of their
replacement. The conflict between Ley and Rust on the one hand and Bormann and
Hess on the other meant that the new regulations for elementary education were
delayed until 1939, while secondary schools were served little better. This had two
unfortunate side-effects for the Nazis. One was the dilution of the content of the
curriculum by more traditional influences than was originally intended. The other
was the persistence of confusion within the schools themselves as to the precise
means of delivering the curriculum. Gestapo reports were full of references to unsatisfactory teachers; but many of these were probably confused rather than deliberately
uncooperative. There was also a serious decline in educational standards. A typical
complaint expressed by the army was that 'Many of the candidates applying for
commissions display a simply inconceivable lack of elementary knowledge.'[56]
Vocational and technical schools frequently claimed that basic ignorance seriously
impeded normal coverage of the curriculum. There were also problems in higher
education: Nazi policies led inevitably to a decline in the standard of scientific
research, especially with the abolition of the 'Jewish Physics' of Albert Einstein.
Ultimately Germany paid a heavy penalty for this straitjacket on academic freedom,
losing against the Western Allies the race to develop the atomic bomb.

Indoctrination was also attempted by means of mobilization through the youth
movements. All young people were to be trained for a future role. In the case of
boys this was military service, while for girls the emphasis was on preparation for
marriage and motherhood. To ensure the martial and marital message did get through,
boys and girls were co-opted into the Hitler Youth. This was subdivided into several
components. Boys joined the Deutsches Jungvolk (DJ) at the age of ten, proceeding
at fourteen into the Hitlerjugend (HJ). Similarly, girls entered the Jungmädelbund
(JM) at ten and the Bund Deutscher Madel (BDM) at fourteen. The whole organization was placed under the control of Baldur von Shirach as the Reichsjugendführer.

In some respects the varied activities had widespread appeal, initially appearing as a challenge to more conservative forms of authority and giving youth a sense of collective power. But again the process suffered through administrative imbalance. This time there were arguments between the Ministry of Education and the Reich Youth Leadership as to underlying objectives and overriding priorities. Consequently the Hitler Youth and the educational system often diverged. The whole system also began to lose the edge of its initial appeal as it came to be seen as part of a new establishment and eventually as merely a nursery for military mobilization. As the best of the youth leaders moved into the army, the official youth programme became more routine and less imaginative. The result was that a growing proportion of German youth was attracted by alternative organizations such as the Edeleweiss Pirates and the Swing Movement (see p. 192), both considered deviant by the authorities.

Education and youth movements lacked a completely clear statement of ideology which, as in other spheres, remained eclectic. As Peukert argues, 'the ideological content of National Socialism remained too vague to function as a self-sufficient educational objective. In practice young people selected from competing information-sources and values which were on offer.'[57] As it turned out, the impact of war meant that the more positive elements of the Hitler Youth disappeared altogether, while alternative subcultures became increasingly influential. In this way Nazi Germany unintentionally gave birth to modern youth culture – not as an integral part of conformity but as an autonomous and sometimes hostile response to it. Nothing could have been further from the intention of the Nazi leadership.

Propaganda and culture

If indoctrination had a significant but limited impact on youth, could the same be said about the effect of propaganda on the rest of the population? A further distinction needs to be made at this point between the control of propaganda *channels*, such as radio, cinema and the press, and the attempts to influence *cultural* output in literature, art and music.

The Nazis gave priority to the radio since this increased the impression of personal contact between the people and their leader, thereby enhancing the effectiveness of the Führer cult. Goebbels argued that modern methods were essential here:

> Technology must not be allowed to proceed ahead of the Reich; the Reich must go along with technology. Only the most modern things are good enough. We are living now in an age when the masses must support policies . . . It is the task of State propaganda so to simplify complicated ways of thinking that even the smallest man in the street may understand.[58]

Increased access to radio sets was, of course, an essential prerequisite for the success of this approach. This was achieved, with ownership of sets increased from 25 per cent of households in 1932 to 70 per cent by 1939, the largest proportion anywhere in the world. These were all brought into a web of the Reich Broadcasting Corporation, over which the government established control in 1933. Radio was also used to generate a feeling of collective loyalty, as was shown in a notice from a local paper in Neu-Isenberg near Frankfurt on 16 March 1934:

> Attention! The Führer is speaking on the radio. On Wednesday 21 March, the Führer is speaking on all German stations from 11.00 to 11.50 a.m. According to a regulation of the Gau headquarters, the district Party headquarters has ordered that all factory owners, department stores, offices, shops, pubs and blocks of flats put up loudspeakers an hour before the broadcast of the Führer's speech so that the whole workforce and all national comrades can participate fully in the broadcast. The district headquarters expects this order to be obeyed without exception so that the Führer's wish to speak to his people can be implemented.[59]

For the vast majority of the population the radio provided the most abiding impression of the Führer that they were ever likely to have. As such this component of propaganda must go down as a considerable success.

Film proved a more difficult medium and the regime used it less effectively than it did radio. The most accomplished film was not necessarily the most influential. Riefenstahl's *Triumph of the Will* was commissioned by Hitler himself as a record of the Nuremberg rallies of 1934. Technically a brilliant achievement, it created a multi-layered image of Nazism which brought in all elements of society and directly fostered the Führer cult. On the other hand, it was too long for most audiences, who sometimes reacted negatively to the repetition of the same types of scene. During the war years the anti-Semitic component of films became more extreme; here, however, Hitler's vision of what was likely to engage the public was less effective than that of Goebbels. *The Eternal Jew*, commissioned by Hitler and directed by Hippler, was so crude that audiences were repelled by the images created. The anti-Semitic message was conveyed more skilfully through a feature film, *Jud Süss*. By this stage, Goebbels had learned how to introduce propaganda as a subliminal message within the context of a story with which the viewers could identify. This applied also to his attempts to engender a spirit of resistance to the Allies with his film on Frederick the Great. But such developments came too late to have anything but a peripheral effect on the morale of a population facing imminent defeat.

Channelling the press for propaganda was also problematic. Because it was based on a more traditional technology, it had had longer than radio to develop within the structure of private ownership; radio, by contrast, could be taken over relatively easily by the state. The proliferation of newspapers during the liberal era of the Weimar Republic accentuated the difficulty: by 1933 there were about 4,700 daily newspapers in Germany, representing a wide variety of political and regional views and loyalties. It is true that the government achieved administrative control. Between 1933 and 1945, for example, state-owned newspapers increased from 2.5 per cent of the total to 82 per cent. The German News Agency, or DNB, provided regulations for the presentation of news and all journalists were made responsible to the state rather than to their editors. But the result was a bland form of journalism which produced a decline in public interest, which was hardly surprising given the type of blatant interference shown in this extract from a press conference in the Propaganda Ministry in 1935:

> The Propaganda Ministry asks us to put to editors-in chief the following requests, which must be observed in future with particular care. Photos showing members of the Reich Government at dining tables in front of rows of bottles

must not be published in future, particularly since it is known that a large number of the Cabinet are abstemious. Ministers take part in social events for reasons of international etiquette and for strictly official purposes, which they regard merely as a duty and not as a pleasure. Recently, because of a great number of photos, the utterly absurd impression has been created among the public that members of the Government are living it up. News pictures must therefore change in this respect.[60]

Throughout the period, the regime was never able to use the press to generate support. The emphasis of its censorship therefore tended to be preventive rather than creative.

The Nazi relationship with culture was ambivalent. On the one hand, it distrusted some of the traditional content. On the other, it never quite succeeded in providing an alternative. In literature, art and music, censorship created a contemporary vacuum which a new and distinctive Nazi culture was intended to fill. The results differed in intensity. Literature produced a complete void; music was less affected; and the vacuum of art was most filled – but with work of distressingly low quality.

Literature was heavily affected by preventive censorship. This involved book-burning sessions, mobilized by the SA, and the removal of over 2,500 German authors from the approved lists. To some extent, destruction was cathartic – the relief of pent-up anti-intellectualism. It could never seriously have been the preliminary to an alternative Nazi literature. It discouraged any diversity of viewpoints and individual experience, seeking instead to stereotype collectivism. Within this atmosphere any chance of creating much of an 'official' literature disappeared, even supposing that the population would have been allowed any time to read it.

If, however, the Nazis gave up on literature as a form of propaganda, they made more effort to use the visual arts to put across basic blood and soil values. Painters like Kampf and Ziegler were able to provide pictorial stereotypes of physical appearance, of women as mothers and home-minders, and of men in a variety of martial roles. Such images reinforced the roles already developed through the institutions of indoctrination, such as the BDM and the HJ. On the negative side, the result was a form of art which was bland and lacking in talent: the vacuum produced by preventive censorship was filled with mediocrity. Much of the 'Nazi' art was derivative and eclectic: for example, Kampf's study of *Venus and Adonis* was a thinly disguised copy of earlier masters such as Rubens and David. The effect of such plagiarism on the public cannot have been anything more than peripheral, especially since there was always more interest in exhibitions of non-Nazi art which were officially classed as 'degenerate'. Of all the art forms, it was architecture which held the deepest interest for Hitler; it would, after all, be the visible measure of the expected millennium of Nazi rule. Hitler made the revealing comment in 1937 that 'the greater the demands the state makes upon its people, the more imposing it must appear to them'. He therefore became obsessively involved in designs for the rebuilding of Berlin and Nuremberg – plans eventually scrapped because of their unsurpassed ugliness.

The Nazi regime ended the period of musical experimentation which had been a major cultural feature of the Weimar Republic. The works of Schoenberg and Berg were considered un-German, while those of Mendelssohn were banned as 'Jewish'.

Yet the majority of German or Austrian composers were unaffected and retained their place as part of Germany's cultural heritage. The Nazis did, however, use certain composers as the spearhead of their cultural penetration: foremost among these was Wagner, whose *Ring* cycle was seen by Hitler as the musical embodiment of *völkisch* values. Contemporary composers like Richard Strauss and Carl Orff had ambivalent attitudes. They managed to coexist with the regime and produce work which outlived the Reich. In this sense the quality of the Reich's musical output was superior to the work of painters like Kampf and Ziegler, but the result was less distinctively Nazi. Overall, Nazi culture was ephemeral and, unlike Socialist Realism in Russia, had no lasting impact.

Indoctrination, propaganda and the test of war

The ultimate test of the success of Nazi propaganda was whether the people of Germany could be brought to accept the experience of war. Throughout the Nazi era there were really two levels of propaganda: one put across Hitler's basic ideology, the other made pragmatic adjustments to fit the needs of the moment. Up to 1939, pragmatism frequently diluted ideology, giving rise to considerable theoretical inconsistency in Hitler's ideas. During this period Hitler was presented as a man of peace and yet all the processes of indoctrination and propaganda emphasized struggle and its martial refinement.

The period 1939–45 tended to bring together more completely the man and his ideas. This occurred in two stages. The first was the acclimatization of the people to the idea of war, achieved through the emphasis on Blitzkrieg, or 'lightning war'. Logically this fitted in with the notion of easy conquest achieved by the 'master race', and while it lasted it was a considerable success: Hitler probably reached the peak of his popularity in 1940, at the time of the fall of France. During the second stage, however, propaganda had to acclimatize the people to the experience of war. At first Goebbels scored a propaganda success in his 'total war' speech in 1941, but in the longer term there was a clear decline in popular enthusiasm. From 1943 the main characteristic shown by German civilians was fortitude in the face of adversity and destruction, not a fanatical desire to achieve a world vision. By this stage, Nazi propaganda and indoctrination had not so much failed but become irrelevant.

Relations with the Churches

Germany has, since the Reformation, been divided between the Protestant north and the mainly Catholic south. Both denominations had been highly suspicious of what they saw as the blatant secularism of the Weimar Republic and were prepared to do a deal with the Nazi regime. Hitler's initial attitude was reassuring. He said in the Reichstag on 23 March 1933 that Christianity was 'the unshakeable foundation of the moral and ethical life of our people'.[61] There was, however, some doubt as to whether this was the real policy of the Nazis or merely a precaution to maintain a measure of support while the regime consolidated. The passage of time soon pointed to the latter.

The Protestant Churches were prepared to welcome the arrival of the Nazi regime, regarding the Weimar Republic as un-German and ungodly. Hitler took only six months to exploit this. In July 1933 the twenty-eight provincial Protestant Churches (Landeskirchen) were centralized into a single Reich Church, which soon came under Reich Bishop Müller. Then, in 1935, the Reich Church was placed under the control of Hans Kerrl, Minister of Church Affairs. There was also increasing evidence of the infiltration of Nazi values, with the establishment of the DC (German Christians). This sect managed to combine Christian beliefs with racism, anti-Semitism and Führer-worship, laying itself open to the accusation that it was the 'SA of Jesus Christ'. In opposition to the DC there emerged the Confessional Church, under the leadership of Pastor Niemoller. It retained its political detachment from the Nazi regime and, perhaps because of this, was banned in 1937, Niemoller himself being interned in a concentration camp.

The Catholic Church was also willing to collaborate with Hitler in 1933. The Centre Party, still a political arm of Catholicism, had supported Hitler's Enabling Act (March 1933) in return for certain religious guarantees from the government. This compromise was followed, in the same year, by the Concordat, drawn up by Cardinal Pacelli for the Church and by von Papen for the political authorities. This promised continuing freedom of worship, the protection of denominational schools and the right to publish and distribute pastoral letters. In exchange, the Church agreed to withdraw totally from active politics; the Centre Party, for instance, dissolved itself voluntarily. The Nazis, however, soon subverted the agreement. Various organizations, like the Cross and Eagle League and the Working Group of Catholic Germans, sought to disseminate Nazi values, while the government deliberately discredited the clergy by holding public 'immorality' trials involving nuns and monks. By 1937 the situation had deteriorated so badly that Pope Pius XI abandoned his earlier neutrality and issued an encyclical called *Mit brennender Sorge* ('With Deep Anxiety') which was strongly critical of government measures. This was followed by growing disillusionment within the Catholic Church and real doubts about ultimate Nazi intentions towards religion.

By the late 1930s these intentions had come out into the open. As the Churches reacted with hostility to government attempts to Nazify them, many party officials inclined increasingly to non-Christian forms of religion. One example was the German Faith Movement, which introduced pagan ceremonies (widely used by SS officials) and virulently attacked the most sacred tenets of Christianity. According to *Sigrune*, the journal of the German Faith Movement, 'Jesus was a cowardly Jewish lout who had certain adventures during his years of indiscretion.'[62] Two prominent Nazis were particularly anti-Christian, Julius Streicher, notorious anti-Semite and pornographer, claimed that the Crucifixion was an instance of Jewish ritual murder. Martin Bormann declared in 1941 that 'The concepts of National Socialism and Christianity are irreconcilable . . . Our National Socialist ideology is far loftier than the concepts of Christianity, which in their essential points have been taken over from Jewry.'[63] Given these extreme viewpoints, it is hardly surprising that the Nazi regime was considering banning the Churches altogether as soon as the war had been won.

Did Nazi persecution inflict any lasting damage? Kershaw provides several examples of the resilience of Christianity in Germany. During the 1930s there was no significant decline in Church membership, while an increase occurred during the war years. Meanwhile, the clergy managed to maintain a considerable influence over the laity. In the long term, the impact of the Churches on politics was strengthened, as was shown in the Catholic base of post-war Germany's CDU (Christian Democratic Union). Everything, therefore, 'points to the conclusion that Nazi policy failed categorically to break down religious allegiances'.[64]

Support and opposition

A considerable amount of research has now been done into the reactions of the German people to the Nazi regime. This partly challenges the traditional view that the population was terrorized into compliance, that support was enforced and that opposition was rare. Recent interpretation has followed two trends. One has been to question the ability of the totalitarian state to impose such total domination. The other shows that the population was far more active in expressing its views than was once thought. The implications of this are, on the one hand, that the regime must have experienced a considerable degree of willing support to enable it to function properly, while, on the other, there were substantial numbers of people who showed varying forms of defiance. Modern studies have put the focus on the people as much as on the institutions, and have come up with some intriguing results.

Support

Support can be either active or tacit, positive or negative. It can mean direct commitment through personal conviction or, alternatively, the absence of opposition through fear of the consequences. Both types existed in Nazi Germany.

The main reason for positive support was the personal popularity of Hitler. To many Germans, he was a direct successor to the populist vision of the Kaiser after 1888 and he made full use of the Führer Principle. His appeal also had a chameleon nature: he offered something different to each class and yet pulled them all together with the uniqueness of his own vision for the future. He struck a chord with the disillusionment with the institutions, parties and leaders of the Weimar Republic. He had, of course, the considerable advantage of a monopoly of the media which was used for the processes of indoctrination and propaganda. In a sense, however, Hitler transcended the image created by Goebbels. The main reason for his popularity – and this may seem surprising – was that he was seen as a moderate. After all, he made sure that his political changes were technically constitutional; he emphasized that he was upholding traditional virtues; and, at least until the late 1930s, he professed to be religious. Although there was considerable unease about others within the Nazi movement, like Röhm and Streicher, Hitler was widely trusted as the man who would control the thugs and tame the radicals. For this reason, he was seen 'practically as a hero' after the Night of the Long Knives in 1934.[65]

Part of Hitler's popularity came through his capacity to reassure. The rest was due to his ability to deliver results. To an extent he was fortunate. He benefited from a series of opportunities, which he seized. One was the cyclical upturn in the economy after 1933, for which he received the credit from a grateful population. He also gained considerable ground in his quest for satisfaction abroad. The German people compared with the rather slow developments of the Stresemann era Hitler's success in remilitarizing the Rhineland in 1936 and annexing Austria and the Sudetenland in 1938 – all without recourse to war. Even those with a vested interest in undermining Hitler's position admitted to the strength of his appeal. For example, the SPD in exile, SOPADE, drew up a number of reports, one of which stated that 'Many people are convinced that Germany's foreign-policy demands are justified and cannot be passed over. The last few days have been marked by big fresh advances in the Führer's personal reputation.'[66]

Not all Germans were taken in by the Führer cult; many saw through the projection of his image as an apparent moderate. Yet those who were not swept along found that there were many constraints on dissent. Constitutional changes had removed all possibility of voting for opposition parties or setting up new ones. Besides, the step-by-step approach of the 'legal revolution' had made opposition appear increasingly illogical. Why should it become justifiable when earlier steps taken by the Nazis within the same process had not been resisted? Hence, opposition, once considered a vital component of democracy, now became synonymous with disloyalty and treason. As such, it came within the scope of the terror applied by the SS and Gestapo. This was intended both to create object lessons and to isolate individuals by smashing the organization which might have given them voice. Terror worked well because it affected only a minority but, at the same time, promoted an unwillingness among the majority to speak out over issues which they considered did not immediately affect them. It made sense for most Germans to accept a trend which seemed inexorable rather than to make themselves a target for certain and terrible retribution.

Looking at the different sectors of the population has, in the past, produced a number of stereotypes. The upper and middle classes, for example, were seen as enthusiastic supporters of the regime, since they had brought Hitler to power in the first place. The working class, by contrast, were oppressed by the Nazi system and had to grow to accept it in the absence of the parties which they traditionally supported, the SPD and the KPD. The female population was repressed but compliant; youth became increasingly radical, even fanatical; and the army was split between fervent Nazi supporters and a substantial layer of higher officers, usually Prussian, who held the Nazis in barely concealed contempt. All this has now been modified by recent research.

The upper middle class, especially the business sector, had initially supported the Nazi Party out of fear of communism. During the Third Reich the great industrialists threw in their lot with Hitler because the regime delivered to them a disciplined workforce deprived of any effective means of collective bargaining. Although Marxist historians have tended to exaggerate the 'monopoly capital' influence on Nazism, there remains little doubt that the industrial barons and the regime saw eye to eye with each other. Mobilization for war brought an even closer identity, and many major industrial enterprises such as Krupp and I.G. Farben became implicated in the worst excesses of Nazi occupation.

The attitudes of the middle classes are more difficult to disentangle. Some sections benefited greatly from Nazi rule and became key elements in the support of the regime. But others were more marginalized. The small landowners or peasantry, for example, found themselves in an ambiguous position. On the one hand, they had been built up by Hitler as the basis of the Nazi blood and soil policy, and therefore as the most crucial component of the Volksgemeinschaft. On the other hand, the peasantry probably experienced the least benefit from the economic recovery from 1933 and had to suffer interference from the state in the form of the Reich Entailed Law, which prevented the subdivision of their estates. Nevertheless, any resentment remained quiescent and there was no direct opposition from this sector. Small businesses also had a mixed record. Those which were reasonably efficient thrived in the atmosphere of the mid-1930s, while those which were struggling went under. Hence, the successful artisanate tended to worship Hitler, while that sector which failed was in effect proletarianized and had to settle for being Nazified through institutions aimed at the working class. The salary-earning and white-collar sector of society, the so-called 'new' middle class, were less attracted by the 'blood and soil' or 'small self-made man' ethos of the Nazi appeal. They were, however, more responsive to the increased opportunities which accompanied economic revival and the rapidly growing bureaucratic complex which was Nazi Germany. The Nazi state was administered by huge numbers of officials who sank their individual identity into an impersonal system.

It was once argued that the working class remained more resistant to Nazi influences under the Volksgemeinschaft. It is true that the workers were less affected than the middle classes by the Führer cult and that they benefited far less from the economic recovery after 1933. After all, their wages were pegged, their working hours increased and their contributions to the GNP unacknowledged in wage increases. They therefore had cause for grievance. Yet the vast majority settled down into tacit support, becoming drawn into the activities and diversions offered by the KdF and SdA. Much of the workforce acknowledged the regime as the source of their economic recovery. Mason argues that 'the Nazi economic "miracle"' convinced many workers that 'things were getting better, especially as, for most of them, the point of reference was not the best years of the Weimar Republic but the more recent depths of the Depression'.[67] In any case, the full-scale use of modern methods, including the assembly-line process, made individual action increasingly difficult. The whole process was accentuated by the mobilization for war, which meant that 'Firm integration into traditional socio-cultural milieux was shaken.'[68] This made possible a growing loyalty to the leadership among the very people who had once been suspicious of it. According to contemporary evidence from SOPADE reports: 'There is no mistaking the enormous personal gains in credibility and prestige that Hitler has made, mainly perhaps among workers.'[69]

Women were for many years seen by historians as a distinct group, forced into compliance to the Nazi regime. Recent historiography, to which major contributions have been made by women, has moved away from this approach by integrating them more fully into the mainstream of German life. As such, women would have had the full range of views about Hitler. Nazism would, on the one hand, have exercised an appeal based on the family and home, reinforced by improved provision for maternity and for family benefits. Against this, of course, was the resentment caused by the removal of women from sectors of employment like the professions. But this was often offset by the creation of new roles within party and public organizations, in which many women became actively involved. Hence, for some women, the Nazi regime brought further opportunities than had been available under the Weimar Republic. This applied especially to women who had few formal qualifications but wished to be involved in political activism. By 1935 about 11 million out of the country's 35 million females belonged to the NS-Frauenschaft and were willing to support the ideas and beliefs of Nazism. Not all of these were meekly subservient: some, who were Nazi activists, challenged the official line on gender subordination. For example, a Nazi feminist, Sophie Rogge-Berne, argued in 1937 that it was misguided to remove women from the professions since 'Women doctors could give aid and comfort to fatigued mothers. Women teachers would be most suited to instruct adolescent girls. Women jurists would be most qualified for dealing with cases involving children.'[70] Overall, women are now accredited with a more active role in Nazi Germany. This places more emphasis on their complicity with, rather than their compliance to, the regime.

The army has always been seen as largely dominated by the Nazi political system, but there has been some shift in interpretation concerning its complicity in German war crimes. The bulk of the army was systematically taken over. Until 1934 at least it always had the option of removing Hitler, as Hindenburg had remained its commander-in-chief. But Hitler won its support by stealth rather than by the confrontation preferred by Röhm. The army was grateful for the action taken by Hitler during the Night of the Long Knives and, on the death of Hindenburg, backed his claim to the presidency. The support of the army was also institutionalized to an unprecedented degree in the oath of allegiance, making any future opposition an act akin to treason. But the influence went further. Every attempt was made to Nazify the army through the adoption of the swastika insignia on uniforms and through a prolonged process of indoctrination. The Waffen SS was also introduced as the elite corps in the invasion and conquest of much of Europe. For many years the view was that it was the SS, not the Wehrmacht, which committed the atrocities in the occupied territories. More recent research, however, has shown that the army played an integral part in the shooting of civilians in Poland and the Ukraine. Indeed, Bartov has argued that even members of the working class, who had once supported the SPD or KPD, could be transformed into 'brutalized and fanaticized soldiers'.[71]

Overall, there has been a recent shift in interpretation about the extent to which the regime was voluntarily supported by the population. More emphasis is now placed on complicity at all levels. Three historians present a particularly disturbing picture. Mallman and Paul argue that the Gestapo relied predominantly on information volunteered by large numbers of people – from all sections of society, including the working class. Many Germans, it seems, were willing to denounce each other.[72] Goldhagen goes further by insisting that a substantial portion of the German army was willing to slaughter Jews in the Ukraine and Russia.[73] It is, of course, possible to go too far in this direction, and notice also needs to be taken of the opposition which developed to the regime.

Opposition and resistance

Much more attention has recently been focused by historians on opposition to Hitler's regime than was the case during the first three decades after 1945. This is due partly to the increase in specialist study on all areas of the Third Reich and partly to the influential thesis that the Nazi system was less efficient than was originally thought. The incomplete nature of German totalitarianism meant that opposition was not only possible but was a reality, and the Gestapo was fully aware of it. It took various forms, ranging from everyday grumbling to complaints about specific issues, more general political activism and, most threatening of all, resistance. The authorities also became increasingly concerned about the growth of social deviance which threatened to undermine the re-education of Germany's youth.

Grumbling and minor dissent were quite widespread. Kershaw has argued that 'The acute perception of social injustice, the class-conscious awareness of inequalities . . . changed less in the Third Reich than is often supposed . . . The extent of disillusionment and discontent in almost all sections of the population, rooted in the socio-economic experience of daily life, is remarkable.'[74] There was considerable oral dissent about a range of issues – the lack of wage increases, increased working hours, compulsory activities within the KdF, and the subordination of consumer interests to rearmament. Yet the type of discontent remained at a remarkably low key, certainly when compared with the resistance of the peasantry to collectivization in the Soviet Union. There was little chance of discontent ever being converted into something stronger. SOPADE reports indicated that most grumbling was sparked by economic conditions, and not by more fundamental reservations about the nature of the regime. 'This is especially so among the Mittelstand and the peasantry. These social strata are least of all ready to fight seriously against the regime because they know least of all what they should fight for.'[75] Most Germans were therefore never likely to turn against a system which, for all it inconveniences, they still preferred to the Weimar Republic.

In contrast to undirected grumbling, several formal complaints were made about specific issues. These might involve individuals, small groups or major institutions. The Churches, for example, came into conflict with the regime on three occasions. One was Pastor Niemoller's objection to the establishment of the Confessing Church. The second instance was the Catholic protest against the government order to replace crucifixes with portraits of Hitler in Catholic schools. A third, and the most significant, stance was taken in opposition to the regime's euthanasia programme from 1939 onwards. These complaints varied in the degree of their success. The Protestant opposition was less likely to succeed than the Catholic, due to the fragmentation of Protestantism into a number of different sects and the fundamental issue on which that opposition was being expressed: the regime could hardly be expected to reverse a major constitutional change. The Catholic Church, by contrast, was a centralized structure, with considerable capacity for exerting pressure at certain specific points. It succeeded over the two issues it contested: the programmes to Nazify Catholic schools and to conduct the clandestine euthanasia programmes were both temporarily suspended. On the other hand, the more general complaints made by the Pope in his encyclical *Mit brennender Sorge* that the regime had broken the provisions of the Concordat across the board were less likely to succeed. There is little doubt that Christianity proved most effective not as a general impetus for opposition but as a residue for the nation's conscience. Despite efforts at the end of the 1930s to eradicate it through the paganism of the Nazi Faith Movement, the majority of Germans remained either Catholic or Protestant and the incidence of church actually increased after 1939.

The expression of more general opposition through political activism was confined largely to the Communists and Social Democrats, as might be expected from the two parties which had previously had the support of the larger part of the working class. The Communists continued to try to oppose the regime actively, but failed badly. This was due in part to the success of the Gestapo in identifying and eradicating Communist cells. As a result, something like 10 per cent of the whole Communist membership was killed and Thalmann, the leader of the KPD, was arrested as early as 1933. The continuing conflict between Communists and Social Democrats meant fewer converts on the shop floor and made it easier for the Gestapo to acquire information. The Communists were also impeded by external constraints such as the foreign policy of Stalin which culminated in the highly pragmatic Nazi–Soviet Non-Aggression Pact of August 1939. It was not until 1941, when Hitler invaded the Soviet Union, that the Communists began to make a comeback, largely under the tutelage of Stalin, who switched his entire emphasis to the direct support of the KPD. The SPD, meanwhile, had been less directly involved in political activism. From its position in exile, SOPADE was organized by Ernst Schumacher, initially from Prague, then from Paris. They were generally more restrained and cautious than the KPD in their actions. They had the advantage of more accurate information on the state of support shown for the regime in the SOPADE reports. By and large neither they nor the Communists succeeded in making any major inroads into the working classes. As we have seen, there was plenty of grumbling but little chance of persuading workers to risk their livelihood, families and lives in the expression of political opposition.

There were, however, small groups who were prepared to make such a sacrifice. The strongest form of opposition took the form of resistance, an attempt to remove the regime altogether. Realistically this could be done only by a coup, since all the constitutional channels had been blocked by Hitler's 'legal revolution' between 1933 and 1934. The key to any chance of success was the army. This had, however, been won over by the process of gradual Nazification during the 1930s. Hence, the only possibility was the defection of disillusioned elements and their linking with individuals and groups prepared to risk everything on a political substitution. These army elements were always there. Ironically, they were nearly always members of the Prussian aristocracy, deeply conservative in their outlook and, in some instances, former enemies of the Weimar Republic. But this should not be taken to the usual extreme that the conservative forces within the army were generally anti-Nazi. Many, as we have seen, welcomed Nazism without reservation. This was one of the basic reasons for the failure of armed resistance: there was simply no depth in numbers to offset the failure of individual attempts like the Stauffenberg bomb plot. A few courageous individuals did become involved. General Beck tried to persuade the General Staff to remove Hitler in 1938, and also urged the British government to resist Hitler's demands over the Sudetenland. Rommel participated in a plot against Hitler's life for which he was forced to commit suicide. Other leading members of the resistance movements were strongly conservative, comprising members of the traditional right, many of whom had served Hitler at one time or another. These included von Hassell, former German ambassador to Italy, as well as Goerdeler, von Koltke and von Wartenburg. Also closely involved were Christian groups such as the Kreisau Circle, which produced a programme entitled 'Principles for the New Order of Germany', and prominent churchmen like Dietrich Bonhoeffer. Ultimately, however, all such resistance failed in its objective – which was to replace Hitler's regime with a more democratic one and to negotiate an armistice with the Allies. There would be no repetition of the situation in October and November 1918, since Hitler himself was head of state and was not open to any attempt to do a deal. In any case, the Allies insisted on unconditional surrender, thereby removing an important component from the programme of the German resistance movement. Hence, Nazism could be removed only by conquering armies, not by internal revolution.

One category of opposition greatly puzzled the authorities. Social deviance was most apparent among younger Germans, especially from the working class, and pointed to the deficiencies of the Hitler Youth as a channel of indoctrination. As the whole structure became more bureaucratized and less imaginative, some of the earlier attractions began to erode. The Hitler Youth came to be seen increasingly as part of the establishment rather than a rival to it. Hence, there developed alternative youth groups and cultures. Deviant behaviour among adolescents during the Third Reich was much wider than was once thought. In 1942 the Reich Youth Leadership stated: 'The formation of cliques, i.e. groupings of young people outside the Hitler Youth, has been on the increase before and, particularly, during the war to such a degree that one must speak of a serious risk of the political, moral and criminal subversion of youth.'[76] Examples included the Navajos, centred largely on Cologne, the Kittelbach Pirates of Oberhausen and Düsseldorf, and the Roving Dudes of Essen. These were all sub-groups within the broader Edelweiss Pirates. They were antagonistic to authority and in particular to the Hitler Youth, whose patrols they would ambush and beat up; indeed, one of their slogans was 'Eternal War on the Hitler Youth'. They also defied restrictions on movement during the war by undertaking extensive hikes, and they maintained a much more liberal attitude to sexuality than the authorities liked. Some also supported the Allies during the war or offered help to German army deserters. Less militant and more cultural in its emphasis was the Swing Movement, which adopted influences from English and especially American jazz. This was particularly provocative to the regime, which regarded jazz as 'negro music' and therefore as 'degenerate'. In all cases the authorities were seriously concerned. Usually, however, they did not know what to do – apart from the occasional salutary public hanging of Edelweiss Pirates. At the same time, the activities of the Edelweiss Pirates and Swing Movement lacked the organizational edge to be anything more than an embarrassment to the regime. Social deviance was, therefore, never likely to amount to serious political opposition.

The overall deduction which can be drawn from these different strands is a complex one. In theory, the Nazi state was a totalitarian one in that it eradicated institutions allowing for the formal expression of dissent and opposition and then proceeded to use the SS and Gestapo to pick off individual manifestations of anti-Nazi behaviour. By and large this combined process was successful: there was, after all, never any real threat to the regime except for the occasional act of violence. And yet the fact that opposition did develop in such a variety of forms indicates that totalitarianism was only partly successful. The regime frequently had to make concessions on specific issues; it faced a general increase in deviant behaviour and during the war it provoked the coalescence of normally incompatible groups. It is possible to go further. Peukert argues that the Volksgemeinschaft had not been achieved by 1939 and that the internal harmony of the system needed increasingly to be maintained by diverting public opinion against minority groups whether inside or outside Germany. 'Terror accordingly bit ever deeper . . . from the margins of society into its heart.'[77]

The Nazi economy

Hitler's main ideas

According to Bracher, 'At no time did National Socialism develop a consistent economic or social theory.'[78] It is true that Hitler was in no sense an economist. Unlike Marxism, the ideology of Nazism had no underlying economic component: there was no equivalent to the notion of political change occurring through the dialectical conflict between classes exerting their economic interest. Nazism was fundamentally racist and *völkisch* in it conception and economic factors were always subordinate. It would therefore be inappropriate to seek in it any autonomous economic strategy.

Nevertheless, Hitler did have ideas which influenced his economic policy. These can be extracted from *Mein Kampf* and the *Second Book*. Four main priorities can be deduced. First, Hitler aimed to create an autarkic system which would enable Germany to sustain a broader hegemony within Europe. He intended, second, to target the lands to the east. Third, since this inevitably involved expansion – and therefore conflict – the economic infrastructure would have to accommodate a considerable increase in military expenditure. But, fourth, he needed the support of the German people and could not therefore risk severely depressing their living standards in any quest for military supremacy.

The emergence of a policy

How did these components fit together? Broadly, the 1920s saw the emergence of Hitler's policy of Lebensraum, which was to provide the infrastructure for all of Hitler's ideas about the ultimate purpose of economic change. Then, after 1933, Hitler had the opportunity to implement these ideas.

An underlying economic approach emerged during the 1920s. There were at first two possibilities. One was socialism, which was championed by Gregor Strasser. The other was nationalism, to which Hitler became increasingly committed. He drew a connection between territorial expansion and self-sufficiency: Lebensraum and autarky became the the the twin pillars of Hitler's strategy. This was shown in the second volume of *Mein Kampf*, published in 1925, and in his *Second Book*, written 1928. In the former he argued that Germany should abandon her former pursuit of economic power through colonies or through attempts to dominate western Europe. Instead, he advocated 'turning our eyes towards the land in the east'. This meant 'finally putting a stop to the colonial and trade policy of the pre-war period and passing over to the territorial policy of the future'.[79] New communities would eventually be established on land carved out of Poland and Russia by the German army. Germany would also have self-sufficiency in raw materials and food, as well as guaranteed outlets for her manufactured goods. Such goals would, of course, involve conflict, but this was another key ingredient of Hitler's thinking. He said in 1923, 'It has ever been the right of the stronger . . . to see his will prevail.' Indeed, 'All of nature is one great struggle between strength and weakness, an eternal victory of the strong over the weak . . . The nation which would violate this elementary law would rot away.'[80]

These ideas have sometimes been dismissed as the vague fantasies of an immature fringe politician. This is a mistake, on two counts. First, there were many on the conservative right who took them seriously in the late 1920s and early 1930s because Lebensraum fitted closely into the pan-German concepts already apparent before 1914 in Imperial Germany. Hitler therefore found ready converts among the so-called respectable sectors of big business, the armaments industry and the military High Command. Many non-Nazis recognized the flow of the argument and were willing to take it seriously. Second, the eventual shaping of German hegemony in Europe bears a close resemblance to the original prototype, even if it was to be implemented by the SS rather than Hitler's state channels. *Mein Kampf* need not be considered the 'blueprint' for Hitler's future projects, as suggested by Trevor-Roper, but it is surely more than the 'daydreaming' attributed to it by A.J.P. Taylor.

The development of Hitler's economic policy, 1933–45

There appear to have been four main phases in the emergence of an economic policy, although these did not follow on logically from each other.

The first, lasting from 1933 until 1936, has been called a period of 'partial fascism'. The state moved into a programme of job creation to reduce the levels of unemployment while, at the same time, seeking to control wages and eliminate trade union powers. In these respects there is some similarity to Mussolini's corporativism. But in other respects the government's economic policy was highly pragmatic, especially while it was under the direction of Schacht (President of the Reichsbank from March 1933 and Economics Minister from June 1934). He gave priority to developing a favourable trade balance by means of a series of bilateral trade agreements with the Balkans and South American states. These underdeveloped areas provided Germany with essential raw materials in return for German investment and credits for German industrial products. The complexities of foreign exchange were dealt with by the New Plan (September 1934), which regulated imports and the allocation of foreign exchange to key sectors of the German economy. Overall, Schacht was convinced that it was essential to raise the level of exports if Hitler's objective of increased military expenditure were to be realized.

By 1936 Hitler had begun to show impatience with Schacht's somewhat cautious approach and opted openly for 'military and political rearmament', to be promoted by 'economic rearmament and mobilization'. The second economic phase therefore opened with the introduction of the 'Four Year Plan'. The basic purpose of the Four Year Plan was to achieve self-sufficiency or autarky, in both industry and agriculture, through increased productivity and the development of substitutes for oil and other key items. This became even more important when, in 1937, Hitler made clear his decision to prepare for war at the meeting with his chiefs of staff recorded in the Hossbach Memorandum. Goering was placed in control of the Four

Year Plan Office; this completely undermined Schacht's position so that the latter felt compelled to resign his post in November 1937. The Plan resulted in a steady increase in military expenditure, from 1.9 billion marks in 1936 to 5.8 billion in 1937, 18.4 billion in 1938 and 32.3 billion in 1939. There were, however, deficiencies. Although some progress was made in the manufacture of substitutes, targets were not met for the production of rubber and synthetic fuels; synthetic petrol, for example, met only 18 per cent of Germany's needs and it was still necessary to import one-third of all the raw materials needed by industry.

Ready or not, the Nazi economy entered its third phase in 1939. The outbreak of war saw the implementation of a military strategy known as Blitzkrieg, or 'lightning war'. The intention was to secure victory as rapidly as possible through preliminary aerial attacks, followed by the advance of panzer divisions of tanks and armoured vehicles. Blitzkrieg was, however, also an economic strategy. It was the means whereby Germany could achieve military victory over its neighbours without mobilizing its economic resources to the full. This lasted until the end of 1941 and saw the collapse and absorption of the economies of Poland, Denmark, Norway, the Low Countries and France. The invasion of the Soviet Union, however, brought the fourth phase – total war. The German economy was now pushed to its limit. War production came under the control of Albert Speer and the Central Planning Board. The result was a more rapid increase in armaments, despite the heavy Allied bombing of German cities between 1943 and 1944. Yet, even at this point, Germany was massively outproduced by the two industrial giants – the Soviet Union and the United States. This was a major factor in the eventual destruction of the Third Reich.

Two of these developments have become the subject of historical controversy. The relationship between Blitzkrieg and total war has attracted interpretations which are virtually opposites in their emphasis.

The development of Hitler's economic policy: interpretation one

One line of argument would stress that the implementation of economic policy was largely pragmatic. Hitler had to modify his theories on the domestic front, just as he did in his foreign policy, until he could be certain of his power base.

The initial policies of Schacht were therefore based on immediate requirements such as job-creation to reduce unemployment and wage controls to prevent the threat of inflation. It also seemed that Schacht's trade agreements with the Balkan states provided sound foundations for future commercial expansion. Hitler needed Schacht until 1936, by which time he had come to place more emphasis on rearmament than Schacht thought wise. By now, Hitler reasoned, recovery from the depression had been sufficiently rapid to allow an acceleration of the rearmament policy which was to be the key factor in the Four Year Plan. This was taken a stage further in his decision in 1937 to prepare Germany for war. The Hossbach Memorandum, together with the Four Year Plan, therefore militarized Hitler's basic economic objectives.

Again, however, Hitler had to settle for a pragmatic course. Several historians have argued that he could not pursue a policy geared to total mobilization and total war. Klein maintains that he still needed the support of the German consumer and therefore had to settle for a compromise – for an economy which would allow a limited degree of rearmament while, at the same time, allowing a reasonable level of consumer affluence.[81] According to Sauer, this balance meant the creation of a 'plunder economy'. The only way in which Germany could expand through limited mobilization was by steadily increasing her economic base through a series of rapid and specifically targeted conquests. Hence, Hitler 'committed himself to starting a war in the near future'.[82] The solution was Blitzkrieg, which was therefore as much an economic as a military strategy. And it seemed to work. By 1941 Blitzkrieg seemed to have produced the base for the early stages of Lebensraum. Germany had gained military and economic control over Czechoslovakia, Poland, the Ukraine and a sizable area of European Russia, as well as direct influence over Hungary, Romania and Bulgaria. With these victories, the economic dimension of Lebensraum became clearer. According to Hiden and Farquharson: 'the economic reorganization of Europe continued also to reflect the durability of National Socialist attempts to bring into being a viable alternative both to centralized state planning, as under Marxism, and to the liberal capitalist order which they had seen collapse in 1929'.[83] The former was repugnant on ideological grounds, while the capitalist system was based on the sort of liberal principles which were incompatible with Nazi rule in Europe. In implementing Lebensraum, the Nazis developed an alternative to both, an expanded economic empire which had similarities with earlier European policies of mercantilism.

Then came total war, which wrecked the new economic order. Total war was not the logical final step in Nazi economic policy, a total mobilization of the economy to make possible total victory, but a response to Hitler's failure to achieve a further rapid victory after 1941 through Blitzkrieg. It was an admission that the previous delicate balance between consumer and military needs could no longer be maintained. Above all, it was a struggle for survival as, from 1942 onwards, the tide began to turn with the military recovery of the Soviet Union and the entry of the United States into the war. Despite the best efforts of Armaments Minister Albert Speer, the German economy proved far less adaptable to total war than did those of her three main rivals. Germany was massively outproduced in terms of war *matériel* by the United States and the Soviet Union, while even Britain, with a smaller economic base, managed a larger per-capita output of aircraft and artillery. It seems, therefore, that total war was a desperate attempt to cling on to that part of Lebensraum already achieved through Blitzkrieg. So it can be said that there was no economic logic in the change from Blitzkrieg to total war.

The development of Hitler's economic policy: interpretation two

It is, however, possible to give an entirely different explanation for the way in which Hitler's economic policy developed. From the start, Hitler moved systematically towards equipping Germany with an economic base capable of achieving Lebensraum. According to Berghahn, 'the rearmament programme which was begun in 1933 amounted . . . to nothing less than a deliberate unhinging of the national economy with the intention of recovering the financial losses by exploiting other national economies of Europe within the confines of a German-dominated empire conquered by force'.[84] It is true that some of Schacht's policies were a continuation of the deflationary approach of Brüning. They were, however, tolerated by Hitler, who saw them as essential for the establishment of autarky. Hence, the trading networks with the Balkans would become the first step in German hegemony; the public works schemes, especially for the autobahns, would help create a military infrastructure; and the controls on wages would create a disciplined workforce which would become increasingly receptive to intensive mobilization. Hitler was therefore using Schacht's New Plan as the first stage in the move towards total war,

But the process was not to be that easy. Hitler's hand was forced by a major economic crisis between 1935 and 1936 in the form of a food shortage which affected the whole of the German workforce. He took what he considered to be the only way out: to impose further constraints on the workforce while, at the same time, accelerating rearmament to achieve Lebensraum and autarky. The whole purpose of the Four Year Plan was therefore to prepare for war; this became clear in the Hossbach Memorandum, which anticipated that 'Our relative strength would decrease in relation to the rearmament which would by then have been carried out by the rest of the world. If we did not act by 1943–45, any year would, owing to a lack of reserves, produce the food crisis, to cope with which the necessary foreign exchange was not available.'[85] It seems logical, therefore, that Hitler was gearing the German economy to the total war which would be necessary in order to achieve the Lebensraum which would provide long-term economic salvation.

There were, however, complications. The outbreak of war with Britain and France in 1939 was premature, which meant that the economy could only support Blitzkrieg military strategies. Blitzkrieg was therefore an emergency response – or, in the words of Overy, 'total war by default'.[86] It was not until 1941 that the economy of Germany had been sufficiently enlarged to enable a full-scale mobilization of resources – the whole point of total war. But total war now went on to produce defeat rather than victory. This was partly because the original mistiming of Blitzkrieg had prevented a proper build-up of resources, and partly because the involvement of the United States meant the dissipation of those resources in a conflict on two fronts. Hence, the total-war economy failed not because it was the reversal of a successful phase of Blitzkrieg, but because it was rendered incomplete by Blitzkrieg as an unnecessary diversion. Overy's view is therefore the reverse of that of Sauer and Klein. He argues that

> If war had been postponed until 1943–5, as Hitler had hoped, then Germany would have been much better prepared, and would also have had rockets, intercontinental bombers, perhaps even atomic weapons. Though Britain and France did not know it, declaring war in 1939 prevented Germany from becoming the super-power Hitler wanted.[87]

Which interpretation?

For once, it is genuinely difficult to synthesize what appear to be two mutually exclusive interpretations. Either the Blitzkrieg economy was the initially successful step towards Lebensraum which was then reversed by the disasters of total war, or the drive for Lebensraum through total war was impeded by the intrusion of Blitzkrieg. Either is possible but, pending further research, the verdict should perhaps remain open.

The social impact of economic policies

How were the German people affected by Nazi economic policies? There were a few overall advantages. By 1938 Germany had completely recovered from the impact of the depression, and national income was 20 per cent higher than the previous peak of 1928. There had also been, since 1932, a rise in wages, a reduction in unemployment, an increase in food consumption and a growth in the turnover of clothing and household goods. These developments, however, need to be seen in context. Two perspectives can be provided: one is the general survey of the different sectors of the population, the other a more specific analysis of various social statistics.

The impact on different social sectors

Different sectors of the population were affected in different ways. The largest single group – the industrial workers – certainly benefited from the decrease in unemployment from 6 million in 1932 to 0.4 million in 1938. It has, however, been shown that the trend was already downwards before Hitler came to power in January 1933. In addition, the collective influence of working-class organizations was steadily eroded, the trade union movement coming under a general ban from May 1933. The gap was filled by a pro-Nazi German Labour Front (DAF) under Robert Ley. Two other organizations were established: Schönheit der Arbeit (Beauty of Labour) and Kraft durch Freude (Strength through Joy), which had the overall effect of regulating leisure as well as working hours and increasing the possibilities for exploitation by employers.

Germany's rural population comprised three sections, all pro-Nazi at the outset of the regime. The peasants, or small landowners, were upheld by Nazi ideology as the backbone of the German race, but there was a tendency to paint an idealized and highly unrealistic picture. The result was a series of damaging attempts by the government to freeze the peasantry into an unchanging class. The Reich Entailed Farm Law of 1933 severely limited the subdivision and sale of peasant plots, which inevitably prevented consolidation, mechanization and more effective use of fertilizers. The second group, agricultural workers, made very few substantial gains. Many continued to experience grinding poverty and migrated in desperation to the towns at a rate of 2.5 per cent per annum (compared with 1.5 per cent per annum before 1933). The third category, the wealthy landlords, were the only real beneficiaries of Nazi rule. The rapid increase in land values enabled them to retain their economic prominence, which partially offset the loss of some of their political influence.

The business sector consisted of two main groups. The small businessman, usually from the middle class, was attracted at an early stage by Nazi promises to protect the 'small man' from the burden of monopolies. This group did benefit initially, mainly from much tighter control over the labour force. On the whole, however, the NSDAP preferred to cultivate the support of big business, which increased its ownership of industry from 40 per cent of the total in 1933 to 70 per cent by 1937; this was accomplished mostly through the absorption of smaller enterprises. It is true that the state exercised greater influence and control during the period of the Four Year Plan. The new Hermann Goering Works, for example, became a major state-owned steel producer. But some of the great names in private enterprise rapidly increased their profits by up to 150 per cent between 1938 and 1942. Great industrialists also collaborated closely with the government over the war effort and worse: several, for example, supplied Auschwitz with equipment for the gas chambers. This co-operation between the government and big business has led some historians to see the Nazi regime as a bastion of capitalism. It would, however, be more appropriate to argue that Hitler decided at the outset to avoid confrontation with capitalism, even if, in the process, it meant subverting a number of earlier economic principles.

Women, as a distinct social group, had a clearly defined place in the Nazi world. In a rally at Nuremberg in 1934 Hitler said that 'man's world is the State', while 'the world of woman is a smaller world. For her world is her husband, her family, her children and her house.'[88] According to Goebbels: 'The mission of woman is to be beautiful and to bring children into the world . . . the female prettifies herself for her mate and hatches the eggs for him.'[89] The initial policy was to ease women out of the top levels of the civil service, law, medicine and politics. Women were induced to stay at home by new 'marriage credits' and child bonuses. The gradual decline of unemployment, however, created a new demand for labour. The result was the steady recruitment of women into both agriculture and industry, the total reaching 5.2 million by 1938. But the highly qualified never regained their former status. They were true victims of Nazi policy.

Statistical evidence

In 1938 a Cambridge economics lecturer wrote after a visit to Germany: 'No-one who is acquainted with German conditions would suggest that the standard of living is a high one, but the important thing is that it has been rising in recent years.'[90] At a superficial level this statement can be supported by statistics of the period. More detailed analysis, however, shows a different picture: that, in relative terms, the standard of living was at best static and, by some criteria, deteriorating.

There seemed to be much to support the view that Germany was experiencing a return to prosperity after the trauma of the depression. For one thing, unemployment was in rapid decline. The figure had stood at 4.8 million in 1933, dropping thereafter to 2.7 million in 1934, 2.2 million in 1935, 1.6 million in 1936, 0.9 million in 1937, 0.4 million in 1938 and a mere 0.1 million by 1939.[91] This was far more rapid than the reduction of unemployment in comparable economies such as the United States and France, while Britain still had 1.8 million on the dole in 1938. Corresponding with the decline in unemployment was an increase in wages. Falling to a low in 1933 of 70 per cent of their 1928 level, these had recovered to 75 per cent by 1934, 80 per cent by 1936 and 85 per cent by 1938.

Thus, by a double criterion increasing numbers of people became increasingly better off during the six years after 1933. They were also part of a general increase in prosperity represented by a steady growth of Germany's national income from 44 billion marks in 1933 to 80 billion in 1938. This was particularly impressive since the 1938 figure was greater than the 72 billion of 1928, despite the fall in the value of the mark in the meantime. The workforce benefited at certain key outlets within the economy as the production of some consumer goods seemed to take off. Germans, for example, became the world's largest per-capita owners of radio sets, while progress was also made in developing the comparatively cheap Volkswagen. Added to these benefits was the vast range of activities provided through the KdF and the improvement of working conditions by the SdA. Certainly the workforce as a whole was far better off than that in the Soviet Union. It was not, by and large, in constant dread of being denounced to the Gestapo or being forced to reach unrealistic targets by being driven to breaking point. Overall, it is easy to see why contemporaries should have seen Nazi Germany as a country undergoing a transformation in its economy to the ultimate benefit of its people.

The underlying assumption of this reasoning, however, is that any improvements after 1933 were due directly and solely to Hitler's policies. This is flawed on two counts. First, there is more continuity between the early policies of the Third Reich and the later policies of the Weimar Republic than is often realized. In economic terms, the dividing line is really in 1929. There was far more difference between the policies of Müller and Brüning than between those of Papen or Schleicher and Hitler. Second, the policy of Brüning created a dynamic which was of double benefit to Hitler. In ruthlessly taking control of the economy, Brüning intended to deal forcefully with the problems as quickly as possible in order to enable Germany to come through the other side of the economic crisis more quickly than any of the other leading industrial powers. This benefited Hitler's reputation by creating a huge peak of unemployment which Hitler could not help but alleviate. And, by the time that Hitler had come to power, the worst was over as Brüning's policies were beginning to have an admittedly belated impact. In other words, Hitler inherited a disastrous situation which was just about on the mend.

Even so, the improvement which did occur was not fully transmitted to the workforce, since it was not consumer-based. The focus of the economy was switched, especially from 1936, to rearmament and an expansion in the size of the armed forces. Declining unemployment was, it could be said, artificially induced. This was also apparent in the calculated use of the unemployed on public works schemes such as the construction of autobahns. Such expedients are rarely possible within a democracy since they remove the element of choice from unemployment. It might be argued that the unemployed have no choice, but it is important for the government of a democratic regime to assume that they do so that it will offer solutions based on persuasion rather than coercion. This was certainly the case with Roosevelt's New Deal. On the other hand, a totalitarian regime can dispense altogether with the very notion of choice and, through coercive measures, generate an immediate impact on unemployment levels. As Germany accelerated the pace of rearmament through the Four Year Plan, unemployment levels were bound to drop like a stone.

Forced employment produced a disciplined workforce which was held to lower wage levels. Pay may have increased relative to the year 1933 but there was no return to 1928: indeed, the percentages for 1933 and 1939 were 77 per cent and 89 per cent, respectively.[92] This was hardly a massive upswing. Besides, the wage earner was actually worse off in terms of the cost of living. This had increased from 71 per cent of the 1928 level in 1932 to 90 per cent in 1939. In real terms, therefore, those in employment had been marginally better off in 1933 than they were in 1939. The workforce received an ever declining proportion of the national income as wages. In 1933, for example, wages amounted to 63 per cent of the national income, while by 1938 this had dropped steadily each year to 57 per cent. It is also significant that these wages were earned through a working week which had been extended on average by over seven hours.

Declining wages were accompanied by reduced attention to consumer needs. It is true that between 1933 and 1938 the level of consumer goods rose by 69 per cent. But, over the same period, industrial goods increased by 389 per cent. In other words, workers were producing proportionately more in terms of heavy industrial goods and armaments than they were consumables. It can also be deduced from import and export figures that the general flow of trade was not in the consumers' interest. Imports in 1935 totalled 4.16 billion marks, compared with 4.18 billion marks for exports. The corresponding figures for 1930 had been 12.4 billion and 12.0 billion, respectively. The consumer suffered in two ways – the imposition of tight import controls by Schacht and the huge drop in consumer goods from abroad.[93]

As to the new employee organizations, these may have had certain benefits and attractions, but they were very much in line with the aims of a totalitarian regime. The workforce was strictly regulated even down to its use of free time. This was done partly to break any desire to revive consumer habits, which would draw off resources from rearmament, and partly to keep open the channels of propaganda and indoctrination. The KdF and SdA were therefore no substitutes for the trade unionism which had been banned by Hitler in 1933. Free collective bargaining, which had been such a prominent feature of the Weimar Republic, had been replaced by the creation of corporate identity and interest. It is true that it lacked the crude terror of the Soviet system, but it was no less pervasive in its destruction of individual values. Exploitation was as much a feature of the Nazi economy as of its Soviet counterpart – even if in Germany the stick was disguised as the carrot.

In reality, therefore, the German workforce was putting in longer hours for a notional increase in wages. In real terms (compared to the cost of living) wages were in decline. The input that workers had into the economy was substantial but largely one-way: it fed into rearmament but received few consumables in exchange. Returning to the Cambridge lecturer's statement, therefore, it now seems that the standard of living was falling, not rising.

Racism and anti-Semitism

Fundamental to all Hitler's policies was his absolute belief in the superiority of the 'Aryan' race and the need to prepare the German people for its role as master of Europe. He categorized mankind into three separate groups: 'founders' of culture, 'bearers' of culture and 'destroyers' of culture. The Aryans, of course, formed the highest group. According to Nazi race theorists, the essential characteristics of the typical Aryan included a tall and slim build, a narrow face and nose, a prominent chin, a fresh complexion, and gold or blond hair. (It is ironical that the only one of the Nazi leaders to fit this description – Heydrich – was obsessed with what he considered to be the 'taint' of a Jewish ancestor.) Hitler aimed gradually to purify the German race so that the majority of people would eventually conform to this ideal appearance. This would be achieved by eliminating racial mixing (miscegenation) and by special breeding programmes undertaken by the SS. Race therefore became a vital part of all indoctrination, the purpose being, in von Shirach's words, to create 'the perfect and complete human animal – the superman!'. The main obstacle to this was what Hitler called 'subman', who threatened to 'pollute' the Aryan race. Among 'submen' were the 'eternal enemy' of the German people, the Jews.

Nazi measures against the Jews unfolded in three main stages, each more radical than the last. The first, between 1933 and 1938, saw extensive legislation imposing a series of limits on the activities of Jews. In April 1933 Jews were excluded from the civil service, prevented from working in hospitals and removed from the judiciary. The Nuremberg Laws of 1935 deprived Jews of German citizenship and banned marriage or sexual relations between Germans and Jews. Between them, these measures were the most comprehensive in modern history. Yet, at this stage, there were still some constraints on Nazi action. President Hindenburg, for example, managed to keep civil service jobs for those Jews who had fought or lost relatives in the First World War. Also, Frick issued a memorandum from the Ministry of the Interior instructing authorities not to exceed the instructions on the Jews. In some instances the authorities were embarrassed by the excesses of militants like Julius Streicher with his virulent tabloid. On the occasion of the 1936 Olympics Hitler ordered the removal from Berlin of all anti-Jewish notices. He was clearly playing safe so as not to alienate the establishment while secretly preparing more comprehensive measures for the future.

From 1938 anti-Semitism became more violent and all remaining constraints on persecution were swept aside. In July 1938 they were banned from participating in commerce, their last preserve. The authorities also attempted to identify and control the movement of Jews by decrees on compulsory 'Jewish' names, identity cards and passports. The law no longer offered any protection, as was all too evident on the night of 9/10 November 1938. 'Kristallnacht' saw the smashing of Jewish shops and other property all over Germany by the SA and the SS in retaliation for the assassination by a Polish Jew of an official in the German embassy in Paris. The mob violence caused some irritation at top levels in the administration which preferred a more systematic and less messy approach, like the confiscation of Jewish assets. At Hitler's instigation several possibilities were now examined for removing the Jewish population from Germany altogether, including a scheme for its resettlement on the island of Madagascar.

But Hitler soon came to the conclusion that emigration was not feasible. Between 1941 and 1945 Hitler's anti-Jewish obsessions were sublimated in the most extreme measures seen in the whole of human history. The programme of extermination appears to have begun in July 1941 with instructions to Heydrich to implement the 'Final Solution'. The first step was the Decree of Identification which forced every Jew to wear a yellow Star of David. This was followed by the mass deportation of Jews to the concentration camps at Chelmo, Auschwitz-Birkenau, Belzec, Sobibor, Treblinka and Maidenek. Exterminations began in earnest from mid-1942 as a total of 3 to 4 million Jews went to the gas chambers. Organized by Eichmann, the whole process was conducted with industrial efficiency; leading German firms competed for contracts to manufacture the gas chambers. Yet the Nazis were constantly aware of the need to maintain secrecy for fear of a public backlash. The details were, however, brought to light early in 1945 as the Russians liberated the camps in Poland and the Allies those in the west.

The role of race and anti-Semitism in the Nazi system

Race is usually seen as the most illogical component of the Nazi system, the one which made it a totalitarian regime capable of committing acts of great evil. This is, of course, the truth; but it is not the whole truth. Race was also the fundamental rationale for all social developments.

The foundation of the Nazi race doctrine was the concept of genetic drive. This was rooted in nineteenth-century ideas of fringe theorists such as Gobineau, Houston and Chamberlain. Collectively known as Social Darwinists, they transferred the scientific concept of the survival of the fittest from the animal to the human world. In 1915 the biologist Haeckel argued that 'the theory of selection teaches us that organic progress is an inevitable consequence of the struggle for existence'.[94] Hitler took this a stage further and based his whole ideology on the premise of struggle, which he saw as 'the father of all things'. From this emerged the right of the strong to triumph over the weak. Indeed, this was essential, since the strong created, while the weak undermined and destroyed. He emphasized that 'All the human culture, all the results of art, science and technology that we see before us today, are almost exclusively the creative product of the Aryan.' Conversely, 'All the great cultures of the past were destroyed only because the originally creative race died from blood poisoning.' The solution was obvious: 'Therefore, he who would live, let him fight, and he who would not fight in this world of struggle is not deserving of life.'[95]

The implications of this theoretical framework were huge. Race, linked to struggle, provided a new approach to the organic development of the Nazi society and state. The racial doctrine had three dimensions: it provided Germany with its purpose, its cohesion – and its victims.

The ultimate purpose of the Nazi system was to transcend the existing limits of the state. Here we can see a contrast with Fascist Italy. Mussolini saw the highest political form as the nation state, which he sought to extend into a revived form of the Roman Empire. In the case of Nazi Germany, etatism was not the main priority: this was the Volksgemeinschaft, or the 'people's community', which was to be the higher form of the state. Similarly, the focus of German expansion was not the establishment of a traditional empire, but rather to provide 'our nation with sufficient living space. Such living space can only be in the east.'[96] Unlike Mussolini, Hitler's emphasis was not imperial, but *völkisch*. Étatism, for Italy the main aim, was for Nazi Germany merely the first step to Aryanism and Lebensraum. The driving force for this was the concept of the master race.

Racial theory also aimed to create a new form of social cohesion – by replacing class divisions with racial unity and racial supremacy. The Volksgemeinschaft would reconcile what Peukert calls a 'society of fractured traditions, social classes and environments'.[97] In place of embittered Germans from competing economic groups, there would emerge healthy, vigorous and productive Aryans. The new stereotype proved attractive to most of the population and therefore ensured their loyalty to a regime which appeared to value them so highly. This, of course, was part of the overall formula. For, in return for their new unity of purpose and elevated status, the people were to be 'primed for self-sacrifice'.[98] Hence, the racial policies were closely connected not only with the propaganda and indoctrination trends within Germany's schools, but with the new work ethic implicit in organizations like the

RAD, SdA and KdF. According to Peukert, racialism was 'a reflection of welfare workers' everyday experience and problems, to which a racialist solution seemed to be the obvious one'.[99]

To be fully effective the Volksgemeinschaft needed to have its 'impurities' removed. The victims were all those who, for genetic reasons, did not fit into the stereotype of Aryanism. This might be for reasons of ethnic origin, physical or mental impairment or social deviance: the concept of racial purity therefore had several forms of inward focus. Those suffering from hereditary diseases were compulsorily sterilized from 1933 as a result of the Law for the Prevention of the Hereditarily Diseased. Between 1934 and 1939 this affected some 0.5 per cent of the population. From 1939 the scope was extended through the introduction of the euthanasia programme: between 1939 and 1941 about 72,000 people were killed in this way. To these can be added large numbers of tramps, vagrants, alcoholics and homosexuals. These were all considered 'alien to the community' (*gemeinschaftsfremd*) and had therefore become race enemies in the broader sense. The Volksgemeinschaft therefore achieved cohesion by replacing class conflict with targeted persecution. 'Thus', argues Schoenbaum, 'Nazi social theory denied equality while at the same time asserting it.'[100]

The largest single group of victims were the Jews. Their persecution provided the regime with its dynamic and with the primitive elements of vicious hatred. In part, German anti-Semitism was the culmination of centuries of discrimination throughout Europe: this had reared its head again after 1880, with violence in Vienna and Berlin, blatant discrimination in the French army and a series of pogroms in Tsarist Russia. H.S. Chamberlain justified such events within the context of tradition. He wrote in 1901: 'The entrance of the Jew into European History had . . . meant the entrance of an alien element – alien to that which Europe had already achieved, alien to all it was still destined to achieve.'[101] Anti-Semitism could therefore be seen as a tidal force: its high-water mark at the turn of the nineteenth century brought Hitler in with its flotsam.

Hitler's own views on Jews were the main driving force behind the whole Nazi ideology and movement; anti-Semitic policies were therefore a sublimation of his personal obsession. *Mein Kampf* and his speeches are full of the most inflammatory references. In the former he created the stereotype of the Jew as a parasite and pollutant: 'Culturally he contaminates art, literature and the theatre, makes a mockery of national feeling, overthrows all concepts of beauty, and instead drags men down into the sphere of his own base nature.'[102] In one of his speeches he fantasized about hanging the Jews of Munich from lampposts until their 'bodies rotted'. There is no doubting the elemental force of his hatred. At the same time, there was also a deliberately pragmatic use of the techniques of scapegoating: the paradox was that anti-Semitism as an irrational force could be used rationally to strengthen the Volksgemeinschaft. There would be numerous occasions on which the regime called for sacrifice. This would elicit two sentiments: a positive effort and negative feelings of resentment at the sacrifice required. The former would be used by the regime, but the latter needed to be deflected away from the regime. For the mentality attuned to Social Darwinism it made sense to target a minority group which had been picked out by the Führer from the taint of many centuries. The methods used to generate hatred were varied. One was the spread of the vilest misinformation, based on Hitler's earlier principle of the 'big lie'. Hence, Streicher's *Der Stürmer* alleged ritual killing of Christian children by Jews: 'The blood of the victims is to be forcibly tapped . . . the fresh (or powdered) blood of the slaughtered child is further used by young married Jewish couples, by pregnant Jewesses, for circumcision and so forth.'[103] Another was Hitler's oratorical device of blaming Jews for all perceived threats, ranging from the economic crisis of 1935–6 to the hostility of Britain and France to German designs on Poland in 1939. A third was the carefully orchestrated 'spontaneity' of Kristallnacht, publicized by Goebbels as the expression of the 'righteous indignation of the German people'.

In summary, Nazi race policy did three things. First, it converted traditional etatism into a more radical Aryanism, the ultimate thrust of which was Lebensraum. Second, it substituted for the older class divisions of German society the new unity of the Volksgemeinschaft. And, third, this unity was maintained at the expense of minorities which had no place within it. Some, the 'community aliens', were removed with as little fuss as possible. Others, especially the Jews, were deliberately set up as targets for any resentment which might be felt by members of the Volksgemeinschaft at the extent of the sacrifice demanded of them. Anti-Semitism was the obvious vehicle for this, since it had deep historic roots and seemed to fit into the Führer's messianic claims. During the period 1933–41, therefore, racism and anti-Semitism were widely accepted, although few could have predicted their eventual outcome.

Interpretations of the Holocaust

No historical topic is immune to controversy. Even the Holocaust, perhaps the most cataclysmic event in history, has produced polarized views.

There are, broadly speaking, three debates. The first is over whether it happened. This can be addressed quickly. The vast majority of historians accept that the evidence for the Holocaust is overwhelming. A small minority, most prominently Irving, consider that the gas chambers were the creation of Allied propaganda in 1945; these historians, however, are pursuing an openly polemical line in support of the neo-Nazi cause and have thereby discredited themselves as serious contributors to the debate. The second controversy is a more genuine one. Was the Holocaust the logical fulfilment of the Nazi policy of anti-Semitism or was it the result not of careful planning but rather of the failure of alternative strategies? The third debate concerns the extent of complicity: how much was the German population involved in the Holocaust and how was it possible for such actions to happen at all?

In considering whether the extermination of the Jews was always intended, or whether it emerged institutionally, few historians have seriously attempted to deny the ultimate responsibility of Hitler. The disagreement between them has arisen over the means by which his anti-Semitism was converted into the 'Final Solution'.

One school, labelled the 'intentionalists', attribute the policy of genocide to the Führer state as a function of a personalized totalitarian regime. Historians who follow this line include Fleming, Jäckel and Hillgruber. They maintain that Hitler implemented the decision in the summer of 1941. The reason was that the collapse of Russia in the wake of the German invasion seemed inevitable and this was the perfect chance to achieve a long-held ambition. Goering therefore ordered Heydrich to bring about 'a complete solution of the Jewish question within the German sphere of influence in Europe'. Although no document has ever been found linking this order directly to Hitler, it makes no logical sense to deny his ultimate authorship. Dawidowicz places this in a more general context, arguing that there was a gradual escalation of persecution from the nineteenth century, through to Hitler's ideas in the 1920s, then to implementation in the 1930s, and ultimately to extermination. Most recently – and forcefully – Goldhagen has argued that there are four clear precursors in Hitler's thought and speeches for the Holocaust. First, 'Hitler expressed his obsessive eliminationist racist antisemitism from his earliest days in public life': this can be seen explicitly in *Mein Kampf*. Then, on coming to power, Hitler 'turned the eliminationist antisemitism into unprecedented radical measures'. Third, in 1939 he 'repeated many times his prophecy, indeed his promise: the war would provide him with the opportunity to exterminate European Jewry'. This, finally, he proceeded to do 'when the moment was ripe'. Hence, Goldhagen concludes, 'The genocide was the outgrowth not of Hitler's moods, not of local initiative, not of the impersonal hand of structural obstacles, but of Hitler's ideal to eliminate all Jewish power.'[104]

There is, alternatively, a 'structuralist' argument that the extermination was a process which was arrived at as a logical sequence of administrative actions rather than as a preconceived plan. This view was pioneered by Hilberg as early as 1961.[105] It was subsequently continued – and refined – by Mommsen and Broszat. The basic argument is that the 'Final Solution' was not the solution originally intended but rather that arrived at because of the failure of all the others. It was the result of growing incompetence, not increased efficiency. The original target had been resettlement, first to Madagascar, then to Siberia. The former had been made impractical by the outbreak of war, which had focused Germany's priorities on Europe itself. The latter was impeded by the nature of the war against Russia. Proposals to transport all Jews over the Urals were set in motion but were then blocked by the growth of Russian resistance to the German advance. This meant an accumulation of peoples in eastern Europe with no obvious long-term destination. The result was the search for a swift solution, first through the SS Einsatzgruppen killings, then through the use of extermination camps.

This debate fits into the broader one of the nature of the Nazi state. It is no coincidence that the intentionalists also argue that the structure of dictatorship in Germany depended on the personality of Hitler himself and that he deliberately exploited any weaknesses and contradictions within it to his own advantage. He would therefore have chosen the time, the method and the institutions for the implementation of a scheme of extermination which had always existed in his mind. The structuralists, by contrast, see consistency in the weakness of Hitler's response to institutional chaos and the disorganized way in which the Holocaust was finally implemented. This makes it possible to conclude that the Holocaust was the administrative response to the failure of earlier policies.

A possible synthesis may be that, while he was out of power, Hitler initially thought in terms of genocide – but then moderated this in order to broaden his support once he was in power. This explains why he limited early measures to the Nuremberg Laws and ordered the removal of discriminatory public notices at the time of the 1936 Berlin

Olympics. It is true that there was a violent acceleration in Kristallnacht (1938). Nevertheless, there was no inexorable move towards extermination. Furthermore, during the first two years of the war, Hitler hoped for a possible peace with Britain and did not at this stage wish to antagonize the United States. The reaction of public opinion in these countries to genocide would have been one of horror, compared to the apparent indifference which had previously prevailed over earlier anti-Semitic policies.[106]

Then total war changed the whole situation. This occurred for two reasons. First, in invading the Soviet Union, Hitler was signalling that he considered that Britain was no longer capable of exerting any real threat: that she was now marginalized and therefore irrelevant. Germany could now focus on the racial struggle which Hitler had always foreseen. The defeat of the Soviet Union could be accompanied by the removal of Jewry – by whatever method. But, with the failure to inflict permanent defeat on Russia in 1941, the struggle for racial conquest became one for racial survival – in which Hitler's ideas of extermination, already strongly hinted at, were crucial. The pursuit of total war against the Soviet Union required the total removal of the perceived racial enemy within. So far the impetus for genocide must be considered Hitler's. The means by which this would be carried out, however, resided with the SS, which alone could provide the degree of organization and commitment that was needed. This implementation of the genocide programme gave the SS an enormously enhanced role so that, after 1941, the Nazi state came to be partly superseded by the SS state.

The debate on the origins of the Holocaust also raises the question of the complicity of the German people. Traditional views place the focus on Hitler and his immediate henchmen. In support of this, it can be argued that much of the population was held in the grip of a dictatorship which had absolute control over information and the capacity to intimidate and terrorize. Both processes were under the control of one institution – the SS. Himmler gave explicit instructions for secrecy: he said of the extermination to an assembly of SS officials in Posen in 1943, 'Among ourselves, we can talk openly about it, though we can never speak a word of it in public.' He added, 'That is a page of glory in our history that never has been and never can be written.'[107] There was therefore a huge barrier of credibility: the idea of genocide was unimaginable to most people. And, if it was denied by the regime, why should rumours to the contrary be believed? Besides, if rumourmongers were disposed of by the SS, this did not necessarily mean that the rumours were true: the use of terror had long been institutionalized for any form of dissent. How, therefore, could the German people reasonably have been expected to know what was going on?

The revised view spreads the degree of involvement and responsibility. Dülffer's view is typical: he argues that the Holocaust was above all due to Hitler, 'But to recognize this is not to exculpate the hundreds of thousands of others who were involved in carrying out the Final Solution.'[108] Goldhagen goes further: Hitler's ideal, he says, was 'broadly shared in Germany'.[109] This can be seen in several ways. The bureaucracy was involved on a huge scale and there was massive collaboration between the SS, the civil service, business corporations and the army. This deprived Jews of their rights and assets, isolated them, deported them and killed them. The army, too, was heavily implicated. In many cases the Wehrmacht actively co-operated with the SS – in contrast, it has to be said, with officers in the Italian army who officially protested against the killing of Italian Jews. The true extent of knowledge about and acceptance of the Holocaust will probably never now be known. But it is undoubtedly wider than was once believed.

This raises the disturbing question of how so many people could allow themselves to be involved in acts of evil. There can be no question that the participants were unaware of the real nature of what they were doing, whether in the Einsatzgruppen or in the camps. Even Rudolf Hoess, the commandant of Auschwitz, maintained that 'Our system is so terrible that no-one in the world will believe it to be possible.'[110] But how could this 'terrible system' have had so many practitioners? One possibility is that a minority of sadists enforced a system from which others knowingly followed through fear of retribution if they disobeyed orders. The impetus here is evil as a positive force, released by psychopathic behaviour. The main example would be the influence of Streicher, who derived sexual gratification from the persecution and torture of helpless people. There is no doubt that thousands of similar characters were attracted to membership of the SS by similar prospects. But it is equally certain that they were a small minority among all those involved in the Holocaust. There must be a better explanation.

The alternative, according to Hannah Arendt, is that the process of extermination was dealt with 'neither by fanatics nor by natural murderers nor by sadists. It was manned solely and exclusively by normal human beings of the type of Heinrich Himmler.'[111] Far from being sadistic, Himmler was squeamish about the details of mass murder and issued official instructions that SS officials were not to torment the inmates of the camps. In 1943 an SS *Untersturmführer* was sentenced to death for succumbing to the temptation to 'commit atrocities unworthy of a German or an SS commander'.[112] Rudolf Hoess always maintained that he was doing to the best of his ability the job allocated to him and that, at the same time, he remained 'completely normal': 'Even while I was carrying out the task of extermination I led a normal family life. I never grew indifferent to human suffering.'[113]

By this route we arrive at a preposterous conclusion. Among the sadists handling the extermination programme were 'normal' family men, who presided over them and tried to do their duty like decent German citizens. The extermination programme was seen as an arduous duty to be carried out. It involved the denial of the preferences of the participant, not their sublimation. But this was the clue. Denial of preference was initially directed by external discipline. External discipline led to internal self-discipline as the participant adapted to a new routine. Routine brought familiarity with the task which, in turn, reduced the chance of rejecting it. Yet in all this some absolute values could remain. These were parallel to and yet entirely cut off from the genocidal tasks being carried out. Hence, men like Hoess, who remained a practising Catholic while commandant at Auschwitz, literally led double lives, neither of which intruded on the other. We are left with the image of evil, in the words of Arendt, as being essentially 'banal'. In its ordinariness it can affect any group of people at any time. This is a far more frightening concept than a system dominated by psychopaths. Yet, for all that, evil can operate as mundanity only in the most extraordinary situations. This brings us full circle, back to trying to understand the nature of the ideology and regime which managed to capture a civilized people.

The Jewish response to persecution

Most studies in racism and anti-Semitism focus on the motivation of the persecutors. Attention is now being given to the reaction of the persecuted.

One view is that there was little resistance – and for a reason. According to Hilberg, the Jews tried to avoid provoking the Nazis into still more radical measures: 'They hoped that somehow the German drive would spend itself.' Furthermore, 'This hope was founded on a two-thousand-year-old experience. In exile the Jews had always been a minority; they had always been in danger; but they had learned that they could avert danger and survive destruction by placating and appeasing their enemies.'[114] This may have been broadly true. Traditionally the Jews had survived by adapting to persecution rather than resisting it. Yet we should not conclude from this that there was no attempt to contest Nazi measures; on the contrary, several measures emerged.

There were, for example, numerous self-help organizations. Comprising lawyers, doctors and artists, these were intended to evade the discriminatory legislation where possible and to minimize its effects. These were also linked to the Reich Association of German Jews which tried periodic public appeals: in 1935, for example, it complained to the Minister of War about the exclusion of Jewish servicemen from the German armed forces. Jewish lawyers also complained to the League of Nations about discrimination in Upper Silesia, still officially under League supervision as a plebiscite area. In this instance the government backed down and withdrew some of its measures (although it reinstated them when the League's supervision ended in 1937). More radical opponents were prominent in the illegal groups organized by the Communists and Social Democrats. These, according to confidential Gestapo reports, contained disproportionately large numbers of Jews. It is unlikely that such reports would have distorted this point, since they were intended to collate information, not to spread propaganda.

Yet in a sense such Jewish activities were counterproductive. Winterfelt argues that the various organizations impeded the full realization of the extent of anti-Semitism. The only real alternative was emigration, which the response actually discouraged. 'Instead of trying to make life for Jews under Nazi tyranny as pleasant as possible, everything, and every possible Pfennig, should have been invested in attempting to get Jews out of the country.'[115] There is some support for this: the United States allowed an immigration quota of 25,000 per annum, which was never filled before 1939.[116] On the other hand, different figures show that there was a major concerted effort to leave Germany: 130,000, or 20 per cent of the Jewish population, emigrated between 1933 and 1937, while a further 118,000 followed them after Kristallnacht, leaving something like 164,000. This occurred despite the upheaval and dislocation, and the loss of up to 96 per cent of emigrants' financial assets. Housden therefore puts a different case to that of Winterfelt: 'If emigration amounted to opposition through escape, the vast majority of the Jews did oppose the Third Reich.'[117]

Perhaps not surprisingly, historical controversy intensifies over the period of the Holocaust between 1941 and 1945. One debate concerns the extent of the Jewish administrative co-operation with the authorities. As the Germans occupied eastern Europe they established Jewish authorities, or *Judenräte*, in areas of heavy Jewish population. In the Ghetto of Lodz, for example, the *Judenräte* organized labour rotas, enforced discipline and prepared people for the resettlement ordered by the Nazis. Hilberg argues that the *Judenräte* aimed to avoid provoking the German authorities by making themselves indispensable to the German war economy and they certainly did a great deal to help the German administration, the resources of which were heavily stretched. 'The Jewish and German policies, at first glance opposites, were in reality pointed in the same direction.'[118] In some cases, Jewish officials even knew the secret of the exterminations but decided to remain silent. While accepting the humanitarian motive behind this, some historians, like Robinson, see it nevertheless as 'collaboration'.[119] Against this, it is strongly arguable that without such co-operation the plight of the victims would have been even worse. The same applies to those *Judenräte* in Upper Silesia which tried to stamp out opposition to the Nazis and sometimes handed offenders over to the Gestapo. But, according to Trunk, 'Under the system of collective responsibility, any act of a single person could lead to collective punishment of the whole ghetto community, whose doom would then be sealed.'[120] What the *Judenräte* were doing, therefore, was governing humanely. The fact that their authority was delegated to them by an inhumane system does not make them complicit.

Much has also been written about compliance within the death camps, especially over the apparent docility with which millions of Jews went to the gas chambers. One argument is the sheer extent of the deception applied by the Nazi authorities. Deportees were led to believe that they were being taken to the camps to be resettled. The next, and cruellest, deception was that those selected for the gas chambers were told that they were to be showered and deloused before taking on new trades allocated to them: they would therefore have been preparing themselves for a revival of the type of existence they had experienced in the ghettos. In these instances the SS and the German administration became expert at avoiding any trouble by building up hopes. Even in such terrible circumstances, however, there were examples of Jewish resistance. In 1942 Jewish inmates in Sachsenhausen rioted in protest against a decision to move them to the east. This was the only instance in Germany but there were also examples in 1943 at Treblinka, with 750 escapes, and at Sobibor, with 300 breakouts. Meanwhile, in Berlin, the Herbert Baum Group co-ordinated Jewish opposition, distributed anti-Nazi propaganda and made common cause with the Communists.

The way in which anti-Semitism developed in Germany therefore made the expression of dissent increasingly difficult. In the 1930s deprivation of any legal status meant that any opposition was by definition illegal and consequently posed all types of moral dilemmas since it endangered the security of the whole community. The period of the Holocaust involved closer administrative co-operation between Nazi authorities and Jewish groups, which served to intensify the dilemma.

GERMAN FOREIGN POLICY, 1919–39

The foreign policy of the Weimar Republic, 1919–33

By far the most important influence behind German foreign policy before the rise of Hitler was the Treaty of Versailles. Since this was fundamental to the mainstream of European diplomacy, its terms and significance have already been examined (see pp. 11–13).

The Treaty of Versailles caused great bitterness in Germany. There it was condemned by the entire range of political opinion, from far left to extreme right. It was seen by Hugo Preuss, a prominent politician and legal expert, as a severe blow to the new republic; he referred to the 'criminal madness of the Versailles Diktat'[121] and claimed that the new constitution 'was born with this curse upon it'. It was hardly surprising, therefore, that the major objective of the republic's foreign policy was to lift the burden of Versailles and seek a revised settlement. The question, of course, was how could this be accomplished?

One of the earliest strategies was that devised by Joseph Wirth, Chancellor for two brief periods in 1921 and 1922. This was the policy of 'fulfilment', a strange approach which, according to Hiden, was 'a necessary expedient based on the premise that to show determined good faith in trying to carry out the peace terms properly would not only demonstrate how impossible a task this was, but would therefore also induce the Allied powers to be more lenient in interpreting the treaty'.[122] In other words, let the treaty discredit and destroy itself through its very harshness. The British government was not unsympathetic, but the French were determined that the treaty should be applied to the letter. Hence, when Germany defaulted on a reparations payment of a specific number of telegraph poles, French troops entered and occupied the Ruhr in 1923. The policy of 'fulfilment' was immediately replaced by one of passive resistance called for by the Chancellor, Wilhelm Cuno. Relations between Germany and the Western powers had therefore reached a dangerous low.

Elsewhere, Wirth had been more successful. He opened up diplomatic relations with Europe's other isolated power, Bolshevik Russia. Representatives of Germany and Russia used the international conference at Genoa (1922) as a front for their own Treaty of Rapallo. This established diplomatic relations between the two states and laid the foundations for commercial contacts and economic co-operation. Rapallo was a diplomatic triumph for the Weimar Republic in eastern Europe, but clearly something had to be done to improve relations with the West.

This was to be the work of Gustav Stresemann. Chancellor in 1923 and Foreign Minister between 1923 and 1929, he pursued a skilful combination of aims. He intended, on the one hand, to rebuild cordial relations with other states and to remove the underlying international tensions which Europe had experienced in the early 1920s. He even saw Germany as 'the bridge which would bring East and West together in the development of Europe'. For his promotion of détente and his condemnation of war, Stresemann has sometimes been called a 'good European'. On the other hand, he was also a patriot who was as convinced as anyone that the Treaty of Versailles must eventually be revised. Much of his diplomacy was therefore double-edged. He once observed: 'We must get the stranglehold off our neck. On that account, German policy, as Metternich said of Austria, no doubt after 1809, will have to be one of finesse.'[123] More specifically, he had three objectives. One was 'the solution of the Reparations question in a sense tolerable for Germany'. A second was the 'protection of Germans abroad, those 10 to 12 millions of our kindred who now live under a foreign yoke in foreign lands.' Third, he hoped eventually for 'the readjustment of our eastern frontiers'.[124] The other face of the 'good European' was, therefore, the 'good German'.

There are three particularly important examples of Stresemann's policy of reconciliation between Germany and the rest of Europe. These were Germany's accession to the Locarno Pact (1925), her membership of the League of Nations (1926) and her involvement in the Kellogg–Briand Pact of 1928. These all seemed to indicate that Germany was now a reformed and rehabilitated power. Yet, at the same time, Stresemann was pursuing covert policies which benefited Germany at the expense of the rest of Europe and which were clearly revisionist in intention. Gatzke refers to Stresemann's 'appeasement abroad' and 'rearmament at home'. A good example of the latter was the 1926 Treaty of Berlin between Germany and Russia. This extended the earlier relationship established by the Treaty of Rapallo. Both powers now agreed to remain neutral if either were involved in a war with a third country. Even more significant, however, was Germany's use of her special relationship with Russia as a means of evading the rearmament restrictions imposed by the Treaty of Versailles. The German army (Reichswehr), under von Seeckt, derived a great deal from secret training and manoeuvres on Russian soil. Stresemann's attitude to Germany's secret rearmament ranged, in the words of Gatzke, 'from passive acceptance to active assistance'.[125] This was because co-operation needed, in Stresemann's view, to be accompanied by an increase in self-confidence and strength. Hence, in Stresemann's words, 'The main asset [of a strong foreign policy] is material power – army and navy.'[126]

What was the extent of Stresemann's success? Between his death in 1929 and the accession of Hitler in 1933, Germany experienced several positive developments. The Allied powers removed in 1930 all the occupying troops still in the Rhineland and, in 1932, the Lausanne Conference judged it expedient to alter radically the method by which Germany should pay reparations. It might, therefore, be thought that revisionism had made substantial inroads into the Versailles Settlement. Yet, during this same period, the Weimar Republic's foreign policy experienced a profound crisis. The Great Depression upset the republic's political stability and caused a swing to the parties of the right (see pp. 156–9). These had always opposed Stresemann's policies of détente and collaboration with the West. Hitler, especially, increased the intensity of his attacks on the republic, reviving the myth that the German army had been 'stabbed in the back' in 1918 and that the republic had always been dominated by the 'November Criminals', the 'traitors' of the First World War. The way was therefore open for the more intensive pursuit of revisionism by a regime which took full advantage of the head start provided by the Stresemann era but which rejected Stresemann's moderation.

Hitler's foreign policy, 1933–9

Hitler assumed responsibility for German foreign policy in January 1933. Although he had a considerable number of preconceived ideas, he decided that his initial strategy should be cautious and moderate. The main reason for this was Germany's still vulnerable position in Europe. The country was regarded by the Western powers as a defeated state, under the constraints of the Treaty of Versailles. Furthermore, the German government still had to contend with the manifest distrust shown by France and with the extensive system of alliances constructed by France in eastern Europe. Germany had not yet developed a counter-alliance, unless the pact with Russia, renewed in 1931, is included. Fascist Italy, perhaps the most likely prospect for an alliance with Germany, was at this stage hostile to Germany's designs on Austria, since Mussolini had not yet abandoned the possibility of expanding Italy's frontiers into the Alps. Between 1933 and 1935, therefore, Hitler had little option but to make conciliatory diplomatic gestures and to lull the suspicions of the rest of Europe. At the same time, he clearly intended to revive Germany's military power; the problem, he told his generals, was that this 'building of the armed forces' was also 'the most dangerous time'.[127] He must therefore avoid any possibility of retaliation.

An example of Hitler's early diplomacy was his attitude to the Geneva Disarmament Conference (1932–3) and its immediate follow-up. The politicians of the Weimar Republic, especially Stresemann, had shown interest in the case for a general reduction of armaments throughout Europe, since this would help offset the one-sidedness of the Versailles provisions. Hitler, however, was less interested in this type of approach for, as Craig points out, he intended to exploit Germany's grievance over arms, not deprive her of it.[128] He certainly wanted to avoid any future limitations on German rearmament but without being blatantly provocative. His opportunity came when the British Prime Minister, MacDonald, proposed a reduction of French troops from 500,000 to 200,000 and an increase in German troops to parity with the French. This was far below Hitler's expectations; he knew, however, that the French would reject the proposal and was therefore able to project a moderate image in supporting MacDonald. When the French did decline the offer, Hitler withdrew from the Disarmament Conference and then from the League of Nations. Realizing that this might provoke some sort of retaliation, he decided to cover his tracks with bilateral agreements which could later be broken. In 1934, therefore, he drew up a Non-Aggression Pact with Poland. This was partly to break the French system of alliances in eastern Europe and partly to allay the suspicions of western Europe that he had long-term designs on Polish territory. In reality, of course, he had no intention of keeping to the pact. He declared, privately, 'All our agreements with Poland have a purely temporary significance.'[129] For the time being, however, he decided to conceal his hand.

Hitler's pretended moderation encountered a setback in 1934 when the Austrian Nazis assassinated Chancellor Dollfuss in an abortive attempt to seize power and achieve a political union with Germany. Hitler was seriously embarrassed by this development which put a brake on the possibility of closer relations between Germany and Italy. He was therefore obliged to play down the activities of the Austrian Nazis, since he was not yet strong enough to use such opportunities to further a more aggressive course. Much would depend on the success of his rearmament policy. What stage had this reached by 1935?

There had never been any question of Hitler abiding by the disarmament provisions of the Treaty of Versailles. When he came to power in 1933 he inherited ten divisions; by the middle of 1934 he had increased the total to 240,000 men, more than twice the number allowed by Versailles. By 1935 there was no longer any point in pretending. On 11 March he formally announced the existence of a German airforce. On 16 March he issued a decree introducing conscription and warning that the military provisions of Versailles would no longer be observed. The reaction of the other powers posed a major diplomatic problem which Hitler needed to resolve. The League of Nations formally censured Germany's unilateral decision to rearm and, in April 1935, Britain, France and Italy formed the Stresa Front. In the following month, France responded of her own accord by drawing up a mutual assistance pact with the Soviet Union. It seemed that Germany had reached the critical phase of almost total isolation.

The period 1935–7, however, provided Hitler with a series of opportunities. He was able to end German isolation, put pressure on Britain and France and bring together a formidable diplomatic combination in central Europe. He was greatly assisted in accomplishing all this by favourable external trends and events.

The first of these was the reluctance of the British government to become involved in continental obligations, which meant that it was always receptive to a deal on armaments levels. In June 1935 Hitler secured an Anglo-German Naval Pact by which he undertook not to build a German fleet beyond 35 per cent of the total British strength. This was another example of Hitler's preference for bilateral agreements and it ruined any chance that the Stresa Front might be able to put concerted pressure on Germany: France and Italy were both furious with Britain's co-operation with Hitler. But the real windfall for Hitler was the involvement of Italy, from 1935 onwards, in Ethiopia (see pp. 140–2). This had several beneficial results for Germany. Imperial expansion diverted Italian attention away from Austria, Hitler's target to the south. It also had considerable diplomatic repercussions as Britain and France antagonized Italy by applying economic sanctions. Above all, Britain now saw Italy as a potentially hostile power and became more apprehensive than ever about commitments in Europe; she needed to be free to deal, if necessary, with Italian threats in the Mediterranean or Africa. Hitler therefore gambled that Britain would not be prepared to back any military action by France to prevent any further breaches of the Treaty of Versailles. He decided to remilitarize the Rhineland ahead of his original target. This he accomplished in March 1936 with only 22,000 troops, against the advice of his generals who feared instant retaliation. His judgement proved correct. The British government, anxious not to become involved, took no action and persuaded the French government to do likewise.

From this stage onwards Hitler was able to construct a new network of partners and satellites. Italy, involved in the Ethiopian adventure and the Spanish Civil War (see pp. 142–3), was no longer a rival in central Europe and gravitated towards Germany in the 'Rome–Berlin Axis' of 1936. At the same time, Hitler extended the scope of his diplomacy to outflank France. He assisted Franco to replace the Spanish Republic with a far-right regime deeply hostile to France. Russia, France's partner since 1935, was the target of the Anti-Comintern Pact, drawn up in November 1936 between Germany and Japan and eventually including Italy. Meanwhile, Germany was also implementing the Four Year Plan and a policy of autarky which involved the economic penetration of Romania, Yugoslavia, Bulgaria and Greece (see pp. 194–5). By the end of 1937, Hitler's position was sufficiently secure for him to consider adopting a more openly aggressive policy.

Therefore, in November 1937, Hitler summoned to a special conference the War Minister (Blomberg), the Commander-in-Chief of the Navy (Raedar), the Commander-in-Chief of the Army (Fritsch), the Commander-in-Chief of the Airforce (Goering) and the Foreign Minister (Neurath). The sixth person present was Colonel Hossbach, whose unofficial record of the meeting is generally known as the Hossbach Memorandum. According to this document, Hitler revealed the underlying purpose of his foreign policy and his hopes for the future, including schemes for the enlargement of Germany. Hitler added that there was some urgency because his plans would be resisted by Britain and France, and Germany's military superiority could not be expected to last beyond the period 1943–5. The Hossbach Memorandum, therefore, clearly indicates a change in the tempo of Hitler's diplomacy. It has been argued that Hitler was now willing to run high risks to attain his objectives and that he was prepared, if necessary, to launch a series of swift military campaigns. His new approach came as something of a shock to some of his subordinates, who inevitably tried to point out the dangers involved. Hitler's response to this was to reorganize the structure of the army and to replace Blomberg, Fritsch and Neurath. He was clearly determined to remove any obstruction to the next phase of his foreign policy.

Two targets were particularly prominent in 1938: Austria and Czechoslovakia. In March he accomplished the long-intended Anschluss and, in defiance of the Treaty of Versailles, incorporated Austria directly into the Reich. The result was a radical change in the balance of power in central and south-eastern Europe. Germany now had a joint border with Italy, completely outflanked Czechoslovakia and had gained direct access to Hungary and the Balkans. Hitler had also scored a major personal triumph: once again he had ignored warnings that his action would provoke foreign intervention and once again he had been proved right. Indeed, the ease with which the Anschluss had been accomplished led inexorably to the next undertaking. This was the removal of the German-populated Sudetenland from Czechoslovakia and its incorporation into the Reich. Again, this has been seen as a 'virtuoso performance'.[130] Hitler used a variety of expedients; these included the use of Henlein's Sudeten Nazis as an internal pressure group, and the serious differences between the provinces of Bohemia and Slovakia. According to Noakes and Pridham, 'Hitler now proceeded to use the ethnic diversity of the country as a lever with which to break it up into its ethnic components.'[131] Above all, he exploited the unwillingness of Britain and France to take direct action in support of Czechoslovakia. The result was the Munich Agreement (29 September 1938) which allowed Hitler to annex the Sudetenland to the Reich. In return Chamberlain, the British Prime Minister, secured a promise that Britain and Germany would 'never go to war with one another again'. The whole episode showed the bankruptcy of collective security, of Franco-Soviet co-operation and of the British policy of appeasement. The Munich Agreement, conversely, built up Hitler's image within Germany and convinced him absolutely of his ability to accomplish the objectives outlined in the Hossbach Memorandum.

There is a school of thought that Hitler saw Munich as something of a failure – that he had allowed himself to be talked into making a diplomatic agreement instead of going ahead with the military option which he had threatened throughout the crisis. He certainly made up for this during the course of 1939. Once again working on an internal crisis, he engineered the break-up of Czechoslovakia and, in March, incorporated Bohemia and Moravia into the Reich. Having accomplished his objectives in central Europe, Hitler turned his attention eastwards, gaining Memel from Lithuania. He was now determined to complete the union of all Germans within the Reich, recover the last vestiges of territory lost at Versailles, and begin the process of Lebensraum.

This meant that his next victim was Poland. Hitler swiftly stepped up the pressure by demanding Danzig and the Polish Corridor, only to meet determined resistance from the Polish Foreign Minister, Beck. By this stage, Poland was bolstered by an Anglo-French guarantee. This had been delivered in March and was a clear indication that the Western powers had finally come to recognize the futility of appeasement. Hitler, however, was utterly confident that he could continue to outwit Britain and France. He was convinced that the British government was bluffing and that France would not go to war alone against Germany. In any case, he made his own position more secure by drawing up in May 1939 the Pact of Steel with Italy (see p. 143) and in August the Non-Aggression Pact with the Soviet Union (see pp. 74–7). The latter was a major diplomatic turnabout which made a nonsense of any undertaking by the West to protect Poland. Hitler still expected to avoid a conflict with Britain by seeming to negotiate further with the Polish government and, through a series of manufactured border incidents, providing evidence of Polish 'aggression'. But his invasion of Poland on 1 September 1939 provoked declarations of war from both Britain and France, much to Hitler's surprise. He was also let down at the last minute by his most important ally: Mussolini felt obliged to inform Hitler that Italy was insufficiently equipped at this stage to undertake direct military action. Despite these unexpected obstacles, Hitler was supremely confident of success and proceeded to demonstrate the awesome power of the new German army operating a Blitzkrieg strategy.

Aims of Hitler's foreign policy

While the statesmen of the Weimar Republic were trying in the 1920s to achieve a revision of the Versailles Settlement and, at the same time, effect a reconciliation with the other powers, Hitler was already devising more elaborate schemes, to which he added substantially in the 1930s and early 1940s. There are three major sources for discerning Hitler's ideas. The first, of course, is *Mein Kampf*, written in Landsberg prison, and subsequently published; it achieved a mass circulation and was read by millions of Germans. The second is Hitler's *Second Book*, which dealt explicitly with foreign policy but remained unpublished in his lifetime. The third source is a series of spoken remarks made by Hitler and edited by Dr Henry Picker as Hitler's *Tischgespräche* (*Table Talk*). Because of the undisciplined and often rambling nature of these works, it is difficult to put together a carefully structured outline of his policy. The basic aims, however, seem clear enough.

He maintained that all previous governments had been restricted in their foreign policy by the notion of the 'fixed frontier'. Even the conservatives and neo-Bismarckians were wrong to aim at recreating the territorial arrangements of 1914, for 'the German borders of the year 1914 were borders which presented something incomplete'. As an alternative to the 'border policy' of the 'national bourgeois' world, the Nazis would follow a 'territorial one', the whole purpose of which would be 'to secure the space necessary to the life of our people'. The limited policies of Bismarck had, perhaps, been necessary to establish and build up the 'power structure' for the future. But Bismarck's successors had denied Germany her natural process of expansion and had pursued an 'insane' policy of alliance with Austria–Hungary and maritime conflict with Britain. Now the mistakes of history should be rectified, Lebensraum could be achieved, and the 'inferior races' could be deprived of the territory to which their low productivity and potential gave them no natural right. 'According to an eternal law of Nature, the right to the land belongs to the one who conquers the land because the old boundaries did not yield sufficient space for the growth of the population.' Returning to the theme of struggle which had permeated *Mein Kampf*, Hitler affirmed: 'Every healthy, vigorous people sees nothing sinful in territorial acquisition, but something quite in keeping with its nature.' The intended direction of this expansion was made abundantly clear in *Mein Kampf*: 'We put a stop to the eternal movement of the Germanic people to Europe's South and West and we turn our eyes to the land in the East.' More specifically, 'In speaking of new territory in Europe, we can, above all, have in mind only Russia and its subjugated border states.'[132]

Did these ideas gradually evolve into an overall programme, a blueprint which Hitler intended to follow? This question has produced one of the major historical controversies within the theme of Nazi foreign policy.

On the one hand, some historians emphasize the fundamental logic of Hitler's designs and acknowledge that he did develop a definite programme and set of intentions. These so-called 'programmists' and 'intentionalists' owe much to the pioneering work of Trevor-Roper, who maintained that *Mein Kampf* was 'a complete blueprint of his intended achievements'.[133] More recently, it has been argued, by Hillgruber, that Hitler pursued his aims systematically 'without, however, forfeiting any of his tactical flexibility'.[134] Similar views are expressed by Jäckel, who claims that Hitler's 'programme of foreign policy' can be divided into three phases:

> During the first phase, Germany had to achieve internal consolidation and re-armament and to conclude agreements with Britain and Italy. During the second phase Germany had to defeat France in a preliminary engagement. Then the great war of conquest against Russia could take place during the third and final phase.[135]

Jäckel also maintains that there is 'ample documentary evidence to prove that he always kept this outline in mind'. There is an alternative 'programme', pointed to by other historians but overlapping that deduced by Jäckel. Hitler's first priority was to destroy the Versailles Settlement and rearm Germany. This would be followed by the creation of an enlarged Reich which would incorporate all of Europe's German population. This, in turn, would be the prelude to the achievement of Lebensraum from conquered territory in Poland and Russia.

The 'intentionalist' school is in broad agreement on Hitler's formulation of a programme or series of objectives. There is, however, a sub-debate between what might be termed the 'continentalists' and the 'globalists'.[136] The former maintain that Hitler's objective was the conquest of Lebensraum in the east. According to Jäckel, 'Hitler's main aim in foreign policy was a war of conquest against the Soviet Union.'[137] But a considerable number of German historians now claim that Hitler had an aim which transcended the defeat of Russia and the achievement of Lebensraum: namely, world conquest. These include Hillgruber, who believes that Hitler's policy geographically 'was designed to span the globe; ideologically, too, the doctrines of universal antisemitism and social Darwinism, fundamental to his programme, were intended to embrace the whole of mankind'.[138] Thies is in broad agreement with this: 'at no time between 1920 and 1945 did [Hitler], as his statements prove, lose sight of the aim of world domination'.[139] Other 'globalists' include Hildebrand and Hauner; according to the latter, Hitler's power would be spread 'in a series of blitz campaigns, extending stage by stage over the entire globe'.[140] As events turned out, of course, Hitler was never able to achieve 'more than the opening moves of the continental phase of his programme'.[141]

There is a school of thought which denies that Hitler pursued a particular programme in his foreign policy. Rather, he was profoundly influenced by the needs of the moment. This case has been put most forcefully by A.J.P. Taylor, who argues that Hitler's projects, as outlined in the Hossbach Memorandum, were 'in large part daydreaming, unrelated to what followed in real life'. In his opinion, 'Hitler was gambling on some twist of fortune which would present him with success in foreign affairs, just as a miracle had made him Chancellor in 1933.'[142] There has been qualified support for this line of thought, although for different reasons. Mommsen, for example, argues that Hitler did little to shape his foreign policy and that his whole approach was spontaneous – a series of responses to specific developments: 'in reality the regime's foreign policy ambitions were many and varied, without any clear aims and only linked by their ultimate goal: hindsight alone gives them some air of consistency'.[143] Broszat, too, points to the lack of any fundamental design and maintains that Lebensraum was basically an expression of the need to sustain a dynamic momentum.

An overall synthesis was suggested by one of the earliest and best-known historians on the Hitler era, Bullock. He submits that both claims – whether for preliminary planning or disorganized spontaneity – have to be combined. Hitler, after all, 'had only one programme: power, first his own power in Germany, and then the expansion of German power in Europe'.[144] Elsewhere, Bullock maintains that 'he was at once both fanatical and cynical'.[145]

Another major debate on Hitler's foreign policy is whether there is an underlying continuity with early periods. The original argument was that there was a fundamental break, both with the foreign policy of the Weimar Republic and with that of the Kaiser's Second Reich. But this earlier consensus was shattered during the late 1960s by Fischer who, in *Germany's Aims in the First World War*,[146] claimed that Germany deliberately engineered the conflict in order to pursue expansionist aims which were really a prelude to those of Hitler. These aims had included: economic dominance over Belgium, Holland and France; hegemony over Courland, Livonia, Estonia, Lithuania and Poland, as well as over Bulgaria, Romania and Turkey; unification with Austria and the creation of a Greater Germany; control over the eastern Mediterranean; and rule over a dismantled Russia. Clearly, in the light of such a programme, Hitler's objectives would appear far from new; they could more appropriately be called a continuation than a radical departure. In addition, there were precedents for the *völkisch* emphasis of Hitler's expansionist policies in a number of pan-German and Lebensraum groups in pre-1914 Germany.

Of course, such plans were never implemented. The Second Reich lost the First World War and was itself replaced by the more moderate Weimar Republic. Here, surely, would be a case for denying continuity. Yet certain trends can be detected linking the Weimar Republic and the Third Reich. In the first place, there was considerable continuity of military and diplomatic personnel which lasted until Hitler's radical changes in 1938. The Weimar Republic had contained, within the Foreign Ministry, men like Neurath and Bülow, who also served Hitler for the first five years of the Third Reich. Much the same applied to Germany's ambassadors abroad, drawn as they were largely from the former aristocracy. This continuity of personnel at first lessened the likelihood of any sudden and dramatic switch of policy. In any case, it could be argued, Hitler was able to continue with the objectives of the republic as long as he concentrated on whittling away the Versailles Settlement. Indeed, by 1938 he had accomplished the targets of the republic's revisionists: Germany had regained full sovereignty over all internal territories, including the Saar and Rhineland; the restrictions on armaments had been ignored since 1935; and the Germans of Austria and the Sudetenland had been incorporated into the Reich.

In retrospect, however, it is obvious that the continuity between the diplomacy of the Weimar Republic and the Third Reich can be misleading. The crucial point which showed that Nazi foreign policy was as revolutionary as its domestic counterpart was that Hitler saw revisionism merely as a step towards projects which were well beyond the ambitions of the republic's statesmen. Although the republic's politicians had a strong element of opportunism, even ruthlessness, they did not share Hitler's Social Darwinism and racialist vision. They also respected the traditions of European diplomacy and, under Stresemann, contributed much to international co-operation. One of Hitler's aims was to smash the multilateral agreements, like the Locarno Pact, which had been carefully built up during the 1920s. As for the continuity of personnel, it suited Hitler to retain the appointments made by the republic, so that he could give his regime a façade of moderation and respectability during the period of maximum vulnerability. As soon as he had accomplished safe levels of rearmament he instituted radical changes, in both his policy and his appointments. The turning-point was clearly the Hossbach Memorandum of 1937 and its follow-up. The developments of 1939, too, went far beyond any republican revisionism. According to Noakes and Pridham, 'It is in the policy pursued in Poland after 1939 and in Russia after 1941 that the distinction between Nazism and conservative German nationalism emerges clearly for the first time.'[147]

Finally, to what extent was Hitler's foreign policy influenced by events within Germany? Recent historians have argued strongly that there is a direct correlation between Germany's economic problems and performance and the pursuit of an expansionist policy in Europe. Sauer, for example, maintains that Blitzkrieg was an economic as well as a military strategy. It enabled Germany to rearm without causing German consumers excessive suffering and thereby depriving the regime of their support.[148] The practical effect was the deliberate dismantling of neighbouring states in order to strengthen the German economic base. Kershaw sees the relationship between the economy and militarism as more problematic. Hitler's Four Year Plan and his Hossbach Memorandum were responses to the economic crisis of 1935–6 and locked Germany into a course of rearmament – and war.[149] The process was less deliberate than Sauer maintains, but no less inexorable. It could also be argued that Hitler accelerated the pace of his foreign policy in order to divert German public opinion from domestic problems, especially economic. This was a well-worn device, used both in the Second Reich and in Mussolini's Italy.

There is a certain logic to all of the views outlined in this section, but they need to be carefully integrated into an overall argument consisting of four components. First, Hitler was not uniquely responsible for creating an entirely personal foreign policy. As Fischer has shown, he inherited the main hegemonist aims from the Second Reich. Nevertheless, second, he played an important part in renovating these within the context of a more forceful ideology based on a racial and *völkisch* vision, contained in *Mein Kampf* and the *Second Book*. He therefore personalized and amended certain historical concepts, and it would be quite wrong to suggest that these were not seriously intended. In this respect, there is much to commend the approach of the 'intentionalists', although whether we can go so far as to accept that Hitler had a 'programme' – continental or global – is more doubtful. Third, Hitler implemented his ideas in his move towards war during the late 1930s partly as a result of domestic issues, especially the shaping of the German economy: the balance between guns and butter required a Blitzkrieg approach to conquest. Hence, the Four Year Plan stepped up rearmament and the Hossbach Memorandum set an agenda for conflict. By 1938 these internal forces had locked Germany into a course which was likely to lead to war. Only at this point can Taylor's thesis be included. With growing confidence provided by his military preparations, Hitler became increasingly opportunistic, playing the diplomatic system with some skill and achieving what he wanted over the Anschluss and the Sudetenland. Why this course resulted in war has generated another controversy.

Hitler and the outbreak of the Second World War

The Nuremberg Judgement maintained that the Second World War was the outcome of Nazi policy and of Hitler's determination 'not to depart from the course he had set for himself'.[150] This raises the fundamental question: was the conflict really Hitler's war?

The majority opinion is that it was. The previous section provided an outline of the various arguments about Hitler's plans for European and world mastery, which are clearly relevant to the debate on the origins of the Second World War. There has also been much emphasis on what Hitler himself had to say about struggle and war. *Mein Kampf*, the *Second Book* and *Tischgespräche* all focus on militarism and unlimited expansion, together with the notion that struggle and war were fundamental human activities and needs. 'War is the most natural, the most ordinary thing. War is a constant; war is everywhere. There is no beginning, there is no conclusion of peace. War is life. All struggle is war. War is the primal condition.' The logical conclusion, therefore, is that Hitler wanted war, not only to achieve the objectives of his foreign policy, but to purify and strengthen the Aryan race. Hitler's responsibility for the outbreak of war is emphasized by a variety of British, German and American historians. Sontag, for example, argues that Hitler's policy in 1939 was, 'like the annexation of Austria and the Sudeten districts of Czechoslovakia, merely preliminary to the task of winning "living space"'.[151] Trevor-Roper believes that 'The Second World War was Hitler's personal war in many senses. He intended it, he prepared for it, he chose the moment for launching it.'[152] Fest affirmed the orthodoxy that 'who caused the war is a question that cannot be seriously raised'.[153] Much the same conclusion has been arrived at by Hillgruber, Hildebrand and Weinberg.

The alternative view, held by A.J.P. Taylor, relates to his argument that Hitler lacked any specific programme or long-term objectives, as outlined in the previous section. Instead of pursuing policies which led inevitably to war, Taylor argues, Hitler was, by and large, continuing those of the Second Reich and the Weimar Republic. He goes further: 'Hitler was no more wicked and unscrupulous than many other contemporary statesmen', although 'in wicked acts he outdid them all'. Hitler's diplomacy was based on short-term expedients and he doubted that a major conflict would be the outcome. Part of the Hossbach Memorandum made it clear that 'He was convinced of Britain's non-participation, and therefore he did not believe in the probability of belligerent action by France against Germany.' According to Taylor, the Hossbach Memorandum contained no plans for war

> and would never have been supposed to do so, unless it had been displayed at Nuremberg. The memorandum tells us, what we know already, that Hitler (like every other German statesman) intended Germany to become the dominant power in Europe. It also tells us that he speculated how this might happen. His speculations were mistaken. They bear hardly any relation to the actual outbreak of war in 1939.[154]

He also maintains that Germany was not really ready for war in 1939 – the levels of armaments confirm that Germany had not developed an advantage over Britain and France.

There has been considerable criticism of the Taylor thesis, both from historians convinced that Hitler did have long-term objectives which included war (for example, Trevor-Roper) and those who, although less convinced about this, feel that Taylor's approach is too narrow. One method of criticism is to remove the debate from the predominantly diplomatic ground which Taylor preferred to occupy and focus, instead, on the economy. Mason, for example, argues that Taylor's view

> leads to an overwhelming concentration on the sequence of diplomatic events, [his judgements] rest very largely upon the diplomatic documents [and that] these documents were primarily the work of conservative German diplomats, who, in dealing with their specific problems, were able to cover up or ignore the distinctive language and concepts of National Socialism. This helps to nurture the illusion that the foreign policy of the Third Reich was much the same as that of the Weimar Republic.[155]

Instead, Mason argues, Hitler deliberately chose war in 1939 as a way out of the difficulties faced by the German economy.

There is, finally, an approach which would apportion at least part of the responsibility for the outbreak of war to the other powers. In this case, however, responsibility is associated less with 'guilt' than with 'misinterpretation', 'inconsistency' and 'default'. It has been argued that Hitler's progress towards war was unintentionally accelerated by Western leaders, paradoxically, because of their very hatred of war. Daladier and Chamberlain, who found war morally repugnant, assumed that the rationale of all diplomacy was the pursuit of peace. Chamberlain, in particular, made the crucial mistake of assuming that even Hitler had fixed objectives and that if these were conceded to him, the causes of international tension would be removed. Hitler, of course, was greatly encouraged by the pressure exerted on the smaller states by the British and French governments and mistook forbearance in the interests of peace for weakness and diplomatic capitulation. This explains the increasingly aggressive stance which he adopted during the Sudeten Crisis of 1938. By 1939 Chamberlain had at last got the true measure of Hitler and decided to extend guarantees to Poland. This sudden switch appeared to be a desperate turn within a bankrupt policy and clearly failed to convince Hitler of Chamberlain's seriousness. Liddell Hart compared the pre-war crises with allowing someone to stoke up a boiler until the pressure rose to danger level and then closing the safety valve. It could certainly be said that the Western powers let Hitler accomplish so many of his objectives before 1939 that they precipitated conflict by eventually trying to stand firm. On the one hand, according to Henig, one cannot argue

> that firmer action before 1939 would have prevented war. It might have precipitated it earlier. Evidence seems to suggest fairly clearly that Hitler was determined to fight in October 1938 to gain Sudeten Czech territory. It might have been better, from a military point of view, for Britain and France to have fought then rather than later. This would not have prevented war but it might well have localized it.[156]

GERMANY AT WAR, 1939–45

German involvement in the Second World War is often divided into two distinct phases. The first was the period of Blitzkrieg or 'lightning war'. This saw a series of rapid military victories over Poland, western Europe and the Balkans, as well as initial success against Russia, bringing most of Europe under German control. The main reasons for the Blitzkrieg strategy are dealt with on pp. 193–7. The second period was one of total war (1942–5). By this time Blitzkrieg had clearly failed to defeat Britain and the Soviet Union and proved helpless against the United States. During this second phase, Germany was slowly but inexorably ground down by the overwhelmingly greater industrial capacity of the Allies (see pp. 231–3), who were much more effectively geared to fight a prolonged war. In retrospect, it is surprising not that Germany lost the war but that she survived so long.

Blitzkrieg and the expansion of the Third Reich, 1939–41

German armies invaded Poland on 1 September 1939, secured by the Non-Aggression Pact from possible retaliation by the Soviet Union. Although Britain and France had both declared war on Germany in support of Poland, they were unable to take direct military action; for them the period 1939–40 was one of inactivity, generally known as the 'phoney war'. The German attack on Poland was the last to be planned entirely by the German generals. It was highly professional and was the first completely mechanized invasion in history, comprising armoured vehicles, tanks and preliminary air attacks on selected targets. The Polish cavalry was routed and Warsaw was taken after a converging drive from East Prussia, Pomerania, Silesia and Slovakia. When Stalin intervened on 17 September to claim the territory set aside for Russia by the Non-Aggression Pact (see p. 75), Poland's fate was sealed. She was partitioned for the fourth time in her history and ceased to exist as an independent state.

The strategy of Blitzkrieg was applied next to the west, with even more spectacular success. The first targets were Denmark and Norway, chosen to consolidate Germany's position before the major assault on France, long considered by Hitler to be Germany's 'natural enemy'. Norway was especially important as it was a major outlet for Swedish iron-ore supplies and had enormous potential for North Atlantic naval bases. Besides, it dominated Germany's submarine route past the Shetlands and could well be used by Britain unless quickly taken. The task, accomplished in April 1940, demonstrated a new version of Blitzkrieg: namely, combined land and sea operations. It seemed that the German war machine was irresistible and there was clear evidence of a sense of defeatism in the Low Countries and France – Hitler's next victims. The Netherlands, Belgium and Luxembourg all fell to a renewed German onslaught in May 1940. This, however, was only the preliminary to Hitler's major objective – the conquest of France. Again, this was accomplished by a variation of Blitzkrieg. This time von Kleist's panzer divisions punched a hole through the Ardennes, supposedly impassable and therefore lightly defended. Guderian's forces then overwhelmed the French Ninth Army. In the subsequent race to the Channel ports, the Germans captured most of Flanders, and the British army was evacuated at Dunkirk. The German offensive then flowed southwards, culminating by the end of June in the capture of Paris and the capitulation of France.

Why was France defeated so easily? It used to be thought that the French armies were overwhelmed by superior numbers. More recent estimates have shown that this was not the case. Against the 103 German divisions on the western front, France mustered 99 which were also supported by British contingents. The Allies had a definite superiority in tanks (3,000 against 2,700), in warships (107 against 13) and in artillery pieces (11,200 against 7,710). The only real deficiency of the Allies was in air power, where the Luftwaffe had the advantage. The real reason for Germany's success has to be sought, therefore, in vastly superior strategic thinking. Hitler's campaign was based on the 'Sichelschnitt' (sickle cut) through the northern plains of France via the Ardennes, as explained above. According to Noakes and Pridham, 'It was perhaps the most brilliant military plan of modern times.'[157] The French, by contrast, were stuck in the mould of their First World War strategy. They assumed that any conflict with Germany would again be defensive and slow moving, a belief which was symbolized by the vast and ultimately useless Maginot Line, constructed at enormous expense between the wars.

By June 1940 Hitler had achieved in the west all his objectives but one – a satisfactory settlement with Britain. Hitler did not intend, at this stage, to undertake a fight to the finish with Britain: his first priority was the quest for Lebensraum in eastern Europe. In any case it might be possible to produce honourable peace terms. His interpretation of recent history was that Britain had always distanced itself from Europe unless it could rely upon a particular power to act as its 'continental sword'. The collapse of France had now removed this sword. It would make sense, therefore, for Britain to resume its traditional position of neutrality and isolation. Hitler did everything possible to encourage this. He made a series of statements that he had no hostile intentions against Britain and that he certainly never intended to seek to destroy the British Empire.[158] When his peace approaches were contemptuously rejected by Churchill, the new British Prime Minister, Hitler considered that he had no option but to give the directive for the invasion of Britain. This would be the most ambitious Blitzkrieg to date, starting with an all-out preliminary air offensive, followed by a massive landing operation which would be codenamed 'Operation Sealion'.

The events of 1940–1 were to prove the first setback in Hitler's war. This was due in part to a lack of total commitment to the task which he had undertaken. He overestimated the possibility of reconciliation with Britain on the one hand while, on the other, underestimating the British capacity for resistance. The result was that Hitler seriously misused Germany's resources and undermined the whole purpose of Blitzkrieg. In the first place, he mismanaged the invasion plan. According to Craig,[159] Goering's direction of the preliminary campaign to knock out resistance from the RAF was amateurish: he frittered away Germany's strength in the air by hitting too wide a variety of targets and not concentrating on British airfields. Hitler's decision to go for British cities also contributed to the survival of the RAF in the early and crucial stage, making possible its eventual victory in the Battle of Britain. The RAF also had the advantage of more effective aircraft in the Spitfire and Hurricane, more experienced pilots, and a better warning system. Once the RAF had confirmed its superiority in the air by 1941, Hitler was forced to postpone Operation Sealion.

But, despite the failure of Hitler's plans, Britain posed no direct threat to Germany in 1941. It did not possess sufficient resources to engage in a major continental war and, in 1941, suffered a number of reverses which built Hitler's confidence to a new peak. The opportunity was, in a sense, unsought. Mussolini had made a series of disastrous mistakes in North Africa, Greece and Yugoslavia (see pp. 146–7), resulting in temporary incursions by British troops. In order to consolidate Germany's southern flank and to rescue Mussolini from defeat, Hitler despatched Rommel to North Africa and German panzer divisions to the Balkans in 1941. Within weeks the British were forced back into Egypt and had to evacuate Greece and the Greek islands in the Mediterranean.

These reverses did not, however, make the defeat of Britain any more imminent. Hitler had already decided to approach the problem from a different angle and to unleash another Blitzkrieg, this time against Russia. In retrospect, this decision seems to be the ultimate in folly. Yet, at the time, it must have had a certain compelling logic. Ideologically, of course, Hitler had a long-standing urge to smash what he regarded as the centre of international Bolshevism and world Jewry – in his eyes synonymous evils. At the same time, Germany would at last achieve Lebensraum in eastern Europe, a design frequently mentioned in *Mein Kampf* and the *Second Book*. The defeat of Russia would also enable him to dominate the Eurasian land mass and accumulate sufficient strength to accomplish the next stage in his quest for world supremacy. Operation Barbarossa was therefore the culmination of all his previous policies – indeed, their logical fulfilment – even though it was introduced against the advice of his High Command.

8 Adolf Hitler, *c.* 1940 (Popperfoto)

One question is frequently asked about this decision. Why did Hitler open up a second front, thereby bringing into action a new enemy, before disposing of Britain? This could be seen as a monumental blunder, one which eventually cost Hitler the war. After all, he had once argued in 1939 that 'we can oppose Russia only when we are free in the West'.[160] On the other hand, it has been argued that he took the decision to invade Russia precisely because he had not managed to defeat Britain. According to Weinberg, this was 'Hitler's answer to the challenge of England – as it had been Napoleon's'.[161] By means of another swift and decisive campaign Hitler was certain that he could deprive Britain of any lingering hope that she might in future be able to use a 'continental sword'. There would also be wider advantages. As early as 31 July 1940 Hitler told his army chiefs: 'If Britain's hope in Russia is destroyed, her hope in America will disappear also, because the elimination of Russia will enormously increase Japan's power in the Far East.'[162]

But there is another possibility: that Operation Barbarossa was a pre-emptive strike against the Soviet Union which was becoming a looming military threat. Stalin had taken the decision during the 1930s to prepare for an offensive war at a time of his choosing and had accordingly stockpiled huge quantities of weapons (see pp. 78–9). If this was the case, and recent historical research suggests that it was a major factor in Stalin's Five Year Plans, then Hitler must have deduced Stalin's intention, or even picked up some of the details through German intelligence. It must have seemed to Hitler that by 1941 the gap was growing rapidly between the military strength of the two powers. Stalin would clearly attack eventually and the best chance Germany had of taking on the Soviet Union was by getting in first, especially since Stalin was prepared to go to great lengths to avoid a war until he was ready. Besides, Hitler's hands were free at the time: France had been smashed and Britain, although undefeated, was unable to bring the war to the continent. The most appropriate time for another major campaign was therefore 1941.

On 18 December 1940, Hitler therefore issued Directive no. 21 for Operation Barbarossa and ordered that 'The German armed forces must be prepared to crush Soviet Russia in a quick campaign even before the end of the war against England.' The invasion was delayed until June 1941 to enable Hitler to rescue Mussolini in the Balkans and North Africa. When it came it was to be a Blitzkrieg on an unprecedented scale, consisting of 4 million men, 3,300 tanks and 5,000 aircraft. At first the Germans encountered little resistance and advanced more rapidly than had any previous invasion force in history. Russian resistance folded (see pp. 79–80) and, by September 1941, the Germans held a line extending from the outskirts of Leningrad to the Black Sea. Hitler now intended to capture the rest of European Russia at least as far as the Urals.

By the end of 1941 Hitler had reached the peak of his power in Europe. Blitzkrieg had been applied in a succession of waves, each more extensive than the last. Poland had been crushed in the initial assault of 1939, followed in 1940 by western Europe. His attempt to apply it to Britain had failed, but the second Blitzkrieg in the east produced even more stunning results than the first. There was, however, one major shortcoming, which was ultimately to prove fatal to the Third Reich. Operation Barbarossa had not fulfilled the objective of finishing off the Soviet Union by the end of 1941, a serious failure since Blitzkrieg depended on instant victory. Thus, although Hitler's mastery over Europe seemed formidable, the tide was about to turn against Germany. From 1942 onwards Hitler's lightning wars were transformed into a more prolonged and destructive war of attrition – total war (see pp. 231–3).

Europe under Nazi rule, 1939–45

After his conquests, Hitler constructed a Reich which was intended to last a thousand years. To ensure this, he considered it essential to build a 'New Order' by which Germany would effectively dominate Europe. The two main elements of Hitler's scheme were, according to Rich,[163] the purification of the Germanic race and the extension of Germany's frontiers in search of Lebensraum in the east. Taken together, these brought about the greatest upheaval in Europe since the collapse of the Roman Empire.

Map 4 shows the extent of Hitler's domination of Europe by 1942. Most of the events leading up to this have been dealt with elsewhere, but it would be useful to draw the various threads together. The first area to be incorporated was Austria, by the Anschluss of 1938 (see pp. 262–3). This was followed by the dismantling of Czechoslovakia, with the absorption of the Sudetenland in 1938 and Bohemia in 1939, the latter as a German protectorate under Heydrich. Slovakia was allowed to become a puppet state under the leadership of Tiso (see pp. 293–4) until direct military occupation by the Germans after the 1944 rebellion.

The situation in south-eastern Europe was highly complex, involving a combination of Italian rule, German 'rescue missions', puppet regimes and outright conquest. On the whole, Hitler was content initially to allow Italian domination of the Balkans and the eastern Mediterranean. Albania, for example, came under Mussolini's rule in 1939. His attempt to subdue Greece, however, failed and in 1941 the Germans had to take over and partition the country. Yugoslavia was also crushed and divided, the southern part being allocated to Italy, Serbia coming under German military occupation and Croatia establishing another puppet government, this time under Pavelić (see pp. 284–5). The other states of the area were more careful or fortunate. Hungary allied herself to Germany until 1944, when Horthy was replaced by Szálasi's pro-Nazi Arrow Cross regime (see pp. 267–8). Bulgaria's alliance with Germany was transformed into almost total Nazi control over Prince Cyril in 1943 (see p. 280). Romania's connection with the Reich was similarly strengthened by Antonescu (see pp. 286–7). The greatest single problem for Hitler in southern Europe was the collapse of Italy in 1943 (see pp. 146–9) and the need to pour German troops into the north to prop up Mussolini's new Salo Republic. Between 1943 and 1945 Axis co-operation and alliances throughout the region were therefore replaced by total German domination.

Western Europe came under Nazi rule in 1940. Denmark experienced least upheaval; she retained her parliamentary monarchy until 1943, although under German 'protection'. Norway was jointly administered by a German commissioner, Terboven, and a Norwegian collaborator, Quisling (see pp. 295–6). The Netherlands were ruled by Reichs Commissioner Seyss-Inquart, who had previously been Governor of Austria, and Belgium by General von Falkenhausen. Luxembourg was, by 1942, incorporated directly into the Reich, along with the Belgian districts of Eupen and Malmédy and the French provinces of Alsace and Lorraine. Finally, France herself was divided after being conquered in 1940. Two-thirds, including

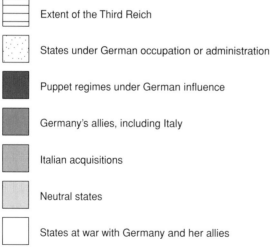

Extent of the Third Reich

States under German occupation or administration

Puppet regimes under German influence

Germany's allies, including Italy

Italian acquisitions

Neutral states

States at war with Germany and her allies

Map 4   Europe under Nazi influence by 1942

Paris and the Atlantic coast, were placed under General von Stülpnagel. The rest was allowed to establish a puppet state under Petain and Laval, based in Vichy (see pp. 296–7).

The greatest changes came in eastern Europe. Poland was conquered, plundered and destroyed in 1939 (see p. 271). This was followed by an attack on the Baltic states (see pp. 272–4) and on Russia. Part of Poland – West Prussia, Southern Silesia and Posen – was incorporated directly into the Reich. The rest formed the General Government of Occupied Polish Territories under the brutal administration of Hans Frank. The second wave of German conquests (1941–2) brought further reorganization, this time in Russia. Two vast new territories were set up, under Rosenberg. The first was Ostland, comprising the Baltic states and White Russia, the second the Ukraine. There were plans for two more, Muscovy and the Caucasus, which would have accounted for Russia up to the Urals. The whole of eastern Europe, therefore, was set aside for future German expansion in accordance with Hitler's designs in *Mein Kampf* and the *Second Book*.

All areas under Nazi rule were intended for maximum exploitation by the Third Reich. The basic justification for Lebensraum in eastern Europe was that the low productivity and cultural achievements of the 'inferior races' deprived them of a right to separate statehood and territory. The Slavs possessed far more land than their history warranted; Frank observed that the Poles 'have no historical mission whatever in this part of the world'.[164] Russia was to be set aside for the resettlement of up to 100 million Germans once the rapid population increase, projected by Hitler, had begun. Meanwhile, the peoples of the occupied countries of both eastern and western Europe would be used to enhance Germany's war effort. A severe shortage of labour had by 1942 become apparent within the Reich. Albert Speer, Minister for Armaments and War Production from 1942, managed to increase economic growth and the production of war *matériel* by deliberately promoting foreign labour both voluntary and forced. By 1944 there were at least 7.5 million foreign civilians working in Germany. A constant supply of labour was ensured by mass deportations. In some cases slave workers were provided by the Plenipotentiary for Labour, Sauckel, for use by the Reich's industrial and armaments firms. According to evidence produced at the Nuremberg Trial in 1945, eastern workers like the Tartars and Kirghiz 'collapsed like flies from bad housing, the poor quality and insufficient quantity of food, overwork and insufficient rest'. Western workers were also badly treated. Krupp of Essen kept its French workers 'in dog kennels, urinals and in old baking houses. The dog kennels were three feet high, nine feet long, six feet wide. Five men slept in each of them.'[165] While people were exploited, the national wealth of the occupied states was systematically plundered. Gold and foreign holdings were removed from all the banks, and industrial produce was requisitioned on a massive scale. It has been estimated that France provided Germany with 60 billion marks and 74 per cent of her steel, while Belgium and the Netherlands lost two-thirds of their national incomes.[166]

The Nazi occupation of Europe was carried out with an unprecedented contempt for the subject peoples. This was due primarily to the racial emphasis of Hitler's rule. There were two distinct aspects here. One was a search for racial purity for the German people. This was entrusted to the SS; Himmler was made head of the RKFDV (the Reich Commissariat for the Strengthening of German Nationhood). One of the results was the large-scale kidnapping of foreign children who fitted the Aryan stereotype. At the other end of the scale were Europe's 'lower orders', including Poles and Russians, considered to be fit only for forced labour. According to Bormann, in 1942, 'The Slavs are to work for us. In so far as we don't need them, they may die. Therefore compulsory vaccination and German health services are superfluous.'[167] At the bottom of Hitler's descending racial scheme came the Jews.

Contempt for the subject peoples bred an unimaginable brutality, evidence of which came to light in 1945 and 1946. Terror was made systematic through the extension of the SS and the SD and through basic legislation. Two examples of the latter, both in 1941, were the 'Commissar and Jurisdiction Decrees' for Russia, and the 'Night and Fog Decree' for the west. The authorities were provided with unlimited powers to uphold security, including the use of torture, arbitrary arrest and summary execution. Large-scale atrocities against the subject peoples were all too common. Three examples will suffice. In 1941, 100,000 civilians in Kharkov were forced to work all day digging a huge pit and were then machine-gunned into it. The reason was that the German authorities felt that they were a threat to the levels of available foodstocks. In 1942 all the men of the town of Lidice, in Bohemia, were executed and the children and women sent to concentration camps. This was in retaliation for the assassination of Heydrich, the Governor of Bohemia. A similar event occurred in 1944 when the inhabitants of Oradour-sur-Glâne, in southern France, were herded into the local church and barns and burned alive as a punishment for resistance activity. It was later discovered to be the wrong village. Vast numbers of people died in various camps, including over 4 million Soviet prisoners-of-war. Many camps, especially in Poland, became extermination factories as part of Hitler's scheme for altering the racial composition of Europe. Auschwitz, for example, killed over 1 million Jews, Treblinka 700,000, Belzec 600,000, Sobibor 250,000, Maidenek 200,000 and Kulmhof 152,000. Among the most horrific of all the Nazi activities were the appalling medical experiments carried out without anaesthetic by the likes of Josef Mengele at Auschwitz. As Foot writes, these 'did not advance human knowledge in any useful way whatever; unless it is useful to know how nasty man can be to man'.[168]

The very awfulness of Nazi occupation implies a high degree of efficiency. In one respect this is true; the regime took human extermination to unprecedented levels. There were, however, severe administrative problems which prevented Hitler from coming even close to establishing uniform control over Europe. There was no overall plan, merely a series of local *ad hoc* expedients, usually lacking any central co-ordination or control. The basic problem was Hitler's own withdrawal from active administration to involve himself in the conduct of the war from the remoteness of Wolfsschanze in East Prussia. As in Germany itself (see pp. 174–6) numerous administrative conflicts developed from the chaos of the conquered areas. Four examples can be cited. The first was France where there was an increasingly complex overlap of authority. The second was Norway, which saw a major conflict between Terboven and Quisling (see pp. 295–6). Third, Poland was the scene of a bitter clash between the new Governor, Hans Frank, and Reich officials like Goering and Himmler, both of whom tried to interfere with policy decisions and administrative detail. Finally, Rosenberg had much the same problem in his attempt to run the Ukraine. As he did with all political disputes, Hitler tended to ignore complaints and allow his subordinates to settle things among themselves. Overall, Hitler's policy towards the east was applied haphazardly and with an almost total lack of underlying discipline. At a conference held in July 1941, Hitler argued for initial caution and for concealing the true intention of Nazism in Russia for as long as possible in order to ease and hasten the conquest: 'we do not want to make any people into enemies prematurely and unnecessarily'. Germany's conduct towards the conquered area, he continued, should be 'first to dominate it, second to administer it, and third, to exploit it'. As events turned out in Russia and elsewhere in Europe, the occupying forces, while ruthless, frequently lacked discipline and purpose, therefore going directly against Hitler's own instructions. The result was administrative confusion and the alienation of huge sections of the population. In Russia the Great Fatherland War was in part provoked by unnecessary German excesses, while in other countries the occupying authorities had to deal with an ever increasing problem of resistance movements.

Total war and the contraction of the Third Reich, 1942–5

From the beginning of 1942 there were indications that the character of Hitler's war was changing. In declaring war on the United States he involved Germany against the world's greatest industrial power, while military reverses in Russia and North Africa severely tested the German economy for the first time.

The initiative for involving Germany in a conflict against the United States came from Berlin, the reverse of Washington's decision to enter the First World War. This is generally seen as one of the most irrational of Hitler's acts, and was taken without consultation with his military staff. Hitler displayed total ignorance of the United States, believing the whole nation to be deeply corrupted by its ethnic mixture and 'permanently on the brink of revolution'. But why provoke a new conflict? Why not dispose of Britain and Russia first? There is a case for saying that Hitler extended the war in order to redress the failure of the previous stage, just as the attack on Russia had been supposed to hasten the end of Britain's involvement. It is possible that Hitler's reasoning was that the United States could be expected to enter the struggle eventually – clearly this would be another major problem for Germany. On the other hand, this would also upgrade the alliance between Germany and Japan since the latter would attack British and American interests in the Far East and the Pacific. This would be of vital importance, for it would divert US attention from Europe for long enough to enable Hitler to complete the destruction of Russia and to force a settlement on Britain. There would therefore be no repetition of 1918, when US troops had broken the deadlock on the western front and tipped the balance in favour of the Allies. It was crucial to ensure that Japan did not withdraw from the war prematurely. Hence, according to Jäckel, 'Japan had to do more than enter the war. It had to be kept from pulling out before victory had been won in Europe.'[169] This was a serious miscalculation by Hitler. President Roosevelt made the decision to concentrate as much on the war in Europe as on Japan, for fear that Russia and Britain might be defeated, leaving the USA to face Germany alone. All Hitler had succeeded in doing, therefore, was to strengthen the war effort against him on the periphery – at sea and in North Africa – at the same time as his life and death struggle in Russia.

During the course of 1942 and 1943 the Wehrmacht suffered a series of reverses which turned the tide of the Second World War. The worst disasters occurred in Russia, with the surrender of Paulus at Stalingrad in one of the most crucial battles in modern history. But there were also crises in North Africa, with the defeat of Rommel at El Alamein. Indeed, the commitment in North Africa had a crucial effect on the campaign in Russia since it prevented Hitler from pouring in sufficient reinforcements to counter the Russian recovery. It also gave the Western Allies a change to attack Hitler's 'fortress of Europe' via its most vulnerable point of access. The result was to be the collapse of Mussolini's regime, the withdrawal of most of Italy from the war and the need for Hitler to deploy, in support of Mussolini's Salo Republic, divisions which were desperately needed in Russia.

Meanwhile, Germany was also failing to win control over the sea and air. At first, Hitler's emphasis was on creating a large surface fleet to challenge Britain's world naval supremacy. Eventually, however, he was converted by his naval commanders to a more specialized form of warfare based on U-boat attacks on merchant shipping in the Atlantic. But, despite heavy losses inflicted on Allied ships, Hitler had, in effect, lost the Battle for the Atlantic by late 1943. This was of vital importance since Hitler was unable to prevent a massive influx of supplies from the United States to Britain under Lend–Lease. He also failed to disrupt the supply route via Murmansk through which the Western Allies made a significant contribution to the Russian war effort.

Aerial warfare affected Germany more directly. The failure of Operation Sealion was due largely to the victory of the RAF in the Battle of Britain and to a rapid increase in British aircraft production. With the entry of the United States into the war came heavier saturated bombing of German targets. This was conducted round the clock, by the United States Air Force during the day and the RAF at night. A deliberate attempt was made to destroy German cities, and hence German morale, and also to knock out key industrial centres. The former included Hamburg, Cologne, Essen, Dortmund, Berlin and Dresden. The main industrial targets were ballbearing plants, armaments factories and communications networks. Two arguments have been advanced as to whether this bombing made a significant difference to the outcome of the war. One is that the Armaments Minister, Albert Speer, pulled together the German economy in 1944 for a final effort; this counteracted the effect of Allied bombing, as German armaments production increased during the period of heaviest destruction. Thus, criticism is often levelled against Bomber Command for, in effect, conducting a war on civilians. On the other hand, it could be argued that, although the attacks of 1944 may not have led to a dramatic decrease in production, they did, nevertheless, prevent the sort of increase which might otherwise have occurred. In addition, catastrophic damage was inflicted by the Allies on Germany's transport and communications network; this was far more important than the destruction of cities in breaking the Nazi war effort.

By 1944 Hitler's 'Fortress of Europe', won by Blitzkrieg, was being breeched from three main directions. The first battering ram was applied by the Red Army, which conquered eastern Europe during the second half of 1944 and the early months of 1945. Meanwhile, the Western Allies were hammering at Mussolini's Salo Republic and, in June 1944, opened up a third front with the invasion of France. Hitler now became increasingly irrational, living on false hopes and drawing comfort from the example of Frederick the Great, an eighteenth-century Prussian king who had held off, in the Seven Years War, a combination of Russia, Austria and France. Hitler firmly believed that sooner or later Russia and the Western Allies could be induced to attack each other. 'All of the coalitions in history have disintegrated sooner or later. The only thing is to wait for the right moment.'[170]

He did manage two last-minute successes. He defeated in September 1944 a British airborne invasion at Arnhem which attempted to capture the bridgeheads of the lower Rhine. He also came close in December 1944 to breaking through the Allied lines at the Ardennes in what is usually called the Battle of the Bulge. But these did no more than slow down the Anglo-American advance. The Western Allies now conformed to Eisenhower's strategy of a slow and methodical thrust on Germany across the whole front rather than the British preference for a quick advance on Berlin. The result was that the Russians reached Berlin first. Hitler committed suicide on 30 April 1945 after entrusting the succession to Commander-in-Chief Admiral von Dönitz. On 7 May the German High Command surrendered: 'The Third Reich had outlasted its founder by just one week.'[171]

Hitler as a war leader

How effective was Hitler as a military leader? We have seen that there were occasions on which Hitler had considerable success, usually in pushing the High Command in a direction where it was reluctant to move. He was especially adept at the use of Blitzkrieg tactics against Poland in 1939 and against the Low Countries and France in 1940. On the other hand, Hitler also made major blunders in military organization and strategy. Perhaps the best evidence for this is provided by four men who served under him and were directly involved in the war effort: all were highly critical. One was Hitler's official war diarist, Percy Ernst Schramm, who subsequently published a detailed account of Hitler's personal life and military leadership, based on first-hand observation. The other three were generals in the High Command: Manstein, Halder and Jodl. Halder, who replaced Beck as Chief of General Staff in 1938, wrote a totally condemnatory tract in 1949 entitled *Hitler as War Lord*. Jodl produced a memorandum in 1946, shortly before being executed at Nuremberg for war crimes. Even allowing for the fact that each of these men had reason to distance himself from Hitler, the combined weight of criticism is formidable.

On the question of Hitler's direction of the war, Halder observed that the Führer destroyed the High Command as the apex of military organization. 'He may have had a gift for mass political leadership. He had none for the leadership of a military staff.'[172] Indeed, his divide-and-rule policy 'destroyed a well organized system of military command which no true leader would ever have given up'. According to Jodl, Hitler allowed little influence and 'resented any form of counsel regarding the major decisions of the war. He did not care to hear any other points of view.' Instead, he had 'an almost mystical conviction of his own infallibility as a leader of the nation and of the nation and of the war'. Schramm maintained that Hitler constantly interfered in military operations. He 'violated the tried and proven principle that subordinate commanders must be allowed a certain limited freedom because they are in a better position to evaluate the prevailing circumstances in their sector of the front and might be able, through swift action, to deal with a sudden crisis'. Overall, Schramm adds, 'Hitler had already made himself dictator of state and society during peacetime. The war consolidated his dictatorship over the military.'[173]

Consequently, Hitler can be blamed personally for all the main strategic blunders. Schramm argues that Hitler's early success was based on huge risks which, even in retrospect, could be considered irresponsible. As the situation deteriorated he was incapable of taking a balanced decision and never saw the need for organized military retreat; he was 'unable to bring himself to make militarily necessary decisions such as the evacuation of untenable outposts'.[174] This can be supported by reference to a range of decisions in the latter phase of the war, from his refusal to let Paulus pull out of Stalingrad to his determination to hold all German outposts in France against enveloping Allied attacks. Hitler found the defensive role utterly distasteful. Instead of an orderly contraction of all his front lines, he adopted what Schramm calls a 'wave break doctrine', whereby positions had to be held even after the enemy had swept past and isolated them; they could always be used as advance posts during the German recovery which Hitler hoped would occur as a result of his determination and willpower. Eventually he lost all sense of perspective. According to Halder, 'The delicate interplay between yielding pliancy and iron determination which is the essence of the art of generalship was impossible to this man, who could be termed the very incarnation of brute will.'[175] Almost exactly the same conclusion was arrived at by Manstein: 'Ultimately, to the concept of the art of war, he opposed that of crude force, and the full effectiveness of this force was supposed to be guaranteed by the strength of will behind it.'[176] Halder drew comparisons between Hitler and men of greater reason and more limited and practical objectives in what he regarded as the true German military tradition: he cited, especially, von Moltke and Bismarck. He concluded of Hitler, 'this demoniac man was no soldier leader in the German sense. And above all he was not a great General.'[177]

Chapter 5

Dictatorship elsewhere

DICTATORSHIP IN PORTUGAL AND SPAIN

Portugal

At the beginning of the twentieth century Portugal was ruled by an authoritarian monarchy. This was, however, overthrown in 1910, to be replaced by a republic which, in 1911, introduced a democratic constitution with a two-chamber parliament, direct suffrage, and an executive with limited powers. Overall, the new regime was by far the most progressive in Portugal's history. Unfortunately, it was also inherently unstable. The sophisticated political system proved inappropriate to a society which was one of the most backward in Europe and in which 70 per cent of the people were illiterate. As in many other parts of Europe democracy foundered on political instability. During the sixteen years of the republic's existence there were nine presidents, forty-four governments, twenty-five uprisings and three temporary dictatorships.[1] This catalogue makes Portugal, in the words of Payne, 'the most politically chaotic of any single European ... state in the twentieth century'.[2]

Political crisis was intensified by economic disaster caused by a series of incompetent budgets, an increase in inflation and a deterioration in Portugal's balance of payments. By the mid-1920s all the influential sectors of society – the professional middle class, the army and the Church – had come to the conclusion that the republic would have to be replaced by a more stable regime. On 17 June 1926 it was therefore destroyed by General Gomes da Costa who installed a *dictadura* (or dictatorship) in its place.

The Estado Novo

The new military rulers, however, proved equally unable to tackle Portugal's economic problems, as the cost of living soared to a level thirty times that of 1914. By 1928 the head of state, President Carmona, handed over complete responsibility for the Portuguese finances to a professor of economics at the University of Coimbra, Dr Antonio de Oliveira Salazar. In 1932 Salazar became Prime Minister, a position he held until incapacitated by a stroke thirty-six years later.

Throughout this lengthy period he remained in complete control, seeing himself as the only person who could reconcile the conflicting trends in Portuguese society or provide an alternative to Portugal's inefficient democracy. His power-base was

9 Antonio Salazar, 1889–1970, photo taken in 1964 (Popperfoto)

a formidable array of groups disillusioned by the anarchy of the republic. These included army officers who felt that the forces had been neglected, the Church who hated the republic's anticlerical policies, the upper bourgeoisie and banking interests who wanted economic stability, and, finally, right-wing intellectuals and monarchists. All trusted this remote academic far more than Portugal's more flashy military leaders.

What sort of person was Salazar? Bruce describes him as a 'devout and Right-wing Catholic, a quiet and an austere man, dressed usually in a rather ill-fitting dark suit'.[3] He had little personal charisma and avoided any hint of a personality cult; in this respect he was the very reverse of Mussolini. He did, however, have a strong character, and as early as 1928 affirmed: 'I know quite well what I want and where I am going . . . When the time comes for me to give orders I shall expect it [the country] to obey.'[4] His ideas were clearly and forcefully stated. He profoundly distrusted parliamentary democracy, for it had 'resulted in instability and disorder, or, what is worse, it has become a despotic domination of the nation by political parties'.[5] He therefore saw his role as establishing a paternalist regime, a government without parties. The individual should submit to this government without seeking to limit its powers. 'Let us place our liberty in the hands of authority; only authority knows how to administer and protect it.'[6] Salazar also sought to revive traditional virtues and loyalties and to develop a national pride based on the glorification of Portugal's history; for this reason his cult of empire assumed major importance. Overall, he tried to develop a state which, although based on tradition and in some ways an escape from the realities of the twentieth century, was nevertheless new in its organic development. Hence, he called his model the *Estado Novo*, the New State.

The basis of the *Estado Novo* was the 1933 constitution which replaced the multi-party system with a 'unitary and corporative republic'.[7] The new lower house – the National Assembly was elected on a list system through a restricted franchise. It also had few powers over the government and could not initiate financial legislation. A one-party system was confirmed, with the National Union (UN) acting as 'a pressure group intended to bind all sections of the community in a corporative movement'.[8] This was the means whereby Salazar hoped to achieve harmony and discipline and to break the long-standing strife between labour and capital. It operated through the upper house of parliament – a corporative chamber – which was selected from various sections of the community, including industry, commerce, agriculture, the army and the Church. Industrial relations were regulated by the National Labour Statute of 1933 which forbade workers' strikes and employers' lockouts. The whole point of corporativism was to present a viable alternative to the liberal idea, which Salazar distrusted, without adopting the collective principle as embodied in communism, which he hated.

Salazar's *Estado Novo* had a mixed record in the period up to 1945. On the positive side, it undoubtedly provided greater political stability; the solid support from the wealthier sections of society brought to an end the pendulum of revolution alternating with counter-revolution. Above all, Salazar achieved a considerable amount in the financial sector. He produced a series of balanced budgets, stabilized the currency, reduced corruption and improved the process of tax collection. According to Gallagher, his methods 'were those of a careful accountant'.[9] On the other hand, the *Estado Novo* attempted few progressive reforms. Salazar was 'not an economic innovator' and balanced budgets became an obsession which served only to discourage foreign investment and loans. Industrial growth was minimal; the proportion of the workforce in industry increased hardly at all between 1920 and 1940. Agriculture, too, experienced neither fundamental changes in methods nor sustained efforts to improve irrigation. Above all, a real barrier to change was exerted by the social elite which upheld the regime. Social reform was held back by a rigid class system, something which concerned Salazar not at all. After all, he had once said quite openly: 'I consider more urgent the creation of élites than the necessity to teach people to read.'[10]

The Second World War and beyond

Salazar was always careful not to tie Portugal's foreign policy to a Fascist line. He avoided the temptation of an alliance with Italy and Germany, believing that 'in accordance with the true interests of the Portuguese nation its foreign policy is always to avoid, if possible, any entanglements in Europe'.[11] His main priority during the 1930s was to remove any possible threat from Portugal's more powerful neighbour, Spain. He was particularly concerned that the Republicans should not win the Civil War, for this might tempt a left-wing government to intervene against Portugal's *Estado Novo*. Hence, Salazar backed the rebel forces under Franco and in 1939 cemented relations with his Nationalist regime in the Iberian Pact. The Second World War threatened to destabilize Salazar's position and he directed his diplomacy towards remaining neutral. An alliance with the Axis would have made a nonsense of Salazar's hope of maintaining the Portuguese Empire intact, since the greatest threat would have been the naval power of Britain. On the other hand, there were clear advantages in not joining the Allies. Salazar was especially concerned about the prospect of the spread of communism in Europe. In 1942 he said that unless Germany defeated the Soviet Union, 'Europe will be engulfed in a wave of communism such as no power of earth can stop.'[12] Salazar, along with Franco, benefited from his country's neutrality by remaining in power after the end of the war in 1945.

Nevertheless, Salazar felt isolated and distinctly vulnerable in the immediate post-war period. His formula for survival was, on the one hand, to contribute as much as possible to the international scene and to make Portugal an indispensable link in Western security while, on the other, insulating his internal dictatorship from Western ideas and influences. The first of these aims was greatly assisted by the climate of the Cold War, in which the United States and Britain were more concerned with what they perceived as the new left-wing dictatorships in the eastern European countries than with the residual right-wing dictatorships of the Iberian Peninsula. Indeed, they held their noses and admitted Portugal to the North Atlantic Treaty Organization in 1949.

Salazar's domestic policies, meanwhile, continued to be deeply conservative; Bruneau maintains that he 'intentionally isolated Portugal from the outside world'.[13] Salazar remained committed to old-fashioned budgetary financing and carefully restricted the use of foreign credit and investment which did so much to rebuild the shattered economies of the other states of western Europe. He was certain that rapid industrialization would weaken the social elites underpinning his regime and hence destroy the balance of the *Estado Novo*. He also emphasized the ever growing danger of internal 'subversion'. The secret police, renamed the Policia Internacional e de Defesa do Estado (PIDE), was expanded, and detention without trial and the use of torture became routine. By the time of his death in 1968, Salazar had done very little to liberalize his authoritarian rule or to admit that there might be valid influences from other European countries.

Throughout its entire existence, the *Estado Novo* had one particular source of strength – and weakness. This was Portugal's overseas empire, which comprised: the Azores; Madeira; the African colonies of Guinea Bissau, the Cape Verde Islands, Príncipe, São Tomé, Cabinda, Angola and Mozambique; Goa, Damao and Diu in India; Macao in China; and East Timor in Indonesia (see Map 5). These possessions played a vital role for four reasons. First, they were of historic importance. According to Armindo Monteiro, Salazar's Minister of Colonies in the 1930s, 'we now feel that we are so much the legitimate heirs of a great tradition that the generation of today is entitled to invoke the past, not as a remembrance of dead things, but as a source of inspiration for the future'.

Second, it guaranteed Portugal a world role. Jorge Ameal emphasized that 'our sovereignty as a small European state spreads prodigiously over three continents and is summed up in the magnificent certainty that we are the third colonial power'. Third, Portugal had a historic obligation to 'civilize' and convert the peoples of

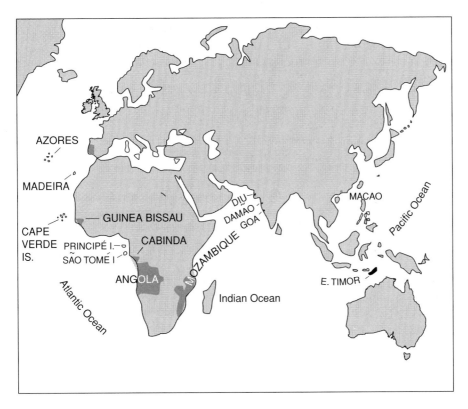

Map 5   The Portuguese overseas empire in the twentieth century

Africa; 'in this heroic element is contained the most noble sentiment of our mission as a chosen people, since the task of civilizing must have, above all else, a spiritual content'.[14] Finally, the overseas empire was of economic importance, supplying Portugal with raw materials and providing markets for its finished goods.

So deep was Salazar's commitment to empire that he resisted with all his strength the trend of decolonization initiated by Britain and France in the late 1950s and early 1960s. The result was a series of colonial wars which had a profound impact on Portugal itself.

The first disaster was the Indian capture of Goa, Damao and Diu, in 1961, made possible by Britain's refusal to put pressure on a Commonwealth partner to exercise restraint. Then, from 1961, the situation also deteriorated in Portugal's African colonies. A series of guerrilla movements emerged, all committed to ejecting Portuguese rule and all receiving assistance from neighbouring Black African states or Eastern Bloc countries. Although there is some controversy as to whether the 'bush war' had been lost by 1974, the real significance lies in its impact on Portugal itself. Up to 45 per cent of the budget was allocated by Caetano (Salazar's successor from 1968) to maintaining 142,000 troops in Africa. The Portuguese army, confronted by heavy casualties in Africa and hostility from the rest of the world, suffered a decline in morale. The war also acted as a catalyst of social change in the officer corps as recruitment extended far down into the lower middle class. The new middle-ranking leadership felt less commitment to the regime and played a prominent part in the overthrow of Caetano in the coup of 25 April 1974.

The passing of the *Estado Novo* had a sense of inevitability. It had outlived its original purpose of stabilizing Portugal and was beginning to threaten, through die-hard economic and colonial policies, whatever limited harmony had been achieved. After 1968 Salazar himself was no longer able to exert his unique blend of authority and reassurance, and his successor attracted far less support. Events in Africa convinced a large part of the population, including the army, that the time had arrived for Portugal to distance itself from its tradition and past achievements and to accept modernization. This fundamental change of attitude enabled Portugal to progress, via the coup of 1974, from dictatorship to democracy.

Portugal compared with other dictatorships

Salazar's regime was typically authoritarian and had many features in common with Austria, Hungary and Franco's Spain – with more than a passing resemblance also to Fascist Italy and Nazi Germany. All the distinguishing features of the *Estado Novo* were from the right of the political spectrum. It was based on the supreme power of Salazar himself; an American diplomat reported in 1936 that Salazar could 'make any decision without necessity for consultation with any other individual in Portugal'.[15] His dictatorship was ensured, like those of most other regimes of the right, by a reduction in the powers of the legislature so that no legal enactments could occur without his personal approval. His position was further underpinned by the establishment of a one-party state and a ban on all forms of political opposition. This was ensured by a secret police force, initially the Policia de Vigilancia e Defesa do Estado (PVDE), later the Policia Internacional e de Defesa do Estado (PIDE). The nation was associated with the glories of imperialism, in defence of which military expenditure was given priority. All of these were characteristic of authoritarian regimes elsewhere. His introduction of corporative institutions also owed much to right-wing ideas before 1914, possibly to the same stream which influenced Mussolini. Above all, Salazar, in common with almost all inter-war dictators, had a deep and profound hatred of communism.

Yet we should not deduce from this that Portugal was one of the regimes of the extreme right between the wars. On the whole, Salazar was much more conservative and less radical than the so-called totalitarian regimes of Germany and Italy. According to Gallagher, 'Although Salazar, like Mussolini and Hitler, set about creating a strong state to fulfil his goals, it was not required to be as drastic as theirs in its regulatory or coercive methods; the aim was merely to strengthen existing social values and modes of behaviour rather than pioneer a radically new social order.'[16] This contrast between Portugal, on the one hand, and Germany and Italy, on the other, was apparent in a number of ways.

There was, for example, a clear ideological difference. Salazar said in the 1934 that he feared that totalitarianism might 'bring about an absolutism worse than that which preceded the liberal regimes'. In particular, 'Such a state would be essentially pagan, incompatible by its nature with the character of our Christian civilization and leading sooner or later to revolution.'[17] His ideological base was traditional and Catholic – more in line with Franco than with Hitler or Mussolini. His personal power was also more discreet and less ostentatious than that of most of his contemporaries. Salazar had no wish to develop a personality cult – he even ended the official use of the term *dictadura*. The one-party state in Portugal was based on a different premise to those in Germany and Italy. The Uniao Nacional (UN) was not intended as a radical means of reshaping political views and of mobilizing political opinion. Rather, it was a device to create consensus, or to demobilize politics altogether. It is true that opponents of the regime were firmly dealt with: repression was effective, but the PIDE made less use of terror than any other secret police system in Europe and Portugal had no death penalty. Minorities were not persecuted as they were elsewhere. Anti-Semitism did not become a feature of Salazar's regime, despite attempts of the Blueshirts to make it so, and Portugal even provided sanctuary for some of the Jewish exiles from Germany. As for expansionism, Salazar always emphasized that Portugal had 'no need of wars, usurpations or conquests'.[18] Unlike the vast majority of right-wing regimes, Portugal was already a satiated power and wanted nothing more than to preserve those territories won in the past. This made the whole notion of empire a traditionalist and conservative one. In the economic sphere, the corporate state involved far less state involvement than in Italy. There was also no drive for industrial expansion, since this did not suit the traditional nature of the Portuguese economy. The purpose of social policy was to conserve existing values; education was therefore not intended to radicalize, which explains why not a great deal was done to extend its range.

Portugal was therefore one of the milder dictatorships of the inter-war period. This, and the cautious foreign policy of Salazar, enabled it to outlive the others on the right, with the single exception of Spain. Its successful longevity served, however, to delay the movement to democracy and to open it to charges that Portugal, along with Spain, provided Europe's last gasp of fascism.

Spain

On paper, Spain had certain assets which could well have equipped her for democracy rather than the dictatorship to which she twice succumbed between the World Wars. For example, the 1876 constitution had given her a parliament with two chambers, one of which was elected from 1890 by universal male suffrage. In practice, however, the political and social fabric faced desperate problems which eventually resulted in the collapse of the parliamentary system in 1923.

One problem was a series of external disasters. Spain became the first power to lose her imperial role, suffering in the process humiliating naval and military defeats. In 1895 Cuba rose in revolt, and Spain was defeated by the United States in the war of 1898. More serious still was a crisis in Spanish Morocco, the only significant colony left to Spain in the twentieth century. Spanish troops were pinned down by indigenous resistance movements and General Silvestre was defeated by the Riffians in 1921 at Anual, losing 12,000 of his contingent of 20,000. Military disasters were accompanied by internal instability which involved the growth of powerful opposition to central government from the left and from the regions. The former consisted of a strong trade union movement, as well as anarchist organizations influenced by the nineteenth-century philosopher Bakunin. Left-wing radicalism frequently

10 Miguel Primo de Rivera, 1870–1930 (David King Collection)

overlapped demands for the independence of regions such as Catalonia; an example was the 1909 revolt in Barcelona in which Catalan nationalism and left-wing ideologies merged in common defiance of Madrid. Although the central government succeeded in suppressing this rebellion, it was unable to restore full confidence in its rule and resorted increasingly to graft and corruption. According to Thomas, 'By 1923 the Spanish parliamentary system was bruised almost to death.'[19]

Dictatorship to republic, 1923–30

The result was that the Spanish king, Alfonso XIII, acquiesced in a military coup in 1923 by Miguel Primo de Rivera. Rivera was a general who, according to Payne, was neither an intellectual nor a politician but who had become 'impatient with constitutions', preferring 'order and simplicity'.[20] He was well meaning but unsophisticated. Depending on intuition rather than reason, he convinced himself that he was most in touch with the needs and aspirations of the Spanish people. 'Your president is vigilant', he proclaimed, 'while you are asleep.' He liked to be portrayed as an Atlas who 'with his stout shoulders unshakeably avoided the collapse of the lofty roof of our beloved fatherland'.[21] He also saw himself as strengthening the Christian base of society and as a sentinel against the threat of communism. The best means of serving Spain, in his view, was to dispense with party politics. He was much influenced by political developments in Italy and was once introduced by Alfonso XIII on a visit abroad as 'my Mussolini'. His regime was not, however, based on ideology; as Blinkhorn maintains, 'In the sense that it rested on prior mass movement and lacked a totalitarian vision, the regime was not a fascist one.'[22] It was, instead, largely pragmatic. He tried at first to manage with a cabinet of military officers but came to the conclusion by 1926 that a broader-based and more systematic government was necessary. He therefore introduced a 'National Assembly', a corporative chamber intended to represent different classes and interest groups. He also developed a new party, the Union Patriotica, to mobilize popular support for the authoritarian system. 'This', he claimed, 'is a national movement which signifies, above all, faith in the destinies of Spain and in the grandeur and virtue of our race.'[23] As it turned out, the whole political system was too diffuse; it was neither one thing nor the other. It was not sufficiently democratic to satisfy the demands for alternative policies, nor was it sufficiently authoritarian to stop these demands from being made.

During the six years in which he was in power, Rivera pursued bold policies, sometimes with notable success. He avoided the humiliation experienced by previous governments in dealing with Morocco and managed to subdue the protectorate in 1927. Internal problems were more complex. He considered Spain's most urgent need to be stability, to be achieved partly through reviving traditional virtues and partly through a process of modernization. He therefore strengthened Spain's infrastructure through the extension of public works. Unfortunately, his policies were handicapped by inadequate financing. One possible method of raising the necessary revenue was a complete overhaul of the taxation system, but this was fiercely resisted by the upper classes and the bankers. He resorted then to the alternative expedient of borrowing and, in his later years, made extensive use of the 'extraordinary budget'. He aimed also at more direct government intervention in economic activity, hoping to create new industries and bring about protection through higher tariffs. There were signs of economic improvement during the 1920s, particularly a steady increase in industrial production. According to Carr, however, 'the continued prosperity was to a large extent the result of favourable outside circumstances for which the regime could take no credit'.[24] It has also been pointed out that any economic reform was accompanied by much needed social changes; there was, for example, no improvement in the conditions of either industrial or agricultural workers. Rivera was not blind to the need for social reform but he was too heavily committed to the wealthier classes, upon whom he depended for support.

Rivera's dictatorship ended in January 1930, the result of overwhelming economic and political difficulties. Spain experienced a slump in share prices in the stock markets and an erosion of the currency. The whole basis of economic growth was threatened so that Rivera had to stop using the extraordinary budget and batten down the hatches. This signalled the end of prosperity, but the regime was not strong enough to withstand the backlash. Rivera had been unable to provide a permanent legitimacy for his government and he fell as a result of an attack from the left and the withdrawal of support from the right. The offensive was launched by Spanish republicans, the press, the universities and socialists, while the conservatives saw nothing to gain in prolonging Rivera's regime. The upper classes, fearing the impact of economic decline, hoped that a change of government would regenerate confidence. Above all, the army was alienated by Rivera's attempts to reform the promotion system and eliminate some of the more blatant privileges. Given this overall lack of confidence, the king requested and received Rivera's resignation in January 1930. The dictator was in poor health in any case and died only two months later.

It used to be thought that Rivera's rule was merely an interlude between the complex political developments before 1923 and after 1930. But more recently the tendency has been to stress his influence on later events. Ben-Ami, for example, sees his regime as a 'most significant turning point in modern Spanish history',[25] a view endorsed by Blinkhorn.[26] In the short term, the backlash against Rivera brought down the Spanish monarchy as well. Rivera's successor, General Berenguer, tried to introduce several reforms. But the republicans who had been so successful against Rivera in 1929 and 1930 were not likely now to be content with a few promises and compromises. Instead, they took full advantage of the restoration of parliament and party politics and won a massive victory in the election of April 1931. This was taken as an overwhelming vote of no-confidence in the monarchy. Fearing revolution if he tried to keep himself in power, Alfonso XIII voluntarily abdicated, expecting, no doubt, to be recalled when the political scene had quietened down. He was replaced immediately by the 'Second Spanish Republic'.

The Rivera regime not only pulled down the monarchy with its own demise; in the longer term it helped prepare the way for a more radical right-wing dictatorship. When the Second Republic, in turn, faced crisis and collapse, it was to be replaced not, as Alfonso had hoped, with a restored monarchy, but with a more ruthless and radical right-wing dictatorship under Francisco Franco.

Republic to dictatorship, 1930–9

The Second Republic lasted eight years: from 1931 to 1939. From 1936 onwards it was confronted by an all-out assault from General Franco, who eventually installed himself as *Caudillo* or dictator.

The opening years of the Republic (1931–3) were dominated by the left, first under Zamora and then Azaña. The early governments introduced a series of major reforms, intending to alter the political and social structure of Spain. Early measures included the introduction of an eight-hour working day, together with benefits and paid holidays. These were followed by attempts to reduce the top-heavy officer corps in the army through early retirement. The momentum increased as the 1931 constitution introduced universal suffrage at the age of twenty-three, abolished the nobility and, in Article 26, took extensive measures against the Church. The republicans regarded the Church as a reactionary force which had become resistant to any progressive ideas and which therefore needed drastic change. The main measures introduced by Article 26 were the right of the state to dissolve religious orders (which now had to register officially), an end to religious education and the forcible introduction of the type of social reform, like divorce, which had been resisted by the Church. Azaña brushed off all criticism with the words 'Do not tell me that this is contrary to freedom. It is a matter of public health.' The next reform was the 1932 statute which granted a degree of autonomy to Catalonia in such functions as education, taxation and the police. Finally, the Law of Agrarian Reform (1932) tried to narrow the gap between the landless peasantry and the enormously

11 General Francisco Franco, 1892–1975 (David King Collection)

wealthy landlords, allowing the state to purchase in certain parts of Castile unworked lands of over 56 acres. Overall, this was the most extensive package of reforms Spain had ever experienced.

Unfortunately, everything went wrong; nearly all the changes aroused bitter opposition from Spain's various vested interests. The army resented the pruning of its ranks. The Church went on to the defensive, finding a champion in Gill Robles, who set up a confederation of Catholic parties (CEDA). The landlords did everything in their power to resist the legislation on land, which was never applied effectively anyway. Azaña therefore failed to benefit Spain's lower orders and succeeded only in terrifying the privileged. In 1933 Azana's government fell after being defeated in a general election. There then followed a swing to the centre-right, with a series of coalition governments. These proceeded to dismantle the previous reforms, or at least did everything possible to render them unworkable. This policy, in turn, provoked action by the left in industrial areas – such as the Asturias Revolt of 1934, which was bloodily suppressed. The government also removed from circulation many left-wing leaders, irrespective of whether they had been responsible for the violence. Even so, chronic instability characterized the whole period. By the time that the Assembly was dissolved in January 1936 the republic had experienced 26 governmental crises, where 72 ministers had served during a period of four and a half years.[27]

There followed one of the most famous elections in modern history, as much of Spain polarized into two political camps – known as 'fronts'. The left-wing parties

(Communists, Socialists, Liberals, Republicans and Anarchists) combined to form the Popular Front, or Republicans. This was countered on the right by the National Front, or Nationalists, which consisted of monarchists (especially the Carlists of Navarre), conservatives and the CEDA. Excluded from these blocs were the centre, the Basques and a new far-right-wing organization, known as the Falange, under José Antonio Primo de Rivera. The result of the election was close, with a victory for the Popular Front with 4.2 million votes to the National Front's 3.8 million.

As Azaña formed a new government, the Nationalists looked on sullenly and awaited an opportunity to seize power. Azaña proceeded to reintroduce all his earlier reforms. He exiled Franco, whom he regarded as the major threat in the army, to the Canaries. Unfortunately, the second Azaña administration did nothing to allay the fears of the right that he was drifting further to communism. Indeed, all his policies seemed openly provocative. The right therefore opted for action and the army hatched a plot to overthrow the republic. The *casus belli* was the murder by the state police of Sotelo, a leader of the Falange and of CEDA. General Franco, who had returned from the Canaries, led seasoned Spanish contingents from Morocco into the south, while Mola advanced from the north with support from Navarre. The republic was to be snuffed out by the two converging forces.

At first the Nationalist offensive moved slowly. Mola gradually established a grip on northern Spain, except the Basque lands, and made Burgos the capital of the new Nationalist government, in direct defiance of Republican Madrid (see Map 6). Meanwhile, Franco invaded from Morocco, using the invaluable airlift facilities provided by the Italians and Germans. In August 1936 the two Nationalist zones linked up along the Portuguese frontier with the capture of Badajoz. The Republicans, however, still controlled the far north, part of the south, almost all the east and, of course, Madrid. Franco made an unsuccessful attempt to grab Madrid and then laid siege to the city from November 1936; the Republicans held out but transferred their capital to Valencia on the east coast.

Meanwhile, foreign interest in the war was growing rapidly. Germany and Italy stepped up their supplies to Franco (Italy's motives are explained on p. 142). France was, at first, openly sympathetic to the Republicans but was manoeuvred by Britain into a more neutral stance. In 1936 the British government promoted the establishment of the Non-Intervention Committee to try to bring the war to an end by denying arms to both sides. All the major powers initially paid lipservice to the principle of the Committee, but Germany and Italy eventually defied its provisions by openly increasing the flow of war *matériel* to the Nationalists. Although the Soviet Union provided some assistance to the Republicans, the disparity between the two sides was considerable. This showed in 1937 when Franco was able to mop up Republican territory in the south, including Malaga. In the far north, meanwhile, occurred an event which provoked an international outcry – the German bombing of the Basque town of Guernica. By October 1937 the Nationalist domination of northern Spain was completed by the conquest of the Asturias.

The Republicans were not finished, however; they had major, if temporary, successes at Guadalajara (March 1937) and Teruel (December 1937). But Franco doggedly persevered, greatly assisted by further Italian and German reinforcements. By 1938 the Nationalists had split the Republic into two, isolating Catalonia in the north-east from what was left of Republican Castile. It was now only a matter of

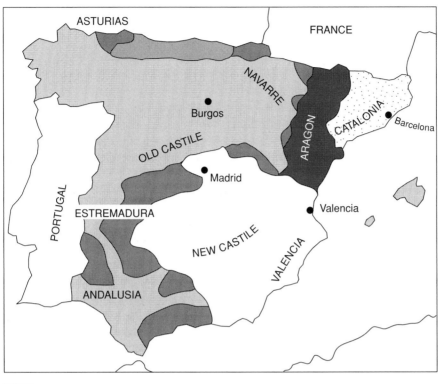

Nationalist gains by September 1936

Further Nationalist gains by March 1937

Further Nationalist gains by October 1937

Further Nationalist gains by July 1938

Further Nationalist gains by February 1939

Map 6   The Spanish Civil War 1936–9

time before the Republic was completely destroyed, especially since the international situation had become even more unfavourable to it. Britain and France, prepared to appease Hitler over Czechoslovakia, were clearly in no mood to confront him over his assistance to Franco. Russia, meanwhile, ended her commitment to the Republic, which was therefore deprived of all foreign help. The Nationalists were free to bomb and starve into submission the three key Republican cities – Madrid, Barcelona and Valencia. By 1 April 1939 Franco's government had been recognized by much of Europe, democracies as well as dictatorships.

Civil war is particularly destructive. The Spanish conflict was no exception. The usual estimate of the total loss is about 1 million dead, although Thomas places the figure at 400,000 casualties and over 100,000 through 'malnutrition, starvation, or disease directly attributable to the war'.[28] There was certainly no shortage of information or publicity. A large number of war correspondents described or photographed battles and massacres, and writers like Hemingway and Orwell provided vivid images, as did artists like Picasso and Dali. Both the Nationalists and the Republicans were responsible for atrocities and terror. The earliest examples were mainly against the Church in the Republican zone; 80 per cent of the clergy were killed in the Barbastro region. On the whole, however, terror was not normally the Republic's policy and formed no systematic part of the ideology on the left. It was the Nationalists who made terror the norm. They inflicted barbaric punishments on the areas they occupied, conducting, for example, a massacre in the bullring at Badajoz. After the end of the Civil War they probably carried out over 250,000 executions. There is therefore no doubt that the 'White Terror' was more total than any 'Red Terror'. It also spelled the end of democracy and submerged Spain into a new and ruthless dictatorship.

What were the sides in the Spanish Civil War?

The Spanish Civil War is often seen as a fundamental divide between right and left – the first major struggle between fascism and communism. This view is now generally seen as an oversimplification and the result of the propaganda labels used by each side of the other. The recent tendency is to examine all the complex issues behind the confrontation. Hence, according to Preston, 'the Spanish Civil War was not one but many wars'.[29] The basic argument of this section is that, on the one hand, there were fundamental differences between the two sides, often expressed in powerful ideological terms. On the other hand, there were also many cross-currents in Spain which tended to complicate the main issues.

As we have seen, the Civil War was fought between broad coalitions of the right (Nationalists) and left (Republicans). The Nationalist aims were the more coherent, largely because of the overwhelming influence of Franco. He projected the whole war as a crusade against the godless left which he felt was trying to subvert the whole of Spanish society; in this respect, Franco emphasized the defensive nature of the uprising. He also caught the imagination of the Church by his talk of crusades, and was careful to associate his army closely with the Catholic religion, even to the extent of making the receiving of communion compulsory among his troops. In place of the corrupt 'communist republic', with its malfunctioning parliament and bickering parties, its declining moral standards and growing secularization, Franco promised to revive Spain's glorious traditions. These included military power, firm personal leadership and overriding religious zeal.

The factions of the right all shared Franco's repugnance of the far left but they disagreed on long-term objectives. The Carlists, for example, hoped that Franco's appeal to tradition would include the eventual restoration of the monarchy. The more moderate right wished to retain at least part of the constitutional structure, while the more radical right, the Falange, aimed to create a classless and corporatist system influenced by the Italian model. Franco steered carefully between these various positions and was able to represent them all.

The left, meanwhile, regarded its enemy with equal abhorrence: as a Fascist regime which would impose terror by means of a permanent military junta. The result would be the total exploitation of labour in the interest of the capitalist classes. The immediate task, therefore, was to defend the republic and what it had so far achieved. The Republicans were, however, at a major disadvantage: they were by no means agreed about what was worth preserving. The moderate Republicans hoped to keep the existing institutions and to move closer towards the Western democratic system once Franco's military threat had been removed. The radical left, however, wanted more fundamental changes, including the establishment of a workers' state. At this point there was a serious division within the Republican camp, as the radical left were unable to agree on a strategy for further change. One section, comprising the CNT (anarcho-syndicalists), left-wing socialists and Trotskyist communists, all felt that the real effort should go into extending the scope of the revolution through rapid collectivization and the creation of workers' militias. This would strengthen the Republic to defeat the right. Hence, according to the anarchist Berneri, 'we shall not win the war by confining the problem to the strictly military conditions of victory but by associating these with its political and social conditions'. Against this was the view of the Spanish Communist Party, on orders from Moscow, that absolute priority must be given to the defeat of Franco. According to the Party Secretary, 'We cannot achieve the revolution unless we win the war; the first thing is to win the war.'[30] To give priority to revolution would only alienate the rest of the left and risk destroying the Popular Front altogether.

To summarize, the Nationalists were fighting to destroy the Republic and impose a system which would be authoritarian, Christian and traditionalist with (via the Falange) elements of fascism. The Republicans were obviously fighting to save the Republic but were divided on whether to keep it in its existing form or to revolutionize it. Those who advocated revolution disagreed over strategy: should priority be given to the revolution in order to win the war, or to the war in order to prepare the revolution? Given these divisions it is hardly surprising that the Republicans were unable to summon up the sort of crusading zeal exhibited by Franco's Nationalists.

How did the various groups within Spain respond to the two sides? Examples particularly worth examining are the Church, the army and the regions.

The Catholic Church was torn. Many of the lower clergy supported the Republicans, partly to preserve democracy and partly for social reasons. Some of the more liberal church leaders also preferred the left to the right – for example the Bishop of Vitoria and the Cardinal of Tarragona. But the majority of the church establishment threw in its lot with the Nationalists. There were two main reasons for this. One was the appeal of Franco's religious crusade which, it was hoped, would arrest the secularization of what had once been Europe's most Catholic country. During the 1930s, for example, over two-thirds of the population never attended church and in some areas the proportion was as high as 99 per cent. Second, Franco seemed to offer the best protection against what was seen as the atheistic left. According to Pope Pius XI, it was the left, not the far right, which posed the main threat to religion in Europe: 'The first, the greatest and now the general peril is certainly Communism in all its forms and degrees.' He considered Spain to be especially at risk: 'Satanic preparation has relighted . . . in neighbouring

Spain that hatred and savage persecution.' Hence, 'our benediction, above any political and mundane consideration, goes in a special manner to all those who assume the difficult and dangerous task of defending and restoring the rights to honour God and religion'. As for Franco himself: 'We send from our hearts the apostolic blessing, propitiator of divine favours.'[31] The Spanish bishops, meanwhile, fully justified Franco's rebellion on the grounds that it was reasonable in the defence of Christianity. They even quoted the Catholic Church's leading medieval theologian, St Thomas Aquinas. This powerful ideological undertone would seem to justify the view of Gallo that this was 'the last of the European religious wars'.

It is sometimes supposed that the Spanish army rose to a man against the Republic. If this had been so, the Republic would have collapsed within weeks. The reality was more complex, as the army contained a mixture of liberal and reactionary influences. Most of the senior officers remained loyal to the Republic, as they had been appointed in the first place because of their political support for the regime. The vast majority of the middle-ranking officers, by contrast, took part in the 1936 uprising. They opposed the reforms of Azana, especially the effort to reduce the size of the officer corps through early retirement. They also came to believe that Azana was a 'pervert who nourished hatred for the virile virtues of the army, which he intended to destroy, leaving Spain helpless and prey to freemasonry and Marxism'.[32] The role of the army was therefore to save the state, whose government, according to General Kindelan was 'in the gutter', and act as 'the guardian of the values and historical constants of the nation'.[33] The army also intended to prevent decentralization and the growth of regionalism, for this would lead eventually to the disintegration of Spain as a military power.

This brings us to the two areas which did aspire to independence from Madrid – Catalonia and the Basque country. Both declared for the Republic against the Nationalists, but for pragmatic rather than ideological reasons. Catalonia's commitment was not to the Republic as such. Rather, it saw the Republic as the only means of preserving the autonomy granted in the 1932 Catalan Statute. Franco, it was well known, intended to reimpose a unitary state. During the course of the Civil War Catalonia resisted bravely and Barcelona was heavily bombed by the Nationalists in 1938 and 1939. The Basques also felt that the Republic would be more likely to uphold the autonomy which had been granted by the statute of October 1933. They, too, suffered at the hands of Franco: the bombing of Guernica became a great symbol of 'fascist' brutality against the Basque people and, indeed, the people of Republican Spain.

To what extent did the sides in the Civil War reflect class divisions? The general trend is obvious. According to Carr, 'Where they were free to choose, the working classes chose the Republic and the upper classes were, with few exceptions, fanatic Nationalists.'[34] The middle classes are more difficult to assess, but it seems that the young intellectuals and members of the professions were inclined to the Republic, their elder peers to Franco. Preston argues that the greatest divide was in the rural areas between the landlords and exploited peasants; this applied especially in Andalusia and Extremadura. The wealthy landlords did whatever possible to destroy the reforming legislation of 1931 and showed a callous indifference to the plight of the poorest peasantry. It is hardly surprising, therefore, that the peasantry and estate owners aligned themselves respectively with the Republicans and Nationalists.

Despite the self-evident political allegiance on the basis of class differences, there were some less predictable cross-currents. One was the generational divide, which affected many families in a tragic way; younger members were more likely to commit themselves to the Republic, the elder members to Franco. Another cross-current was loyalty to regional patriotism or to the Catholic Church, both of which might displace the priority of class loyalty. Finally, the accident of where they lived decided for many people which side they supported. As in any civil war, it was taken for granted that the population of the occupied zones would act as cannon fodder for the victors.

Why did Franco win the Spanish Civil War?

A combination of factors can be used to explain the success of Franco and the Nationalists in overcoming the Second Republic and installing a dictatorship in 1939.

The first of these was the contrast between the disunity of the Republicans and the cohesion of the Nationalists. The Second Republic suffered from serious divisions which undermined its war effort and military capacity; it has been argued that it experienced a 'civil war within the civil war'. There was, for example, a three-sided conflict between liberal constitutionalists, authoritarian socialists or communists, and far-left anarchists. The ideological range was considerable, the two extremes being Western democratic theories on the one hand and the revolutionary left on the other. The latter, in turn, was divided over the primary objective of the war. One strategy was to maintain the Popular Front and to put all the effort into the defeat of Franco; this was backed by most socialists, Marxists and pro-Stalin communists. The alternative emphasis was that of the CNT, a trade union of anarcho-syndicalists, and the POUM, a union of ultra-left communists and Trotskyists. They wanted to progress with the 'revolution' in the belief that compromising on this would weaken the war effort. Hence, in their irreconcilable ideological conflict, the groups found themselves 'polarized between war and revolution, revolution and war'. The disagreements were sometimes violently expressed; fighting, for example, broke out in Barcelona in 1937 between anarchists, socialists and communists.

All this contrasted with the unity in the nationalist ranks. This was due largely to the leadership of Franco. Jackson describes Franco as 'an authoritarian leader of immense contradictory forces within his camp [who] made good use of the diplomatic and administrative talent at his disposal'.[35] Gallo sees him as 'competent and determined',[36] but Franco certainly had shortcomings. According to Puzzo, 'His head was a cemetery of dead ideas.'[37] Nevertheless, he showed remarkable determination and commitment to his principles; these, according to Crozier, were 'Duty, Discipline and Order'.[38] His basic programme was single-minded and simplistic. It assumed the nature of a crusade which was fired by bigoted passion.

One of Franco's main tasks was to create unity among his supporters. As Gallo maintains, 'Like the parties of the Popular Front, the Nationalists were originally a collection of heterogeneous clans, their political diversity reflected in a variety of uniforms.'[39] Franco managed to overcome internal disputes and to balance the different Nationalist groups. He satisfied the Carlists by leaving open the question of the monarchy and in catering for their demand for legislation which favoured the Catholic Church. These moves, admittedly, were not to the liking of the more radical Falangists, but they were pacified by being allowed to direct propaganda and to influence those characteristics of a mass movement which Franco was prepared to allow; they were also pleased with his close relations with Italy and Germany. The army, bereft of any real ideas of its own, depended completely on Franco to maintain its position and influence. Franco skilfully ensured an adequate representation between the various Nationalist interests. His first National Council of October 1937 combined twenty Falangists, eight Carlists, five generals and seventeen others.[40] He was able to bind them together while, at the same time, preventing any of them from becoming too dominant and introducing embarrassingly radical policies. He therefore managed to avoid the sort of problems confronting Republican leaders.

Another significant reason for the victory of the Nationalists was their superior military structure and organization. The Republicans had a fair share of loyal generals but a severe shortage of middle-ranking officers, which meant that it was necessary to promote numerous inexperienced NCOs to this vitally important level. The Nationalists had a more systematic method: their twenty-eight military academies turned out a total of 30,000 trained officers. The Republican army also suffered from being less cohesive, largely because it depended on militias and elected officers. A serious disadvantage of this system was that all strategy was discussed at length, which reduced speed and efficiency and encouraged insubordination. The Nationalists had no such problems, as Franco brought all the militias under centralized control in December 1936 and imposed rigorous military discipline on all his forces. He also developed a far more efficient military administration. Carr maintains that 'Its notable achievements notwithstanding, the Popular Army, as a military machine that could be deployed by a unified command, was inferior to the Nationalist Army.'[41] As for battle strategy, Franco's was unimaginative but solid. The Republican commanders often had more dash and launched several brilliant attacks which initially succeeded. But Franco's great strength was his cautious and thorough preparation. He would never start an offensive unless he was certain that he could see it through to the end. He was often criticized by his allies abroad for his slowness but, in the end, he got results.

There is a consensus among historians that the Nationalists probably would have been unable to win the war without assistance from outside, especially from Italy and Germany. There is, therefore, agreement with Hitler's belief that 'without the help of both countries there would be today no Franco'.[42] Italy's contributions were considerable. They included over 50,000 ground troops, 950 tanks, 763 aircraft and 91 warships. Germany provided 16,000 military advisers, the latest aircraft and the services of the Condor Legion. This support proved of vital importance on three occasions. The first was the transporting of Franco's troops from Morocco into southern Spain in German and Italian aircraft, enabling Franco to conquer Andalusia in 1936. The second was the boost given to Nationalist morale, after a series of Republican victories in 1937, by a sudden increase in Italian equipment. The third was another massive flow of armaments in 1939 which made it possible for Franco to crush Catalonia.

How was all this aid paid for? At first the Nationalists faced a massive problem, for all of Spain's gold reserves were in Republican hands. But Italy and Germany soon offset this in a series of financial agreements; these, according to Vinas, were 'the principal way in which the Burgos [Nationalist] government could manage to make the international payments necessary to strengthen the war sector of its economy'.[43] Italy provided aid worth a total of $263 million, while Germany contributed arms worth $215 million. Altogether, Franco may well have received as much as $570 million from abroad. A significant amount of business was also done with multinational companies in the Western democracies; Whealey cites as examples the Texas Oil Company, Texaco, Shell, Standard of New Jersey and the Atlantic Refining Company. Their role was vital; according to Whealey, 'without oil, the Generalissimo's war machines would have ground to a halt'. They also deprived the Republic of its last chance of survival: 'Multinational corporations in the sterling dollar countries . . . helped to crush the Spanish Republicans' hopes.'[44]

The Republic suffered more from the obstructive policies of the other powers than Franco, who could rely on more consistent support. Its most consistent ally was Stalin, though even he proved eventually to be unreliable. Stalin was always unwilling to commit Russia too fully in case he should leave himself vulnerable to invasion by Germany. In any case, his involvement in Spain was partly intended to stiffen the West against fascism but, once it became clear that appeasement was the order of the day, he lost interest. Munich finally convinced Stalin that he should withdraw. Meanwhile, France was reluctant to become involved in assisting a fellow republic. A series of governments, headed by Blum and Daladier, kept out of the conflict for fear of alienating important groups, like the Catholics, in France. The United States also kept its distance, largely to avoid complicating relations with right-wing, and pro-Franco, regimes in Latin America.

But by far the greatest obstacle to the Republic's war effort was Britain. The governments of Baldwin and Chamberlain still hoped to come to terms with Germany and also to revive Anglo-Italian friendship. Besides, in ideological terms the real enemy was considered to be communism, not fascism, and therefore Stalin, not Franco. There was no question of support for the Nationalists, many of whose policies were considered repugnant. Equally, however, there appeared to be a strong case against risking a general European war for the sake of bolstering up a Republic which was inclining increasingly to the left. Hence, Britain put heavy pressure on France to ban all arms sales to the Republic and was also the main influence behind the formation of the Non-Intervention Committee in 1936, the purpose of which was to prevent support being given by any country to either side in the conflict. Unfortunately, while the rules of the Non-Intervention Committee were observed by the democracies, they were openly flouted by the dictatorships, who gave Franco what he wanted. Britain's role was therefore vital. According to Puzzo: 'The conclusion is inescapable that the defeat and destruction of the Spanish Republic must be attributed as much to British diplomacy in the years 1936 to 1939 as to German aircraft and Italian infantry.'[45]

The Republicans, it is true, had certain benefits; but these gradually dwindled as those of the Nationalists grew. The greatest initial advantage of the Republic was that it owned the world's fourth largest gold reserve – sufficient, it might be thought, to finance military operations against Franco. Added to this was government control over the main cities and industrial areas. The Republic, however, soon met serious difficulties in paying through normal international banking channels for arms shipments. The main reason for this was the reluctance of bankers to defy government orders on neutrality. Eventually, the Soviet Union agreed to make necessary provision. The price, however, was the transfer of Spain's gold reserves to Moscow; Stalin refused point-blank to provide the Republic with the credit being made available to Franco by Hitler and Mussolini. The Republic bought from Stalin 1,000 aircraft and 200 tanks, together with the services of between 500 and 5,000 advisers (who, however, arrived with Stalin's instructions to 'keep out of artillery range'). In addition, the Comintern organized the International Brigades which provided a total of 40,000 volunteers from France, Britain, Canada, Yugoslavia, Hungary, Czechoslovakia, Sweden, Switzerland, Germany, Austria, Italy and fifty-three other countries.[46] These fought bravely but suffered heavy casualties. They were finally disbanded in 1938 as Franco made a final and successful thrust against Catalonia and Madrid.

Franco's regime, 1939–75

Franco owed an enormous debt to the fascist states who put him in power. It might therefore be thought that his future should inevitably have been linked to theirs and that their fate would be his. And yet, by 1945 both Nazi Germany and Fascist Italy lay in ruins, with their leaders dead. Franco, by contrast, was still firmly in control and managed to impose his will until his death thirty years later.

The basic reason for this was that Spain never became totally involved in the Second World War, therefore avoiding catastrophic military defeat. There was never any doubt about Franco's sympathies for the Axis cause. General Aranda said on 5 June 1939: 'Franco is deeply and firmly convinced that his path lies by the side of Italy and Germany. He openly detests the French and does not love the British.' In August 1940 Franco assured Mussolini of his intention 'to hasten our preparations with a view to entering the war at a propitious moment'.[47] But when in 1940 Hitler met Franco at Hendaye in the Pyrenees he found the Caudillo evasive and determined to avoid any specific military commitments. Indeed, Hitler seems to have had a bad time and later observed that he would 'rather have four teeth pulled out' than have to deal with Franco again. Franco was motivated less by caution than necessity; he had no option but to remain neutral. The Spanish economy had been ruined by the Civil War and the disruption of international commerce caused by the Second World War was enough to make recovery impossible. The army was rundown and war-weary and there was a major possibility that Britain and the United States would seize Spain's Atlantic islands the moment Franco made an alliance with either Germany or Italy. He was, therefore, grateful when his neighbour and fellow-dictator, Salazar, suggested an Iberian neutrality pact.

Franco did, however, make one notable exception to his policy of non-belligerency. He referred to the existence of two wars: the one in the west was clearly beyond Spain's resources, but the war in the east involved a powerful ideological principle. Franco's Foreign Minister, Suner, maintained that 'Russia is to blame for our civil war' and that 'the extermination of Russia is a demand of history'.[48] Hence, Franco sent 18,000 volunteers in the 'Blue Division' to assist the German invasion of Russia. By 1943, however, it had become evident that Hitler was bogged down at Stalingrad; Franco cut his losses and withdrew his remaining troops from the Russian front. He was therefore the one European dictator who managed to pull out of the Russian flame without burning his fingers. In fact, he was able to extricate himself from all hostilities so that the Western Allies, much as they disliked Franco's regime, had no reason to overthrow it in their onslaught on the Axis powers.

All the same, Spain was seriously isolated in the 1940s, which meant that Franco's foreign policy was based on the search for diplomatic recognition. At first this was provided only by Salazar's Portugal and Peron's Argentina, the latter agreeing to provide grain and meat on special terms. The rest of the world was hostile. The 'Big Three' at Potsdam opposed any possible bid by Franco to join the United Nations since Franco's government did not 'in view of its origins, its nature, its record and its close association with the aggressor states, possess the qualifications necessary to justify such membership'.[49] A United Nations communiqué endorsed this view in December 1946, referring to 'a Fascist regime patterned on, and established largely as a result of aid from Hitler's Nazi Germany and Mussolini's Fascist Italy'.[50] Nor were individual European countries likely to be receptive, most of them having recently elected left-wing governments. For a while Franco shrugged off this ostracism as a deliberate conspiracy which revealed just how necessary his authoritarian regime was. 'Spaniards know what they can expect from abroad, and as history teaches them, ill-will against Spain is not something which began today or yesterday.'[51]

Gradually the situation began to improve as Spain became less obnoxious in the eyes of the Western states. The basic reason was the escalation of the Cold War with the perceived threat of world communism sponsored by the Soviet Union and China. The Berlin Crisis (1947–8) and the Korean War (1950–3) both gave Franco his opportunity to end Spain's isolation and he played his diplomatic role with some skill. The result was the 1953 Madrid Pact between Spain and the United States. This provided Spain with $226 million of aid and military equipment, in return for the use of three air bases and naval facilities. According to Gallo, this agreement was a 'triumph for the regime'. It was renewed in 1963, when it stated that any threat to Spain would be 'a common concern' to the United States. Relations also improved with West Germany and the new French Fifth Republic. Even so, Spain was still not regarded as a desirable partner in various international organizations; it was not admitted to NATO or the EEC until, in the decade after Franco's death, it had proved itself capable of sustaining basic democracy.

While he ruled Spain Franco's power was virtually absolute. He dispensed with any formal constitution, maintained complete control over the administration, dominated the courts and crippled the parliament. His authority was strongly personalized. 'I am', he once said, 'the sentinel who is never relieved.' The inscription on Spain's coinage read 'Caudillo of Spain by the Grace of God'.[52] Clearly he saw himself in historic succession to the great Spanish monarchs of the past, especially Philip II, with whom he often identified. For this reason he sought to revive the glories of Imperial Spain and, in the words of Gallo, 'appropriated Spanish history'. This powerful pull of tradition is an argument against applying too loosely the term 'fascist' to Franco. Orwell, with characteristic insight, observed as early as 1937 that Franco's mutiny 'was an attempt not so much to impose fascism as to restore feudalism'.[53] Franco lacked commitment to any radical ideology and certainly did not have a mass party base. In fact, he maintained his position by balancing against each other the main groups supporting the regime. These were the army, the Church, monarchists, industrialists, financiers and the nearest Spain came to a fascist movement – the Falange. Hence, according to Gilmour, Spain was governed by 'a limited pluralism . . . not by a single party but by a reluctant coalition of diverse groups'.[54]

It would be a mistake to assume that no political changes occurred during the long period between Franco's victory and his death; the regime did eventually dispense with some of its earlier horrors. Immediately after the Civil War Franco introduced the most appalling repression, with mass executions, three-minute trials, concentration camps and confessions under torture. According to Carr, 'the firing squad and prison replaced the dungeons and fires of the Inquisition'.[55] By the 1960s, however, there was evidence of some relaxation. Although Franco's personal power remained intact, much of the old bureaucratic repression was dismantled. His basic aim was no longer to terrorize the population but, rather, to neutralize and depoliticize it, encouraging it to make the most of the economic boom which Spain was experiencing during the 1960s.

This boom took some time to materialize, and only after a false start. The initial problem confronting the regime was reconstruction after the Civil War. The method chosen was autarky, or self-sufficiency, involving heavy government intervention in wage levels, import quotas and the regulation of industry. The emphasis was on industrialization. The result was predictable hardship, which included widespread poverty, threatened starvation and the spread of accompanying diseases such as tuberculosis. Franco used characteristically tough words to justify his policy: 'We do not want an easy, comfortable life . . . we want a hard life, the difficult life of a virile people.'[56] Arguably, industry benefited. By 1950 it had regained its level of pre-war production, and between 1950 and 1957 doubled its output.

This growth was, however, beset with serious problems which revealed the utter inadequacy of autarky. According to Carr, 'Autarky had ceased to be a stimulus; it had become a straitjacket.'[57] Industrial growth, for example, led to an increased demand for imports which, in turn, put a strain on the balance of trade. The government therefore recognized the necessity of creating a more balanced economy by reducing controls and depending more openly on market forces. In 1959 it introduced a Stabilization Plan to bring the economy into line with others in the West. The measures included deflation, control of the money supply, reductions of public expenditure, wage controls, the promotion of foreign investment and the reduction of trade restrictions.[58] Initial hardship was followed between 1961 and 1966 by a so-called 'economic miracle'. The government ascribed the new-found prosperity to the Stabilization Plan and its successors, the Development Plans from 1964. It is, however, equally likely that the major cause of this recovery was indirect. Abandoning autarky promoted two vitally important foreign exchange earners which helped stimulate growth. One of these was tourism; the total number of foreign visitors to Spain increased from 6 million in 1959 to 21 million in 1969 and 34 million in 1972. The other boost was the large Spanish workforce abroad which sent its earnings back to the mother country. The existence of such a large Spanish workforce abroad, however, was also an indication of one of the main shortcomings of the economy: the lack of full employment. Other persistent problems were the depressed condition of agriculture and the iniquitous system of taxation which prevented the state from extracting sufficient revenue from the sectors of society which most benefited from the boom. The result was that the gap between rich and poor increased as the new-found wealth was inadequately redistributed.

What condition was the regime in by 1975? Carr refers to the 'Agony of Francoism, 1969–75', an apt description of the era of growing dissent, economic strain and doubts about the future. Although opposition was still illegal, it welled up through the system in the form of working-class activism and student unrest. A more violent form was Basque separatism, the violent tactics of the organization known as ETA provoking the government into issuing the 1975 Anti-terrorist Law. Even the Church, once a loyal ally, now distanced itself from the regime. Its change of attitude went back to the Second Vatican Council (1962–5) when Pope John XXIII made a stand on the protection of human rights. By the 1970s the upper clergy finally withdrew their support from Franco, leaving his regime bereft of the religious sanction it had once been able to take for granted. To make matters worse, Spain was experiencing the economic problems common to other parts of Europe in the wake of the 1973 oil crisis; this threatened to cut away one of Franco's main boasts – that he had presided over unprecedented economic growth. Now the question in everyone's mind was: what type of regime would succeed the ageing and ailing dictator?

Franco's own intention was to ease the way for the return of the monarchy by grooming Prince Juan Carlos for future authority. He did not, however, have the chance to complete this to his own satisfaction. On 17 October 1975, Franco collapsed in a cabinet meeting. Doctors were summoned to the palace and performed a tracheotomy to enable him to breathe. Rumours circulated that Franco was dying, but these were officially denied. Indeed, the surgeons made every effort to prolong Franco's life. They succeeded until 20 November, by which time he was permanently on a respirator and a kidney machine and his stomach had been removed. It was almost as if Spain dared not let him die for fear of the subsequent uncertainty.

A character as diverse and complex as Franco has inevitably been the subject of historical controversy. Two very different viewpoints can be cited. On the one hand, Franco has his defenders. One of these, Crozier, maintains that Francoist Spain was not a totalitarian state and was therefore much freer than the Soviet Union or eastern Europe. Franco's achievements were substantial, including economic well-being and all the preconditions necessary for future stability and growth. He should, therefore, be judged by the standards of Spanish history and not those of more developed countries.[59] At the other end of the spectrum, Preston denounces any attempt to defend Franco. He argues that it is a basic misconception that Franco provided social peace, for this ignores his labour camps and executions, signs of his 'brutal efficiency'. In this respect, Preston insists, 'Franco stands comparison with the cruellest dictators of the century.'[60]

DICTATORSHIP IN CENTRAL AND EASTERN EUROPE

Introduction

At the beginning of the twentieth century over three-quarters of the total area of Europe was ruled by three empires: Turkey, Austria-Hungary and Russia. By 1914 the Balkan provinces of Turkey had splintered into six independent states; their treatment after the First World War and subsequent problems are dealt with on pp. 8–18. Central and eastern Europe underwent a similar transformation in 1918 as a result of the defeat of Tsarist Russia and the disintegration of Austria-Hungary. From the territory of these two empires no fewer than eight 'successor states' were established as a result of the Treaty of Brest-Litovsk and the Paris Settlement. The former (dealt with in Chapter 2) destroyed Russian sovereignty over Finland, Poland and the three Baltic states of Estonia, Latvia and Lithuania. The Paris settlement, comprising the Treaties of St Germain (1919) and Trianon (1920) acknowledged the collapse of the Habsburg monarchy and the establishment of Austria, Hungary and Czechoslovakia.

The Paris Settlement ensured that Austria and Hungary were now merely the German and Magyar rumps of the old empire. The provinces of Bohemia, Moravia and Slovakia were converted into the state of Czechoslovakia. Galicia was ceded to Poland, Transylvania to Romania, Croatia and Bosnia-Herzegovina to Yugoslavia, and South Tyrol and Trentino to Italy. These provisions have been the subject of vigorous debate ever since and three arguments seem to represent the full range of opinion. At one extreme, the new Czech leader, Masaryk, welcomed the changes which had 'shorn nationalism of its negative character by setting oppressed peoples on their feet'. At the other extreme, some observers looked nostalgically back to the days of the multinational empire of the Habsburgs. One of these was Eyck, the German historian, who saw the 'dismemberment of the Austro-Hungarian state' as 'a basic error'.[61] More recently, A.J.P. Taylor pointed to the transitory nature of the empire, but also to the difficulty of managing without it: 'The dynastic Empire sustained central Europe, as a plaster cast sustains a broken limb; though it had to be destroyed before movement was possible, its removal did not make movement successful or even easy.'[62]

An analysis of the problems confronting the 'successor states' should enable the reader to weigh the relative merits of these views. It should also explain why this part of Europe should have become the scene of a series of domestic crises, which promoted dictatorship, and of international confrontations, which precipitated general war.

The first of these problems was the ethnic composition of the 'successor states'. In theory, the Paris Settlement was eminently reasonable; President Wilson's principle of 'national self-determination' ensured that the Slav peoples all received their own homelands, whether in Czechoslovakia, Poland or Yugoslavia. In practice, however, the settlement discriminated against both Austria and Hungary by so drawing the new boundaries that large minorities of Germans and Magyars were separated from their respective homelands. Hence 3.1 million Sudeten Germans came under Czech rule, as did the Hungarian population of Slovakia. The justification was that the Sudetenland was an industrial area which was indispensable to the economic viability of Czechoslovakia. In any case, to have left the province with Austria would have created a geographic impossibility and the Allies could hardly transfer it to Germany. There was therefore a tendency among the peacemakers to shrug off such anomalies; King Albert of the Belgians asked, 'What would you have? They did what they could.'[63] Unfortunately, the policy of favouring the Slavs at the expense of non-Slavs did not always work, for there was serious friction between the various subgroups who were brought together as co-nationals. Slovaks, for example, accused Czechs of monopolizing power, and some historians consider that the nationalist tensions which existed in the Danube area were worse after the dissolution of the empire than they had ever been before.

Ethnic conflicts were compounded by economic difficulties resulting initially from the manner in which the resources of the empire were carved up. The 'successor states' received disproportionate shares of the industries and agricultural land of Austria-Hungary. Czechoslovakia, for example, inherited only 27 per cent of the empire's population but nearly 80 per cent of its heavy industry, sufficient to enable it to compete successfully with many Western industrial states. Hungary was less fortunate. Although it received between 80 and 90 per cent of the specialized engineering and wood-processing plants, these had access to 89 per cent less iron ore and 85 per cent less timber. There was also a serious disruption in what had been a free-trade area of some 55 million inhabitants in which certain areas had specialized. In the textile industry, for example, most of the spinning was concentrated in Austria and the weaving in Bohemia. From 1919, however, each of the newly independent states was forced to build up those areas of its economy which had previously been undeveloped, the purpose being to create a more balanced agricultural and industrial base. Therefore, Austria had to build up her weaving and Bohemia her spinning. This, in turn, precipitated a round of tariff increases in order to protect infant industries from competition from neighbours; in their struggle for survival, many of the 'successor states' had to accept the principle of self-sufficiency even if it meant tariff wars and reduced exports. For a short period, in the second half of the 1920s, most governments managed a respectable rate of economic growth. This, however, was reversed, from 1929 onwards, by the onset of the Great Depression.

Political instability was due, in part, to economic crisis, in part to institutional defects. A great deal of thought had gone into the preparation of the constitutions of the 'successor states' in 1918 and 1919 and all the most advanced features of Western democratic thought had been enshrined in the new regimes, including universal suffrage, proportional representation and strict legislative control over the executive. One of the great disappointments of the inter-war period was that these constitutions failed to work properly in any country in central and eastern Europe, with the single exception of Czechoslovakia. In most cases there was a steady slide towards authoritarian regimes. In 1926 Piłsudski installed himself as Polish leader after a military coup, as did Smetona in Lithuania in the same year. By 1934 Austria had moved to the right under Dollfuss, while Estonia had succumbed to Päts and Latvia to Ulmanis. Hungary experienced more drastic changes, which resembled violent swings of the pendulum: within the space of twenty-six years it was ruled by a radical left-wing 'dictatorship of the proletariat' under Béla Kun, a conservative–authoritarian regime under Horthy, and a far-right, pro-Nazi dictatorship under Szálasi. None of these states had experience of the subtleties of a constitutional democracy, since they had previously experienced only the autocracy of Tsarist Russia or the milder but authoritarian monarchy of the Habsburgs. It was, therefore, unduly optimistic to expect a country like Poland or Austria to operate the type of constitution which baffled even the experienced politicians of the French Third Republic.

The fourth problem was even more serious than the ethnic conflicts, economic difficulties and institutional defects. Feuds developed between the 'successor states' which soon interacted with the rivalries between the major powers in the area. The motives varied. Hungary followed a revisionist course, spurred on by an irredentist policy which aimed to reclaim her lost Magyar territories from Slav neighbours. Austria, deprived of her role as a major power, sought an Anschluss, or union, with Germany, while Poland aimed to expand her frontiers to those of 1772, at the expense of the Soviet Union and Lithuania. The Baltic states had to focus their attention on basic survival. After 1920 these policies resulted in the emergence of two blocs. One, which consisted of Austria and Hungary, sought to revise the Paris Settlement, and gravitated rapidly towards Italy and Germany. This trend was completed by the Anschluss and Hungary's membership of Hitler's Anti-Comintern Pact. The second bloc comprised Poland, Czechoslovakia, Yugoslavia and Romania. These states formed close diplomatic links with each other and, during the 1920s, could depend on French guarantees against the aggression of other powers. During the 1930s, however, French influence collapsed in central and eastern Europe. As a result, this 'Little Entente' was undermined as various states hastened to make their own additional arrangements with Germany. Czechoslovakia tried to hold out against German influence, but she was set upon in 1938 by Germany, Hungary and Poland, all intent on claiming their fellow-nationals in the Sudetenland and Southern Slovakia. The failure of the West to support Czechoslovakia was a catalyst for Soviet aggression. In August 1939 Stalin sought to wipe out the memory of Brest-Litovsk by agreeing with Hitler the partition of Poland and the division of eastern Europe into German and Soviet spheres of influence. This pact enabled Hitler to launch his Blitzkrieg on Poland and, in so doing, to complete the destruction of the Paris Settlement.

Austria

In 1919 Austria was the German remnant of the Austro-Hungarian monarchy. It contained a population of a mere 8 million people, of whom over one-third lived in Vienna. This transition from a major power to a state not much larger than Switzerland was so sudden that it caused 'a terrifying array of problems',[64] both internal and external. By 1933 the search for solutions in a democratic context had clearly failed and Austria drifted into a period of authoritarian government under Dollfuss (1932–4) and Schuschnigg (1934–8), which was ended by the absorption of Austria into Germany and the imposition of the Nazi dictatorship.

Austria's political problems were intensified by a loss of identity; Austrians had never wanted to be a separate entity, preferring instead Anschluss, or union with Germany. According to Bauer, one of the leaders of the Austrian Social Democrats, 'If we stay independent, then . . . we shall live the life of a dwarf-state.'[65] In the event, Austrians had no choice, for Anschluss was explicitly forbidden by the Treaties of Versailles and St Germain. But they developed no real commitment to the separate identity thus forced upon them. The 1920s saw the steady decline of democracy; although the 1920 constitution provided for a federal republic and a strong legislature, it was rendered unworkable by the constant rivalry between the left-wing Social Democrats, under Bauer and Renner, and the conservative Christian Socialists under

12 Dr Engelbert Dollfuss (left), 1892–1934 (Popperfoto)

Bishop Seipel. Initially in coalition until 1922, the two had drifted apart and the Christian Socialists dominated most of the governments of the 1920s and 1930s. Unable to achieve a majority in parliament, the Christian Socialists were constantly looking over their shoulders at the Social Democrats, whom they accused of trying to introduce a programme of 'Austro-Marxism'. Indeed, fear of the socialist left eventually induced the Christian Socialists to rely on a paramilitary force called the Heimwehr, the activities of which became increasingly sinister.

The main catalyst for the change from democracy to dictatorship was economic crisis which, according to Stadler, prevented 'a reasonably intelligent, civilized and industrious nation from settling down and making a success of their new state'.[66] Much of the blame has been placed on the terms of the 1919 Treaty of St Germain; according to the Austrian delegation, 'what remains of Austria could not live'.[67] Austria was now able to produce only one-quarter of her food and was obliged to import most of her coal and raw materials. By 1922 the situation had deteriorated badly, with rampant inflation and hunger riots. Chancellor Seipel offered a series of solutions in the form of international loans and careful budgetary controls and, for a while, Austria experienced a small boom. This did not, however, reverse the permanent trade deficit and was, in any case, wiped out by the Great Depression. In 1931 the entire Austrian banking system, Credit Anstalt, collapsed under the strain which, in turn, resulted in the withdrawal of all foreign investment. Industrial production declined in 1932 to 61 per cent of its 1929 level, while the unemployment rate rose, in the same period, from 9.9 per cent to 21.4 per cent.[68]

Austria now entered an authoritarian phase as her leaders, unable to do much about the financial and economic crisis, sought to minimize the symptoms of political instability. The Christian Socialist leader, Dollfuss, became Minister of Agriculture in 1931 and Chancellor in 1932. This 'physically tiny and excessively vain man'[69] was a devout Catholic and implacable opponent of the left, determined to rid the country of 'godless Marxism'. Highly critical of 'so-called democracy', he aimed to establish a 'Social Christian German state of Austria, on a corporative basis, under strong authoritarian leadership'.[70] His subsequent measures certainly showed the seriousness of his intentions. In 1933 he severely weakened the Austrian parliament and made it possible to rule by executive decree. He then turned on the parties and movements, apart from the Christian Socialists. His measures against the Social Democrats (to 'remove the rubbish accumulated under the Republic'[71]) precipitated the 1934 civil war, from which Dollfuss emerged victorious. Meanwhile, under the influence of Mussolini, he had set up a mass party, the Fatherland Front, and went on in 1934 to introduce a corporative system similar to that in Italy. His own power increased dramatically as, in imitation of Mussolini, he accumulated for himself no fewer than five cabinet posts. His personal rule was abruptly terminated by his assassination in 1934, but the system was maintained in its essentials by his successor, Schuschnigg, until the latter's replacement by Nazi rule in 1938.

The main issue from 1935 onwards was the future of Austria in relation to Germany. To some extent, the obstacle to voluntary Anschluss was the Austrian leadership itself. Both Dollfuss and Schuschnigg were fully in favour of union with Germany, but within the traditional model of Austro-German dualism rather than under the more recent Prussian domination. Schuschnigg, especially, distrusted German militarism, the influence of Hitler and, of course, the intentions of the Austrian Nazis whom he saw as an enemy in the midst. He therefore pursued a policy of maintaining Austrian independence for the moment by manoeuvring diplomatically between Hitler and Mussolini and avoiding direct dependence on either Italy or Germany. Italy, however, soon lost the will to counter German influence in Austria as her own attention was diverted to the campaign in Ethiopia and the war in Spain. There was little, therefore, to prevent German ascendancy in Austria. The 1936 Austro-German Treaty tightened the link and, in 1938, Hitler summoned Schuschnigg to Germany, charging him with having broken this pact. Convinced that Hitler was trying to find an excuse to take over Austria, Schuschnigg announced a national plebiscite for a 'free', independent and united Austria. Hitler, however, moved too quickly for Schuschnigg. The Austrian Nazis caused so much internal unrest that Schuschnigg was forced to resign before the plebiscite could be held. He was succeeded as Chancellor by the Nazi leader, Seyss-Inquart, who promptly requested German intervention. There was no resistance to the German invasion and Hitler was given a rousing welcome in Vienna. The plebiscite held on 10 April 1938 returned a vote of 99.75 per cent in favour of the Anschluss as carried out by Seyss-Inquart and the German government.

The next seven years were probably the worse in Austria's history. Her very name was expunged and she was subordinated totally to the interests of the Third Reich. The administration was Nazified, the opposition was purged by the Gestapo and SS, and special courts were set up to deal with political cases. The entire economy was plundered for the German war effort, including Austria's gold reserves. Indeed, Austria suffered more severely as a result of Hitler's military ventures than did most other parts of the Reich. It is generally agreed that this experience cured for ever Austria's desire to be united with Germany. In the words of the Social Democrat Renner: 'In just three months Austria was liquidated as a state and a nation, but therewith the people's sympathies for the German Reich were also extinguished.' By 1943, Barker maintains, the vast majority of the population desired total independence. Resistance was attempted by a variety of groups, including communists, socialists, Catholics, factory workers and intellectuals; three movements of particular importance were the Austrian Freedom Movement, the Austrian Freedom Front and the Anti-Fascist Freedom Movement for Austria. There was therefore little regret when the Allies ended the Anschluss in 1945. Austria recognized that her future lay in accepting that she was a small non-aligned state and not part of a massive German monolith.

Was there an 'Austro-fascist' regime?

Throughout the period Austria experienced a complex pattern of right-wing influences which calls for some explanation. The first major movement was the Heimwehr, a radical mass movement which was, however, increasingly used by the political right, the Christian Socialists. As the regime became, under Dollfuss, more rigidly authoritarian, it developed, in the Fatherland Front, its own mass base, which overlapped many of the activities of the Heimwehr. The relationship between these components in the governments of Dollfuss and Schuschnigg have been the subject of two very different interpretations.

On the one hand, Lewis maintains that the Christian Social Party destroyed the democratic republic and established, from 1934 onwards, an 'Austro-fascist' regime. The whole purpose of the dictatorship of Dollfuss was to eradicate the left in Austria, rather than to establish control over all parts of the political spectrum. 'Parliamentary democracy in Austria was destroyed in order to wipe out the Social Democratic movement, not to protect the country against fascism. The result was a form of fascism itself: Austro-fascism.'[72] The regime, or *Standestaat*, had many of the hallmarks of fascism: the Christian Socialists had a strong populist tradition which 'fostered a distinct form of fascist thought' which contributed to the creation of the *Standestaat*;[73] the parliamentary system was replaced by a series of councils, a typical example of corporatism; and the Heimwehr played an integral part in the Christian Socialists' control rather than being a competitor. In other words, fascism was operating at the centre of the Austrian state rather than on its fringes.

The reverse is usually asserted. Payne and others maintain that the dictatorship of Dollfuss and Schuschnigg was traditional rather than fascist. Indeed, part of their motive was to prevent more radical groups like the Heimwehr from seizing the initiative. Hence, in Payne's view , 'the non-fascist forces of the right were able to organize a pre-emptive authoritarian government of their own'.[74] The main inspirations for Dollfuss were the authoritarian regimes and styles of leadership shown by Primo de Rivera in Spain and Piłsudski in Poland. The corporatist constitution of 1934 was similar to that introduced in Portugal in 1933 and had very little to do with Italian influences. Similarly, the emphasis of Dollfuss was always Catholic and Western, and he frequently criticized the racist values of Nazi Germany. It is true that some fascist trappings were introduced, such as the Sturmkorps set up in 1937; although this has been likened to the SS, it was closer to Assault Guards formed in pre-Franco Spain. Any youth movements were rooted firmly in Catholicism and there was no reference to militarism, expansion or 'new man'.

It is also significant that the movement which was unquestionably fascist, the Austrian Nazis, bitterly opposed the traditionalist dictatorship, to the extent of assassinating Dollfuss. There was no question of their leader, Seyss-Inquart, coming to terms with what he saw as a different system altogether; to him the only real option was to impose Nazism through the Anschluss which the traditionalists had come to oppose. Hence, Dollfuss and Schuschnigg were perceived as fundamentally anti-fascist.

Hungary

Between the wars Hungary experienced a more complete range of regimes than any of the other 'successor states'. The collapse of the Habsburg monarchy in 1918 was followed by the establishment of a democratic republic under Károlyi. This, in turn, was replaced in 1919 by the Soviet Republic of Béla Kun, one of the very few communist dictatorships established outside Russia between the wars. This, however, soon succumbed to a counter-revolution which was based on reactionary terror. This was stabilized by Admiral Horthy, who established a more permanent right-wing regime between 1920 and 1944; although there was some alternation between moderate and radical governments, there was little evidence of direct fascist influence. Then, in 1944 Horthy was overthrown by the Germans and a Nazi-style dictatorship under Szálasi was installed; during this period the whole regime was radicalized and became particularly brutal. With the defeat of Germany in 1945 Hungary came under a second and, this time, more durable communist administration.

Hungary's political experience was therefore similar to the swing of a pendulum: it moved from the centre violently to the left, through the conservative right to the extreme right, before returning to the far left. In the process, it experienced dictatorship under communism, traditional conservatism and radical Nazism. More than any other country in Europe, it provided a microcosm of the different movements and regimes experienced by inter-war Europe.

The different styles of dictatorship

Hungary seceded from the Austro-Hungarian Empire once it had become clear that the defeat of the Central powers was inevitable. In October 1918, a new Hungarian National Council was set up under Károlyi, which was intended as a progressive and democratic parliamentary system based on universal suffrage, secret ballot, freedom of the press and land reform. This experiment was never given a chance to work. Hungary was invaded by Czech and Romanian detachments seeking to extend the boundaries of states, and the Western Allies denounced Károlyi for his refusal to allow his territory to be used as a base for operations against Soviet Russia. Károlyi was even denounced as a Bolshevik; this was a major blunder which served only to bring about the very communist regime which the Allies had hoped to avoid.

For Károlyi, under severe external pressure, now felt impelled to bring the communists into collaboration with his own Social Democrats and even thought in terms of seeking assistance from Russia to support the new regime against its numerous enemies. In March 1919 he resigned in desperation and a new, far-left coalition was set up, dominated by Béla Kun. A new Revolutionary Governing Council heralded the formation of a Soviet Republic and introduced a string of new institutions and policies, including a 'Red Army', revolutionary tribunals, a network of councils and extensive nationalization. Béla Kun made no secret of the narrow base of his power. He had, he said, set up 'a dictatorship of an active minority on behalf of the by and large passive proletariat'. He also considered it necessary to 'act in a strong and merciless fashion . . . at least until such time that the revolution spreads to the [other] European countries'.[75]

The Kun regime was not without its achievements; it introduced an eight-hour working day, increased pay and guaranteed rights for ethnic minorities in Hungary. But it collapsed, after only 133 days, for a combination of external and internal reasons. By July 1919, the invading Romanians had broken through the Hungarian lines and were advancing on Budapest. At this time of crisis the government lacked extensive popular support, largely because of mistakes in its strategy; it had been too doctrinaire and had neglected to exploit national sentiment, it had failed to win over the peasantry by refusing to redistribute, to their private ownership, the land confiscated from the nobility, and it had ignored the need to maintain the support of the non-Communist left. Kun was therefore forced to flee Budapest and go into exile. He was eventually shot, ironically, in the Soviet Union during Stalin's purges.

The swing to the left was now followed by a lurch to the right. The 'Red Terror' was replaced by an infinitely more savage 'White Terror' as 'officers' detachments' prowled those parts of the country not occupied by the Romanians, slaughtering workers and Jews and torturing to death any suspected members of the Béla Kun regime. This appalling phase of Hungarian history was ended in 1920 with the emergence of Admiral Horthy as the head of state, or Regent. A convinced anti-communist, Horthy constructed an authoritarian system which rested on the traditional power bases: the landed gentry, the industrial capitalists and the government bureaucrats. It was not, however, totalitarian; he retained the Hungarian constitution and allowed most of the parties to function, although with carefully restricted powers. Of all the 'dictatorships' covered in this book, the Horthy regime was probably the most borderline; indeed, it might be possible, for the 1920s, to dispense with the term altogether.

The lengthy period of Horthy's rule is usually divided into two distinct phases: the moderate conservatism of the 1920s and the more complex zigzags between caution and radicalism which characterized the 1930s.

After the bloodbath of the 'White Terror', Horthy concentrated on providing the new regime with an aura of legitimacy. He chose as his Prime Minister Count Bethlen, a leading aristocrat who had the confidence of the capitalists and landowners. Bethlen was suspicious of democracy as applied in those countries which had not, as yet, acquired political maturity and sophistication, and hoped to reach a position halfway between 'unbridled freedom and unrestrained dictatorship'.[76] He considered it safest to return to the limited democracy of pre-war Hungary and was willing to allow many components of a constitutional system.

13 Admiral Miklos Horthy, 1868–1957 (Popperfoto)

But his concessions were cosmetic rather than functional; his franchise, for example, drastically reduced the size of the electorate. He should, nevertheless, receive some credit for a period of relative political stability and economic progress. By 1929 industry had recovered from its dreadful performance of the early 1920s and had exceeded the production figures of 1913.

The Bethlen era was ended by the Great Depression which hit Hungary as seriously as any country in Europe. The industrial growth of the late 1920s had depended heavily on foreign capital investment which was withdrawn following the collapse of the banking system in central Europe. To make matters worse, Hungary's agriculture suffered disastrously under the strain of low prices and foreign tariffs against food exports. The overall result was large-scale poverty and, in some areas, people starved to death. Bethlen, unable to cope with the inevitable outbursts of discontent, resigned in 1930. Horthy was now faced with a dilemma about the style of rule which he should adopt. He ultimately opted for an increased personal role. But he experienced difficulties with his choice of prime ministers. Basically, there were two types of premier: those who were in the conservative tradition of Bethlen, and those who had radical, even fascist, leanings. Horthy manoeuvred uncertainly between the two styles. Between 1932 and 1936 Hungary was governed by Gömbös, a radical and, according to Pamlényi, 'an uncompromising advocate of arbitrary, totalitarian forms of government'. His real aim was the 'realization of a less concealed, total form of fascist rule free of parliamentary trappings'.[77] His death in

1936 was followed by a zigzag sequence of conservatives like Daranyi (1936–8) and Teleki (1939–41) and radicals such as Imrédy. It seemed that Horthy was unable to decide which style of right-wing rule was more appropriate to Hungary's needs.

Much the same could be said of his foreign policy. The basic influence behind Hungarian diplomacy was a powerful revisionist urge resulting from the Treaty of Trianon (1920). This had deprived Hungary of two-thirds of its territory and consigned 3.3 million Hungarians to Yugoslavia, Romania and Czechoslovakia. According to Sinor, Hungary was a 'mutilated, dismembered, disarmed country, surrounded by strong and hostile neighbours'.[78] The immediate priority was to emerge from isolation. The first major development was the 1927 Treaty of Friendship with Italy, and it seemed that Mussolini was the obvious ally for the future. Then, after 1933, Hitler emerged as a real alternative. The Horthy regime oscillated between distancing itself from Germany (because of its fear of German expansionism) and collaborating with Hitler in the hope of smashing the Trianon settlement. After much dithering, Prime Minister Imrédy settled for the latter course and, by the First Vienna Award (1938), Hungary benefited territorially from Hitler's destruction of Czechoslovakia.

At the same time, a succession of premiers thought that they could prevent Hungary from being sucked into Germany's European war. Teleki went so far as to refuse to German troops access via Hungary to Poland's southern frontier, and he even provided asylum for Polish refugees from Hitler's Blitzkrieg. But again irredentism or perhaps territorial greed prevailed. With German support, Hungary acquired, in the Second Vienna Award, some 17,000 square miles of Romania, together with 2.5 million people. Inevitably, Hitler expected in return a commitment from Hungary and this was fulfilled when, in 1941, Premier Bardossy provided Hungarian troops for the invasion of Yugoslavia and the Soviet Union. At first it seemed that Hungary would have no cause to regret her deeper involvement, for the Axis powers appeared invincible in 1941. By 1943, however, all illusions had been destroyed in the shattering defeat inflicted on the Hungarians by the Soviet army at Voronezh, to the north of Stalingrad. Horthy tried to extricate Hungary from the war by opening negotiations with the Allies. Hitler's response, in March 1944, was the occupation of Hungary and the enforcement of the full rigours of Nazi policies, including the deportation of Hungarian Jews to the extermination camps in Poland. Horthy, in desperation, signed an armistice with the Soviet Union in October 1944. He was immediately arrested by the Germans and confined to Dachau and Buchenwald. After the end of the war he found refuge in Portugal where he lived for the rest of his life. He escaped extradition and trial for 'war crimes' largely through Stalin's intervention: 'Leave him alone; after all, he did ask for an armistice.'[79]

Horthy was succeeded by one of the most fanatical regimes of the period – the Fascist dictatorship of Szálasi. Founder of a blatantly Nazi-style movement called the Arrow Cross, Szálasi formulated a programme of 'Hungarism' or the construction of a Greater Hungary which would cover the whole of the Danube Basin.[80] He was also committed to introducing a corporate state and to nationalizing industry and mechanizing agriculture. He achieved none of this. He lost control over his movement which plundered, pillaged, tortured and murdered over 10,000 people in the Budapest area alone before the arrival of the Russians put paid to their activities.

Szálasi eventually met the fate which Horthy escaped. He was put on trial in Hungary in 1946, condemned to death and executed. By 1945 Hungary had established, as in 1919, a coalition government dominated by communists. This time, however, the regime did not collapse, as it had behind it the full support of Soviet military power. The communists had also learned, from the failure of Béla Kun's 'dictatorship of the proletariat', the importance of patriotism and efficient organization as well as ideology. The other parties were steadily undermined and eliminated so that, by 1948, the Communist Party ruled alone. This remained the case until liberalization occurred in 1989.

Reasons for Hungary's instability

The most important catalyst behind this experience of so many different styles of dictatorship was the break-up of the traditional Hungarian state. Many Western politicians and intellectuals warned of the effects of depriving Hungary of so much territory by the Treaty of Trianon – and they were proved right. The overall impact was massive dislocation and a huge sense of collective grievance. This was the more unbearable since Hungary had achieved autonomy and nationhood by the Ausgleich of 1867. In accommodating the minority Slav populations, the powers reduced pre-war Hungary by almost two-thirds. Like Austria, Hungary became a 'dwarf state'. Unlike Austria, it had no large ethnic neighbour with which it could now identify: there was never any possibility of a Hungarian Anschluss.

All parts of the population were affected. The working classes faced the prospect of mass unemployment through the loss of key industries to Hungary's newly emergent or enlarged neighbours. This meant that they were susceptible to radicalization, initially by the communist left, later by the fascist right, especially by the Arrow Cross. The latter process was accelerated by the severe impact of the Great Depression on an economy which was already struggling to come to terms with its dislocation. The middle classes were doubly damaged. They were hit by the decline of industry and commerce and also by the impact on the machinery of government. The pre-1914 civil service in Budapest had been among the largest in Europe. Although it was no longer strictly necessary, every effort was made after 1919 to maintain it at its existing size. The result was that employment was bought at the cost of lower salaries and the creeping impoverishment of state employees. The upper levels of society faced a further crisis. They too resented the settlement which deprived many of them of their estates and reduced their landed wealth. But there was also a deep fear of the way in which the settlement threatened to radicalize the working and middle classes. There was therefore a powerful reason to pursue conservative policies in an attempt to preserve what was left of traditional Hungary; the extent of the threat meant that Horthy's conservatism merged with reaction and, as measures became more extreme under Gömbös, some of the methods associated with fascism began to appear. This explains the zigzag between moderate and radical governments in the 1930s.

The tragedy of Hungary was that it was impossible to pursue consistent political moderation. Even the intelligentsia suffered a sense of cultural alienation by a process which seemed to cut Hungary off from its past. A form of cultural irredentism helped make the Hungarian equivalent to German *völkisch* influences not only influential but respectable. These were adapted by extremists within Hungary's 101 far-right parties and eventually converted into the equivalent of German Lebensraum in the form of Szálasi's 'Hungarism'. Hungarian irredentism was diluted only by the savage experience of Nazi domination, war and post-war communist rule. Modern Hungary has resumed its democratic course within its restricted frontiers. It is, however, ironical that two of the three states given Hungarian territory in 1919 have since broken up.

Poland

The First World War proved to be the turning-point in modern Polish history. It smashed the three empires which held it captive (Russia, Germany and Austria-Hungary) and created a power vacuum which a new state in eastern Europe could fill. The core of independent Poland was the former province removed from Russia by the Treaty of Brest-Litovsk (1918). To this was added territory from Germany by the Treaty of Versailles (1919) and from Austria and Hungary by the Treaties of St Germain and Trianon (1919 and 1920). The Polish government, however, considered the eastern frontier to be too restrictive; hence, in 1919, Poland launched an attack on the Soviet Union and captured much of the Ukraine, including Kiev. The Soviet army soon recovered and drove the invaders back to Warsaw, which was subsequently besieged. Poland now appeared to be in dire peril but, with French assistance, managed to rout the Russians and reoccupy western Ukraine, possession of which was confirmed by the Treaty of Riga (1921). To this substantial slice of territory was added Vilna, seized from Lithuania, and parts of Upper Silesia. Overall, Poland, with an area of 150,000 square miles and a population of 27 million, was one of Europe's more important states.

Unfortunately, it was confronted by a series of desperate problems. The first was the mixed composition of its population. Poles comprised only two-thirds of the total; the rest included 4 million Ukrainians, 3 million Jews, 1 million Germans, 1 million Belorussians, and small numbers of Russians, Lithuanians and Tartars.[81] The second problem was political instability. The constitution proved inappropriate to the ethnic structure since it provided for a centralized rather than a federal state. In theory, Poland was an advanced democracy, with guarantees of individual freedoms. Unfortunately, proportional representation encouraged the growth of small parties and prevented the formation of stable governments; altogether, there were fifteen cabinets between November 1918 and May 1926, an average lifespan of only five months. The whole situation was aggravated by a major economic crisis in which inflation led to the Polish mark sinking to a level of 15 million to the dollar. This inevitably hindered the task of reconstruction, promoting shortages and unemployment. This unstable period came to a dramatic end when, in May 1926, General Piłsudski led several regiments of the Polish army into Warsaw. He replaced the democratic government with an authoritarian regime which lasted, beyond his own death in 1935, until the eventual liquidation of Poland in 1939.

Piłsudski was already something of a national hero. He had organized the Polish legions which had fought for the country's independence in the First World War. He had then become head of state between 1919 and 1922, leading the Polish offensive against Russia and organizing the defence of Warsaw in 1920. He had voluntarily stepped aside in 1922 into semi-retirement. Between 1922 and 1926, however, he watched with disgust the deteriorating political scene. At first he was not disposed to take drastic action because 'If I were to break the law I would be opening the door to all sorts of adventurers to make coups and putsches.'[82] Eventually, however, he became convinced that direct action was unavoidable. His solution was a call for national unity and a common moral sense, to be promoted by a grouping called Sanacja.

Piłsudski's achievements related mainly to the restoration of the Polish state after a century and a half of foreign rule. He strengthened the executive through his changes of 1926 and the constitution of 1935 (which he did not live to see), and made the administration more professional and efficient. He revived the morale of the army and, through a skilful foreign policy, strengthened Poland's standing in Europe. On the other hand, his regime witnessed serious financial and economic problems. The Great Depression had a particularly devastating effect on Polish agriculture and, as elsewhere, caused a sudden spurt in industrial unemployment. Piłsudski resorted to an unimaginative policy of financial constraints and drastic deflation. But this only aggravated the problem, and even by 1939 Poland's per capita output was 15 per cent below that of 1913. 'Thus,' observes Aldcroft, 'Poland had little to show economically for 20 years of independent statehood.'[83]

Piłsudski also showed serious flaws in his character. His rule became increasingly irksome as he himself became increasingly petty. Rothschild argues that Piłsudski's best years were behind him and that he had become 'prematurely cantankerous, embittered and rigid'.[84] Overall, it could be said, he completely lost the will to temper discipline and constraint with progressive reform; his emphasis on continuity therefore precluded any possibility of meaningful change. Piłsudski was one of the few dictators to die before the general upheaval of 1939–40. The authoritarian regime which he had established continued for the next four years, but it became less personal and more ideological. The reason for this was that, cantankerous though he had been, Piłsudski proved irreplaceable; the likes of Slawek, Rydz-Smigly and Beck lacked his popularity and charisma. Faced with ever growing pressure from the right, the Sanacja after Piłsudski was forced to collaborate with Poland's semi-fascist movements, since it lacked Piłsudski's confidence to defy them.[85] Whether Poland would eventually have become a fascist state is open to speculation, but it is interesting to note that its movement in that direction was due to the lack of leadership rather than to any personality cult. Polish 'fascism' therefore served to conceal mediocrity rather than to project personal power.

Piłsudski and his successors were faced with the problem of upholding the security of the new Polish state. This was given some urgency by the resentment of all her neighbours against Poland's territorial gains. At first Piłsudski sought safety in an alliance with France and Romania in 1921. Gradually, however, the will of France to assist Poland grew weaker. In 1925 France signed the Locarno Pact which, alongside Britain, Italy, Belgium and Germany, guaranteed the 1919 frontiers in western Europe but not in the east. By the early 1930s Piłsudski felt that he could no longer depend upon France and therefore sought accommodation with the powers which threatened Poland; he formed non-aggression pacts with Russia in 1932 and Germany in 1934. After Piłsudski's death, however, Poland slid towards destruction. There was a dreadful inevitability about the whole process: given Hitler's policy of Lebensraum and Stalin's determination to wipe out the memory of Brest-Litovsk, Poland did not stand a chance. According to Syrop, 'It is clear now that once Hitler and Stalin had jointly decided to wipe Poland off the map, no Polish policy and no power on earth could avert disaster.'[86]

Foreign Minister Beck showed courage in defying Hitler's demands for a Polish corridor and was bolstered by the Anglo-French guarantee of March 1939. He clearly felt that Poland stood a chance of holding off Germany, as Piłsudski had fended off Russia in 1920. This time, however, Poland was crushed by Hitler's Blitzkrieg. The Polish cavalry, which had triumphed over Soviet infantry, was now shot to pieces by German tanks and aircraft. By mid-September the western half of Poland had been conquered by the Nazi war machine. The Polish government transferred to the east, only to be trapped by Soviet troops who were moving into position to take up the territory agreed in the Nazi–Soviet Non-Aggression Pact. Poland was therefore at the mercy of her two historic enemies. Stalin proceeded to impose communist institutions in the east, while the German zone was divided in two. The north-west and Silesia were absorbed directly into the Third Reich and were immediately Germanized; Gauleiter Forster said that his intention was 'to remove every manifestation of Polonism within the next few years'.[87] The rest was placed under Governor-General Hans Frank, who stated that no Polish state would ever be revived. The German occupation of Poland was to prove more horrifying and destructive than that in any other conquered territory. Six million people died out of a total population of 35 million; many of these were Jews who perished in extermination camps set up at Auschwitz-Birkenau, Maidenek, Sobibor, Belzec and Treblinka. The Polish capital, Warsaw, was the only occupied city to be pulled apart, systematically, by ground demolition squads.

The devastation did not destroy the Polish national spirit and three resistance organizations had come into existence by mid-1941. The first was a government in exile under Sikorski which established an army abroad and integrated Polish servicemen into the American and British forces. The second was the underground Home Army (AK), the third the Polish Workers' Movement (PPR), a communist organization led by Gomułka. At first there was co-operation between Sikorski and the Soviet Union but, as the Soviet victory over Germany became increasingly likely, Stalin did everything possible to weaken Sikorski and the AK. His task was made easier by the Yalta and Potsdam conferences of 1945. The Western Allies were, of course, unhappy about Poland falling under Soviet influence, but they were unable to prevent it. Hence, when recreated, Poland eventually became one of Stalin's satellite states, with a regime which was far more systematically pervasive than Piłsudski's had ever been. It was not until 1989 that the monopoly of the Communist Party was broken.

The nature of the Polish right wing

Poland is rightly seen as the victim of the aggression of Europe's two leading dictatorships in 1939. At the same time, however, Poland had itself become a dictatorship and had spawned a number of far-right parties. In this respect it followed an experience similar to that of Austria and Portugal. As in these countries, a distinction needs to be made between a conservative authoritarian establishment and semi-fascist minority groups which wanted to radicalize the right.

Authoritarian dictatorship is normally associated with Piłsudski. His assumption of power in 1926 was a reaction to the political chaos of the mid-1920s. He was in no sense a radical. His aim was to reconcile, not to radicalize. According to Rothschild, the purpose of the Sanacja was to form a 'non-political phalanx of all classes and parties supposedly prepared to elevate general state interests above particular partisan and social ones'.[88] This new order would be kept together by Piłsudski himself. Ironically, he did not resume the presidency in 1926, serving, instead, in the humbler capacity of Foreign Minister with two brief spells as premier. Yet no one doubted that ultimate power lay in his hands: 'I am a strong man and I like to decide all matters by myself.'[89] To emphasize this point, he reduced the power of the legislature, arguing that 'The Chicanes of Parliament retard indispensable solutions.' He saw Western-style party political manoeuvres as highly destructive in Poland, since they had produced a parliament which was in reality a 'House of Prostitutes'. He therefore broke the back of the party system and surrounded himself with loyal followers. Yet his dictatorship was never complete; his aim was not to set up a totalitarian state and a new political consciousness, but rather to depoliticize Poland and to create unity through heightened moral awareness. His successors were somewhat less restrained than Piłsudski and, in the words of Payne, 'accentuated state control and authoritarianism'.[90] Between 1935 and 1939 the authoritarian regime was becoming more involved in regulating the economy and mobilizing popular support behind a new government organization, the Camp of National Unity, or OZN. This took on several outward appearances of proto-fascism.

Even so, the post-Piłsudski governments were less radical than most other non-fascist dictatorships in Europe. More open to far-right influences were the minority movements such as the National Democrat Party; strongest in western Poland, this was violently anti-Semitic, strongly nationalistic and sympathetic to both Fascist Italy and Nazi Germany, even though the latter was widely perceived as the national enemy. From this developed the even more extreme National Party (OWP) and Camp of National Radicalism (ONR). But the most explicitly fascist group was the Falanga, which was strongly influenced by the Spanish Falangist movement; it also had similarities to Codreanu's Legion and Iron Guard in Romania.

As elsewhere, the traditionalist authorities were not prepared to tolerate the excesses of these minority groups and at various stages during the 1930s resorted to banning them. Even though they stood no chance of coming to power they did, nevertheless, provide a core for that section of the Polish population which was prepared to collaborate with the Nazis, especially in implementing their anti-Semitic policies.

Estonia, Latvia and Lithuania

The Baltic enclaves Estonia, Latvia and Lithuania, originally provinces of Tsarist Russia, had been occupied by Germany in the First World War. Like Poland, they filled the power vacuum left by the defeat of both Germany and Russia. By 1920, the last foreign troops had been withdrawn and the newly independent republics could concentrate on internal consolidation.

In this they appeared to be assisted by liberal constitutions guaranteeing individual freedoms, rights for ethnic minorities, proportional representation and powerful parliaments. Unfortunately, in the Baltic republics, as elsewhere, these principles proved extremely difficult to operate. One of the main problems was the proliferation of parties competing for power; in 1925, for example, the Latvian parliament (Saeima) contained no fewer than twenty-six parties. The result was political instability, as Estonia saw seventeen governments in fourteen years, Latvia sixteen in the same period and Lithuania eleven in seven years. All this occurred at a time when political continuity was particularly important to tackle a wide range of economic and social problems, especially land reform and industrialization.

The first move to the right occurred in Lithuania in 1926. After a prolonged economic depression many prominent Lithuanians questioned the relevance of democratic institutions. The most important of these was Smetona, who seized power with the help of the military and established an authoritarian regime similar to that of Piłsudski in Poland. Democracy lasted somewhat longer in the other two states but was wrecked eventually by the Great Depression which caused a decline in exports, an increase in unemployment, and misery in the rural areas. In 1934 they followed Lithuania's example. Dictatorships were set up by Päts in Estonia and Ulmanis in Latvia.

The three regimes had much in common. All imposed the usual measures associated with dictatorship, including restrictions on political parties, the strengthening of presidential powers and dependence on the army. Smetona went further than either of his contemporaries, transforming Lithuania into a one-party state and developing the aura of a personality cult – he was known as Leader of the People (*Tautos Vadas*). But none of the regimes had an ideological base. Indeed, all were as suspicious of the extreme right as they were of the radical left. The fascist movements which developed in the Baltic states (the Thunder Cross of Latvia, the Estonian Freedom Fighters and the Lithuanian Iron Wolf) were regarded as a major danger, to be disciplined or even banned.

The three Baltic dictators have attracted far less condemnation than the others. Vardis argues that 'As dictatorships go . . . their rule was the mildest in Europe.'[91] The repressive measures were by no means complete and left considerable room for manoeuvre. The press, for example, was less constrained than elsewhere and was still able to convey left-wing views. There was no attempt to introduce a complete corporate system and private enterprise continued to flourish. The Baltic peoples recovered reasonably well from the worst impact of the depression and certainly enjoyed a higher standard of living than their contemporaries in the Soviet Union. By the late 1930s two of the three, Estonia and Latvia, showed signs of returning to a more obvious democratic base. Payne maintains that 'Both of these regimes exercised policies of very moderate authoritarianism and may well have had the support of the majority of the population.'[92] Yet, in 1939, the independence of all three Baltic republics was snuffed out, never to be rekindled. Two contrasting explanations have been provided for this.

One is that the three states were, like Poland, condemned by their geo-political position in Europe, strategically placed as they were between Germany and the Soviet Union. Dallin argues that their demise was as near as possible inevitable and that 'whatever these countries did or failed to do was ultimately immaterial'.[93] It could certainly be argued that the situation which brought the states into existence at the end of the First World War was unique and never to be repeated – the almost simultaneous collapse of major powers in the region. But it was hardly to be expected that this power vacuum would remain or that Russia would countenance the permanent loss of her Baltic territories. Hence, the fate of the republics was decided when the Nazi–Soviet Non-Aggression Pact of August 1939 allocated Estonia and Latvia to Stalin, and Lithuania to Hitler.

An alternative view is that the Baltic states did too little to help themselves. They failed to set up an effective security system or to co-operate sufficiently to mobilize the 500,000 men available. Any attempts which were made at alliance were unsatisfactory. A pact was drawn up in 1921 but Latvia and Estonia refused to admit Lithuania because they were afraid of being drawn into a border conflict between Lithuania and Poland. The 1934 Treaty of Friendship and Co-operation did include Lithuania but provided only for consultation on foreign policy and not on military planning. By 1939 there were three divergent approaches: Latvia wanted to remain strictly neutral, Estonia was primarily anti-Russian and Lithuania anti-German. Anderson has argued:

> It would be idle to pretend that the Baltic states were a factor of first importance in European affairs; nevertheless, placed as they were between Russia, Poland and Germany, if united, they could have played a respectable role in north-eastern Europe. Their fate during the months that followed, then, would probably have been somewhat different.[94]

Late in 1939 Estonia, Latvia and Lithuania had to sign pacts with the USSR allowing the Red Army to be stationed on their territory. Stalin systematically tightened his grip, assisted by Hitler's transfer of Lithuania to the Soviet sphere in exchange for an additional slice of Poland. In 1940 the area was brought under direct Soviet rule but proved extremely difficult to govern. Revolts occurred in all three states and the Baltic peoples had high hopes of independence when, in 1941, Germany attacked the Soviet Union. But Hitler's plans were even more unpleasant than Stalin's. All three states came under Rosenberg's Ministry for the Occupied Eastern Territories and experienced systematic terror and exterminations. The Nazi dictatorship ended in 1944 with the fall of Tallinn and Riga to the Red Army but the price was the reimposition of Stalinism and their transformation into Soviet Socialist Republics. The Baltic republics were, therefore, the only creations of the Brest-Litovsk and Paris settlements not to be revived at the end of the Second World War.

DICTATORSHIP IN THE BALKANS

Introduction

The one common link between all the Balkan peoples was their historic subjugation to the Turks; all of the states of south-eastern Europe were originally part of the Ottoman Empire. Greece became independent in 1830, followed by Serbia and Romania after the Crimean War, Bulgaria in 1878 and Albania in 1912. The First World War saw a division of loyalties. Bulgaria allied herself to Germany, Austria-Hungary and Turkey (known collectively as the Central powers). Serbia and Albania were invaded and occupied by the Central powers, while Romania and Greece opted to join the Allies. All but Bulgaria emerged from the peace settlement either intact or enlarged. It seemed that their futures were guaranteed and that they would benefit from liberal and progressive rule.

Appearances were, however, deceptive and this initial optimism was not fulfilled. The Balkan states faced massive economic, social and political problems which led inexorably to dictatorship.

The first failures occurred in the agricultural policies of the various governments. The immediate post-war priority was to redistribute land to the peasantry but, in every case, the reform programme was either incomplete or did not affect a high enough proportion of the population. There remained a large and discontented rural proletariat which placed intolerable pressure on the land and aggravated the problem of low productivity. The other half of the economy, industry, also experienced difficulties. The most serious were inadequate domestic sources of investment, which made most of the Balkan states prey to external influence; Albania, for example, came to depend too heavily on Italy, while Romania and Bulgaria found themselves ensnared by Germany.

Although it is hazardous to generalize about an area as complex as the Balkans, there does seem to have been an identifiable political trend. At first the Balkan states operated as democracies, with radical governments (like that of Stambuliski in Bulgaria) attempting radical reforms. There followed a drift to the right as the parliamentary system was undermined by bickering parties and a rapid sequence of weak governments. The eventual outcome was a series of authoritarian regimes. Albania was the first to succumb as Ahmed Zogu proclaimed himself President in 1924 and King Zog in 1928. Yugoslavia, too, came under a royal dictatorship, in the form of Alexander I, from 1929. Romania's equivalent was King Carol (1903–40) and Bulgaria was ruled with an iron hand by King Boris from 1935. Greece experienced a more ideologically based dictatorship under General Metaxas (1936–41).

All of these regimes found themselves caught up in hectic diplomacy and bitter rivalry. Before the First World War the Balkans had been the 'powder keg' of Europe, always threatening to transform a local crisis into a general conflagration between the major powers. After 1918 the area of greatest potential danger shifted to central Europe but the south-east remained unstable and volatile as some of the defeated states sought to reconstitute their former power. Bulgaria and Hungary, in particular, advanced revisionist claims against their neighbours. The latter, fully conscious of the resentment of Bulgaria and Hungary, sought security in two major multilateral agreements. The first was the Little Entente (1920–1) in which Romania, Yugoslavia and Czechoslovakia sought to isolate Hungary and to prevent the possibility of a Habsburg restoration. The second was the Balkan Pact of 1934, comprising Romania, Yugoslavia, Turkey and Greece and directed, among other objectives, towards the containment of Bulgaria. There was also a considerable amount of bilateral diplomacy between individual Balkan states. The overall result was that, by 1939, a precarious balance of power had been achieved in which uneasy détente had come to replace active confrontation. What happened was that this balance was destroyed by the involvement of the great powers, and the Balkan states were sucked one by one into the Second World War.

A final point is worth a mention. The politics of the right were particularly complex in the Balkans, especially the relationship between conservatism and fascism in the formation of dictatorships. Each state had a different experience. In Yugoslavia the conflict was regionalized: conservatism was centred on Serbia, while fascism became strongly established in Croatia as a radical opposition. Eventually there were to be two dictatorships. In Romania the conservative right and the fascist right clashed continuously. Although fascism was eventually eliminated as an organized movement, the conflict had pulled conservatism so far to the right that it even secured the approval of Hitler. In Bulgaria the conservative right remained in control throughout the 1930s and was hardly challenged by fascism. In Greece some have claimed that traditionalism and fascism came together in the person of Metaxas. All of these issues will be looked at further in the following sections.

Albania

The main developments in Albania between the wars were the internal dominance of Ahmed Zogu, later proclaimed King Zog, and the ever growing influence of Fascist Italy, resulting in 1939 in direct rule.

Albania established itself as an independent state in 1912, after the First Balkan War. Almost immediately it encountered external threats to its very existence. During the First World War, for example, it was occupied by no fewer than seven armies, while both Greece and Italy had expectations of Albanian territory as a

14 King Zog, 1895–1961, photo taken on 6 April 1939 (Popperfoto)

reward for having joined the Allies. Their claims to territory so delayed international consideration of the future of this tiny state that the Albanians impatiently took matters into their own hands. Setting up a Regency Council and a Committee of National Defence, they managed to evict an Italian occupation force of 20,000 men. By 1920 Albania was a fully independent state and a member of the League of Nations. Indeed, a report commissioned by the League was full of optimism about Albania's future: 'It seems clear that the essential elements of a prosperous Albania exist' and that 'it possesses all the conditions necessary for the formation of a politically and economically independent state.'[95]

Unfortunately Albania was to suffer from serious instability which led to political chaos and dictatorship. The problem was partly socio-economic: inadequate development and the long-standing conflict in the south between the Muslim landowning aristocracy and the Christian agricultural workers. It was also political. Albania was torn by the rivalry between Bishop Noli and Ahmed Zogu, the former much influenced by Western ideas, the latter entirely indigenous. At first they served in the same government but, in 1922, Noli withdrew to form an opposition. In 1924 Zogu did badly in an election and considered his position so perilous that he fled to neighbouring Yugoslavia. Noli, who now replaced him, attempted to introduce a series of reforms but his government lacked internal unity and effective leadership. In 1924, therefore, Zogu was able to make a sudden comeback. Invading Albania with his followers, a thousand Yugoslav volunteers and forty officers of the White Russian army, he overthrew Noli and had himself proclaimed President. He took immediate action to consolidate his power and, in 1928, elevated his title to 'Zog I, King of the Albanians'. He was backed by a new constitution which remained in existence until 1939.

There is little disagreement about the nature of Zog's rule. Pollo and Puto argue that 'Zogu's return meant the establishment of a totally reactionary dictatorship in Albania.' It is true that order was restored, but 'it was the worst possible kind of stability'.[96] Logoreci maintains that the monarchy was 'a pitiful incongruity' which made Albania 'the laughing stock of Europe'.[97] Stavrianos, too, believes that any reforms attempted were only 'skin deep'.[98] Zog did make a superficial effort to retain the parliamentary system but, at the same time, rigged elections, eliminated opponents and even hired assassins to deal with prominent Albanians in exile. He was determined, in his own words, to 'establish exemplary order and discipline throughout the country'.[99]

Much, of course, would depend on economic stability. This, in turn, provided a link between domestic and foreign policy. Zog identified Albania's main need as foreign aid, and Italy as the most likely source. He therefore signed a series of agreements with Mussolini. The first, in 1925, allowed the Italians to finance a new National Bank and a Company for the Economic Development of Albania. In return, Mussolini expected to be given increased control over Albania's military security and foreign affairs. Zog went further down this perilous road in the 1926 Treaty of 'Friendship and Security' and the 1927 defensive military alliance. By 1933 he was uncomfortably aware of Albania's dependence on Italy and openly defied the Italian dictator by refusing his demands for a customs union. Mussolini, however, won his point because, by 1935, Albania was in urgent need of further Italian loans to wipe out the large budgetary deficit which had accumulated during this brief period of conflict. The process of Italian colonization was well advanced by 1939. It remained only to transform this into direct political control. Feeling the need to keep up with the hectic pace of Hitler's foreign adventures, Mussolini invaded Albania on 7 April 1939 and overthrew the Zog regime. Albania came under the direct rule of Victor Emmanuel III, and the diplomatic corps and army were united with those of Italy. This arrangement continued until the surrender of Italy in September 1943. From this date Germany was the occupying power, a transition which marked an increase in the number of savage atrocities.

The Albanians are, historically, the most fiercely independent of the Balkan peoples. A powerful resistance movement developed in 1941, with the assistance of Yugoslavia, and based on Hoxha's Albanian Communist Party. The military arm was the National Liberation Front (NLC), which co-ordinated a series of successful guerrilla attacks against German units and increased its own numbers by the end of 1944 to about 70,000. Hoxha aimed for a social revolution to be accomplished alongside the eviction of the Germans and his new government was dominated from the start by the Communists. He remained in firm control until his death in 1984, establishing in the process the sort of personality cult which had completely eluded Zog. Unfortunately, his rigid brand of communism also delayed the prospect of economic modernization and political democracy.

Bulgaria

Bulgaria was the only Balkan state to have allied itself during the First World War to the Central powers. As one of the defeated combatants, Bulgaria was treated severely by the Allies, losing Western Thrace to Greece, the Dobruja to Romania and several key frontier areas to Yugoslavia. The Treaty of Neuilly (1919) also ended military conscription, reduced Bulgaria's army to 33,000 and imposed an indemnity of 450 million dollars, payable over thirty-eight years. Bulgaria's leaders, therefore, faced considerable problems in adjusting to the country's loss of territory, prestige and status; this was reflected in the wide variety of regimes experienced between the wars. Bulgaria's first government, under Stambuliski, was radical and reformist. After this had been overthrown in 1923, Bulgaria reverted to a more traditional style of politics. This, however, proved so chaotic that another coup, this time in 1934, set up a right-wing regime which was gradually converted by King Boris into a royal dictatorship. After a period of German influence, Bulgaria emerged from the Second World War with all the components of a pro-Moscow communist system.

Between 1919 and 1923 Bulgaria was led by Stambuliski, son of a peasant and a former schoolteacher. He intended to transform Bulgaria into 'a model agricultural state'[100] by means of a programme which redistributed land to benefit the poorer peasantry; by 1926 about 80 per cent of the rural masses owned plots. Stambuliski's popularity was apparent in the 1923 elections, in which his Agrarian Party won 212 of the 245 seats in the legislature. But this could not guarantee the survival of his government. He was confronted by numerous enemies which included liberals, the army (which was concerned about his leftist leanings) and a terrorist group called the Internal Macedonian Revolutionary Organization (IMRO). In June 1923 Stambuliski was ousted by a military coup. He was handed over to the IMRO, at whose hands he met a horrifying end: he was tortured, mutilated and finally shot.

15 King Boris of Bulgaria, r. 1918–43 (Popperfoto)

He was succeeded by a series of short-lived coalitions led by nonentities. Between 1923 and 1934 the incidence of violence rapidly increased as the IMRO intensified its activities. Relations with neighbouring states also caused concern; in October 1925, for example, the Greeks invaded Bulgaria to settle a frontier dispute and left only when confronted by a rare show of collective unity in the League of Nations. In 1934 Bulgaria's vulnerability increased as a result of the formation, among her neighbours, of the Balkan Entente. Meanwhile, of course, the economy had been shattered by the impact of the Great Depression. The whole unstable edifice was eventually brought down on 19 May 1934 by a coup conducted by Colonel Velchev.

At first the new regime was faceless; Stavrianos has called it 'dictatorial but not fascist'.[101] It did not have the ideological base of fascism, and Premier Georgiev had little upon which to construct a personality cult. Waiting in the wings, however, was a more ruthless and dynamic figure. King Boris intended to take control of the new regime when the opportunity presented itself. According to Ristelhueber, he showed 'a combination of flexibility and subtlety'.[102] In 1935 he issued a manifesto which announced major changes. There would, he insisted, be 'no going back' to the unstable era of party politics; hence, all political parties were banned. In 1937 he drew up a new constitution which guaranteed the place of a legislature in the Bulgarian system but placed tight conditions on the purpose and conduct of elections. It was possible, for example, to elect only candidates who had no party attachment and voting was made into something of an ordeal as a result of heavy police surveillance. In defence of Boris, it has been argued that he did much to reduce the level of political extremism and terrorist violence. For example, he banned fascist movements such as the Home Defence, the National League of Fascists, the Ratnitsi, or Warriors, and the Bulgarian National Legions. On the other hand, Bulgaria became, in effect, a police state in which terror now came from above. Boris also sought to pull Bulgaria out of the grips of the depression. But the cost was almost total dependence on Nazi Germany which was by 1939 taking 68 per cent of all Bulgaria's exports and providing 66 per cent of her imports. This, in turn, pulled Bulgaria directly into the Axis's political and diplomatic orbit.

Like most other states in eastern Europe and the Balkans, Bulgaria sought at first not to become involved in Hitler's war. Then, in 1941, Boris allowed the Germans to use his country as a base for operations against Greece and Yugoslavia, in return for territory to be extracted from these two victims. By 1943, however, Boris's commitment to the Axis cause was being questioned and he died in suspicious circumstances in August 1943 after an interview with Hitler. His place was taken by Prince Cyril who acted as regent for the six-year-old king, Simeon. Cyril strengthened the links with Germany, effectively transforming Bulgaria from an autonomous dictatorship into a puppet regime under full Nazi control. This was eventually disposed of in 1944 as a result partly of internal resistance from the Fatherland Front under the leadership of Dimitrov and partly of the Russian invasion. By 1946 it had become clear that Bulgaria would be a communist state with close links with the Soviet Union. It was not until 1989 that this was liberalized sufficiently to allow for opposition groups.

Yugoslavia

Yugoslavia was one of the most heterogeneous of the smaller states of Europe. Its original core was the pre-war kingdom of Serbia, to which was added a significant number of territories in 1918. These included provinces of the former Austro-Hungarian monarchy, like Croatia, Slavonia, Dalmatia, Carniola, Styria, Carinthia, Istria, Baranja, Backa, the Banat, Prekomurje, Medjurmurje and Bosnia-Herzegovina. Small but important frontier areas were received by the Treaty of Neuilly from Bulgaria and, finally, the previously independent state of Montenegro was added in the south. The result of these gains was a considerable ethnic mix. The new nation had a total of twelve linguistic groups, of which three were predominant. These were the Serbs, Croats and Slovenes which, between them, accounted for 10 million out of the total population of 12 million.[103] The generous boundary changes meant that there were also significant numbers of Germans, Magyars, Albanians and Turks.

This conglomerate was at first called the 'Kingdom of the Serbs, Croats and Slovenes'. It adopted a new constitution in 1921 which provided for a parliamentary monarchy under King Alexander, recognized the existence of political parties and based the electoral system on proportional representation. This constitution could not, however, provide a guarantee of permanent stability. The country faced two sets of serious problems, economic and political. Serbia had been devastated during the First World War and had experienced, proportionately, one of the heaviest population losses in Europe. Post-war recovery was made extremely difficult by the impoverishment of the peasantry, and the persistent threat of economic instability served only to destabilize the political scene. This, in any case, was threatening enough. The main problem was the mutual distrust, often hatred, between the Serbs and Croats. The former were Orthodox in religion and socially conservative; the latter tended to be Catholic and more open to progressive Western influences. The main area of conflict between them was the type of regime to be established. The Serbs wanted a centralized state (in effect a Greater Serbia), which they won in the 1921 constitution. The Croats, by contrast, aimed at a decentralized federation and did everything possible to undermine the predominantly Serb governments of the 1920s. A major crisis occurred in 1928 when the Croatian leader, Radich, was assassinated in the parliament, the Skupshtina.[104] In the riots that followed there were open demands for an end to the power of Serbia and for the creation of a 'free Croatia'.

At this point King Alexander seized the initiative and imposed the sort of royal dictatorship which was to set the pattern for other Balkan states. He moved rapidly to close the parliament and abolish the 1921 constitution. He was motivated by an impatience with party bickering, which he found repugnant; he had, in any case, developed a profound suspicion of Western democratic systems from his earlier contacts with the court of Imperial Russia. According to Dedijer, he was 'autocratic by temperament'[105] and unable to share power: he frequently screamed at his ministers. He saw himself as the saviour of his state, which he decided to rename Yugoslavia. In his proclamation of 6 January 1929 he observed, 'I am sure that all, Serbs, Croats and Slovenes, will loyally support my efforts, whose sole aim will be to establish as rapidly as possible such administration and organization of the state as will best conform with the general needs of the people and the interests of the state.'[106] To accomplish this he scrapped the old local government boundaries and set up nine new units, or *banovine*, which were superimposed across the old ethnic areas. He failed, however, to draw the sting of the problem. In 1931 the numerous Croatian exiles appealed to the League of Nations, making allegations that Alexander had imposed a reign of terror in Croatia and was making systematic use of brutality and torture.

In fact, Alexander tried to modify his rule by granting in 1931 a new constitution which officially ended the period of dictatorship. Two views have been put forward to explain his action. One is that this was a phased return to normality after a period of tough discipline. An alternative view is that the new concessions were 'merely a fig leaf for the royal dictatorship, which continued as before'.[107] Several points seem to support the second argument. The 1931 constitution greatly reduced the power of the parliament, maintained the structure of the police state, introduced an Italian-style electoral system, and abolished the secret ballot. Far from leading Yugoslavia back to democracy, Alexander only narrowed the base of his regime. In the process, he alienated not only the Croats but a large number of the more progressive Serbs. At the same time, he faced a growing economic crisis which included a trade deficit, a collapse of agricultural prices and the end of foreign investments and credits. The picture looked bleak indeed when, in October 1934, Alexander was assassinated, while on a visit to Marseilles, by a Macedonian terrorist.

He was succeeded by his son Peter, who, at eleven, was too young to rule. The regent was Prince Paul, who, according to Stavrianos, was 'ill suited for his task, being a dilettante and more interested in his art collection'.[108] Paul delegated most of his powers to his Prime Minister, Milan Stoyadinovich, who inclined towards fascism and built up a mass movement of green-shirted youths. Stoyadinovich also projected himself as the *Vojda*, or leader, but failed the ultimate test of maintaining law and order. The threat from Croatia grew increasingly serious until, in 1939, Stoyadinovich was replaced by Tsvetkovich, who had a more moderate and less repressive answer to Croatian separatism. On 26 August 1939, Croatia was given full autonomy and her own assembly, within, of course, a Yugoslav federation.

Among the reasons for this concession were developments elsewhere in Europe. Hitler, for example, had shown the utmost ruthlessness in Czechoslovakia, turning the Slovaks against the Czechs and promoting internal dissolution to make possible external invasion and German occupation. The Yugoslav government wanted to avoid the same thing happening between Croatia and Serbia. The solution seemed to be to remove the sort of irritants which had encouraged the Slovaks to connive at the destruction of their partnership with the Czechs. To make doubly sure that the Czech experience would not be repeated, Yugoslavia maintained and intensified her already close relations with the Axis powers. This process had been under way since the early 1930s and had involved a shift of original policy. During the 1920s Yugoslavia had depended on French support to offset the threat of Italy over the Fiume issue. Then, during the last year of his life, King Alexander had taken the initiative of moving closer to Germany. During the regency of Paul, Yugoslavia became increasingly dependent on German economic aid, as was shown by the trade agreements of 1934 and 1936. By 1939 Yugoslavia seemed a willing enough client state to Germany, although extremely wary of Hitler's habit of exploiting the resentment of ethnic minorities. It seemed, therefore, that the safest course of action was to keep close links with Germany, somehow satisfy the Croats, and sit tight.

By 1941 Paul had become sufficiently confident to follow a more active policy. He was now convinced that the Axis powers would win the war and that the best guarantee of Yugoslavia's external security would be to join the Tripartite Pact between Germany, Italy and Japan. This, however, had drastic consequences. Paul's regime was overthrown in a wave of anti-Axis feeling, intensified by fears that Yugoslavia was about to be forced into war on the orders of Hitler. In fact, the immediate threat now came from Italy. Mussolini used the internal chaos in Yugoslavia as an opportunity to launch an invasion from Albania, which Italy had already occupied in 1939. Mussolini had always expressed the most profound contempt for Yugoslavia, regarding this new country as an 'artificial contrivance of Versailles'.[109] The Italian offensive, however, was not entirely successful, and needed German assistance. Eventually the Yugoslav state was dismembered (see Map 7). Slovenia in the north was partitioned between Germany and Italy, the southern provinces were added to Bulgaria and Italian Albania, Serbia passed under German administration, and Croatia became a pro-Nazi puppet regime under its own *führer* (*poglavnik*) – Pavelić. The collapse of Yugoslavia was accompanied by serious disorder and appalling massacres as old ethnic scores were settled. No other state in Europe must have appeared so unlikely ever to be resurrected in the future.

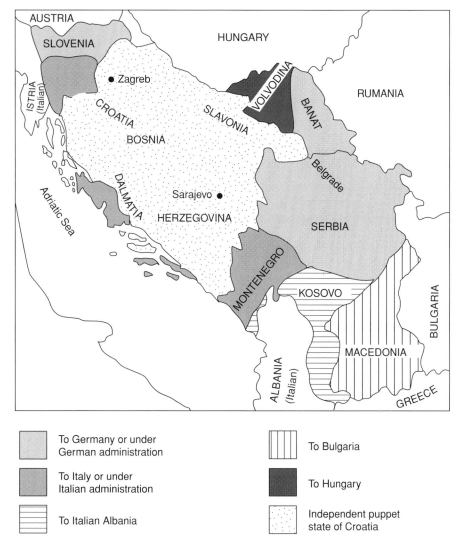

Map 7 The dismemberment of Yugoslavia 1941

To Germany or under
German administration

To Italy or under
Italian administration

To Italian Albania

To Bulgaria

To Hungary

Independent puppet
state of Croatia

Yet Yugoslavia became the centre of the most effective partisan activity in Europe. According to Dedijer, this was the 'first massive uprising in Hitler's "Fortress of Europe", one of the high points in the history of struggle against tyranny'.[110] The two main branches of resistance were the right-wing and predominantly Serbian-based Chetniks, under Mihailovich, and the communist partisans under Josip Broz, better known as Tito – himself a Croatian. Of the two resistance movements, Tito's partisans were the more successful. Tito followed a non-doctrinaire strategy and tried to attract as wide a range of support as possible. He employed highly effective hit-and-run tactics and made maximum use of Yugoslavia's mountainous terrain. He devised a political programme which was likely to appeal to all parts of Yugoslavia, with emphasis on federalism and self-determination. The partisans were, it is true, helped by Hitler's constant need to drain off German troops from Yugoslavia to fight on the Russian front; they also received direct aid from the Red Army in 1944 and 1945. But it is usually acknowledged that the prime credit for the liberation of Yugoslavia should go to the partisans. Yugoslavia was, in effect, one of the very few occupied states to free itself.

This was of enormous importance in Yugoslavia's post-war history. Tito carried out his promises, by introducing a federal structure, but also determined that Yugoslavia should never again fall under the influence of a great power. His independent line resulted in Yugoslavia being excluded from the Soviet orbit in 1949 and Yugoslavia eventually emerged as one of Europe's very few neutral states and as a key member of the world's 'non-aligned movement'.

Conservatism and fascism in Yugoslavia

We have seen that dictatorship emerged in two main forms in Yugoslavia. One was the conservative type which sought to maintain the new status quo, mainly in favour of Serbia. The other was the radical style which sought separate national fulfilment – this took the form of proto-fascism in Croatia.

Before the First World War, Serbia had been an expansionist state, gaining territory as a result of the Balkan Wars of 1912 and 1913. The peace settlement, however, fulfilled any remaining irredentism and gave Serbia the task of coming to terms with all the other ethnic groups attached to it in the new state of Yugoslavia. This automatically led to the search for a new balance. The monarchy, itself Serbian, was therefore anxious to avoid radicalism. This meant that the dictatorships of Alexander and Paul were essentially conservative – similar in some respects to that of Boris of Bulgaria. There were more radical elements in Serbia, such as the Zbor under Ljotic, but the authorities were always wary of them because of their potential for disruption.

The real manifestation of the radical right occurred in the province which deeply resented its close association with Serbia. Croatian nationalism came to be connected with the far right because it was radicalized by its hatred of Serbian traditionalism. Pavelić's Ustashi aimed at nothing less than the complete independence of Croatia with expanded frontiers to include Croatia, Dalmatia and Bosnia. The Ustashi were also racial and *völkisch* in their ideas: they were deeply anti-Semitic and exclusive, claiming that the Croats were 'Western' and 'Gothic' not 'Eastern' and 'Slavic'.[111] They were also one of the most violent of all the terrorist movements, organizing assassinations and sabotage during the 1930s. They even set a modern precedent in collaborating with a foreign organization, the IMRO, to assassinate the head of state in 1934.

All of these influences were crucial to the pattern of Pavelic's dictatorship in the puppet state of Croatia set up in 1940. The Ustashi became a radical mass movement, recruiting especially from the urban population. Croatia was, of course, a one-party state under the leadership of the *poglavnik*, who adopted all the paraphernalia of fascism. Above all, it used terror on a massive scale to convert, expel or exterminate the various minorities in Croatia, especially Serbs and Jews. Of all the regimes outside Germany and Italy, Ustashi Croatia was probably the most genuinely fascist. It was also the most ruthless and arguably the most totalitarian. In both the Serbian and Croatian cases, however, the developments were strongly influenced by external ideologies and methods, adopted as a means to achieve frustrated internal ethnic aspirations.

Romania

Romania entered the First World War in August 1916 and was rapidly defeated by Austria-Hungary, but, on the latter's collapse, ended up as one of the main beneficiaries of the peace settlement. By the Treaty of Trianon Romania received 31.5 per cent of the area of the former kingdom of Hungary and emerged as the largest of the Balkan states.[112]

The political scene, however, was to prove extremely unstable. The first stage was a coalition government between the Nationalist Party of Transylvania and the Peasant Party of Wallachia, under the leadership of Vaida. This was committed to a policy of economic and social reform. It failed, however, to gain the approval of King Ferdinand, who dismissed the entire government in a royal coup in 1920, substituting a more authoritarian regime under Averescu. This, in turn, was replaced in 1922 by a liberal government under Bratianu, which had some major achievements to its credit; a new constitution was drawn up in 1923, based on Western democratic principles. Unfortunately, the reforming impetus broke down and, in 1928, the government was resoundingly defeated by the main opposition, the National Peasants. The new Prime Minister, Maniu, hoped to revive a policy of social and economic reform. This time, however, good intentions were destroyed by the impact of the depression and the emergence of another royal dictator.

Ferdinand died in 1927, leaving the succession open. The main claimant was Carol who had, however, been excluded from the throne earlier because of widespread disapproval of his sexual activities. The National Peasant government now pursued an ultimately fatal policy. Hoping to win Carol's permanent support and wanting to demonstrate that it was not morally prudish, it assisted Carol's return to Bucharest. Soon after his coronation, however, Carol dismissed Maniu and his cabinet. He was convinced that the only solution to Romania's political and economic problems was a regime based on 'dynastic authoritarianism'.[113] He expressed strong reservations about parliamentary systems and openly admired Mussolini's regime. He therefore proceeded to install a series of puppet governments and, in 1938, abolished the 1923 constitution, introducing, instead, an imitation of Mussolini's corporate state. He also replaced the traditional party structure with his own 'Front of National Rebirth'.

Meanwhile, Romania had seen the emergence of an indigenous fascist movement. This originated, in 1927, with the formation by Codreanu of the League, or Legion, of the Archangel Michael. In 1930 it developed a paramilitary organization known as the Iron Guard. The 'Guardists' were violently anti-Semitic and typically fascist in offering a 'third way' between middle-class capitalism and communism. Codreanu also stressed the importance of mass enthusiasm. Describing a campaign in 1930 he said, 'We looked like crusaders. And crusaders we wanted to be, knights who in the name of the cross were fighting the godless Jewish powers to liberate Romania.'[114] At first King Carol was prepared to ally himself with the fascist right and even to make use of its mass base. Soon, however, he found it an encumbrance and a threat to internal security. In 1938, therefore, he took the drastic step of banning the Iron Guard, along with Romania's political parties. Codreanu was prosecuted for treason and sentenced to serve ten years in prison. There, along with other imprisoned Legionaries, he was strangled by the guards. The whole episode provides an example of the bitter distrust between the reactionary right, in the form of royal absolutism, and the radical right, in the form of fascism.

Subsequent events were even more tortuous. King Carol had to abdicate in 1940, in utter humiliation. The immediate reason was that Romania was forced to give up territory to three aggressive neighbours: Bessarabia and Northern Bukovina to Russia, Northern Transylvania to Hungary, and Southern Dobrudja to Bulgaria. Carol was succeeded by Michael, who tried to prevent the complete disintegration of Romania by entrusting power to a military dictatorship under General Antonescu. At first Antonescu was prepared to collaborate with the revived Iron Guard, now under Sima. Indeed, he went so far as to proclaim a National Legionary State with himself as Leader, or *Conducator*. Before long, however, the Iron Guard once again became troublesome, seeking total power and a more extreme regime. Antonescu therefore purged the Guard, dismissed Sima and destroyed, once and for all, the influence of homegrown fascism in Romania.

At the same time, Antonescu strengthened links with Germany. Romania played a significant part in the invasion of Russia and was largely responsible for the conquest of the Crimea. Then, at Stalingrad, the Romanian army was shattered, and with it

16 Ion Antonescu, 1882–1946 (Popperfoto)

Antonescu's reputation. By 1944 Romania was under threat of Soviet attack. Michael tried at the last minute to win the support of the Western Allies by sacking Antonescu and installing, in turn, Generals Senatescu and Radescu. In the process, he deliberately distanced Romania from Germany, thereby reversing Antonescu's policy.

Michael's initiative was doomed. The Western Allies had already secretly consigned Romania to the Soviet sphere of influence, in return for a Soviet guarantee of the security of influence, in return for a Soviet guarantee of the security of Greece. Under Soviet influence a new National Democratic Front was established, coming increasingly under the control of the Communists. The previous leaders were dealt with one by one: Antonescu, for example, was tried and executed as a war criminal in 1946, and Michael was forced to abdicate in 1947. Finally, in 1948, a new constitution was drawn up, based on that of the USSR. The country remained under a neo-Stalinist regime until the overthrow of Nicolae Ceaușescu in December 1989.

The Romanian right wing

The right wing in Romanian politics was especially complex, giving rise to three conservative dictatorships – under Ferdinand, Carol and Antonescu – and a number of fascist movements, the most prominent of which was the Iron Guard.

The reason for this complexity lies in a combination of continuity with the period before 1914 and the transformation of Romania in 1919. There had already been social dislocation in the form of a massive peasant rebellion in 1907, along with ethnic disturbances and outbreaks of anti-Semitism. These had been sufficient to incite the sort of conservative reaction which was common throughout the Balkans. But, more than anywhere else in the area except Yugoslavia, it was the impact of the First World War which helped shape the form of Romania's subsequent politics and dictatorship.

These changes have been described by Livezeanu as a 'national revolution' in which conservative responses became more extreme. Hence, 'the postwar "status quo" represented a profoundly revolutionized state of affairs, "conservation" of which demanded more than traditional conservative measures'.[115] There were bound to be problems in converting the old state of 138,000 square kilometres and 7.8 million people into a new nation of 295,000 square kilometres and 14.7 million people, especially since the additions tended to dilute the ethnic predominance of the Romanians themselves. This made it extremely difficult to practise progressive parliamentary politics, which made it very likely that there would be a right-wing reaction. This, in turn, was influenced by the far right, which fed off the social discord resulting from Romania's enlargement. It was all part of a vicious circle.

The reactionary right and the radical right had a stormy relationship, with the regimes of Carol, Michael and Antonescu alternating between tolerating and banning the Legion and Iron Guard. But the cumulative influence of the Legion had a ratchet effect on the official regime, forcing it to institute increasingly ruthless forms of dictatorship. They were, however, distinctively different. Fascism, especially in the form of the Legion and Iron Guard, was visionary in its extremism, whereas the conservative regimes were largely pragmatic, using ideas when it suited them but preferring not to be permanently committed to them.

During the 1930s Romanian fascism was highly complex: it consisted of several movements and layers which varied in intensity from proto-fascism to the genuine article. By far the most important, however, was the Legion and Iron Guard, Codreanu providing the sort of charismatic leadership which was more commonly associated with Hitler and Mussolini. His ideas also had much in common with Nazism. He emphasized eternal struggle, constant war against the enemies of the *Tara*, or Fatherland. The Romanians were biologically distinct from other ethnic groups and therefore superior to minorities such as Hungarians and Jews. The latter were a particular target and members of the Legion were already sympathetic to the idea of their extermination during the 1930s. From 1937 Codreanu also spoke increasingly of the expansion of Romania into the south-western part of the Ukraine ('Transnistria') and for the establishment of a Danubian–Carpathian Federation under Romanian rule.

Most of this cut little ice with those in power: the monarchy, the army officers and traditionalist politicians. They were less concerned about mobilization of opinion than about the accumulation of power and about dealing with opponents; increasingly, Codreanu came to be seen as a dangerous radical who would destabilize the regime. Although some observers claim that Carol was a 'monarcho-fascist', this term is not particularly appropriate. Carol was never inclined to any systematic ideology and remained traditional and conservative in his policies. This also applied to Michael and the *Conducator*, Antonescu. Yet, when the latter did finally succeed in destroying the Legion, he ruled, in Payne's words as 'a right radical nationalist dictator with the support of the military'.[116]

Strangely, this was preferred by Hitler since Antonescu offered more security as a Romanian satellite. This was understandable because Hitler's main concern in 1941 was the military use of Romania rather than its complete ideological conversion. Hence, a conservative regime which had been radicalized by its contact with fascism was an ideal balance. In any case this radicalized conservatism proved to be one of the most extreme of all the European states in its policies towards the Jews.

Greece

Greece was the oldest of the Balkan states, winning her independence from the Ottoman Empire in 1830. Her territory had been greatly extended by the Treaty of Sèvres (1920), by which she received from Turkey Eastern Thrace, many of the Aegean islands and the administration of Smyrna. From Bulgaria she gained Western Thrace (see Map 8). Yet, despite being one of the victors in the First World War, Greece deteriorated into prolonged chaos during the 1920s and 1930s, eventually succumbing to the dictatorship of Metaxas.

Her problems were both external and internal. The external crisis was the more immediate and urgent. The Greek government found its territorial gains from Turkey difficult to digest. In 1920 the Ottoman Sultan was overthrown and a dynamic leader, Mustapha Kemal, set up a new Turkish republic in Ankara. Kemal's main objective was to destroy the Treaty of Sevres and, in particular, to drive the Greeks out of Turkish territory. The Greek government found itself isolated diplomatically from its former allies, and fought a disastrous war in Turkey. The Greek army was

Greece before 1918

Ceded by Bulgaria; Greek possession confirmed by Treaty of
Neuilly 1919

Ceded by Turkey by Treaty of Sèvres 1920; restored to Turkey by
Treaty of Lausanne 1923

Map 8 Greece after the First World War

badly equipped and had severe problems of communication. By 1922 the Greeks
were defeated and, by the Treaty of Lausanne (1923), were obliged to give up
Eastern Thrace. The whole episode was a triumph for rejuvenated Turkish nationalism over Greek pretensions to imperialism.

Foreign problems acted as a catalyst for internal political instability as Greece
experienced numerous changes of regime between 1920 and 1935. At first the
conflict was between a discredited monarchy and the republicans, but the abdication of King Constantine in 1922 did little to guarantee peace as his successor,

George II, also had to renounce the throne. Party politics in the new republic, formed in 1924, became so chaotic and boisterous that the military decided to intervene, with General Pangalos imposing a brief dictatorship in 1926. Democracy had a second chance when Venizelos was elected to power in 1928, but the parliamentary system was destabilized by the disastrous impact of the depression on the Greek economy, especially on shipping and tourism. Greece reverted in the early 1930s to a series of short and unstable regimes, punctuated by attempted coups and counter-coups. This sorry state of affairs continued until 1935 when General Kondyles forced the Greek parliament to abolish the republic. He then arranged a plebiscite which produced a suspiciously large majority in favour of the return of the monarchy – in the person of George II. The new king dispensed with the services of Kondyles but, in 1936, appointed an even more authoritarian premier in the form of General Metaxas, who dominated Greece for the next four years. The type of regime established by Metaxas has been the subject of historical debate, which is examined in the next section.

Metaxas tried to maintain an independent foreign policy and to avoid becoming a mere puppet of the Axis powers. He was initially more suspicious of Italy than of Germany, largely because of Mussolini's aggressive designs on Corfu (see Chapter 3). Then, in 1939, he came to the conclusion that Germany, too, needed watching: Hitler's designs on Czech and Polish territory caused a wave of apprehension even in states which sympathized ideologically with Nazism. Hence, shortly after the Italian invasion of Albania, the Greek government, along with Romania,

17 General Ioannis Metaxas, 1871–1941 (Popperfoto)

accepted an Anglo-French guarantee of security of the kind which had already been extended to Poland. The hollowness of this promise was, however, demonstrated in September 1939, when nothing could be done to prevent the German invasion of Poland. Metaxas decided that his only course of action was to keep Greece neutral no matter what happened elsewhere in Europe.

But this was to prove impossible. In October 1940 Mussolini issued an ultimatum to Metaxas demanding Italian military bases on Greek territory. When Metaxas refused, Mussolini launched a full-scale invasion. At first, Metaxas showed effective leadership and organized a successful military counter-offensive. He emphasized that Greece 'has a debt to herself to remain worthy of her history'.[117] The Italians encountered a series of defeats, the worst at Metsovo. By the end of 1940 Greece had succeeded in liberating itself. The worst, however, was yet to come, although Metaxas did not live to see it. In spring 1941 Hitler launched a German onslaught to rescue Mussolini from total humiliation. Despite help from British troops, the Greek mainland and islands were rapidly conquered. The country was partitioned between Germany, Italy, Albania and Bulgaria, and ruled by puppet regimes led by Tsolakoglou, Lotothetopoulos and Rhalles. Like Metaxas, these men were ideologically sympathetic to Nazism. Unlike Metaxas, however, they lacked the Hellenic drive which placed Greek nationalism above all other considerations.

They also failed to gain from the Greek people the sort of collaboration received from the puppet regimes of Hungary, Croatia, Romania and Bulgaria. Part of the reason was that the Greek population suffered more severely than almost any other: 7 per cent of all Greeks died under German occupation and 30 per cent of the national wealth was removed. Greeks, it has been argued, were driven to resistance.[118] Certainly there was massive support for the National Liberation Front (EAM) and its National Popular Liberation Army (ELAS). These organizations scored a number of notable successes against the occupying forces and, by 1944, were setting up administrations in newly liberated areas. The Greek effort was assisted not by the Russians, as elsewhere in the Balkans, but by the British, who made a series of landings from 1943 onwards.

The anti-German Greek government in exile returned to Athens in October 1944, but the eviction of the Nazis did not mean the end of Greece's internal problems. Between 1946 and 1949 the country lapsed into civil war as the various ex-resistance groups competed for power. The main threat was from the Greek communists, supported by Greece's neighbours and the Soviet Union. Eventually the communist insurgency was overcome by a pro-Western government, largely with American political and economic support under the label of the Truman Doctrine. Between 1950 and 1967 Greece followed a democratic course but fell to a vicious military junta which is sometimes compared with the earlier dictatorship of Metaxas. This nightmare lasted until 1974, when defeat in the Cyprus War discredited the colonels' regime and made possible the restoration of a parliamentary system.

Metaxas: conservative or fascist?

There has been some debate about the style of regime introduced by Metaxas. According to Hondros, the Metaxas regime was 'a royal bureaucratic dictatorship'.[119] Payne argues, 'Though the regime used the fascist salute and sometimes employed the term *totalitarian*, it was neither generically fascist nor structurally totalitarian [but rather] a primarily bureaucratic form of authoritarianism.'[120] Against these views, Kofas maintains that the regime of Metaxas had a powerful 'quasi-fascist' element.[121]

There is a strong case for the traditionalist nature of Metaxas's dictatorship. His anti-liberalism was autocratic rather than totalitarian, as was his dislike of parliamentary politics which, he thought, would 'throw us into the embrace of communism'.[122] He was also elitist in his support of a pyramid class structure with a nobility at the apex. Nor did he have any revolutionary doctrine as such. The ideas of Metaxas, like those of Franco and Salazar, were based on reviving his country's historic role: 'We owe it therefore to revert backwards in order to rediscover ourselves.'[123] Although his regime was inspired by nationalism, this was not associated with militarism. This meant that the irredentism of the early 1920s was not reactivated in the late 1930s and Metaxas did not seek closer connections with the Axis powers as a means of preying on Greece's neighbours. It is true that there was a brutal system of police interrogation and that political opponents were ruthlessly deal with. In this sense, there was a real terror. But this was not accompanied by systematic targeting of minorities. Indeed, the condition of the Jews improved during his administration; he even forbade discrimination against them and criticized those regimes where anti-Semitism was practised. The Metaxas regime had little difficulty in gaining recognition from the political establishment at home and abroad. It was not in conflict with the traditional Greek monarchy and was also acceptable to Britain and France, who guaranteed Greek security in 1939. Finally, Metaxas himself denied that he was a fascist. He told a British official that 'Portugal under Dr Salazar, not the Germany of Hitler or the Italy of Mussolini, provided the nearest analogy.'[124]

On the other hand, Metaxas went further than the other Balkan leaders in the style of his leadership and the totality of his vision. He fostered a personality cult, proclaiming himself Leader (*Archigos*), 'First Peasant' and 'First Worker'. He aimed to replace constitutional democracy with an entirely new system, the keynote of which would be the suppression of individualism to the interests of the state; his programme would therefore be radical rather than conservative. The spirit behind his changes would be historic and racial: he aimed to revive the glories of the Greek past. He spoke of the three phases of Greek civilization. The first was the Golden Age of Pericles in the fifth century BC, the second was medieval Byzantium. The third would be the emergence of a racially pure Hellenic order under Metaxas himself. He began his dictatorship with a proclamation of martial law and a ban on normal political activity: 'There are no more parties in Greece . . . The old parliamentary system has vanished for ever.' He also imposed a censorship which was so severe that it applied even to blank spaces in newspapers. Gradually he constructed a network of terror and indoctrination which was clearly influenced by the Third Reich; the Athens police headquarters displayed pictures of Hitler and Goebbels, and Greek security was based heavily on the SS and Gestapo. *Mein Kampf* was widely read and became a major influence behind the National Organization of Youth (EDN), which, according to Kofas, provided the regime with a 'fascist base'.

This is perhaps taking things too far. The view of Close is that what Metaxas really aimed at was to maximize the efficiency of the state machinery, which was not unnatural since he had risen through the ranks of the army and been in a family with strong civil service traditions.[125] Hence, his authoritarianism was exercised through intensifying traditional methods rather than inventing new ones. It is true that he borrowed ideas from Nazism, but these were in the quest for efficiency rather than for ideological change. In any case, fascism was associated with Italy which, after Mussolini's invasion of Corfu in 1923, was seen, along with Turkey, as the principal national enemy. The conclusion might therefore be that Metaxas was attracted by the style of power rather than the ideology behind it; although he used elements of fascism he was not overtly or latently a fascist.

PUPPET DICTATORSHIPS FROM DEMOCRACIES

Introduction

All of the states dealt with so far in this chapter developed their own dictatorships before the Second World War. Some, like Romania, Hungary and Bulgaria, became German satellites and allies. Others, like Poland, Albania, Greece, Yugoslavia and the Baltic states, were conquered and partitioned. Two – Spain and Portugal – managed to remain neutral.

The experience of the democracies also varied. A few, like Britain, Ireland, Sweden, Switzerland and Finland, remained intact. The others were conquered and came under foreign military occupation for the duration of the war (these are dealt with on pp. 227–31). Three of these, however, form a special category. Slovakia, Norway and Vichy France all became collaborationist regimes with home-produced dictators who, having failed to achieve power democratically, owed their sudden change of fortunes to German victory. Two of these leaders Quisling and Laval, were among the most detested of the period.

Slovakia

Czechoslovakia was the only state in central and eastern Europe, apart from Finland, to hold on to a genuine parliamentary government during the 1920s and 1930s. Under her two presidents, Masaryk and Beneš, she rose above serious internal difficulties and survived the depression and regional separation. What she could not do was resist the intolerable pressure applied from outside by Hitler, who was clearly determined to destroy the Czechoslovak nation. His initial strategy was to use the German minority in the Sudetenland to make massive demands on the Czech government. At the same time, he used the threat of war to deter Britain and France from supporting Beneš. The result was a series of three visits to Germany by the British Prime Minister, Chamberlain, which culminated in the Munich Settlement. This meant the cession to Germany of 10,000 square miles of territory and 3.5 million people. By the same agreement Poland received Teschen, and Hungary Southern Slovakia. The Munich Settlement was clearly a major step towards the disintegration of Czechoslovakia. In March 1939, Hitler despatched German troops to occupy Prague and bring the whole of Bohemia into the Third Reich. At the same time he backed the claim of the province of Slovakia to autonomy and established a German protectorate under the presidency of Monsignor Jozef Tiso, a cardinal in the Catholic Church.

The new republic did possess certain advantages: it had a fairly widespread support, particularly from the Church, and gained a positive response to the new constitution of July 1939. Tiso hoped to maintain a considerable degree of independence from Germany and to promote conservative Christian values like those of Dollfuss and Schuschnigg in Austria or Salazar in Portugal. Increasingly, however, Tiso was pressurized by the radicals in his Slovak People's Party. His Prime Minister, Tuka, and other leading politicians, like Mach and Durcansky, were openly pro-Nazi. Despite Tiso's efforts, Slovakia came increasingly under Germany's influence. The armaments industry was subordinated to the Nazi war effort and Slovakia contributed over 50,000 men to the invasion of Russia in 1941. Above all, the Nazis had a major say in the treatment of Slovakia's Jews. At first Tiso and the pro-Nazi radicals in his government constructed a package of limited anti-Semitic policies such as the exclusion of Jews from business and the professions. Then Tuka and Mach seized the initiative, pursuing a Nazi scheme for the resettlement of Slovak Jews in Poland. Although Tiso went along with this, he called a halt on the orders of the Pope and for two years resisted a resumption of the deportations. The fate of the Jews, however, was sealed when Slovakia was brought under direct German military administration in September 1944.

Whatever Tiso's claims to the contrary, the Slovak republic was closely tied to the fortunes of Germany. From 1943 onwards this made for extreme vulnerability. As the German military machine was breaking down in Russia, domestic resistance grew against Slovakia's involvement in this futile war. The banned parties collaborated, in exile, to form a Slovak National Council which was committed to ending the link with Germany and to reinstating Czechoslovakia, this time as a federation. In 1944 several army officers hoped, with popular support, to overthrow the pro-Nazi government. By October, however, the Germans had succeeded in crushing the rebellion. They had also installed, under Stefan Tiso (a relative of the previous President), a more subservient regime. This was described by Hoensch as 'a mere puppet of, and executioner for, the German occupation force'.[126] German occupation was ended by the arrival of Soviet troops in April 1945. The Slovak republic was instantly liquidated and the former state of Czechoslovakia revived, with Beneš installed as the first post-war President. Under Soviet influence, the early broad-based and multi-party governments gave way between 1948 and 1949 to an exclusively communist regime which remained until brought down by popular movements in 1989. During the next decade Slovakia separated from the Czech Republic.

Norway

Norway had been a typical example of Scandinavian political stability. The country had survived the Great Depression, through consensus rather than confrontational politics, a model of the effective operation of proportional representation. Norway had also been strongly committed to peace and neutrality. In 1938, a neutrality pact had been signed with Denmark, Sweden, Finland and Iceland. Unfortunately, this was not based on strength; Norway's defences had deteriorated badly during the

18 Vidkun Quisling, 1887–1945 (Popperfoto)

1920s and 1930s. The Norwegian government tried to keep out of the Second World War but the Germans launched a surprise attack in April 1940, drawn by Norway's mineral resources and strategic position in the North Atlantic. The Norwegian armed forces resisted for as long as possible but were eventually forced to surrender in June. King Haakon withdrew in temporary exile to London and the whole country fell to German control.

This was exercised by two dictators. One was Josef Terboven, previously *Gauleiter* of Cologne, now appointed Reich's Commissar for Norway. The other was Vidkun Quisling. He had set up a Norwegian Nazi Party in the 1930s but this had never been popular with the electorate: it seemed, therefore, that he had no chance of attaining power by his own merits. He made secret contacts with Germany in the period 1939–40 and was suitably rewarded after the German conquest in 1940. He acquired greater responsibility until, in February 1942, he became Minister President of Norway, in the process competing directly with his official superior, Terboven. According to Larsen, 'Quisling was allowed to do as he pleased in most internal affairs, and became more and more brutal and tyrannical.'[127]

Quisling's ideas were strongly influenced by Nazism, and in particular by Alfred Rosenberg. He had a vision of the regeneration of Norway under his own leadership as *Forer*; he developed a private army which was similar to the SA and SS; and he totally condemned parliamentary politics, probably as a result of his own disastrous showing in the 1936 elections. He also projected extreme views on race. He was strongly anti-Semitic and believed in the utmost importance of Nordic racial purity and supremacy. His initial hope was that Norway could work to promote peace and co-operation between Britain and Germany to form a great Nordic peace union. By 1940, however, he had become convinced that Britain had succumbed to Jewish influence and was therefore no longer worthy of such a destiny. He therefore decided to throw in Norway's lot entirely with Germany: 'in the Greater German community we shall have a leading position in the working of the New Order'.

Under Quisling and Terboven, Norway was heavily exploited to meet the needs of Hitler's war effort in Europe. The Germans appropriated the funds of the Norwegian national bank, depleted the industrial stock and increased the national debt ninefold. Most of the population remained quiet, if sullen and resentful, but a variety of resistance activities developed. Non-violent forms included Church manifestos, protesting against the occupation and style of leadership, and a massive increase in the number of illegal publications. Military resistance, meanwhile, was co-ordinated in London, and conducted on behalf of the government in exile. Commando groups, for example, carried out daring raids on German positions. The Norwegian merchant navy also played an important role in the war against Germany. Those ships which had escaped German hands carried vital supplies across the Atlantic, assisted at the evacuation of Dunkirk in 1940, and convoyed troops for the Normandy landings in 1944. Even so, Norway did not have the strength to liberate itself and the main impetus of the attacks of the Western Allies was in the Mediterranean and France, not Scandinavia. Norway therefore had to wait until the final surrender of the German armed forces in May 1945.

As soon as this happened, King Haakon returned Norway to her customary democratic government. The general election of October 1945 produced a coalition government which gave priority to reconstruction. It also dealt with the collaborators. Terboven had already committed suicide but Quisling was captured. He was put on trial and eventually executed for treason. It has been pointed out that Quisling's role was no worse than that of the other collaborators elsewhere in Europe. Still, it is he rather than they 'who is remembered above all as the archetypal traitor'.[128]

France

Like Norway, France became a dictatorship as a direct result of military defeat by Germany in 1940. It is difficult to see how fascism could have come to power in any other way. Although France was in some respects the seedbed of fascism (see pp. 104–5), she had managed to sustain democracy throughout the inter-war period, usually through broad-based governments either of the right or the left. These included the Bloc National under Clemenceau (1919), the Cartel des Gauches under Herriot (1924), Poincaré's National Union (1926) and Blum's Popular Front (1936). These had compensated for the Third Republic's tendency towards political instability. What destroyed this republic was the most catastrophic military reverse in the whole of France's history. This resulted from the triumph of the German Blitzkrieg strategy over the French defensive system based on the Maginot Line.

France's humiliation was followed by an armistice with the Germans. A new government under Marshal Pétain, a hero of the First World War, secured partial independence for Vichy France, the rest of the country coming under direct German administration. The Vichy government also contained French fascists like Pierre Laval and Raphael Alibert, who sympathized openly with Nazi ideas. Pétain and Laval introduced a 'National Revolution', the tone of which was unmistakably authoritarian, with the emphasis on 'Work, Family, Country' rather than 'Liberty, Equality, Fraternity'.[129] The democratic past was denounced, especially the Third Republic, which had brought France to defeat and ruin.

There is some evidence to show that Pétain was reasonably popular in 1940, offering as he appeared to do a way out of total defeat and disaster. But gradually the Vichy regime lost all credibility. The Germans imposed greater demands on the French economy and looked to Laval to maintain the closest possible co-operation between Vichy and Berlin. Pétain tried to retain at least some autonomy by dismissing Laval in December 1940 but was forced by strong German pressure to reinstate him in April 1942. From this time onwards Laval was the real dictator, but also a Nazi puppet. He thought in terms of a German-dominated Europe, with France playing an important peripheral supporting role. He also hoped for a negotiated peace with the United States which would enable Germany to finish off Russia and, perhaps, reduce its heavy demands on France. His dreams dissipated when, later in 1942, the Germans occupied Vichy and reduced the once autonomous area to the level of the rest of France.

The reason for this was the growing resistance to the regime, and the threat from outside. Up to 1942 Vichy had kept up at least the pretence of independence and had even possessed colonies in North Africa. These, however, were conquered by British and American troops and the Vichy government was deprived of any significant role. Many Frenchmen therefore switched their support to resistance movements like General de Gaulle's Free French. A great impetus came with the invasion of France by the Western Allies during the course of 1944, the north falling in June, the south in August. De Gaulle was allowed by the British and Americans to liberate Paris. He subsequently introduced a programme for national recovery which included the construction of the Fourth Republic and the involvement of France in key diplomacy on the future of Germany. One of the Allied leaders, President Roosevelt, considered de Gaulle a possible danger. He pointed to certain authoritarian tendencies and warned that de Gaulle might establish another dictatorship. Time was to show that de Gaulle avoided this trap, settling instead for a leadership which was paternalist but firmly rooted in democracy.

Chapter 6

Dictatorships compared

TOTALITARIAN AND AUTHORITARIAN DICTATORSHIPS

Throughout this book references have been made to the terms 'totalitarian' and 'authoritarian' dictatorships. The purpose of this chapter is to draw together these references and to attempt an overall distinction between the two types of regime. It is, however, necessary first to settle upon a working definition.

Disputes over terminology

'Authoritarian' is a term which has attracted comparatively little debate. It can be seen in two main senses. Generically, it is a system of government which is based on heavily centralized control and which dilutes or dispenses with a properly functioning parliamentary democracy. Chronologically, it was part of a phase of conservative right-wing governments in the late nineteenth century,[1] often based on monarchy, whose ideas and methods continued to influence the period between the World Wars. The first definition would apply to any dictatorship, whereas the second would establish the boundaries beyond which most dictatorships did not go after 1918.

'Totalitarian' is a much more controversial term. According to Laqueur, it was 'coined to cover common features of communist and fascist states', even though Mussolini had used it during the 1930s to describe the type of regime he was hoping to establish over the Italian people. Laqueur's statement was more relevant to the period immediately after the Second World War, when Western governments came to fear the Soviet Union – their former ally against Hitler – and to see much in common between communism and fascism. In the atmosphere of the Cold War, two systems were therefore conjoined under one classification. This amounted to pinning 'a "boo" label on a "boo" system of government'.[2] In an attempt to move away from loose generalization into more structured definition, historians since the 1950s have explained totalitarianism in a variety of ways.

Two views have been particularly influential. According to Friedrich and Brzezinski,[3] totalitarianism was a combination of 'an ideology, a single party typically led by one man, a terroristic police, a communications monopoly, a weapons monopoly, and a centrally directed economy'.[4] The ideology and the whole aim of the regime is 'total destruction and total reconstruction'.[5] Hence, the true totalitarian system moves step by step towards the achievement of its goals through the effective manipulation of the population. This makes full use of modern techniques of propaganda and indoctrination as well as of force. For Arendt the process is less orderly.[6] Radical ideology, she agrees, forms the basis of the totalitarian regime. There is, however, no coherent programme – only a restless movement 'to organise as many people as possible within its framework and to set and keep them in motion'.[7] The result is chaos rather than order, with new institutions overlapping traditional ones. The most important method used to bring the population into line is terror, since it cannot be assumed that other forms of socialization will be fully effective.

Other historians have, for several reasons, questioned the usefulness of the term 'totalitarian' at all. One argument is that conceptions of totalitarianism have been shaped by the political one-sidedness of the Cold War. Another is that recent research on Nazi Germany and Stalinist Russia have revealed so many deficiencies in the structure of their power that it can be doubted whether there ever has been a regime which can be properly described as 'totalitarian'. The problem with this approach to terminology is that almost every word could be thrown out by purists, thus severely depleting the historian's vocabulary. As Tormey believes, it therefore 'seems as pointless to write off the concept of totalitarianism as it is to write off the concept of democracy'.[8]

A more constructive development has been the classification of totalitarianism into two different types, the so-called 'strong' and 'weak' models. In the strong model, totalitarianism achieves total control over the population through conversion by methods such as socialization, indoctrination and force. The most important criterion for success is the degree to which the ideology and objectives of the regime are accomplished; the word 'strong' therefore reflects the structured or projective approach to change. By contrast, the weak model focuses on the way in which the regime exercises its power. The emphasis is on 'the practices of rule rather than its effects'. It stresses 'the actions of the regime, what the regime does as opposed to the degree of control it is able to wield'.[9] The word 'weak' is a reflection on the regime having to react to changes rather than being in control of them.

Of the two, the weak model seems to offer more scope for effective analysis. For one thing, it is extremely difficult to define objectively how far a population within a totalitarian regime has been imbued with its ideology. It is far easier to assess the methods by which the regime has tried to achieve conformity. Second, the strong model implies that the regime is always in control, that power and decisions about the exercise of power are part of a 'top-down' process. The weak model, by contrast, allows for the existence of administrative confusion and for the influence of sectors of the population on the development of policy: this makes possible a 'bottom-up' analysis. Third, the strong model would logically characterize an effective totalitarian regime as one which made decreasing use of terror. In the most extreme cases of totalitarian rule, the reverse happened, which also adheres more closely to the weak model.

A suggested approach

This approach will attempt two things. First, it will distinguish between 'authoritarian' and 'totalitarian' dictatorships. Second, it will provide a more detailed framework of totalitarianism – referring to the strong and, more particularly, the weak models.

Both types of dictatorship – authoritarian and totalitarian – dispensed with the normal process of parliamentary government and were critical of democracy. But their basic intentions differed. Authoritarian regimes used dictatorship in a conservative way, aiming to preserve traditional values and often the traditional social structure. This was to be accomplished neither by revolution nor by rousing the masses. Quite the contrary. As Bracher argues, authoritarian regimes arrived at the neutralization or 'immobilization of all other forces in the state'.[10] Totalitarian regimes, by contrast, had a more radical programme of change, and deliberately mobilized the masses to serve a 'revolutionary monopolist movement'. They were also permeated by an ideology or 'a quasi-religious philosophy with a claim to exclusivity'.[11]

More specifically, totalitarian regimes possessed a distinctive ideology which formed a 'body of doctrine covering all vital parts of man's existence'.[12] Everything was in theory subordinated to it and attempts were to be made to restructure society according to its goals. Second, the political system was under the control of a single party, presided over by a leader who was invested with the cult of personality. This party aimed at mobilized mass support, particularly among the young, and generated paramilitary activity. Party politics were ended and the legislature brought under the control of the executive. Third, the individual was completely subordinated to the dictates of the state through a process of coercion and indoctrination. The former could involve 'a system of terror, whether physical or psychic, effected through party and secret police control'.[13] Indoctrination sought the destruction of cultural pluralism and the shaping of education, literature, art and music to the objectives of political ideology. Fourth, the totalitarian state sought to impose complete control over the economy by establishing the basic objectives and providing 'bureaucratic co-ordination of formerly independent corporate entities'.[14]

Using these criteria, it should be possible to establish which of the dictatorships can be described as 'totalitarian' and to which the term 'authoritarian' would be more appropriate.

In some respects the most 'totalitarian' of all the regimes may appear to have been Stalin's Russia, since it fulfilled all the categories mentioned. Marxism–Leninism was an all-embracing ideology which was used extensively as a social-engineering force. The political structure was dominated by the CPSU, in turn subordinated to a leader who took the personality cult to an unprecedented extreme. Stalinist purges accounted for the elimination of millions, while indoctrination was accomplished through the medium of Socialist Realism. The economy, of course, was regulated by a series of Five Year Plans. In theory, this points to a typically strong model of totalitarianism. Yet appearances were deceptive. As we saw in Chapter 2, Stalin adapted his economic policies to the immediate needs of his power-base, he had difficulties in securing the implementation of any of his policies at local levels, and he felt impelled to increase the degree of force. By this revised analysis, Stalinist Russia provides the best example of the weak model, in that the application of terror was more comprehensive than in any other state. We now also have the advantage of hindsight. Decades of indoctrination did not prevent the unseemly collapse of the Soviet Union in 1991; a successful regime by the strong model would surely have lasted longer.

The situation in Germany is also complex. On the one hand, the Nazi regime seemed to adhere to the strong model of totalitarianism. It was based on an ideology which was more extreme than any yet devised and which was imposed upon the population by extensive coercion and indoctrination. The masses were radicalized and mobilized in support of a single party under the personal authority of an irreplaceable Führer. And yet, it has been argued, Germany was an example of 'imperfect totalitarianism'. The Nazi revolution swept away fewer of the institutions of the previous regime than did the Bolshevik Revolution and Hitler was satisfied with a less rigidly centralized and planned economy. The chaos of opaque and overlapping competences, described by Bracher and Broszat, was more symptomatic of the weak model. In Italy, Mussolini's objectives were undoubtedly inconsistent, as is shown in Chapter 3. There was, it is true, a more systematic economic theory than in Germany, but even the so-called corporate state was incomplete. In virtually every sector – political, social and economic – radical theory was undermined by a remarkably persistent status quo. This places Fascist Italy on the borderline between the weak model of totalitarianism and authoritarianism.

Of the lesser states, two might be described as partially totalitarian for the brief period they were ruled by fascist regimes under the protection of Nazi Germany. These were Croatia under the Ustashi regime and Szálasi's Hungary. All the others are more aptly termed authoritarian. It is true that some had common features with the totalitarian states. Greece, for example, sometimes imitated the Nazi security system and Metaxas was partly influenced by Hitler's ideology. Hungary under Gömbös and Poland after Piłsudski flirted with milder forms of fascism, while Austria under Dollfuss and Salazar's Portugal tried out local variants of corporativism. Several factors, however, prevent these and the other regimes from being regarded with Italy as even partly totalitarian. With the possible exception of Greece, they lacked any consistent attempt to mobilize the masses behind the regime. In fact, quite the reverse: they aimed to neutralize and depoliticize. This was partly because leaders like Salazar and Franco relied upon traditional ideas, although in a regenerated form, and distrusted anything which was remotely radical or revolutionary. Finally, authoritarian leaders were content to let the individual remain within his traditional social context and there was rarely any attempt at mass indoctrination.

The rest of this chapter will develop these points and draw general comparisons, under four main headings, between the various regimes covered by this book.

THE IDEOLOGICAL BASIS OF DICTATORSHIP

The term 'ideology' is normally understood to mean an organized set of ideas and ideals intended to deal with problems and, perhaps, to institute sweeping change. The totalitarian ideologies had in common a desire to destroy the existing system and to recreate it according to an ideal form often called a Utopia. In fact, Friedrich and Brzezinski believe that 'totalitarian ideologies are typically utopian in nature'.[15] Authoritarian regimes, by contrast, were usually unable to produce a distinctive ideology. Although they often aimed to change the existing political system, they were much more prepared to adapt to more traditional influences and ideas. Hence, they tended to be backward looking, even reactionary, in contrast to the revolutionary nature of totalitarian ideologies.

It is usual to categorize three inter-war ideologies as potentially totalitarian: Marxism–Leninism, Nazism and Fascism. Of these, Marxism–Leninism was the most coherent, based on a systematic doctrine derived from the ideas of Hegel, Marx and Engels, as redefined by Lenin and Stalin. It incorporated an economic theory (economic determinism), a series of historical laws (dialectical materialism) and a belief in eventual progress towards a higher form of human organization called the 'classless society' (see Chapter 1). Fascism and Nazism owed to nineteenth-century writers like Nietzsche, Gobineau and H.S. Chamberlain such concepts as racial inequality and the inevitability of struggle. But neither possessed the disciplined structure of Marxism–Leninism, partly because, in the words of Bracher, neither had 'the kind of classic bible that Marxism possessed'.[16] Hitler's ideas, for example, were expounded very loosely in *Mein Kampf*, which was little more than an autobiography, while Mussolini's most explicit doctrinal statement was confined to an article in *Encyclopedia Italiana*. Neither of these sources had the coherence and weight of Marx's *Das Kapital* or Lenin's *The State and Revolution*. Bracher goes so far as to call Nazism 'an eclectic "ragbag" ideology, drawn from a multitude of sources'.[17]

As for the lesser dictators, few even attempted a systematic statement of beliefs beyond a simple reformulation of traditional ideas. This applied to all authoritarian leaders, whether military men like Franco and Piłsudski or academics like Salazar. Some of the more radical, potentially totalitarian dictators, who came to power as Nazi puppets during the Second World War, did have a go at organizing their thoughts. A typical example was Szálasi of Hungary; but, as Weber points out, Szálasi's writing is unsystematic and 'steadfastly ignores grammar, style and sense'.[18]

Marxism–Leninism, Nazism and Fascism had in common the desire to transform the previous system through revolution. All three involved the manipulation of history and the movement towards an ideal. There were, however, major differences in the nature of that ideal. The Marxist Utopia involved two distinct phases (see Chapter 1). The first was the 'dictatorship of the proletariat', which was intended to eliminate all obstacles to achieving the second, and very different, phase: the 'classless society'. Force and struggle were therefore a means to an end. This end was fundamentally different in that it would see the decline of organized coercion and the conclusion of the 'prehistoric phase' of man's existence. According to Engels, there would be 'a leap from slavery into freedom; from darkness into light'.[19] In complete contrast Nazi and Fascist Utopias envisaged one state only – uninterrupted and unending movement towards total domination and power. Fascism has been described as a 'national–imperial mission ideology' which made a 'powerful state the highest value';[20] this process, the opposite to the 'classless society', is sometimes called 'etatism'. It also involved the perpetual glorification of war and struggle for, in Mussolini's words, 'war is to the man what maternity is to the woman'.[21] Nazism also focused on struggle, although the vehicle was race rather than the state, Aryanism rather than etatism. According to Hitler, 'All of nature is one great struggle between strength and weakness, an eternal victory of the strong over the weak.'[22] The victims were to be the race enemies, for 'All eugenic progress can begin only by eliminating the inferior.' These ideas were to be sublimated in the most horrifying way in the gas chambers of Auschwitz-Birkenau.

Elsewhere the purpose of ideology was less to transform than to revive. It was therefore less forward-looking and more traditional, even nostalgic. History was regarded less as a transition to a higher phase, more as providing examples for imitation. The clearest example of this was Salazar's stress on 'Deus, Patria, Familia' ('God, Country, Family') and on the historic role of Portuguese imperialism 'to defend western and Christian civilisation'.[23] Franco, in turn, aimed quite consciously at reviving the virtues of the historic Spain destroyed, he considered, by the Second Republic; he regarded himself therefore as the political reincarnation of Philip II. Even the more radical 'Hungarism' of Szálasi and the 'Hellenism' of Metaxas were essentially glorifications of national pasts. In other states presidential or royal absolutism lacked any systematic ideas and based itself on pragmatic common sense and an appeal to patriotism.

Which of the main ideologies proved to be of the most practical use? Marxism–Leninism certainly appears the most elusive in its ultimate aim: the 'classless society' and the 'withering away' of the state could occur only after profound change in human nature. Nazism and Fascism, by contrast, intended to exploit and accentuate the most basic human instincts – the struggles for survival and domination. And yet events proved Marxism–Leninism a more efficient tool than either Fascism or Nazism for transforming society, the economy and political institutions. The reason was that the practical application of Marxism–Leninism by Stalin stopped well short of the ultimate ideal of the 'classless society' and concentrated on the organization and coercion necessary for the phase of the 'dictatorship of the proletariat'. Fascism and Nazism lacked the capacity for complete institutional reorganization and for the mobilization of the economy for total war, even though the latter featured so strongly in their scheme. On balance, therefore, Stalin had at his disposal a more adaptable ideological weapon than had either Hitler or Mussolini.

THE POLITICAL STRUCTURE OF DICTATORSHIP

Totalitarian regimes aimed to transform the political establishment. The three states normally seen as totalitarian went about this in very different ways.

The Russian leadership introduced the most extensive changes, aiming to eradicate all previous institutions. The three constitutions of the period provided for a system of soviets, dominated at all stages by the Communist Party. The party was able to exercise total control through its Central Committee, which, in turn, was subdivided into the Orgburo, Politburo and Control Commission. The Nazi leadership also sought political change, although in practice it stopped short of the sort of transformation seen in the Soviet Union. Instead of sweeping away the old system altogether, Hitler carried out some drastic surgery on it; for example, he perpetuated the emergency powers of the executive by means of the Enabling Act and, by merging the presidency and chancellorship, destroyed the checks and balances within the constitution. Mussolini's Italy followed the German rather than the Soviet pattern. The effect, however, was still less complete; the superstructure of the monarchy remained intact and was eventually to become the focal point of opposition to the regime. Elsewhere the dictators were less ambitious. One of the characteristics of authoritarian regimes was to stabilize and restore rather than transform, even though constitutional amendments were often involved. Examples of attempts to emphasize tradition and order can be seen in Salazar's *Estado Novo* (1935) and the constitutions in the various Balkan states which granted increased powers to their respective monarchs.

What importance did the dictators attach to a party base and to radicalizing the masses? Again, the approach in the totalitarian states varied. Russia used the 'vanguard' method, by which the Communist Party dominated the entire system. Rather than attempting to generate mass involvement, it operated through the principle of 'democratic centralism', whereby a small elite acted on behalf of the whole population. Membership of the Communist Party was strictly limited and, during the 1930s, Stalin was able, through his purges, to reduce this further. The Nazi and Fascist parties possessed more genuine mass bases, which did much to radicalize politics and promote right-wing revolutionary fervour. But penetration by the parties of state institutions was less complete than in Russia. Elsewhere the development of a one-party system was intended to neutralize, defuse and depoliticize rather than to create a resurgent mass. This, for example, was the motive behind Salazar's National Union (UN), Rivera's Union Patriotica (UP), the Fatherland Front of Dollfuss and Piłsudski's Sanacja.

All the dictatorships covered by this book depended upon the leadership of a single commanding figure. The most extreme cases of this were Russia, Germany and Italy. In theory Stalin was subject to collective leadership and the ideology of communism was supposed to prevent any excessive accumulation of personal power. In practice he elevated his authority to heights which were unprecedented even in a country with an almost uninterrupted history of autocracy. At the same time, his power was often constrained by the problem of enforcing his orders in the localities. The situation in Germany was partly similar, partly different. In theory Hitler was in total command, with no conceivable constraints. According to Broszat, 'Hitler's power as Führer exceeded that of any monarch. The notion of "divine right" was replaced by the claim that the Führer was the saviour appointed by Providence and at the same time the embodiment and medium of the unarticulated will of the people.'[24] In practice, however, Hitler was frequently isolated at the pinnacle of the party and state apparatuses. Mussolini's power was never as strong as Hitler's, even in theory. He remained, officially, not the appointee of Victor Emmanuel and it was to the King, not to the *Duce*, that the army and state officials owed their ultimate allegiance. The 'authoritarian' states also depended on the strong-man image. Both Rivera and Franco used the imagery of the 'sentinel', while a range of titles sprang up, all loosely translatable as 'Leader'. Franco was known as *Caudillo*, Smetona as *Tautos Vadas*, Antonescu as *Conducator* and Metaxas as *Archigos*. None of these 'leaders', however, found it necessary to adopt the cult of personality which played so important a part in the totalitarian states. This was because they aimed to quieten the population, not to rouse it; this could be more successfully accomplished by a more remote type of authority.

No dictatorship could have survived without the support of the army. There was, however, a contrast between those regimes which tried to absorb the military and those which allowed the army to remain as an independent and privileged institution. Once again, the most complete transformation was achieved in Russia. The Bolshevik regime built an entirely new army and subordinated it to the Communist

Party by means of commissars; under Stalin these were known as *zampolits* (deputy commanders for political affairs). At the head of the whole system was the GPUVS or the Main Political Administration of the Soviet Armed Forces. In Germany control over the army was accomplished more gradually. Hitler had to earn its support in 1934 in the Night of the Long Knives but, by 1938, felt sufficiently confident to reorganize the High Command. He subsequently used the Waffen SS to politicize the army and infuse it with Nazi ideology. Italy, never a good example of a totalitarian state, did not experience a comparable process. Mussolini, in fact, claimed that he did 'not intend to use the army as a political arm'.[25] He also failed to produce an equivalent to the Waffen SS, which meant that there was nothing to prevent the officers from taking part in a plot to depose him in 1943. Elsewhere the army achieved or retained a high status. In Portugal it had a special relationship with Salazar, until, that is, it was destabilized by the experience of the African wars. In Spain it was directly elevated and protected by Franco who was, of course, the Commander-in-Chief. The same applied in Poland, although Piłsudski was less able than Franco to adjust to a civilian role. These and other leaders did whatever was necessary to prevent the penetration of the armed forces by radical right-wing groups, realizing that a disaffected officer corps could engineer a military coup.

THE STATE, SOCIETY AND INDIVIDUAL

The individual exists within a society; the society is contained within a state. An important characteristic of a totalitarian state is that it aims to subordinate both the individual and society. According to Buchheim, 'Totalitarian rule attempts to encompass the whole person, the substance and spontaneity of his existence, including his conscience.'[26] In Russia, both Lenin and Stalin intended to create a 'new type of man', the purpose of society being to impart to him the new political values and culture as directed by the state. There was a similar emphasis in both Germany and Italy, on a radical change of attitudes and beliefs. In the smaller states there was no place for social transformation. The intention, instead, was to restore the traditional social balance. One example was Salazar's Portugal, of which Bruce writes, 'the state was never to swallow up the groups – hence it was never to be "totalitarian" – it was simply to act as the co-ordinating agent of these groups'.[27] Franco's regime, according to Payne, followed the 'intolerant, ultra-Catholic norms of Spanish history',[28] while the main influence on Piłsudski's Sanacja was Polish civic virtue, based very much on social tradition.

How completely did the totalitarian regimes reach the individual? One of the most important methods used was propaganda. According to Friedrich and Brzezinski, 'The nearly complete monopoly of mass communication is generally agreed to be one of the most striking characteristics of totalitarian dictatorship.'[29] Each state had its own means of achieving this monopoly. Within the Soviet Union state ownership prevailed, in contrast to private ownership under state licence, as sometimes existed in Italy and Germany. The Nazi and Fascist systems placed greater emphasis than the Soviet Union on the use of radio, probably because Hitler and Mussolini were more adept than Stalin at the use of the spoken word. All systems tried to manipulate culture, whether through Socialist Realism or Aryanism;

as shown in Chapter 3, Italy was probably the least successful in this respect. All redesigned the structure and function of education, although in different ways. The Nazi and Fascist approach was to close minds in order to make them unreceptive to anything but carefully programmed propaganda. The result would be a simplification of the whole intellectual process. Soviet education was based, in theory, on expanding the intellect so that it could deal with the complexities of the dialectic and other elements of Marxist ideology. In practice, however, Soviet education under Stalin stultified the intellect by demanding the complete acceptance, as an act of faith, of the ideas passed down from the leadership.

Propaganda and indoctrination were invariably backed up by terror. Totalitarian states, indeed, made a permanent connection between the two processes. Authoritarian states, although never strong on indoctrination, often pursued a brutal form of repression. The purpose of terror in the totalitarian states was the identification and elimination of all enemies, whether 'racial' as in Germany or 'class' as in Russia. The methods used included some of the most notorious institutions ever devised. Russian security evolved through the Cheka, GPU, OGPU, NKVD, MGB, MVD and, after the death of Stalin, the KGB. German institutions comprised the SA, SS, SD and Gestapo. Of the two systems, Germany's committed the more appalling atrocities – sinking, in the process, to the depths of barbarism. Stalin's, however, proved more widespread in its operations and eliminated more people – even if its efficiency has been much exaggerated. Italy's system, based on the OVRA, never achieved the same notoriety; according to Friedrich and Brzezinski, it was 'less total, less frightful, and hence less 'mature" than in Germany and the Soviet Union'.[30] Elsewhere, methods varied considerably. Some states had no organized terror as such: examples included Horthy's Hungary, the Baltic states, Austria under Dollfuss and Piłsudski's Poland. Others developed a machinery for repression which was more efficient than Italy's: Franco executed far more people than Mussolini, Salazar introduced the notorious PIDE, while Metaxas patterned his security system directly on the Gestapo.

The main devices of terror were purges and penal camps. The use of purges was most extensive in Russia. The reason was that Stalin was the most obsessed about the security of his position: unlike Hitler and Mussolini, he had not been the original inspiration behind the new system and needed to place firmly upon himself the mantle of Lenin. Stalin was also confronted by a huge range of local initiatives and inertias which needed to be spurred into action or, alternatively, reined back. The extent of Soviet terror is therefore in part a sign of administrative malfunctioning. In Germany purges served a more restricted purpose. The Night of the Long Knives was Hitler's method of rooting out the radical wing of the Nazi movement in order to guarantee military support for the new regime. It was not, however, followed by a clean sweep through the rest of the party leadership. One can only speculate on whether this would have happened had the Third Reich outlived Hitler. Would Goering, Himmler, Bormann or Goebbels eventually have become a Stalin?

One of the most notorious features of the Hitler and Stalin regimes was their use of camps. More details are known about the German camps because of the publicity given to them during the Nuremberg Trials, although the opening of the former Soviet archives after 1991 is now adding to the information about the Stalinist system. The overall conception of the German camps was the more horrifying because of their eventual connection with the deliberate extermination of 6 million people. There was no Soviet equivalent to the RHSA, to Auschwitz-Birkenau, to the gas chambers or ovens. Stalin's camps were more traditional; they were labour or concentration camps, not designed for mass killings. In terms of overall numbers, more victims were processed through the Gulag system than through the SS network and many more people died in captivity in Russia than in Germany. These deaths, however, were the result of neglect and overwork rather than a policy of genocide. The Stalinist system always retained a theoretical emphasis on correction and reha-bilitation while the Nazi ideology was ultimately geared to a policy of disposal.

THE ECONOMIES OF THE DICTATORSHIPS

Within the totalitarian states the government sought to impose overall economic control. Most was attempted in the Soviet Union, where, as in the political sphere, the previous system was largely destroyed. Stalin's method was the Five Year Plan, co-ordinated by Gosplan, which, by 1938, had been subdivided into fifty-four depart-ments. His basic intention was to impose upon all sectors of the economy the principle of collective ownership while, at the same time, preparing the Soviet Union to resist an invasion from the West. The fascist states, by contrast, aimed to adapt rather than destroy the previous system. Germany's programme was based on *Gleichschaltung*, Italy's on the corporate state. In both cases the emphasis was on state direction but with a degree of private enterprise; the state allied with big busi-ness rather than seeking to destroy it. The ultimate objectives of both Hitler and Mussolini were autarky and the pursuit of Lebensraum, the assumption being that only territorial expansion would enable the German and Italian economies to reflect the industriousness of their respective people.

Elsewhere, the smaller states varied in their economic policies. Some, like Spain, Austria and Portugal, were clearly influenced by Mussolini's corporate state, although they avoided some of its Fascist connotations. Others struggled on with open economies based on private enterprise and minimal state direction; eventu-ally, however, the impact of the depression forced Bulgaria, Romania, Yugoslavia and Greece into making trade agreements with Germany. These, in turn, dragged them into the vortex of German diplomatic and political influence.

The key test of the success of the planned economies was their capacity for mobi-lization in wartime. The Soviet system of the 1930s has been reinterpreted. It was once thought to have made the most successful adjustment to the demands of total war and that Soviet success against Nazi Germany from 1943 onwards was due to the full implementation of the Five Year Plans. It now seems that the Soviet recovery was made possible by the suspension of economic planning (see pp. 81–4) – the very reverse of Stalin's original intention. Even so, it could be argued that Stalin had geared the Soviet economy directly to the demands of total war; the problems were how best to generate the necessary resources and how to make the best use of them. The experience of the fascist states was very different. The Italian economy reacted badly to being stretched by conflict in the 1930s. The Ethiopian campaign and the Spanish Civil War brought it close to collapse, while the campaigns in the Balkans and North Africa finished it off. Germany was geared specifically to a war of conquest followed by the absorption of large areas to consolidate the economic base. But since Hitler never dared inflict on the German consumer the sort of demands taken for granted by Stalin in Russia, this conquest had to be rapid. As long as Germany could depend upon a successful Blitzkrieg the economy functioned smoothly and efficiently. Faced with the prospect of total war, however, Germany fell far behind the Soviet Union in armaments production. By the time that Speer had managed to introduce more radical measures it was already too late: Soviet troops were closing in on the Third Reich.

All of the totalitarian regimes were severely tested by the special problems posed by agriculture. Tight, centralized control was particularly difficult in an economic activity which was essentially local and which required the exercise of on-the-spot initiative. It might have been possible more or less to co-ordinate decision-making in the industrial sector, but how could the same process take into account the diverse and unpredictable conditions faced by agriculture? The Soviet experience was catastrophic. Stalin's enforced collectivization alienated huge sections of the peasantry, and his determination to use agriculture to subsidize industrial development created an imbalance which permanently crippled the Soviet economy. Mussolini's policies were similarly disastrous for Italy. Although he avoided a social upheaval by not seeking to alter the pattern of land ownership, he did cause serious disruption to agricultural productivity. By insisting that farmers should switch to crops like wheat to enable the government to win its 'Battle for Grain', he created an imbalance which post-war Italy has struggled to resolve. Hitler managed to avoid the direct disruption inflicted by Stalin and Mussolini. It could, however, be argued that his belief in a strong peasantry underlay his policy of Lebensraum: he envisaged the settlement of German rural communities across the whole of eastern Europe. Lebensraum, in turn, conditioned Hitler's whole economic and military strategy, with all the implications examined in Chapter 4.

Some of the smaller states experienced agricultural reforms in the early 1920s; Stambuliski, for example, sought to redistribute land among the peasantry of Bulgaria in what was really the reverse of Stalin's policy. But the onset of the depression forced the authoritarian regimes to abandon virtually all attempts to direct agriculture. The smaller dictators valued the support of the landed gentry too much to risk incurring their wrath by interfering with the status quo. In this respect, as in many others, they considered that things were best left as they were.

Postscript: Europe since 1945

The period between the two World Wars saw an unprecedented variety of regimes. These can be classified in two ways. First, it is possible to make a three-way distinction between democracies, left-wing dictatorships (Russia) and right-wing dictatorships (Germany, Italy and many smaller states). The alternative division is between democracy and dictatorship, the latter subdividing into totalitarian regimes (Stalinist Russia, Nazi Germany and possibly Mussolini's Italy) and authoritarian states. This book has looked at both types of classification. The first was considered explicitly in Chapter 1, the second in Chapter 6. Both were used implicitly throughout Chapters 2 to 5.

The post-war period saw major political changes and shifts in the meaning of dictatorship. At the millennium, two major phases were discernible.

1945–89

After 1945 the regimes of the far left were greatly strengthened while, elsewhere, parliamentary democracy was revived. The far right, by contrast, was gradually squeezed out of Europe altogether. The collapse of the right-wing dictatorships was a direct result of military defeat in the Second World War at the hands of the Western democracies and the Soviet Union. The scope and extent of this defeat utterly discredited fascism as a doctrine or as a vehicle for political activism. It is true that the word itself survives. It is normally used to describe small parties of the far right which aspire, so far unsuccessfully, to revive a totalitarian form of nationalism. It is also sometimes used as a term of abuse against regimes or governments more appropriately called reactionary or traditionalist. Between 1945 and the 1980s Europe saw only three manifestations of the far right, all of which were authoritarian rather than fascist. Spain and Portugal survived as dictatorships, against the general trend, because they had avoided involvement in the Second World War. Neither, however, was able to outlive its founder: Portugal moved towards democracy after the 1974 revolution, Spain more gradually under the guidance of King Juan Carlos. Greece presents a different case. Between 1967 and 1974 the colonels briefly recreated the Metaxas era, but their regime was eventually doomed by its isolation, ostracism and defeat in war.

As a result of the decline of the far right, Europe initially polarized between parliamentary democracy and the communist left. The reason was that western

Europe felt vulnerable after the Second World War to the threat which it perceived from the new Soviet superpower and came to depend on a renewed connection with the United States in the form of NATO. The Soviet Union, in turn, tightened its control in eastern Europe by means of Comecon and the Warsaw Pact. The West saw itself as the 'free world' and the Soviet bloc as the remaining source of dictatorship threatening this freedom.

SINCE 1989

This situation lasted well into the 1980s, when a change occurred. Imperceptible at first, this accelerated with breathtaking speed towards the end of the decade. Gorbachev dismantled much of the remaining neo-Stalinist apparatus in the Soviet Union, while the period 1989–91 saw a political transformation. Communist dictatorships were toppled in Poland, Czechoslovakia, Hungary, East Germany, Bulgaria and Romania. The Warsaw Pact was disbanded, the Cold War formally ended and the Soviet Union was replaced by sixteen independent states; those in Europe were Russia, Belarus, Ukraine, Moldova, Estonia, Latvia, Lithuania, Armenia, Georgia and Azerbaijan.

The implications were mixed. There was a great deal more scope for political instability as national identities were revived after decades of suppression by communism. The result was a proliferation of nationalist and right-wing movements throughout eastern Europe, some of them consciously proto-fascist, and of ethnic conflicts which saw the break-up of Yugoslavia and the emergence of authoritarian regimes in Serbia, Belarus and Ukraine. On the other hand, some of the new states looked to closer association with NATO and the European Union as a means of avoiding any possibility of a return to ideologically based dictatorship, whether of the communist left or of a reborn far right. By the millennium, totalitarian dictatorship was being seen in Europe as a thing of the past. Many political theorists were referring to the 'end of ideology' and, in view of the end of the Cold War and the growth of European integration, some were even anticipating the 'end of history'. The twenty-first century is likely to prove both assertions rash. The seeds of many twentieth-century developments were sown in the 1890s. The 1990s could have been similarly productive and it remains to be seen whether dictatorship will regenerate in the future.

Notes

A comment on the term 'dictatorship'

1 H. Buchheim: *Totalitarian Rule: Its Nature and Characteristics* (Middletown, Conn. 1968), Ch. 1.
2 M.R. Curtis: *Encyclopedia Americana*, s.v. 'Dictatorship'.

1 The setting for dictatorship

1 See Z. Sternhell: 'Fascist Ideology' in W. Laqueur (ed.): *Fascism: A Reader's Guide* (Berkeley 1976).
2 J.S. Hughes: *Contemporary Europe* (Englewood Cliffs, NJ 1961), Ch. 2.
3 K.D. Bracher: *The Age of Ideologies* (London 1984), Part II, Ch. 2.
4 S.G. Payne: *A History of Fascism* (London 1995), p. 79.
5 J.A.S. Grenville (ed.): *The Major International Treaties* 1914–1973 (London 1974), Document: President Wilson's Fourteen Points, 8 January 1918.
6 A. Cobban: *The Nation State and National Self-determination* (London 1969), Part I, Ch. 4.
7 H. Köhn: *Political Ideologies of the Twentieth Century* (New York 1949), Ch. 13.
8 K.J. Newman: *European Democracy between the Wars* (trans. K. Morgan) (London 1970), Ch. 3.
9 H. Köhn: op. cit., Ch. 12.
10 Quoted in R.C. Macridis: *Contemporary Political Ideologies* (Boston 1983), Ch. 9.
11 Quoted in D. Smith (ed.): *Left and Right in Twentieth Century Europe* (Harlow 1970), Ch. 1.
12 E. Weber in W. Laqueur (ed.): *Fascism. A Reader's Guide* (Harmondsworth 1979).
13 P. Fearon: *The Origins and Nature of the Great Slump 1929–1932* (London 1979).

2 Dictatorship in Russia

1 A. Ascher (ed.): *The Mensheviks in the Russian Revolution* (London 1976), Introduction.
2 Quoted in E.H. Carr: *The Bolshevik Revolution* (London 1950), Vol. I, Ch. 4.
3 E. Acton: *Rethinking the Russian Revolution* (London 1996), p. 183.
4 Quoted in A.E. Adams (ed.): *The Russian Revolution and Bolshevik Victory* (Lexington, Mass. 1974), extract by m. fainsod.
5 E.H. Carr: op. cit., Vol. I, Ch. 4.
6 Quoted in A.E. Adams (ed.): op. cit., extract by m. fainsod.
7 Quoted in S.N. Silverman (ed.): Lenin (New York 1966), Ch. 2.
8 See G. Swain: *The Origins of the Russian Civil War* (London 1996); S. Smith: 'The Socialists-Revolutionaries and the Dilemma of Civil War', in V.N. Brovkin, (ed.): *The Bolsheviks in Russian Society* (New Haven and London 1997); L. Heretz: 'The Psychology of the White Movement', in V.N. Brovkin, (ed.): op. cit.; E. Mawdsley: *The Russian Civil War* (London 1987).

9 The argument in this section is partly derived from G. Swain: *The Origins of the Russian Civil War* (London 1996).

10 Ibid., p. 252.

11 Ibid., p. 8.

12 L. Heretz: op. cit., p. 106.

13 P. Kenez: 'The Ideology of the White Movement', Soviet Studies, xxxii, l, January 1980.

14 E. Mawdsley: op. cit., p. 283.

15 J.L.H. Keep (ed.): *The Debate on Soviet Power: Minutes of the All-Russian Central Executive Committee of Soviets* (Oxford 1979), Introduction.

16 Quoted in A. Ascher (ed.): op. cit., Introduction.

17 Quoted in S.N. Silverman (ed.): op. cit., Ch. 2.

18 Quoted in A. Ascher (ed.): op. cit., Introduction.

19 J.L.H. Keep, (ed.): op. cit., Introduction.

20 R. Gregor (ed.): *Resolutions and Decisions of the Communist Party of the Soviet Union,* Vol. 2, *The Early Soviet Period 1917–1929* (Toronto and Buffalo 1974), Document 2.9.

21 Quoted in G. Leggett: 'Lenin, Terror and the Political Police', *Survey*, Autumn 1975.

22 Quoted in E.H. Carr: op. cit., Ch. 7.

23 G. Leggett: *The Cheka: Lenin's Political Police* (Oxford 1981), Epilogue.

24 Quoted in G. Leggett: op cit., Ch. 14.

25 Quoted in D. Lane: *Politics and Society in the USSR* (London 1970), Ch. 3.

26 R. Medvedev: *The October Revolution* (London 1979), Part IV.

27 Quoted in A. Erlich: *The Soviet Industrialization Debate 1924–1928* (Cambridge, Mass. 1967), Ch. 1.

28 Quoted in A.G. Mazour (ed.): *Soviet Economic Development: Operation Outstrip 1921–1965* (Princeton, NJ 1967), Ch. 2.

29 L. Trotsky: *History of the Bolshevik Revolution*, Vol. 1.

30 A. Kerensky: 'The Policy of the Provisional Government of 1917', *The Slavonic and East European Review*, xi, 31, July 1932.

31 R. Gregor (ed.): op. cit., Introduction.

32 C. Hill: *Lenin and the Russian Revolution* (London 1947), Ch. 8.

33 E. Mandel: 'Solzhenitsyn, Stalinism and the October Revolution', *New Left Review*, 86, 1974.

34 G. Leggett: op. cit., Epilogue.

35 E.H. Carr: 'The Russian Revolution and the West', *New Left Review*, iii, 1978.

36 E. Mandel: op. cit.

37 L. Schapiro: *1917: The Russian Revolutions and the Origins of Present Day Communism* (Hounslow 1984), Epilogue.

38 Quoted in T.H. Rigby, (ed.): *Stalin* (New York 1966).

39 M. McCauley: *Stalin and Stalinism* (Harlow 1983), Ch. 1.

40 L. Colletti: 'The Question of Stalin', *New Left Review*, 61, 1970.

41 S.N. Silverman: op. cit., Ch. 2.

42 N. Krasso: 'Trotsky's Marxism', *New Left Review*, 44, 1967.

43 Quoted in E.H. Carr: *Socialism in One Country 1924–1926* (London 1958), Ch. 4.

44 N. Krasso: op. cit..

45 Quoted in E.H. Carr: *The Bolshevik Revolution*, op. cit., Vol. 1, Ch. 4.

46 Ibid..

47 J. Arch Getty: 'The Politics of Stalinism', in A. Nove (ed.): *The Stalin Phenomenon* (London 1993), p. 128.

48 Ibid., p. 129.

49 R.C. Tucker: *The Soviet Political Mind* (London 1972), Ch. 3.

50 A. Ulam: 'The Price of Sanity', in G.R. Urban (ed.): *Stalinism. Its Impact on Russia and the World* (London 1982).

51 I. Deutscher: *Stalin. A Political Biography* (London 1949), Ch. 9.

52 L. Viola: 'The Second Coming: Class Enemies in the Soviet Countryside, 1927–1935', in J. Arch Getty and R.T. Manning (eds): *Stalinist Terror. New Perspectives* (Cambridge 1993), pp. 69–70.

53 J. Arch Getty: 'The Politics of Stalinism', in A. Nove (ed.): op. cit., p. 132.

54 R. Thurston: 'The Stakhanovite Movement: Background to the Great Terror in the Factories, 1935–1938', in J. Arch Getty and R.T. Manning (eds): op. cit., p. 160.

55 See R.R. Reese: 'The Red Army and the Great Purges', in J. Arch Getty and R.T. Manning (eds): op. cit.

56 See S. Fitzpatrick: 'How the Mice Buried the Cat: Scenes from the Great Purges of 1937 in the Russian Provinces', in C. Ward (ed.): *The Stalinist Dictatorship* (London 1998).

57 Ibid.

58 G.T. Rittersporn: 'The Omnipresent Conspiracy: On Soviet Imagery of Politics and Social Relations in the 1930s', in J. Arch Getty and R.T. Manning (eds): op. cit., p. 114.

59 R.G. Suny: 'Stalin and his Stalinism: power and authority in the Soviet Union, 1930–53', in I. Kershaw and M. Lewin (eds): *Stalinism and Nazism: Dictatorships in Comparison* (Cambridge 1997), p. 50.

60 R.R. Reese: op. cit., p. 199.

61 Ibid., p. 210.

62 Ibid., p. 213.

63 V. Brovkin: *Russia after Lenin. Politics, Culture and Society 1921–1929* (London 1998), p. 222.

64 M. Lewin: *Russian Peasants and Soviet Power: A Study of Collectivization* (New York 1968), pp. 516–17.

65 J. Arch Getty: op. cit., p. 140.

66 Quoted in M. Lynch: *Stalin and Khrushchev: The USSR 1924–64* (London 1990), p. 30.

67 R. Hutchings: *Soviet Economic Development* (Oxford 1967), Ch. 6.

68 See D.R. Shearer: *Industry, State and Society in Stalin's Russia 1926–1934* (Ithaca and London 1996), p. 235.

69 Ibid., p. 236.

70 Quoted in D. Lane: op. cit., Document 15.

71 Ibid., Ch. 11.

72 Quoted in R. Hingley: *Russian Writers and Soviet Society 1917–1978* (London 1979), Ch. 2.

73 Ibid., quoted in Ch. 9.

74 Quoted in M. McCauley: op. cit., Part II.

75 Quoted in A. Fontaine: *History of the Cold War from the October Revolution to the Korean War, 1917–1950* (trans. D.D. Paige) (London 1968), Ch. 1.

76 G.F. Kennan: *Soviet Foreign Policy 1917–1941* (Princeton, NJ 1960), Document 8.

77 Quoted in R.C. Tucker: 'The Emergence of Stalin's Foreign Policy', *Slavic Review*, xxxvi, 4, December 1977.

78 Quoted in A.Z. Rubinstein: *Soviet Foreign Policy since World War II* (Cambridge, Mass. 1981), Ch. 1.

79 Quoted in R.C. Tucker: 'The Emergence', op. cit.

80 Quoted in W. Laqueur: *Russia and Germany: A Century of Conflict* (London 1965), Ch. 11.

81 Quoted in T.J. Uldricks: 'Soviet Security Policy in the 1930s', in G. Gorodetsky, (ed.): *Soviet Foreign Policy 1917–1991* (London 1994), p. 73.

82 Quoted in R. Hutchings: *Soviet Economic Development* (Oxford 1967), Ch. 6.

83 Quoted in R.C. Tucker: 'The Emergence', op. cit.

84 Ibid.

85 Ibid.

86 J. Haslam: *The Soviet Union and the Struggle for Collective Security in Europe*, 1933–39 (New York 1984), pp. 52–3.

87 J.A.S. Grenville: *The Major International Treaties 1914–1973* (London 1974), pp. 195–6.

88 G. Roberts: *The Soviet Union and the Origins of the Second World War* (London 1995), p. 97.

89 *A Short History of the Communist Party of the Soviet Union* (Moscow 1970), p. 247.
90 See W. Laqueur: op. cit., Ch. 12.
91 I. Grey: *Stalin: Man of History* (London 1979), Ch. 24.
92 G. Roberts: op. cit., p. 121.
93 Quoted in A. Bullock: *Hitler: A Study in Tyranny* (London 1952), Ch. 12.
94 J. Sapir: 'The Economics of War in the Soviet Union during World War II', in I. Kershaw and M. Lewin (eds): op. cit., p. 210.
95 B. Bonwetsch: 'Stalin, the Red Army and the "Great Patriotic War"', in I. Kershaw and M. Lewin, (eds): op. cit. p. 196.
96 Ibid., p. 193.
97 G. Fischer: *Soviet Opposition to Stalin* (Harvard 1952), p. 45.
98 J. Sapir: op. cit., p. 234.
99 G.S. Kravchenko: 'Stalin's War Machine', in Purnell's *History of the Second World War*, Vol. 3 (London 1966).
100 Quoted in V.M. Kulish: 'Russia Strikes Back', in Purnell's *History of the 20th Century*, Vol. 5 (London 1968), p. 1936.
101 See M. von Hagen: 'From "Great Fatherland War" to the Second World War: New Perspectives and Future Prospects', in I. Kershaw and M. Lewin, (eds): op. cit.
102 A. Fontaine: op. cit., Ch. 8.
103 J. Ellenstein: *The Stalin Phenomenon* London 1976), Ch. 5.
104 *History of Soviety Society* (Moscow 1971), p. 273
105 C. Ward: *Stalin's Russia* (London 1993), p. 188.
106 Ibid., p. 187.
107 Quoted in C. Seton Watson: 'The Cold War – Its Origins', in J.L. Henderson, (ed.): *Since 1945: Aspects of Contemporary World History* (London 1966).
108 A.Z. Rubinstein: op. cit., Ch. 3.
109 C. Kennedy-Pipe: *Russia and the World 1917–1991* (London 1998), p. 211.
110 C. Ward: op. cit., p. 188.
111 R.C. Tucker: *The Soviet Political Mind*, op. cit., Ch. 6.
112 This subject is covered thoroughly in R.C. Tucker: 'The Rise of Stalin's Personality Cult', *American Historical Review*, 1979.
113 A. Ulam: op. cit.
114 I. Grey: op. cit., extracts from Preface and Ch. 23.
115 M. McCauley: op. cit., Part III.

3 Dictatorship in Italy

1 Quoted in A. Cassels: *Fascist Italy* (London 1969), Ch. 4.
2 A.J.P. Taylor: *The Origins of the Second World War* (London 1961), Ch. 3.
3 A.J.P. Taylor: video of *Men of Our Time: Mussolini* (Granada Television 1987).
4 J. Pollard: *The Fascist Experience in Italy* (London 1998), p. 10.
5 Ibid., p. 18.
6 A. de Grand: *Italian Fascism: Its Origins and Development* (Lincoln, Neb. 1982), Ch. 1.
7 D. Mack Smith: *Italy: A Modern History* (Ann Arbor, Mich. 1959), Ch. 37.
8 The ideas in this section are based on a lecture given at Bromsgrove School, 29 April 1997, by Dr Richard Robinson: 'The Origins and Emergence of Fascism in Italy'.
9 See Z. Sternhell: *Neither Right nor Left: Fascist Ideology in France* (Berkeley 1986).
10 A.J. Gregor: *Young Mussolini and the Intellectual Origins of Fascism* (Berkeley, London and Los Angeles 1979), Ch. 10.
11 See A. Cassels: op. cit., Ch. 2.
12 A. de Grand: op. cit., Ch. 2.
13 R. de Felice: *Interpretations of Fascism* (Cambridge, Mass., and London 1977), p. 56.
14 A. Lyttelton: 'Italian Fascism' in W. Laqueur (ed.): *Fascism: A Reader's Guide* (London 1976).
15 J. Pollard: op. cit., p. 32.

16 Ibid., quoted on p. 42.

17 Ibid., quoted on p. 41.

18 Ibid.

19 Quoted in J. Whittam: *Fascist Italy* (Manchester 1995), p. 2.

20 Quoted in L. Barzini: 'Benito Mussolini', *Encounter*, July 1964.

21 M. Gallo: *Mussolini's Italy* (New York 1973), Ch. 5.

22 C. Hibbert: 'Fallen Idol', *Spectator*, 19 June 1964; a review of Sir I. Kirkpatrick's *Mussolini, Study of a Demagogue*.

23 Sir I. Kirkpatrick: *Mussolini, Study of a Demagogue* (London 1964), Ch. 6.

24 See D. Mack Smith: *Mussolini* (London 1981).

25 P. Morgan: *Italian Fascism 1919–1945* (London 1995), p. 155.

26 B. Mussolini: 'The Political and Social Doctrine of Fascism', *International Conciliation*, 306, January 1935.

27 A. de Grand: op. cit., Ch. 10.

28 Quoted in J. Whittam: op. cit., p. 2.

29 From *Encyclopedia Italiana*, XIV, 1932, quoted in J. Pollard: op. cit., p. 119.

30 Quoted in M. Gallo: op. cit., Ch. 7.

31 J. Pollard: op. cit., p. 50.

32 S.G. Payne: *A History of Fascism* (London 1995), p. 114.

33 Quoted in J. Pollard: op. cit., p. 52.

34 Quoted in S.G. Payne: op. cit., p. 116.

35 Quoted in J. Whittam: op. cit., p. 43.

36 Ibid., quoted on p. 153.

37 Ibid.

38 S.G. Payne: op. cit., p. 118.

39 E. Tannenbaum: *Fascism in Italy: Society and Culture, 1922–1945* (London 1973), p. 73.

40 S.G. Payne: op. cit., p. 117.

41 Ibid., p. 119.

42 A. Lyttelton: op. cit.

43 See P. Melograni: 'The Cult of the Duce in Mussolini's Italy', in G.L. Mosse (ed.): *International Fascism: New Thoughts and New Approaches* (London and Beverly Hills 1979).

44 Quoted in M. Gallo: op. cit., Ch. 5.

45 Quoted in R. Wolfson: *Years of Change* (London 1978), Ch. 11.

46 J. Pollard: op. cit., p. 67.

47 See S.G. Payne: op. cit., p. 224.

48 P.V. Cannistraro (ed.): *Historical Dictionary of Fascist Italy* (Westport, Conn. and London 1982), s.v. 'Cinema'.

49 See R.J.B. Bosworth: *The Italian Dictatorship: Problems and Perspectives in the Interpretation of Mussolini and Fascism* (London 1998), Ch. 7.

50 Quoted in J. Pollard: op. cit., p. 64.

51 P. Morgan: op. cit., p. 87.

52 S.G. Payne: op. cit., p. 117.

53 Ibid.

54 J. Whittam: op. cit., p. 56.

55 J. Pollard: op. cit, p. 65.

56 *Historical Dictionary of Fascist Italy*, s.v. 'Antisemitism'.

57 M. Callo: op. cit., Ch. 13.

58 Quoted in R.J.B. Bosworth: op. cit., p. 102.

59 J. Pollard: op. cit., p. 127.

60 Ibid.

61 M. van Creveld: 'Beyond the Finzi-Contini Garden. Mussolini's "Fascist Racism"', *Encounter*, February 1974.

62 *Historical Dictionary of Fascist Italy*, s.v. 'Antisemitism'.

63 J. Whittam: op. cit., p. 99.

64 P. Morgan: op. cit., p. 161.
65 *Historical Dictionary of Fascist Italy*, s.v. 'Antisemitism'.
66 B. Mussolini: *My Autobiography* (London 1928), p. 276.
67 P. Morgan: op. cit., p. 96.
68 R.J.B. Bosworth: op. cit., p. 145.
69 Quoted in E. Tannenbaum: op. cit., Ch. 7.
70 Quoted in P.C. Kent: *The Pope and the Duce* (New York 1981); overall argument summarized in Preface.
71 Quoted in G. Jackson (ed.): *Problems in European Civilization: The Spanish Civil War* (Lexington, Mass. 1967; extract by F.J. Taylor.
72 A. Cassels: op. cit., p. 58.
73 J. Pollard: op. cit., p. 84.
74 E. Tannenbaum: op. cit., p. 100.
75 A. de Grand: op. cit., Ch. 8.
76 P. Morgan: op. cit., p. 129.
77 *Historical Dictionary of Fascist Italy*, s.v. 'Industry'.
78 Quoted in D. Mack Smith: *Italy*, op. cit., Ch. 28.
79 Quoted in A.J. Gregor: *Italian Fascism and Developmental Dictatorship* (Princeton, NJ 1979), Ch. 8.
80 V. de Grazia: *How Fascism Ruled Women: Italy 1922–1945* (Berkeley 1992), p. 275.
81 A.J. Gregor: op. cit., Ch. 8.
82 J. Pollard: op. cit., p. 80
83 P. Morgan: op. cit., p. 113.
84 C. Duggan: *Fascism and the Mafia* (New Haven 1989), p. 264.
85 E. Tannenbaum: op. cit., Ch. 7.
86 G. Salvemini: *Prelude to World War II* (London 1953), p. 10.
87 A.J.P. Taylor: *The Origins of the Second World War* (Harmondsworth edition 1964), p. 85.
88 See S. Marks: 'Mussolini and Locarno: Fascist Foreign Policy in Microcosm', *Journal of Contemporary History*, July 1979.
89 See P.G. Edwards: 'Britain, Mussolini and the Locarno–Geneva System', *European Studies Review*, January 1980.
90 Quoted in R.B. Bosworth: 'The British Press, the Conservatives and Mussolini 1920–34', *Journal of Contemporary History*, April 1970.
91 H. Thomas: *The Spanish Civil War* (London 1961), Appendix 3.
92 Quoted in W. Shirer: *The Rise and Fall of the Third Reich* (London 1960), Ch. 9.
93 G. Ciano: *Diary 1937–38* (trans. A. Mayor) (London 1948), p. 29.
94 R.B. Bosworth: 'The British Press', op. cit.
95 P. Morgan: op. cit., p. 136.
96 R. de Felice: *Fascism: An Informal Introduction to its Theory and Practice* (New Brunswick, NJ 1976), quoted in D. Smyth: 'Duce Diplomatico', *Historical Journal* 21, 4, 1978.
97 Ibid.
98 G. Carocci: *Italian Fascism* (trans. I. Quigly) (Harmondsworth 1974), Ch. 7.
99 A. de Grand: op. cit., p. 99.
100 D. Mack Smith: *Mussolini's Roman Empire* (London 1976), Preface.
101 M. Knox: *Mussolini Unleashed 1939–1941* (Cambridge 1982).
102 J. Whittam: op. cit., p. 122.
103 P. Kennedy: *The Rise and Fall of the Great Powers: Economic Change and Military Conflict from 1500 to 2000* (London 1988), p. 430.
104 Ibid., p. 458.
105 P. Morgan: op. cit., p. 177.
106 D. Mack Smith: *Mussolini's Roman Empire*, op. cit., Ch. 17.
107 J. Pollard: op. cit., p. 108.
108 Quoted in C. Leeds: *Italy under Mussolini* (London 1968), Ch. 5.
109 J. Pollard: op. cit., p. 109.

110 Quoted in *Historical Dictionary of Fascist Italy*, s.v. 'Italian Social Republic'.
111 J. Pollard: op. cit., p. 114.
112 G. Procacci: *History of the Italian People* (London 1970), p. 374.
113 L. Barzini: 'Benito Mussolini', *Encounter*, July 1964.

4   Dictatorship in Germany

1 The concept of 'revolution', as applied to Germany in 1919, has sometimes been challenged, although consideration of the arguments would not be appropriate in a section which is here a background to another issue. For further details of the arguments on the 'German revolution' see S.J. Lee: *The Weimar Republic* (London 1998), Ch. 1.
2 Quoted in L. Snyder (ed.): *The Weimar Republic* (Princeton, NJ 1966), Reading No. 3.
3 Ibid., Readings to No. 18.
4 Ibid.
5 Quoted in A. Bullock: *Hitler: A Study in Tyranny* (London 1952), Ch. 2.
6 Quoted in J. Noakes and G. Pridham: (eds): *Documents on Nazism 1919–1945* (London 1974), Ch. 1, Document 12.
7 Ibid., Ch. 3, Document 4.
8 Quoted in K. Sontheimer: 'The Weimar Republic and the Prospects of German Democracy', in E.J. Feuchtwanger (ed.): *Upheaval and Continuity* (London 1971).
9 E. Fraenkel: 'Historical Handicaps of German Parliamentarianism', in idem.: *The Road to Dictatorship 1918–1933* (London 1970).
10 H. Mommsen: 'Government without Parties. Conservative Plans for Constitutional Revision at the End of the Weimar Republic', in L.E. Jones and J. Retallack (eds): *Between Reform, Reaction and Resistance: Studies in the History of German Conservatism from 1789 to 1945* (Providence, RI 1993), p. 350.
11 Quoted in S. Taylor: *Germany 1918–1933* (London 1983), Ch. 4.
12 J.W. Hiden: *The Weimar Republic* (Harlow 1974), p. 21.
13 A. Hitler: *Mein Kampf*, Vol. 2, Ch. 11.
14 Ibid., Vol. 1, Ch. 6.
15 P.D. Stachura: 'Who Were the Nazis? A Sociopolitical Analysis of the National Socialist Machtubernahme', *European Studies Review*, ii, 1981.
16 R.F. Hamilton: *Who Voted for Hitler?* (Princeton, NJ 1982).
17 H. Trevor-Roper: *The Last Days of Hitler* (London 1947), Ch. 1.
18 T. Childers: 'The Middle Classes and National Socialism', in D. Blackburn and R.J. Evans (eds): *The German Bourgeoisie* (London 1991), p. 326.
19 P.D. Stachura: op. cit.
20 D. Mühlberger: 'The Sociology of the NSDAP: The Question of Working Class Membership', *Journal of Contemporary History*, 15, 1980.
21 C. Fischer: *The Rise of the Nazis* (Manchester 1995), p. 108.
22 E. Eyck: *A History of the Weimar Republic* (Cambridge, Mass. 1962), Vol. 1, Ch. 10.
23 H. Boldt: 'Article 48 of the Weimar Constitution, Its Historical and Political Implications', in A. Nicholls (ed.): *German Democracy and the Triumph of Hitler: Essays in Recent German History* (London 1971).
24 J. Hiden: *Republican and Fascist Germany* (London 1996), p. 60.
25 Quoted in D.G. Williamson: *The Third Reich* (Harlow 1982), Ch. 3.
26 J. Noakes and G. Pridham: op. cit., Ch. 5, Document 7.
27 M. Broszat: *The Hitler State: The Foundation and Development of the Internal Structure of the Third Reich* (London 1981), Ch. 3.
28 J. Noakes and G. Pridham: op. cit., Ch. 7, Document 2.
29 Ibid., Ch. 8, Document 1.
30 M. Broszat: op. cit., Ch. 6.
31 J. Noakes and G. Pridham: op. cit., Ch. 8, Document 4.
32 Quoted in Sir J. Wheeler-Bennett: *The Nemesis of Power: The German Army in Politics 1918–1945* (London 1953), Part III, Ch. 2.

33 Quoted in J. Remak (ed.): *The Nazi Years* (Englewood Cliffs, NJ 1969), p. 52.
34 See K. Hildebrand: *The Third Reich* (trans. London 1984), Concluding Remarks.
35 Ibid.
36 J. Noakes and G. Pridham: op. cit., Part III.
37 Information from M. Broszat: op. cit. and J. Noakes and G. Pridham: op. cit.
38 See K.D. Bracher: *The German Dictatorship* (New York 1970).
39 See K. Hildebrand: op. cit.
40 See M. Broszat: *Hitler and the Collapse of the Weimar Republic* (Oxford 1987).
41 See extracts from H. Mommsen in K. Hildebrand: op. cit., p. 137.
42 Information from J. Noakes and G. Pridham: op. cit., Ch. 10.
43 Ibid., Ch. 10, Document 8.
44 Ibid., p. 497.
45 Ibid., Ch. 10, Document 30.
46 H. Höhne: *The Order of the Death's Head* (London 1972), p. 12.
47 Quoted in K.M. Mallman and G. Paul: 'Omniscient, Omnipotent, Omnipresent? Gestapo, Society and Resistance', in D. Crew, (ed.): *Nazism and German Society 1933–1945* (London 1994), p. 169.
48 Ibid., p. 169.
49 Ibid., pp. 169–70.
50 Ibid., p. 174.
51 J. Hiden: op. cit., p. 181.
52 Quoted in J. Noakes and G. Pridham: op. cit., p. 381.
53 Quoted in K.D. Bracher: op. cit., Ch. 5.
54 Quoted in M.J. Thornton: *Nazism 1918–1945* (London 1966), Ch. 7.
55 Quoted in K.D. Bracher: op. cit., Ch. 5.
56 Quoted in R. Grunberger: *A Social History of the Third Reich* (London 1971), Ch. 19.
57 D.J.K. Peukert: *Inside Nazi Germany* (Harmondsworth 1989), p. 15.
58 Quoted in J. Noakes and G. Pridham: op. cit., p. 384.
59 Quoted in J. Remak: op. cit., p. 54.
60 Quoted in J. Noakes and G. Pridham: op. cit., p. 185.
61 Quoted in ibid., Ch. 12.
62 Quoted in R. Grunberger: op. cit., Ch. 29.
63 Ibid.
64 I. Kershaw: op. cit., Ch. 7.
65 This was the view of a report by the Social Democratic Party in Exile (SOPADE); quoted in D.J.K. Peukert: op. cit., p. 71.
66 Ibid., p. 69.
67 Quoted in D.F. Crew: op. cit., pp. 4–5.
68 Ibid., p. 6.
69 Quoted in D.J.K Peukert: op. cit., p. 69.
70 Quoted in R. Grunberger: op. cit.
71 O. Bartov: 'The Missing Years: German Workers, German Soldiers', in D.F. Crew, (ed.): op. cit., p. 46.
72 See K. Mallman and G. Paul: op. cit., pp. 180–9.
73 See D.J. Goldhagen: *Hitler's Willing Executioners: Ordinary Germans and the Holocaust* (London 1997), especially Ch. 15.
74 I. Kershaw: *Popular Opinion and Political Dissent in the Third Reich* (Oxford 1983), p. 373.
75 Quoted in ibid., p. 126.
76 Quoted in D. Peukert: 'Youth in the Third Reich', in R. Bessel (ed.): *Life in the Third Reich* (Oxford 1987), p. 29.
77 D.J.K. Peukert: op. cit., p. 248.
78 K.D. Bracher: op. cit., Ch. 7.
79 A. Hitler: *Mein Kampf* (1925), quoted in J. Laver (ed.): *Nazi Germany* (London 1991), p. 82.

80 Quoted in J. Remak: op. cit., pp. 32–3.
81 See extract in R.G.L. Waite (ed.): *Hitler and Nazi Germany* (New York 1965).
82 Ibid.
83 J. Hiden and J. Farquharson: *Explaining Hitler's Germany: Historians and the Third Reich* (London 1983), p. 151.
84 V.R. Berghahn: *Modern Germany: Society, Economy and Politics in the Twentieth Century* (Cambridge 1987), p. 149.
85 Quoted in J. Noakes and G. Pridham: op. cit., p. 684.
86 Quoted in G. Layton: *Germany: The Third Reich 1933–45* (London 1992), p. 72.
87 Ibid.
88 Quoted in D.G. Williamson: op. cit., Document 7.
89 Quoted in J. Noakes and G. Pridham: op. cit., Ch. 12.
90 C.W. Guillebaud: *The Economic Recovery of Germany from 1933 to the Incorporation of Austria in March 1938* (London 1939).
91 V.R. Berghahn: op. cit., p. 284, Table 18.
92 Ibid., p. 290, Table 25.
93 V.R. Berghahn: op. cit., p. 279, Table 10.
94 Quoted in J. Remak: op. cit., p. 4.
95 A. Hitler: op. cit.
96 A. Hitler: *Second Book* (1928).
97 D.J.K. Peukert: op. cit., p. 208. See also T.W. Mason: *Social Policy in the Third Reich. The Working Class and the 'National Community'* (Oxford 1993), pp. 279–80.
98 Ibid.
99 Ibid., p. 233.
100 D. Schoenbaum: *Hitler's Social Revolution* (New York 1980), p. 55.
101 Quoted in J. Remak: op. cit., p. 5.
102 A. Hitler: *Mein Kampf*, op. cit.
103 J. Streicher: *Der Sturmer*.
104 D.J. Goldhagen: op. cit., p. 162.
105 See R. Hilberg: *The Destruction of the European Jews* (Chicago 1961).
106 See M. Kitchen: *Nazi Germany at War* (London 1995), p. 200.
107 Quoted in J. Remak: op. cit., p. 159.
108 J. Dülffer: *Nazi Germany 1933–1945: Faith and Annihilation* (trans. London 1996), p. 179.
109 D.J. Goldhagen: op. cit., p. 162.
110 Quoted in R. Breitman: 'The "Final Solution"', in G. Martel: *Modern Germany Reconsidered* (London 1992), p. 197.
111 Quoted in H. Höehne: op. cit., p. 352.
112 Quoted in ibid., p. 353.
113 Quoted in J. Noakes and G. Pridham: op. cit.
114 R. Hilberg: op. cit., pp. 666–7.
115 Quoted in A. Barkai: *From Boycott to Annihilation* (London 1989), p. 141.
116 C. Koonz: *Mothers in the Fatherland. Women, the Family and Nazi Politics* (New York 1987), p. 363.
117 M. Housden: *Resistance and Conformity in the Third Reich* (London 1997), p. 125.
118 R. Hilberg: 'The "Judenrat": Conscious or Unconscious Tool?', in Y. Vashem: *Patterns of Jewish Leadership in Nazi Europe 1933–45. Proceedings of the Yad Vashem International Conference* (Jerusalem 1977).
119 J. Robinson: 'Some Basic Issues that Faced the Jewish Councils', in I. Trunk: *Judenrat. The Jewish Councils in Eastern Europe under Nazi Occupation* (London 1972), p. xxxi.
120 I. Trunk: 'The Attitude of the Judenrats to the Problems of Armed Resistance against the Nazis', in Y. Vashem: op. cit., p. 205.
121 J.C.G. Röhl: *From Bismarck to Hitler* (Harlow 1970), Ch. 5, Document 1.
122 J.W. Hiden: op. cit., Ch. 4.
123 J.C.G. Röhl: op. cit., Ch. 5, Document 7.

124 Ibid.
125 H.W. Gatzke: *Stresemann and the Rearmament of Germany* (Baltimore 1954), Ch. 6.
126 Quoted in ibid.
127 Quoted in H. Holborn: *A History of Modern Germany*, Vol. 3, *1840–1945* (London 1969), Ch. 12.
128 G.A. Craig: *Germany 1866–1945* (Oxford 1978), Ch. 19.
129 Ibid.
130 Ibid.
131 J. Noakes and G. Pridham: op. cit., Ch. 18.
132 Quotations in this paragraph are from *Mein Kampf* and the *Second Book*. Material and quotations also from H. von Maltitz: *The Evolution of Hitler's Germany* (New York 1973), Ch. 3.
133 Quoted in D.G. Williamson: op. cit., Ch. 9.
134 A. Hillgruber: *Germany and the Two World Wars* (trans. W.C. Kirby) (Cambridge, Mass. and London 1981), Ch. 5.
135 E. Jäckel: *Hitler in History* (Hannover and London 1984), Ch. 2.
136 See I. Kershaw: op. cit., for summary of debate and for quoted extracts.
137 E. Jäckel: op. cit., Ch. 4.
138 A. Hillgruber: 'England's Place in Hitler's Plans for World Dominion', *Journal of Contemporary History*, 9, 1974.
139 See I. Kershaw: op. cit., for summary of debate and for quoted extracts.
140 Ibid.
141 A. Hillgruber: 'England's Place in Hitler's Plans for World Dominion', *Journal of Contemporary History*, 9, 1974.
142 Quotations from A.J.P. Taylor: *The Origins of the Second World War* (London 1961), Ch. 7.
143 Quoted in K.H. Jarausch: 'From Second to Third Reich: The Problem of Continuity in German Foreign Policy', *Central European History*, 12, 1979.
144 A. Bullock: op. cit., Ch. 8.
145 A. Bullock: contribution to *Hitler and the Origins of the Second World War*, *Proceedings of the British Academy*, liii (Oxford 1967).
146 See F. Fischer: *Germany's Aims in the First World War* (London 1967).
147 J. Noakes and G. Pridham: op. cit., Ch. 16.
148 See extract in R.G.L. Waite: op. cit.
149 I. Kershaw: lecture at Aston University, 1997.
150 J.L. Snell (ed.): *The Outbreak of the Second World War* (Boston 1962); extract from the Nuremberg Judgement.
151 R.J. Sontag: 'The Last Months of Peace, 1939', *Foreign Affairs*, xxv, 1957.
152 H. Trevor-Roper: 'A.J.P. Taylor, Hitler and the War', *Encounter*, xvii, 1961.
153 J. Fest: *Hitler* (London 1974), Interpolation Three.
154 Quotations from A.J.P. Taylor: op. cit., Ch. 7.
155 T.W. Mason: 'Some Origins of the Second World War', *Past and Present*, 1964.
156 R. Henig: *The Origins of the Second World War* (London 1985), Section III.
157 J. Noakes and G. Pridham: op. cit., Ch. 19.
158 D.G. Williamson: op. cit., Ch. 10.
159 G.A. Craig: op. cit., Ch. 20.
160 Quoted in W.L. Shirer: *The Rise and Fall of the Third Reich* (London 1960), Ch. 19.
161 Quoted in D.G. Williamson: op. cit., Ch. 10.
162 Quoted in K. Hildebrand: op. cit., Ch. C1.
163 N. Rich: *Hitler's War Aims: The Establishment of the New Order* (London 1974), Vol. II.
164 Quoted in K. Syrop: *Poland: Between the Hammer and the Anvil* (London 1968), Ch. 16.
165 W.L. Shirer: op. cit., Ch. 27.
166 M.J. Thornton: op. cit., Ch. 9.
167 Ibid.

168 M.R.D. Foot: 'Nazi Wartime Atrocities', in Purnell's *History of the Twentieth Century*, Vol. 5 (London 1968).
169 E. Jäckel: op. cit., Ch. 4.
170 Quoted in T.L. Jarman: *The Rise and Fall of Nazi Germany* (London 1955), Ch. 15.
171 A. Bullock: *Hitler*, op. cit., Ch. 14.
172 F. Halder: *Hitler as War Lord* (trans. P. Findley) (London 1950).
173 P.E. Schramm: *Hitler: The Man and the Military Leader* (London 1972), Ch. 2.
174 Ibid.
175 F. Halder: op. cit.
176 Quoted in J.P. Stern: *Hitler, The Führer and the People* (London 1975), Ch. 22.
177 F. Halder: op. cit.

5   Dictatorship elsewhere

 1 N. Bruce: *Portugal: The Last Empire* (London 1975), Ch. 1.
 2 S.G. Payne: 'Epilogue', in L.S. Graham and H.M. Makler (eds): *Contemporary Portugal: The Revolution and its Antecedents* (Austin, Tex. 1979), p. 345.
 3 N. Bruce: op. cit., Ch. 1.
 4 Quoted in T. Gallagher: *Portugal: A Twentieth-Century Interpretation* (Manchester 1983).
 5 Quoted in H. Kay: *Salazar and Modern Portugal* (London 1970), Ch. 5.
 6 Quoted in ibid.
 7 T. Gallagher: op. cit., Ch. 4.
 8 H. Kay: op. cit., Ch. 4.
 9 T. Gallagher: op. cit., Ch. 3.
10 Quoted in ibid., Ch. 5.
11 Quoted in R.A.H. Robinson: *Contemporary Portugal: A History* (London 1979), Ch. 3.
12 Quoted in T. Gallagher: 'Conservatism, Dictatorship and Fascism in Portugal, 1914–45', in M. Blinkhorn, (ed.): *Fascists and Conservatives* (London 1990), p. 166.
13 T.C. Bruneau: *Politics and Nationhood: Post-revolutionary Portugal* (York 1974), Ch. 1.
14 J.E. Duffy: *Portuguese Africa* (Cambridge, Mass. 1959), Ch. 9.
15 Quoted in T. Gallagher: 'Conservatism', op. cit., p. 164.
16 Ibid., p. 167.
17 Quoted in ibid., p. 163.
18 Quoted in ibid., pp. 164–5.
19 H. Thomas: *The Spanish Civil War* (London 1961), Ch. 2.
20 S.G. Payne: *Falange: A History of Spanish Fascism* (Stanford, Calif. 1961), Ch. 1.
21 Quoted in S. Ben-Ami: 'Dictatorship of Primo de Rivera: A Political Reassessment', *Journal of Contemporary History*, January 1977, pp. 65–84.
22 M. Blinkhorn: 'Conservatism, Traditionalism and Fascism in Spain, 1898–1937', in idem. (ed.): op. cit., p. 123.
23 Quoted in S. Ben-Ami: op. cit., pp. 65–84.
24 R. Carr: *Modern Spain 1875–1980* (Oxford 1980), Ch. 7.
25 S. Ben-Ami: op. cit., pp. 65–84.
26 See M. Blinkhorn: op. cit.
27 H. Thomas: op. cit., Ch. 10.
28 Ibid., Appendix II.
29 P. Preston: 'War of Words: The Spanish Civil War and the Historians', in idem. (ed.): *Revolution and War in Spain 1931–1939* (London 1984).
30 Quoted in R. Carr and J.P. Fusi: *Spain: Dictatorship to Democracy* (London 1979), p. 26.
31 Quoted in F. Jay Taylor: *The United States and the Spanish Civil War* (New York 1956).
32 Quoted in M. Alpert: 'Soldiers, Politics and War', in P. Preston: op. cit.
33 Quoted in R. Carr: op. cit., Ch. 8.
34 Ibid., Ch. 9.

35 G. Jackson: *The Spanish Republic and the Civil War 1931–39* (Princeton, NJ 1965), Ch. 24.
36 M. Gallo: *Spain under Franco* (trans. J. Stewart) (London 1973), Introduction.
37 D.A. Puzzo: *The Spanish Civil War* (New York 1969), Ch. 2.
38 B. Crozier: *Franco: A Biographical History* (London 1967), Part IV, Ch. 6.
39 M. Gallo: op cit., Introduction.
40 S.G. Payne: *Falange*: op. cit.
41 R. Carr: op. cit., Ch. 9.
42 Quoted in D. Smyth: 'Reflex Reaction: Germany and the Onset of the Spanish Civil War', in P. Preston: op. cit.
43 A. Vinas: 'The Financing of the Spanish Civil War', in P. Preston: op. cit.
44 R. Whealey: 'How Franco Financed his War – Reconsidered', *Journal of Contemporary History*, 12, 1977.
45 D.A. Puzzo: *Spain and the Great Powers 1936–1941* (New York 1962), Conclusions.
46 Information on International Brigades from H. Thomas: op. cit., Appendix III.
47 Quoted in M. Gallo: op. cit., Part I, Ch. 2.
48 Quoted in R. Carr: *Spain 1808–1975* (Oxford 1966), Ch. 18.
49 Quoted in M. Gallo: op. cit., Part II, Ch. 2.
50 Ibid., Part II, Ch. 3.
51 Quoted in J.D.W. Trythall: *Franco: A Biography* (London 1970), Ch. 8.
52 Ibid., Ch. 11.
53 Quoted in D. Gilmour: *The Transformation of Spain: From Franco to the Constitutional Monarchy* (London 1985), Ch. 1.
54 Ibid., Ch. 2.
55 R. Carr: *Spain 1808–1975* op. cit., Ch. 18.
56 Ibid., Ch. 20.
57 Ibid.
58 Ibid.
59 B. Crozier: op. cit., Part VII.
60 P. Preston: 'From Rebel to Caudillo: Franco's Path to Power', *History Today*, November 1983.
61 E. Eych: *A History of the Weimar Republic*, Vol. I, Ch. 4.
62 A.J.P. Taylor: *The Habsburg Monarchy* (London 1948), Epilogue.
63 Quoted in S. Marks: *The Illusion of Peace* (London 1976), Ch. 1.
64 E. Barker: *Austria 1918–1972* (London 1973), Part I.
65 Quoted in K.R. Stadler: *Austria* (London 1971), Ch. 4.
66 Ibid.
67 Quoted in ibid.
68 E. Barker: op. cit., Ch. 9.
69 K.R. Stadler: op. cit., Ch. 4.
70 E. Barker: op. cit., Ch. 9.
71 Ibid.
72 J. Lewis: 'Conservatives and Fascists in Austria, 1918–34', in M. Blinkhorn: *Fascists and Conservatives*, op. cit., p. 114.
73 Ibid., p. 103.
74 S.G. Payne: *A History of Fascism 1914–45* (London 1995), p. 250.
75 A.C. Janos: *The Politics of Backwardness in Hungary 1825–1945* (Princeton, NJ 1982), Ch. 4.
76 Ibid., Ch. 5.
77 E. Pamlényi (ed.): *A History of Hungary* (London 1975), Ch. 9.
78 D. Sinor: *History of Hungary* (London 1959), Ch. 32.
79 Quoted in P. Ignotus: *Hungary* (London 1972), Ch. 9.
80 E. Weber (ed.): *Varieties of Fascism* (New York 1964), Reading 3A: Ferencz Szalasi: *The Way and the Aim*.
81 K. Syrop: *Poland: Between the Hammer and the Anvil* (London 1968), Ch. 14.

82 J. Rothschild: *Pilsudski's Coup d'Etat* (New York and London 1966), Conclusion.
83 Z. Landau and J. Tomaszewski: *The Polish Economy in the Twentieth Century* (London 1985) in D.H. Aldcroft: Editor's Introduction.
84 J. Rothschild: op. cit.
85 See J. Holzer: 'The Political Right in Poland 1918–39', *Journal of Contemporary History*, 12, 1977.
86 K. Syrop: op. cit., Ch. 15.
87 Ibid., Ch. 16.
88 J. Rothschild: op. cit., Conclusion.
89 K. Syrop: op. cit., Ch. 15.
90 S. Payne: op. cit., p. 322.
91 V.S. Vardis: 'The Rise of Authoritarian Rule in the Baltic States', in V.S. Vardis and R.J. Misiunas (eds): *The Baltic States in Peace and War 1917–1945* (University Park, Pa., and London 1978).
92 S.G. Payne: op. cit., p. 325.
93 B. Meissner: 'The Baltic Question in World Politics', in V.S. Vardis and R.J. Misiunas: op. cit. Also A. Dallin: 'The Baltic States between Nazi Germany and Soviet Russia', in V.S. Vardis and R.J. Misiunas: op. cit.
94 E. Anderson: 'The Baltic Entente: Phantom or Reality', in V.S. Vardis and R.J. Misiunas: op. cit.
95 L.S. Stavrianos: *The Balkans since 1453* (New York 1958), Ch. 36.
96 S. Pollo and A. Puto: *The History of Albania* (trans. C. Wiseman and G. Cole) (London 1981), Ch. 9.
97 A. Logoreci: *The Albanians* (London 1977), Ch. 3.
98 L.S. Stavrianos: op. cit., Ch. 36.
99 S. Pollo and A. Puto: op. cit., Ch. 9.
100 B. Jelavich: *History of the Balkans*, Vol. 2, *Twentieth Century* (Cambridge 1983).
101 L.S. Stavrianos: op. cit., Ch. 33.
102 R. Ristelhueber: *A History of the Balkan Peoples* (trans. S.D. Spector) (New York 1971).
103 F. Singleton: *Twentieth-century Yugoslavia* (London 1976), Ch. 5.
104 L.S. Stavrianos: op. cit., Ch. 32.
105 V. Dedijer: 'Yugoslavia between Centralism and Federalism', in idem. (ed.): *History of Yugoslavia* (New York 1974).
106 R.W. Seton-Watson and R.G.D. Laffan: 'Yugoslavia between the Wars', in S. Clissold (ed.): *Short History of Yugoslavia* (Cambridge 1966).
107 L.S. Stavrianos: op. cit., Ch. 32.
108 Ibid.
109 Quoted in V. Dedijer: 'The Subjugation and Dismemberment of Yugoslavia', in idem.: op. cit.
110 Ibid.
111 S.G. Payne: op. cit., p. 405.
112 L.S. Stavrianos: op. cit., Ch. 30.
113 S. Fischer-Galaţi: *Twentieth Century Rumania* (New York and London 1970).
114 F.L. Carsten: *The Rise of Fascism* (London 1967), Ch. 5.
115 I. Livezeanu: 'Fascists and Conservatives in Romania: Two Generations of Nationalists', in M. Blinkhorn: *Fascists and Conservatives*, op. cit., p. 220.
116 S.G. Payne: op. cit., p. 000.
117 Quoted in B. Jelavich: op. cit., Ch. 6.
118 L.S. Stavrianos: op. cit.
119 J.L. Hondros: *Occupation and Resistance. The Greek Agony, 1941–4* (New York 1983), p. 26.
120 S.G. Payne: op. cit., p. 319.
121 J.V. Kofas: *Authoritarianism in Greece: The Metaxas Regime* (New York 1983).
122 Quoted in ibid.
123 Quoted in S.G. Payne: op. cit., p. 319.

124 J.V. Kofas: op. cit., p. 186.
125 D. Close: 'Conservatism, Authoritarianism and Fascism in Greece, 1915–45', in M. Blinkhorn: *Fascists and Conservatives*, op. cit.
126 J.K. Hoensch: 'The Slovak Republic', in V.S. Mamatey and R. Luza (eds): *A History of the Czechoslovak Republic 1918–1948* (Princeton, NJ 1973).
127 K.F. Larsen: *A History of Norway* (Princeton, NJ 1948), Ch. 21.
128 P.M. Hayes: *Quisling* (London 1971), Ch. 9.
129 H. Tint: *France since 1918* (London 1970), Ch. 7.

6 Dictatorships compared

1 K.D. Bracher: *The Age of Ideologies* (London 1984), Part II, Ch. 1.
2 F.J. Fleron: 'Soviet Area Studies and the Social Sciences: Some Methodological Problems in Communist Studies', *Soviet Studies*, 16, January 1968, p. 339.
3 See C.J. Friedrich and Z.K. Brzezinski: *Totalitarian Dictatorship and Autocracy* (Cambridge, Mass. 1956).
4 Ibid., p. 9.
5 Ibid., p. 88.
6 See H. Arendt: *The Origins of Totalitarianism* (London 1986).
7 Ibid., p. 326.
8 S. Tormey: *Making Sense of Tyranny: Interpretations of Totalitarianism* (Manchester 1995), p. 186.
9 Ibid., p. 188.
10 K.D. Bracher: op. cit., Part II, Ch. 1.
11 Ibid.
12 C.J. Friedrich and Z.K. Brzezinski: op. cit., Ch. 2.
13 Ibid.
14 Ibid.
15 Ibid., Ch. 7.
16 K.D. Bracher: op. cit., Part II, Ch. 4.
17 Ibid.
18 E. Weber: *Varieties of Fascism* (New York 1964), Reading 3, Introduction.
19 Quoted in R.C. Macridis: *Contemporary Political Ideologies* (Boston 1983), Ch. 5.
20 K.D. Bracher: op. cit., Part II, Ch. 3.
21 Quoted in H. Kohn: *Political Ideologies of the Twentieth Century* (New York 1966), Ch. 10.
22 Quoted in J. Remak: *The Nazi Years* (Englewood Cliffs, NJ 1969), Ch. 3.
23 T. Gallagher: *Portugal: A Twentieth-century Interpretation* (Manchester 1983).
24 M. Broszat: *The Hitler State* (London 1981), Ch. 6.
25 Quoted in C.J. Friedrich and Z.K. Brzezinski: op. cit., Ch. 26.
26 H. Buchheim: *Totalitarian Rule: Its Nature and Characteristics* (Middletown, Conn. 1968), Ch. 1.
27 N. Bruce: *Portugal: The Last Empire* (London 1975), Ch. 2.
28 S.G. Payne: *Franco's Spain* (London 1968), Ch. 2.
29 C.J. Friedrich and Z.K. Brzezinski: op. cit., Ch. 11.
30 Ibid.

Select bibliography

The previous section listed the works which have been used in compiling this book. This final section is intended to select from these a few titles to introduce the reader to further study.

GENERAL ISSUES (INTERNATIONAL RELATIONS, INSTITUTIONS AND IDEOLOGIES)

The various foreign policies are covered in the context of the individual states. The most accessible collection of documents on international relations covering the whole period is J.A.S. Grenville (ed.): *The Major International Treaties 1914–1973* (London 1974). Now under increasing pressure, still invigorating is A.J.P. Taylor: *The Origins of the Second World War* (London 1961). Two introductions to the period can be strongly recommended: R. Henig: *Versailles and After* (London 1984) and R. Henig: *The Origins of the Second World War* (London 1985). A more detailed analysis is provided by S. Marks: *The Illusion of Peace, International Relations in Europe 1918–1933* (London 1976) and a reinterpretation of the Versailles Settlement is contained in M. Trachtenberg: *Reparation in World Politics* (London 1980). Several titles in the series Problems in European Civilizaton (Lexington, Mass.) provide a useful survey of different viewpoints, although they do not always include the latest research. Examples include: I.J. Lederer (ed.): *The Versailles Settlement*; L.F. Schaeffer (ed.): *The Ethiopian Crisis*; J.L. Nell (ed.): *The Outbreak of the Second World War*.

On institutions and ideologies I found the following particularly informative and enlightening: K.J. Newman: *European Democracy between the Wars* (trans. E. Morgan) (London 1970); H. Buchheim: *Totalitarian Rule: Its Nature and Characteristics* (Middletown, Conn. 1968); K.D. Bracher: *The Age of Ideologies* (London 1984); R.C. Macridis: *Contemporary Political Ideologies* (Boston 1983); C.J. Friedrich and Z.K. Brzezinski: *Totalitarian Dictatorship and Autocracy* (Cambridge, Mass. 1956); G.L. Mosse (ed.): *International Fascism* (London and Beverly Hills 1979); E. Nolte: *Three Faces of Fascism* (New York 1963); M. Kitchen: *Fascism* (London 1976); F. Carsten: *The Rise of Fascism* (London 1967); S.J. Woolf (ed.): *Fascism in Europe* (London 1981); and I. Deutscher: *Marxism in Outline* (London 1972).

The second edition of this book has been greatly assisted by Z. Sternhell: *Neither Right nor Left: Fascist Ideology in France* (Berkeley 1986); S. Tormey: *Making Sense of Tyranny: Interpretations of Totalitarianism* (Manchester 1995); and S.G. Payne: *A History of Fascism* (London 1995); these contain many examples of reinterpretation.

DICTATORSHIP IN RUSSIA

Since the late 1980s there have been fundamental changes in the interpretations of the Leninist and Stalinist periods. The second edition of this book has aimed to show how these have developed and to contrast new with original views. It has drawn heavily on material in S.J. Lee: *Stalin and the Soviet Union* (London 1999) to attempt a synthesis.

The more traditional works are still of enormous value to the student. On the Lenin era these include: E.H. Carr: *The Bolshevik Revolution 1917–23* (3 vols, London 1950); E.H. Carr: *The Russian Revolution from Lenin to Stalin 1917–1929* (London 1979); C. Hill: *Lenin and the Russian Revolution* (London 1974); L. Schapiro: *1917: The Russian Revolutions and the Origins of Present Day Communism* (Hounslow 1984); L. Fischer: *The Life of Lenin* (London 1965); and R. Medvedev: *The October Revolution* (London 1979). Two more detailed works which can be recommended are: A. Ascher (ed.): *The Mensheviks in the Russian Revolution* (London 1976) and G. Leggett: *The Cheka: Lenin's Political Police* (Oxford 1981). The basic works on Stalin include: I. Deutscher: *Stalin: A Political Biography* (Oxford 1949); A.B. Ulam: *Stalin: The Man and his Era* (London 1973); T.H. Rigby (ed.): *Stalin* (Englewood Cliffs, NJ 1966); I. Grey: *Stalin: Man of History* (London 1979); R. Hingley: *Joseph Stalin: Man and Legend* (London 1974); A. Nove: *Stalinism and After* (London 1975); and M. McCauley: *Stalin and Stalinism* (London 1983). More specific material can be found in: R. Conquest: *The Great Terror* (London 1968); R. Hutchings: *Soviet Economic Development* (Oxford 1967); D. Lane: *Politics and Society in the USSR* (London 1970); G.F. Kennan: *Soviet Foreign Policy 1917–1941* (Princeton, NJ 1960); R. Hingley: *Russian Writers and Soviet Society 1917–1978* (London 1979).

Revisionist works now provide a fascinating contrast and have been heavily drawn upon for the second edition of this book. They include: E. Acton: *Rethinking the Russian Revolution* (London 1996); G. Swain: *The Origins of the Russian Civil War* (London 1996); V.N. Brovkin (ed.): *The Bolsheviks in Russian Society* (New Haven and London 1997); E. Mawdsley: *The Russian Civil War* (London 1987); A. Nove (ed.): *The Stalin Phenomenon* (London 1993); J. Arch Getty and R.T. Manning (eds): *Stalinist Terror. New Perspectives* (Cambridge 1993); C. Ward (ed.): *The Stalinist Dictatorship* (London 1998); I. Kershaw and M. Lewin, (eds): *Stalinism and Nazism: Dictatorships in Comparison* (Cambridge 1997); V. Brovkin: *Russia after Lenin. Politics, Culture and Society 1921–1929* (London 1998); D.R. Shearer: *Industry, State and Society in Stalin's Russia 1926–1934* (Ithaca and London 1996); and C. Kennedy-Pipe: *Russia and the World 1917–1991* (London 1998). There are, no doubt, many more new approaches in the offing.

DICTATORSHIP IN ITALY

Although less noticeable than in the case of Russia, there have also been some changes in the interpretation of Fascist Italy.

The most valuable of the works reflecting scholarship before 1990 are: A. Cassels: *Fascist Italy* (London 1969); D. Mack Smith: *Mussolini* (London 1981); M. Gallo: *Mussolini's Italy* (New York 1973); R. Macgregor-Hastie: *The Day of the Lion* (New York 1963); Sir I. Kirkpatrick: *Mussolini: Study of a Demagogue* (London 1964); C. Hibbert: *Mussolini* (Harmondsworth 1975); R. Collier: *Duce!: The Rise and Fall of Mussolini* (London 1971); A. de Grand: *Italian Fascism: Its Origins and Development* (Lincoln, Nebr. 1982), A.J. Gregor: *Young Mussolini and the Intellectual Origins of Fascism* (Berkeley, London and Los Angeles 1979); P.V. Cannistraro (ed.): *Historical Dictionary of Fascist Italy* (Westport, Conn., and London 1982); P.C. Kent: *The Pope and the Duce* (New York 1981); A.J. Gregor: *Italian Fascism and Developmental Dictatorship* (Princeton, NJ 1979); R. De Felice: *Fascism: An Informal Introduction to its Theory and Practice* (New Brunswick, NJ 1976); G. Carocci: *Italian Fascism* (Harmondsworth 1974); D. Mack Smith: *Mussolini's Roman Empire* (London 1976); and M. Knox: *Mussolini Unleashed* (Cambridge 1982).

The following works, published since 1990, have been used to try to update the historiography of the period in the second edition of this book: J. Pollard: *The Fascist Experience in Italy* (London 1998); J. Whittam: *Fascist Italy* (Manchester 1995); P. Morgan: *Italian Fascism 1919–1945* (London 1995); S.G. Payne: *A History of Fascism* (London 1995); and R.J.B. Bosworth: *The Italian Dictatorship: Problems and Perspectives in the Interpretation of Mussolini and Fascism* (London 1998).

DICTATORSHIP IN GERMANY

As with the chapter on dictatorship in Russia, I have drawn extensively on one of my books in the Questions and Analysis series. S.J. Lee: *Hitler and Nazi Germany* (London 1998) is an attempt to provide a synthesis between traditional and post-1990 interpretations. Some of it was transferable to the present volume.

The best known of the long-established texts are: A. Bullock: *Hitler: A Study in Tyranny* (London 1952); W.L. Shirer: *The Rise and Fall of the Third Reich* (London 1960); J. Fest: *Hitler* (London 1974); N. Stone: *Hitler* (London 1980); and A.J. Nicholls: *Weimar and the Rise of Hitler* (London 1968).

Especially recommended as overall interpretations of the Nazi era are: M. Broszat: *The Hitler State* (London 1981); K.D. Bracher: *The German Dictatorship* (New York 1980); E. Jäckel: *Hitler in History* (Hannover and London 1984); A. Hillgruber: *Germany and the Two World Wars* (Cambridge, Mass., and London 1981); K. Hildebrand: *The Third Reich* (London 1984); J. Hiden and J. Farquharson: *Explaining Hitler's Germany: Historians and the Third Reich* (London 1983); and I. Kershaw: *The Nazi Dictatorship: Problems and Perspectives of Interpretation* (London 1985).

More recent works, which have had a strong influence on some of the views in the second edition of this volume are: C. Fischer: *The Rise of the Nazis*

(Manchester 1995); J. Hiden: *Republican and Fascist Germany* (London 1996); D.J.K. Peukert: *Inside Nazi Germany* (Harmondsworth 1989); G. Martel: *Modern Germany Reconsidered* (London 1992); R. Bessel (ed.): *Life in the Third Reich* (Oxford 1987); D.F. Crew (ed.): *Nazism and German Society 1933–1945* (London 1994); J. Dülffer: *Nazi Germany 1933–1945: Faith and Annihilation* (trans. London 1996); I. Kershaw: *Popular Opinion and Political Dissent in the Third Reich* (Oxford 1983); M. Kitchen: *Nazi Germany at War* (London 1995); L.E. Jones and J. Retallack (eds): *Between Reform, Reaction and Resistance: Studies in the History of German Conservatism from 1789 to 1945* (Providence, RI 1993); D. Blackburn and R.J. Evans (eds.): *The German Bourgeoisie* (London 1991); A. Barkai: *From Boycott to Annihilation* (London 1989); and D.J. Goldhagen: *Hitler's Willing Executioners: Ordinary Germans and the Holocaust* (London 1997).

By far the most useful collection of primary sources is J. Noakes and G. Pridham (eds): *Documents on Nazism 1919–1945* (London 1974). Others include L. Snyder: *The Weimar Republic* (Princeton, NJ 1966); J.W. Hiden: *The Weimar Republic* (Harlow 1974); and D.G. Williamson: *The Third Reich* (Harlow 1982).

DICTATORSHIP ELSEWHERE

Limited space prevents a detailed list of works on the other dictatorships. I found the most readable books on Salazar's Portugal to be T. Gallagher: *Portugal: A Twentieth-century Interpretation* (Manchester 1983); and H. Kay: *Salazar and Modern Portugal* (London 1970). Among the plethora of books on Spain there are several standard works. These include H. Thomas: *The Spanish Civil War* (London 1961); G. Jackson: *The Spanish Republic and the Civil War 1931–39* (Princeton, NJ 1965); and S.G. Payne: *Franco's Spain* (London 1968). Of R. Carr's general works I found *Modern Spain 1875–1980* (Oxford 1980) the most useful. Among other publications, a series of particularly interesting essays can be found in P. Preston (ed.): *Revolution and War in Spain 1931–1939* (London 1984).

Central and eastern Europe are effectively covered in E. Barker: *Austria 1918–1972* (London 1973); K.R. Stadler: *Austria* (London 1971); E. Pamlényi: *A History of Hungary* (London 1975); D. Sinor: *History of Hungary* (London 1959); K. Syrop: *Poland: Between the Hammer and the Anvil* (London 1968); and V.S. Vardis and R.J. Misiunas (eds): *The Baltic States in Peace and War 1917–1945*. The Balkans and south-eastern Europe are dealt with comprehensively in L.S. Stavrianos: *The Balkans since 1453* (New York 1958) and B. Jelavich: *History of the Balkans*, Vol. 2, *The Twentieth Century* (Cambridge 1983). Books on individual countries are mentioned in the Notes for Chapter 5.

In the process of updating this chapter, I gained a great deal from M. Blinkhorn (ed.): *Fascists and Conservatives* (London 1990) and S.G. Payne: *A History of Fascism* (London 1995).

INDEX